# RAVENS TALKING

## Indigenous Feminist Legal Studies

*Edited by Val Napoleon, Emily Snyder, Rebecca Johnson, and Debra McKenzie*

While awareness of the sexual and gendered colonial violence faced by Indigenous women, girls, and 2SLGBTQI+ people has grown, the field of Indigenous law and beyond has yet to engage with Indigenous feminisms, gender, and sexuality in a sustained way. *Ravens Talking* challenges this gap, treating Indigenous feminisms as essential, insightful, and deeply transformative.

Through critical feminist analyses, this book examines key issues in Indigenous law, demonstrating how legal understandings shift when gender is consistently, meaningfully, and creatively engaged. The contributors confront the forms of power shaping these essential conversations and bring to the fore intergenerational Indigenous feminisms; Indigenous law and gender; the forms of expression and translation between and across legal and political worlds; and the rich array of disagreements and conflicts between Indigenous women. *Ravens Talking* intends to capture the complexities arising from Indigenous feminisms in living contexts to provoke questions and develop critical perspectives.

Both intellectually rigorous and practically grounded, *Ravens Talking* is a vital contribution that encourages dialogue on Indigenous legal traditions, justice, and sovereignty.

VAL NAPOLEON is a professor and Law Foundation Chair of Indigenous Justice and Governance at the University of Victoria.

EMILY SNYDER is an associate professor of sociology at the University of British Columbia.

REBECCA JOHNSON is a professor of law and associate director of the Indigenous Law Research Unit at the University of Victoria.

DEBRA MCKENZIE is a research coordinator in the Faculty of Law at the University of Victoria.

# Ravens Talking

## *Indigenous Feminist Legal Studies*

Edited by
VAL NAPOLEON, EMILY SNYDER, REBECCA JOHNSON, AND DEBRA MCKENZIE

UNIVERSITY OF TORONTO PRESS
Toronto Buffalo London

Toronto Buffalo London
utppublishing.com
Printed and bound by CPI Group (UK) Ltd, Croydon, CR0 4YY

ISBN 978-1-4875-5142-1 (cloth)
ISBN 978-1-4875-5147-6 (paper)
ISBN 978-1-4875-5824-6 (EPUB)
ISBN 978-1-4875-5572-6 (PDF)

**Library and Archives Canada Cataloguing in Publication**

Title: Ravens talking : Indigenous feminist legal studies / edited by Val Napoleon, Emily Snyder, Rebecca Johnson, and Debra McKenzie.
Names: Napoleon, Val, 1956– editor | Snyder, Emily, 1981– editor | Johnson, Rebecca, 1963– editor | McKenzie, Debra, editor.
Description: Includes bibliographical references and index.
Identifiers: Canadiana (print) 20250268930 | Canadiana (ebook) 20250268949 | ISBN 9781487551421 (cloth) | ISBN 9781487551476 (paper) | ISBN 9781487558246 (EPUB) | ISBN 9781487555726 (PDF)
Subjects: LCSH: Feminist jurisprudence. | LCSH: Indigenous women – Legal status, laws, etc. | LCSH: Indigenous people – Legal status, laws, etc. | LCSH: Feminism.
Classification: LCC K349 .R38 2025 | DDC 346.01/3082 – dc23

Cover art: Val Napoleon
Cover design: Kristjan Buckingham

We wish to acknowledge the land on which the University of Toronto Press operates. This land is the traditional territory of the Wendat, the Anishnaabeg, the Haudenosaunee, the Métis, and the Mississaugas of the Credit First Nation.

This book has been published with the help of a grant from the Federation for the Humanities and Social Sciences, through the Awards to Scholarly Publications Program, using funds provided by the Social Sciences and Humanities Research Council of Canada.

University of Toronto Press acknowledges the financial support of the Government of Canada, the Canada Council for the Arts, and the Ontario Arts Council, an agency of the Government of Ontario, for its publishing activities.

Canada Council for the Arts | Conseil des Arts du Canada

ONTARIO ARTS COUNCIL
CONSEIL DES ARTS DE L'ONTARIO
an Ontario government agency
un organisme du gouvernement de l'Ontario

Funded by the Government of Canada | Financé par le gouvernement du Canada

Canada

# Contents

RAVENS TALKING

# Prologue: Indigenous Women Talking: The Work of Indigenous Feminisms in the World

VAL NAPOLEON

> Welcome to pleasure; welcome to fun. Welcome to the Trickster and his [or her] sense of humour. Welcome to our world of rampant insanity. Kwayas kamoo-chigee-taanaa-wow. (Boy, are you going to have one good time.)[1]

> The straight line is godless and immoral.[2]

Raven is perched in an arbutus tree at the top of Pkols,[3] a little mountain in Victoria. It is dawn and the sun is still muffled through the dense fog. The world is a soft palette of greys and whites. The rain now a fine mist. Raven thinks about her most recent reading, *Women Talking*, by Miriam Toews.[4] Hmmm. She has recently heard it was made into a movie directed by Sarah Polley. So exciting to see and with popcorn too.

So many thoughts. The importance of conversations, the many forms of power, about intergenerational Indigenous feminisms, about Indigenous law and gender, about the forms of expression and translation between and across legal and political worlds, and of course, about the ubiquitous invisibility of Indigenous male privileging. Then there is the rich array of disagreements and conflicts between Indigenous women. Agency and political diversity. Mmmm, mmmm. So necessary and exciting, and even healthy she thinks. Chewy and delicious too. And then there are those niggling discomforts.

Might she take up the pen, the keyboard? She is a trickster after all, able to transcend her current raven form which, quite frankly, she has found to be somewhat limiting to her writing goals.[5] How about "Indigenous Handmaid's Tales"? Raven chuckles to herself, but then becomes

---

This paper originated as a keynote address to the Feminist Legal Studies Conference at the Faculty of Law, Queen's University, on 6 March 2020.

serious as she sadly thinks about the many forms and embodiments of Indigenous handmaids' tales across Great Turtle Island, and beyond too. She consoles herself that there is always the hope of *The Testaments*. Maybe that Margaret Atwood is a trickster too.[6] She sure writes like one. And such a wicked and clever sense of humour. And she is so complicated too.

I could be a literary trickster, Raven thinks. Look at that Tomson Highway writing about laughing with the trickster, he is so funny, well mostly anyway.[7] And look at what that Eden Robinson does.[8] She is such a strong Indigenous literary trickster and so funny too. And Raven thinks about what she could do with "Indigenous Women Talking." Different circumstances and starting places, of course. She wants to shake all this up though. What would our conversations look like in a world where Indigenous feminisms are bold and wildly on the loose and in everyone's face? Where Indigenous feminisms are the norm and not the exception?

What follows are a series of conversations, some imagined and dreamed, that are woven together with fragments drawn from experiences over the years. These are snippets intended to capture some of the complexities arising from Indigenous feminisms in living contexts to provoke questions and develop perspectives. To accompany these conversations, I have drawn liberally on the great Tomson Highway, who reminds us to laugh even when facing great odds and despair.

> Where the Elders, the priests, and the shamans of Greek, Christian, and Indigenous mythologies – that is, the mythologies inventors – got these stories is beyond the reach of human comprehension. Who was there, for example, to hear the King of the Sky intone the immortal line, "Let there be light"? By the same token, who was there to hear a [Cree] red-nosed clown cackle, "Let there be laughter," thus kicking life into the universe?[9]

## Conversation One (circa 2040)

Clara is sitting on her deck waiting for Lucy. She reads the article again, just to be sure. Yes, there it is. That Tomson Highway, he really did say that life has to be breathed into the new trickster, who is "passed out under some bar table at Queen and Bathurst, drunk out of his mind, to pitch him off the floor, make him stand up, back on his own two feet – so we can laugh and dance again."[10]

"I knew it!" Clara giggles to herself. When Lucy arrives and after many hellos and the pouring of tea, and when Lucy is seated in her lounge chair, Clara hands her the Tomson Highway article. Lucy starts chortling, "Geez, there must be quite a few tricksters around the country."

"No kidding," Clara is really enjoying herself, "I love Tomson Highway! Now, *he* is one heck of a trickster!" After sharing a good chuckle and thinking about tricksters, they both lean back to relax in their lounge chairs.

Lifetime friends, Lucy and Clara are closing in on eighty now. Both have deep laugh lines and soft wrinkled skin. Lucy has assembled her long grey hair into a neat bun that sits atop her head. Clara appears to have made no effort and her crazy white hair goes in all directions, causing her to resemble a dandelion seedhead just at the point of becoming wind-blown across the land. Both are comfortably dressed in different-coloured tunics with leggings, and they sport the latest jazzy orthopaedic shoes. Bright rainbow grannies.

Today, they are watching a raven perched nearby in a large spruce tree. The raven is watching them back, obviously curious.

"You know something?" says Clara, "That raven looks like she's listening to us."

Lucy squints through her dark horn-rimmed glasses, "You think? Why would she be interested in our little talks? It is not as if we're that interesting anymore. She should go listen to the younger activists and leaders that matter today, not us old timers. All we do now is drink tea. What a nosy thing." She sniffs at the raven.

Then she squints again at the raven, "But hey, I think you're right. Let's give her something to listen to!"

"Like what?" Clara smiles, "We used to be more exciting – today, not so much. Remember when I used to have a motorcycle? I never used to worry about my joints or limbs – not like now. Heck, I didn't even know I had ankle bones."

"Yeah, you sure thought you were hot stuff!" chuckles Lucy, taking a slurp of her tea.

"I was hot stuff! And we used to party like nobody's business. I sure miss the dancing – I just wouldn't dance on the tables now. I would be a little more restrained." Clara is smiling and shaking her wild hair and snapping her fingers to an old rock-and-roll tune playing loudly in her head, "Now I worry about breaking a hip or something else!"

Lucy considers, "I wonder if we'd be treated so wonderfully as elders if the young 'uns knew about how nuts we used to be. Well, you really, not me. Okay – maybe we were both crazy."

"I don't know, sometimes I feel like such a caricature. One-dimensional, as if we were born old tea-drinking grannies with no former lives. As if we hadn't been on the front lines of so many political actions over the years. I loved the blockades up north when we used to camp out. I used to be so sure that the revolution was right around the corner. Hah, them young 'uns wouldn't have been able to keep up!" Clara is smiling at visions of the now-distant past.

"But don't all young people think their elders and previous generations are simple? We did. Like we were the only ones that were really alive while the previous generations were simply dull and probably never really had any excitement of any kind. Hard to put my finger on it. But I think that's how my grandchildren and great grandchildren see me now. Just dull. Feels so weird to be on this side of being old," Lucy muses.

"Maybe it is us that's the problem." Clara starts talking directly to the raven, "Maybe we've lost the pulse of the world. Maybe it is us who don't take the young ones seriously, as if they have nothing new to teach us. Maybe we should still be dancing!"

"And aren't you the little ray of sunshine? I'm usually the optimist here." Lucy takes another slurp of tea. "Wish I could smoke."

"Me too. I loved smoking." Clara mimes holding a smoke and taking a drag. "Not that it solved any problems. Do you know that you start slurping before your tea actually reaches your lips?"

"It's more fun that way and I like the sound effects. You know, geezer talk is really boring, Clara." Lucy is growing impatient. "Even the raven looks bored."

Clara continues, "Once when I was teaching, I tried an experiment to get at some of the various unstated perceptions of age and the various forms of stereotyped elderism. So, I was scheduled to do a guest lecture on Indigenous law. I walked into the classroom wearing a long wrap-around skirt and granny blouse over my regular business clothes. I wore a little kerchief over my hair too. Then after a bit, while talking about Indigenous law, I undid the side clasp of the skirt, slipped the blouse over my head, and took off the kerchief. I set these aside. I didn't say anything about the clothing while doing this.

"I continued to talk about Indigenous law, and after a while, I put on a beaded and fringed leather motorcycle jacket over my T-shirt. It was really a kick-ass jacket. After another bit, and still talking, I took off the motorcycle jacket and put on a suit jacket. All the while, I didn't acknowledge what I was doing. Just kept talking about Indigenous law.

"At the end of the talk, I asked the students how they heard me and whether they had different responses to what I said depending on what I was wearing – you know, the suit jacket, the bad-ass motorcycle gear, or the granny outfit."

She laughs. "Oh, I thought I was really clever, figuring out a way to encourage some critical questions and deeper reflections about stereotypes of Indigenous women and elders – all the romantic idealism." She pauses, thinking back and reliving the class.

Clara shakes her head back into the present conversation and continues, "But there was no response. Not even any questions about why I bothered with all this extra activity. I didn't know what to think. I remember being more than a little deflated." She sighs deeply. "Really nuts. Did they just think I changed my clothes every time I taught a class? Did they really think that this was a normal" – she pauses to create air apostrophes – "'Indigenous way' to teach, like an Indigenous pedagogy? Geez!"

Laughing, Lucy suggests, "Maybe they were uncomfortable 'cause they thought you were doing some kind of crazy-old-woman striptease." She is trying to hold back her laughter, but it erupts into a belly-shaking laugh that caused the raven to tilt her head in a side glance at Lucy.

"What! Jeez, Lucy!" splutters an indignant Clara, but she also starts to giggle at the burlesque image that came to mind. "Wait, was that a raven giggle?"

Still laughing so she is somewhat breathless, Lucy offers, "Or maybe they just didn't have any different responses to your outfits – like they didn't see any real difference."

"That can't be it! You know people treat us differently if they know we're law professors, or if they think we are spiritual folk, or hunters, or academics, or some stereotypical version of elders." Clara is indignant. "I hate the assumptions that we're so simple we can only be one thing at a time – like we can't be a spiritual law professor or we can't be a critical feminist elder or an intellectual hunter." Clara is irate and her face is starting to get red.

"Jeez, take it easy. Calmmm … down." Lucy's holds out her hands palms down making slow downward motions. She is concerned about her friend's blood pressure, and she acknowledges, "It *is* frustrating, and it's exactly what leads to us being conflated to the simple – lacking any depth or complexity."

Lucy continues, "And it's true that people often talk down to me when they don't know I used to be a law professor. They assume that I'm always an agreeable and maternal elder, and that I'll be naively supportive no matter what. That I'm only interested in the spiritual and emotional, and that I don't think critically."

Clara slaps her knee. "You know what, I just hate the 'dearie' thing. Is it rude to slap someone when they call me 'dear'? A good ole bannock slap! I am nobody's dear! Ack! Bleck!"

The raven appears to be nodding along with Clara and Lucy. She cocks her head, listening for more.

"Ready for a margarita, Lucy?"

"Is it three o'clock already? Yes, this tea is cold. And let's go dancing someplace!"

Realizing that neither the margarita offer nor the dancing invitation included her, the raven flies off in search of other conversations, and maybe a margarita.

> The world came about, at least in Cree, as the result of the efforts of a female force of energy called Oomaa-maa, which translates roughly to the Great Mother, a miraculous entity that eventually came to be known in English as Mother Earth. And she, without acknowledgment to the act of conception, gave birth first to the Thunderbird, who would protect the other creatures from the mysterious and destructive sea serpent Kinee-pick.[11]

**Conversation Two (circa 2020)**

Maria and her cousin Charlie are in her living room, kicking back after dinner. Charlie has just returned from his many extensive travels.

Charlie notices a raven perched in the camelia tree. "How come that raven is sitting there right outside your window? Why is she looking at us?"

Maria glances at the raven. "She often comes around. I think she listens only to conversations that really interest her. I wish she would talk to me. I just make up what I think she would say instead."

Charlie lies back on the couch, but with his tall frame, his feet are hanging over. "I took some chilli down to the protesters supporting the Wet'suwet'en at the legislature last night. It felt so good to see all those young people standing up to government and corporate oppression."

Maria also has her feet up. "I'm so conflicted with that situation. I hate the way the issues are reduced to a false dichotomy between hereditary chiefs and elected band councils. Every Wet'suwet'en person is born into her or his mother's kin group, they are all part of the Wet'suwet'en system which includes all the band councillors."

She sits up. "You do know that the current elected chief is also a Wet'suwet'en hereditary chief? He worked with *Delgamuukw*[12] as a Wet'suwet'en interpreter and organizer as a young man. And for decades many of those same band council people have been also involved in past political actions all over Gitxsan and Wet'suwet'en lands, and beyond too."

"I just hate sell-outs," Charlie growls from the couch. "I hate all of them. They don't care about the land. They're just out for themselves!! I even hate looking at them, so smug."

Maria is a little taken aback at Charlie's vehemence. She decides that she has to keep her cool no matter what. "The problem is the way Wet'suwet'en law is just declared by everybody. What is legal here according to Wet'suwet'en law? For instance, we don't know whether and how the chiefs who agreed with the pipeline were and are acting legally within Wet'suwet'en law."

Charlie grumbles to himself, "Here we go again, always about law."

Maria ignores Charlie and takes a big breath. "Nor do we know whether and how the people who are protesting are acting legally according to Wet'suwet'en law, though arguably, as a starting place, they would have the legal obligation to protect their kinship group's territories."

Maria glances at Charlie, who is rolling his eyes as she is speaking. She continues: "What are the consultation and inclusion obligations according to Wet'suwet'en law? Do you know what these legal obligations are? The most important conversations are among the Wet'suwet'en – those folks for and against the pipeline. Canada, the companies, the protesters, and everybody else just need to get out of the way!"

Charlie sits up, and his voice starts to rise just a tiny bit. "What are people supposed to do? Do nothing while the land continues to be destroyed? While the animals lose more habitat? While the water is polluted? While the RCMP violates Indigenous protestors' civil rights? We know what we have to do!"

Maria raises her voice a little too. "Just because I'm asking questions doesn't mean I support the government or oil companies or RCMP here. I am disagreeing with the too-simple story that is being told about Indigenous law and about Indigenous people. As if everything can be reduced to a narrative about good and evil.

"Who should be involved in decisions about a kinship group's lands? What are the legitimate legal processes of reasoning? What are the institutions through which Wet'suwet'en law (as with all law) necessarily operates to solve problems and manage conflict?"

Maria takes a breath, and forces herself to lower and steady her voice. "Every once in a while, there are glimpses of Wet'suwet'en law as real law in the conversations, but the issues get so flattened. You know, even though the media focuses on polarized views, on the ground, there are actually pretty good communication lines among and between the Wet'suwet'en. The media is not much help."

"There is no time for all that now, that can all be done later! We have to protect the land now!" Charlie gets up and starts pacing, "What is going on now just proves that the so-called reconciliation and even democracy in Canada are a farce!"

Maria breathes out heavily, speaking levelly. "Let me be clear, I have the greatest respect for those folks out on the land, especially those that have been out there for an entire decade.

"But if we can't talk about the hard questions now, even between you and me, when can we? The way this protest is playing out is only perpetuating the anti-intellectualism that is sadly becoming part of Canadian politics, including Indigenous politics." Maria gets up and puts another log on the fire.

"Maria, you keep making it too complicated. People don't want to think." Charlie pauses in his pacing, perhaps embarrassed by his own statement. Then undeterred, he continued, "Back home, I got so frustrated with our own community. Every political action would just fizzle out in no time, and as soon as I was gone, people were signing agreements left, right and centre. Money, that was all they cared about. They all sold out! Bastards!"

Charlie is now waving his arms around while continuing to pace. "That's why I support this protest. People are really caring about what is going on. And yes, I know I am acting emotionally!"

Maria smiles, "There was this Dene elder who told me once, 'If there were a bunch of Crees in the room, and a piece of paper blew in one window, they would sign that paper before it blew out the other window!' I don't know, but I am guessing that Crees would probably say the same thing about the Dene! So easy to categorize and dismiss each other – even in the name of fun."

She continues quietly, "I didn't say I didn't support the protest. I said I was worried at the oversimplification of the disputes. I'm also concerned about the long-term effects of this conflict on the collective lives of Wet'suwet'en families and people, and for other Indigenous peoples. Our communities are already so conflicted, it seems all we do is fight." She turned to watch the curious raven who is still listening.

Maria turns back to Charlie. "There is some improvement, I think. For example, there was some better news coverage with more accurate information about who the Wet'suwet'en are as a people with their governance structures. There appear to be more serious steps being taken by state representatives. But it's still a horribly problematic situation.

Horrible, and Wet'suwet'en and other Indigenous peoples are caught right in the middle of the mess.

"One thing I am encouraged by is the recent statement of claim filed by the Wet'suwet'en Likhts'amisyu clan who are making climate change arguments under both Canadian constitutions.[13] That is an inclusive collective action for all clan members with a more meaningful articulation of Wet'suwet'en law and legal processes. There are still Likhts'amisyu members who disagree with the Likht'amisyu chiefs and the other members who are part of this action, but that's okay. There will always be disagreements – the main thing is that people need a legitimate way to sort out the disputes according to their own legalities." Maria is aware that Charlie is practically snorting with impatience.

Exhaling noisily, Charlie sits back down heavily. He shakes his head. "You just don't get it, do you? There are people that want to kill us. They don't care about Indigenous law or even Canadian law. I am willing to fight. We all have to be willing to fight! I know what side I am on. You don't and that is your problem! That is the problem with academics, actually!"

Maria turns away from Charlie and talks directly to the raven, who is now sitting in the dark, but still alert and listening. "You're starting to sound like the freedom convoy truckers or Ford Nation or the Trump supporters! Don't bother me with details, my mind is made up and there is only one way forward. Is that really what you want for Indigenous people?" The raven looks sympathetic.

Encouraged by the raven's response, Maria holds makes a sweeping motion with her arm. "First of all, we have to engage at all levels – what will help to address the very destructive internal conflicts? Vilifying some people and valourizing others according to your own expectations and emotions will just further undermine Wet'suwet'en law! And it will further divide families, kinship groups, and the communities – as if we aren't conflicted enough,"

She continues: "Second, we need to consider the actual dispute and how the damaged relationships between Wet'suwet'en kinship groups can be restored. The hardest conversations are going to be within the Wet'suwet'en – the rest of us have to provide support without imposing our own stereotypes and judgments."

Maria dramatically waves her arm again. "Third, how will the pipeline issue actually be resolved? I hope the Likhts'amisyu legal action finds some traction – it broadens the scope of legal argument to explicitly include Wet'suwet'en law and legal obligations, climate change and the rights of future generations.[14] We need economic imagination too. What is beyond our earth-killing economy?

"We do see some positive changes, like some of the amazing Canadian court judges who are starting to reason with Indigenous law as law – not as merely fact or evidence. We know that answers for Indigenous peoples can't rely entirely on Canadian law."

Charlie stands up and puts his coat on, "You done now? How will anything you're talking about now or those so-called positive changes make a difference for the Wet'suwet'en today or even tomorrow? You are just too darn preachy with no action. Words, just words!"

The raven watches, her head tipped to one side like she is thinking hard. Maria is feeling defeated. "Probably there will be no difference today. But these are exactly the kind of issues and disputes that Indigenous law has to deal with. This is the work of law – if we can't do this together as Indigenous people, then what?

"Indigenous legal orders included requirements of civility – historically, when that broke down, we had wars. We can see this from our oral histories. What about our obligations of civility to one another according to our own laws – including those others we disagree with?" Maria is following Charlie to the front door as he is shrugging into his coat.[15]

Maria tries again: "We have to keep talking, Charlie!"

"I know, but you give me such a headache! I'm going home! I'll see you later," and Charlie heads out the door into the night.

"Charlie," Maria calls out to his back, "There are outstanding issues here!"

But Charlie has already started his pick-up truck. Maria stands on the steps for a few minutes watching his tail lights disappear down the street.

On reflection, Maria decides that she is not unhappy. After all, a least a conversation has been started. Every conversation can be an exploration. There has to be a starting place someplace.

Maria watches as the raven flies off, and wonders if the raven is heading to a meeting of her peers or, better yet, to a party.

### Conversation Three (circa 2023)

> Mother Earth also gave birth to women. And then men, as an afterthought, as they weren't necessary to the act of creation. And mosquitos, by the way. And blackflies … She is far from perfect. Yes, she is beautiful; yes, she is grand. And she is generous, she is bountiful, she is kind and ever-loving and supportive and affectionate. But like the mother goddess Hera in Greek mythology, when tried to the limit by the masculine side of her that is not quite in working order, she can be one jealous, furiously angry force from hell.[16]

Long-time colleagues Jimmy and Mack are having coffee at the university club. Their table is outside by the pond. It is a warm spring day. Turtles and ducks and robins carry on with their busy lives. The sun is streaming through the leaves. The air smells like new cottonwood buds and is filled with energetic robin songs. For years, Jimmy and Mack's working relationship has been friendly and caring, but not really close.

Both have grey hair and grandchildren, and some would even consider them elders. However, neither considers themselves to be elders.

Mack is frustrated, and she has been for a long time. "You know, Jimmy, we've had so many conversations about gender and male privilege, and you care about these issues, and you always agree, but you still don't get it."

Jimmy, who has been watching the ducks, takes a deep breath. "I get so tired of you saying that. What more can I do? What do you expect? Can't we just focus on the positive and do the work that is important to both of us? Why are you so focused on the negative questions?"

"Maybe our conversations are as tired as I am." Mack notices a raven that has landed in the tree nearest their table. The raven begins to watch them. She cocks her head and seems to be listening.

Mack is inexplicitly heartened by the raven's apparent interest. "Let's try this conversation again. I'm feeling optimistic this time!"

Mack starts to recount. "Now, let's see. You remember that gathering in Saskatchewan when I got asked to wear a longer skirt, and then I was told where and how I had to walk in the ceremonial space? But you, your behaviour and your clothing weren't questioned or policed because you're a boy. Remember that?"

Jimmy is looking back through his memories, and slowly nods.

Mack continues, "And the female chief who was publicly chastised by a male elder. Remember? That only happened because she was female, and he needed a public place to stand. She provided his way into the public forum as a stepping-stone, and that is what he did, stepped on her to establish his starting place. That has happened to me lots of times with male elders and leaders in public spaces."

The raven swoops down from the tree to the next table; she lands on the back of a deck chair. Then she vigorously nods using her whole body.

Encouraged, Mack smiles, and recounts, "At conferences, I have had male national leaders, or professors or lawyers, who aggressively and noisily picked up on some tiny or irrelevant aspect of what I said, only to launch into their own topic and rant. They didn't give two poops about my presentation – they were just trying to look smart, and I was dispensable. I was the stepping-stone into the meeting.

"And the audience completely misses the dynamics. They unquestionably accept the male leaders' actions as normal and legitimate. They just ask why that leader or that elder was so mad at me!" Mack thinks for a minute, then says, "I think that people often confuse confidence for intelligence, especially when it is male confidence."

Jimmy has been listening intently. "But aren't we supposed to respect the protocols of the people we are working with? And it was women elders who directed you in that ceremony. He pauses to reflect. "Actually, I don't remember thinking about any of this at the time, now that you mention it."

"Come on, Jimmy, you know that the normalization of sexism and its attendant practices is often enforced by women, including Indigenous women. After all, remember that bell hooks said patriarchy has no gender – she was observing the widespread hostility that surfaces in relation to empowered women.[17] And as women, we can be the absolute meanest to each other and we can also cause the worst lateral damage to each other. Audre Lord wrote about this same phenomenon among Black women. She said that Black women 'have been taught to either ignore our differences or to view them as causes for separation and suspicion rather than forces of change.'"[18]

"Recently, I had a talk with this insightful white guy about his male privilege. Some years ago, he realized that when he walks into a room, people are likely to agree with him and they will do as he suggests, just because he is male. And an older white male at that, who can speak as if he has accepted authority in any situation. I was amazed that he was so self-reflective."

Mack laughs. "And I was amazed that he even noticed his privilege. The privilege is not noticing, not having to notice because sexism and its attendant benefits are so normalized. He only started noticing in the first place because his partner is a strong, outspoken leader – she is the powerhouse in their relationship."

Jimmy sighs, obviously put out. "Haven't I always opposed violence against women and sexist fundamentalism? Haven't I been supportive of you and our other female colleagues? When is enough, enough?" Agitated in his chair, he looks like he is about to storm off.

"Hey, it's not about you being a bad guy!" Mack throws up her hands. "Nice Indigenous men are still blind to their male privilege! So are other non-white men – I can think of some professors, for instance, and white women don't say anything lest they be called racist. We have shameless, normalized sexism in our communities, and we reproduce that sexism wherever we go – in education, government, and business. Everywhere!"

Mack is still smiling but her teeth are gritted, and her face is starting to feel frozen. "Sexism and its many forms, and misogyny, are on a spectrum. At the one end are consequences of male privilege in women's lives – that is sexism. At the other end is the violence against Indigenous women and girls – that is misogyny. One can be sexist but not misogynistic – it's an important distinction.[19]

"And yes, of course there is colonial violence against Indigenous men and boys, but what I focus on is the violence against Indigenous women and girls because of their gender, and gender-diverse peoples too – from both Indigenous and non-Indigenous males."

Jimmy is shaking his head. "What more can I do?" He is feeling unexpectedly discouraged. And even though he likes Mack, he is growing impatient with what he sees as her persistent negativity. And he was feeling so good before lunch.

Mack doesn't want to lose him as an ally and she cares about him as a friend. "You know there are lists of male privilege benefits online … just saying. For starters, pay attention to your privilege and stop taking it for granted. I know you are supportive of me and the other Indigenous women here, but you have to stop assuming that you have simply earned all your special treatments and advantages while none of the Indigenous women around you have."[20]

Jimmy is curious. "What do the online resources on male privilege say? Anything on Indigenous male privilege?"

Mack carefully chooses not to point out that he could have looked these up at any time. Instead, she laughs: "Let's start our own little list of Indigenous male privileges":

1. "Students – male and female, Indigenous and non-Indigenous – will imbue you with authority and will defer to you. They will generally behave better in your classes. They will save their scepticism and disbelief, their bad behaviours and disrespect for their Indigenous female law professors.
   And of course, you should know by now that this does not mean that you just have a 'better classroom manner.'
2. "It will be assumed that as a male, you are the head of all things Indigenous at the university, that you are the boss man, and therefore the absolute expert on all Indigenous matters.
3. "It will be assumed that you should be the principal investigator of any research grants because your stature ensures securing the necessary approvals, and your Indigenous female colleagues will do the actual work. You don't question this; rather you accept that this is okay and normal.

4. "Your behaviours and clothing will not be policed at communities or at universities that are trying to 'Indigenize.' It is less likely that people, including students, will feel free to comment on your clothing or appearance.
5. "Your female colleagues will have full (aka unshared) and unrelenting loads of family care-giving responsibilities for ageing parents, kids, grandkids, extended families, and their communities. They will likely find it difficult to schedule blocks of time for writing, research, and other academic responsibilities.
6. "You will likely not have male elders and leaders making inappropriate comments or trying to grab you in the shadows. This used to be the norm for me, and it's still the norm for many young Indigenous women.
7. "The extent of sexual harassment you experience will be significantly lower than that of your female counterparts."

Mack has been ticking things off on her fingers. She takes a deep breath, wondering how Jimmy will take this, then: "That's a start. Can you think of anything else?"

Jimmy is listening; so is the raven. "There is this Indigenous professor at the University of Alberta who hired a feminist leadership coach. He said it profoundly changed how he related to his female colleagues, and he is really glad of this. But you know, he also said he now ends up listening to sexist jokes on the part of those same Indigenous female professors."

Mack is nodding, sadly, "I know. We have a long way to go, but it doesn't mean we shouldn't start to take this on. All of us."

Unexpectedly, Jimmy smiles. "Hey Mack, since you like uncomfortable conversations so much, let's talk about divas or diva-ism next time!"

Mack is caught off guard. "Wait, what?"

Jimmy is still smiling; in fact, he looks quite happy to have caught Mack by surprise. "You know we do have our Indigenous divas, right? What are the power politics of that?"

Mack breaks out in a loud laugh as she puts her coat on. "You saying I'm a diva, Jimmy? Absolutely, let's talk divas next time!"

"I wouldn't dream of suggesting that you're a diva, Mack! How could you think that?" But Jimmy is looking just a little sly.

The raven is suddenly looking positively diva-ish, then does a raven strut back and forth on the back of the chair. She glances at Mack and Jimmy and takes to the sky. Mack wonders what conversation she will fly to next.

## Conversation Four (circa 2050)

> Sometime in the first half of the twentieth century, the local missionary priest … once asked a Dene girl of not much more than ten years of age, "What is the most miraculous thing we can see in this life?"
>
> "The caribou," answered the girl …
>
> Arrogantly, the old priest chortled, "No my dear, no. It is the angels."[21]

I have four grandsons. When Hawk was six, he asked me why women weren't smarter in movies. We had just watched his movie choice, *Indiana Jones*. I was not sure how to respond to a six-year-old on this question.

Now imagine about thirty years from now when this next conversation takes place. The setting is the entrance foyer of the rebuilt Faculty of Law at the University of Victoria. The fog swirls by the large windows and rain streaks down and sometimes across the glass. The weather is big today, as is necessary to occasionally put humans in their place, a more frequent event now with climate change. Just outside, hanging onto a branch swaying vigorously in the wind, is a raven. She is muttering to herself as she smooths down her glossy blue-black feathers that keep getting disarranged by the wind.

There is a prominent student-made sign over the doors: "Indigenous feminisms are medicine for Indigenous peoples and for Indigenous law." Below the sign in an alcove two brothers are seated, both of whom work with Indigenous law and with Canadian law. Hawk Napoleon is a law professor in the JD/JID (Juris Doctor and Juris Indigenarium Doctor, aka the dual law degree program with both Indigenous law and Canadian law). Owl Napoleon, KC, is a prominent lawyer specializing in Indigenous land and constitutional law. They are meeting early one morning to prepare a thirty-year-anniversary retrospective paper for the JID/JD, and they have decided to focus on the importance of Indigenous feminism to Indigenous law throughout their respective careers.

Hawk leans back in the comfy chair. "OMG, where do we start on this? What were we thinking when we agreed to do this? Why did you talk me into this anyway?"

"As if I could talk you into anything, Hawk. Anyway, quit complaining, we're here so let's do some work." Owl pauses as he glances out the window. "I don't know, but I think the spirit of our law professor Kokum is in the form of that raven over there. She's really watching us." Owl waves at the raven through the window. In response, the raven nods, or was that the wind swaying the branch?

Hawk looks at the raven a little distractedly and nods back, but he wants to get started. "Come on, bro, I have a class to teach soon, and I have so much work to do before then. And then I'm picking up the kids from school, and the baby didn't sleep well last night. I wonder if she's teething?" He yawns and pulls out his computer.

"I hear you, Hawk. The twins had a pajama party last night with friends and kept sneaking out of their room for endless snacks." Owl already has his computer balanced across his knees, and his fingers are tapping across the keyboard. "Okay, I sketched out some governing principles from my law practice. Our Indigenous law group has been working with communities to articulate and develop citizenship legislation and inclusive governing processes."

Hawk has his computer out. "So what does it mean to have Indigenous feminisms as the starting place and foundation of Indigenous law? You know, it's hard to imagine how it used to be in Kokum's day. No wonder she was so pissed off! Well, sometimes anyway." He glances worriedly at the raven, who is watching very intently.

"Remember Kokum's maxim, 'People will live in the worlds they believe to exist, so the work of Indigenous law is to expand the legal imagination.'[22] If people don't see or understand Indigenous feminisms, they simply have a narrower lens through which to see Indigenous law, or any law for that matter." Owl leans back and stretches.

"She also said law was a lens, a grid of intelligibility through which things were visible or invisible.[23] Okay, today, Indigenous feminisms are the norm for Indigenous law. What is different from how it used to be?" Hawk is typing.

"Wait, what are you writing down?" Owl hates getting left behind by his big brother.

"Just looking at the grandfather of Indigenous law, John Borrows – this is important." Hawk is scrolling down his screen. "Hmm, still so true," he reads:

> If an over-exalted view of a tradition is applied, it could limit ordinary people from connecting to it when faced with their messy and often mundane circumstances. Legal traditions must have an air of reality about their present-day applications. People will have trouble making their laws work for them if a hard-edged realism is not combined with the necessary idealism that underlies most legal systems.[24]

"We should include that quote," Hawk notes, then asks, "But what exactly is different today from thirty years ago? First, most Indigenous nationalisms no longer include idealized stereotypes of Indigenous women as being important only because they're mothers or because they form the so-called cultural or spiritual heart of the people. Remember how these essentializations just gave permission to be violent to women who failed to live up to the idealized stereotypes? Didn't Kokum write about that?"[25]

Owl joins in: "For white people, these sexist nationalisms were imagined and expressed in the *Handmaid's Tale* by literary trickster Atwood. But for Indigenous people, this nationalist rhetoric was supposed to define us. Hard to imagine people buying into that kind of rhetoric now!" He holds up his hand to prevent Hawk from jumping in. "I know, I know, don't tell me, humans are always susceptible because of our desperate search for easy answers to everything."

He continues, "Another change is that the stand-in for Indigenous people is no longer the Indigenous male. Now we start with both the reasonable Indigenous woman and the reasonable Indigenous man,[26] and of course we also have the reasonable Indigenous trans-person, and bisexual, gays and lesbians too. Kokum called this the "raven's garden" back in the day."[27]

Hawk's morning coffee finally kicks in and he starts to wake up. He wonders if the raven's presence means he should be more creative. "Indigenous reasoning is explicitly understood as including the whole cisgendered person and LGBTQ+ person – and as being contextualized and informed by emotion and ethics and context. What else?" He snaps his fingers for effect.

Owl catches his brother's energy. "Okay, one starting place for Indigenous feminism is citizenship conversations and Indigenous personhood. In one of her papers, Kokum asked:"

> What is the Gitxsan legal imaginary? According to Gitxsan law, only a Gitxsan person or legal personality has rights, protections, privileges, responsibilities, and legal liability, although there are a range of legal mechanisms for extending such recognition to non-Gitxsan peoples for various purposes.
>
> So how might women and girls have understood themselves historically and today as legal persons in Gitxsan society in accordance with Gitxsan law?[28]

Hawk continues, "And when we teach Indigenous or state law today, we ensure students see all law as always being gendered and relational. One way I do this is by switching genders when analysing oral histories and cases. This always raises a lot of questions and debate but not like before. Remember Kokum was called blasphemous when she did that?"

Owl turns to the raven. "Kokum, are we getting anywhere? Yes, there are still many outstanding issues. I know we still haven't recovered from the Indigenous dark ages with the missing and murdered Indigenous women and girls. But then I don't know how a people can really recover from that."

Hawk jumps in. "We haven't recovered as Indigenous peoples. I think that this is a really complicated issue. I heard a quote from a Holocaust survivor that applies here: 'The past I have not lived, but that lives in me.'[29] That quote could be about the colonial violence documented by the Truth and Reconciliation Commission of Canada[30] and the Missing and Murdered Indigenous Women and Girls Inquiry,[31] you know, from back in the day?"

Owl is looking thoughtful. "I think this connects to the whole genocide denial of Jewish people, and the denial of the violence of settler colonialism, including all misogynist violence documented by the Missing and Murdered Indigenous Women and Girls inquiry. There's a lot of literature about all this, including on the continuing intergenerational trauma.[32] Hawk, we have to make sure none of this is ever forgotten or denied."

Hawk is squinting at his computer. "Right on, brother. I think Kokum's article had something on this. Here it is:"

> To remember this history is not for the sake of keeping alive the memories of old tyrannies, but to recognize present tyranny, for these patterns are still in us. It would be strange if they were not. It is these patterns that I believe we should study, become conscious of, and recognize as they emerge in us and in the societies we live in.[33]

The raven bobs her head. Then she smooths down her feathers again.

Owl turns back to Hawk. "We know that there are still too few Indigenous women and LGBTQ+ folk who are partners in law firms – in Canada and elsewhere. How are the numbers for full professorships?"

Hawk is shaking his head. "Sadly, they're still way too low. I think many Indigenous women are still bearing most of the heavy loads of family and communities. There is still so much work to do at the family and community levels."

Owl has turned back to the raven. "I always thought that we only had to do one seismic feminist shift to move us past the rigid, fundamentalist approaches to gender and law. But it's ongoing, and we still resist real questions about power relations. We still need more practical and productive legal deliberation. We also need to keep space open to support people holding various opinions."

The raven flies away. What was that? Something about generations and law?

Owl laughs. "Hawk, she's gone. I think we're done here. Wait, was she laughing?"

Hawk is looking at his phone. "Hey, I have to go to the school. My youngest is not feeling well."

Owl gathers his things and stuffs his computer in his bag. "See you later, bro!"

**Conversation Five (circa 2023)**

> "Will God let my father in?" I ask this of Father Cheepootaat [Thiboudeau] – which-rhymes-eemataat (which is what I sometimes call him myself).
>
> "No," snaps Father Cheepootaat. "Sorry. Accordions are not allowed in heaven."
>
> Distraught that my father might have to change instruments or go to hell, I vow to help him keep his accordion.[34]

In the early 1800s, six Indigenous women from across Canada were buried at the Ross Bay Cemetery in Victoria, British Columbia. These women were married into the five founding families of Victoria, and for an all-too-brief period of time they were politically, economically, legally, and socially important.[35] When I look at that graveyard now (and since this is Victoria, there are often deer snoozing and resting up against the tombstones), I imagine the spirits of these Indigenous women taking the form of trickster Grandmother Ravens – as contemporary feminist tricksters. And we all know that Indigenous tricksters are the first law teachers who teach by slapping us upside the head when we take ourselves too seriously, but who can also teach with humour and love too.

So, imagine that this murder of Kokum[36] Ravens have gathered in this oceanside cemetery. Gnarly and twisted Garry oaks, elegant elms, and various graceful evergreens provide shade. It is always a beautiful place, rain or shine, misty or windy. The Kokum Ravens perch on the tombstones and are enjoying the lovely sea breezes but disdainfully look down their beaks at the lounging deer. Their innovative research methodology is that of eavesdropping.[37]

Josette is wearing a purple kerchief over her head Kokum-style. "Hey, I was in northern BC last week attending a treaty meeting and you won't believe what happened! It was so funny! Leonard was going on and on about how the young people did not properly respect him as an elder. Just quacking on, he was, then Tough Bugger[38] stood up across the room and said, 'They don't respect you 'cause you're an asshole, Leonard!' I laughed so hard that I just about fell off the window ledge. Everybody else was laughing too, 'cept Leonard of course." At this, all the other Kokum Ravens break out in a good belly laugh.

Josette is still laughing. "You should have seen the faces of the white lawyers. They didn't know what to do, or whether it was okay for them to laugh. Just hilarious!" The Kokums break out in another round of laughter.

Sighing, Isabella, whose kerchief is red, begins, "Ah, it feels so good to laugh. Okay, we've been lamenting the rise of anti-intellectualism. I heard you can get inoculated against the polarized thinking in the infodemic?"

"What the …?" Matilda looks astonished. "A vaccination against stupidity? Where did you hear this? It sounds too good to be true."

Isabella is nodding. "I heard it on CBC radio so it must true. This guy said that we've suffered not one but two outbreaks. One was the biological epidemic of COVID-19, the other he called an 'infodemic' of political, medical, and scientific misinformation."

Amelia is intrigued. "How does it work? Everybody should get this shot."

"It's not a shot," Isabella explains. "This guy, Sander van der Linden, tested this inoculation on YouTube. He found that if he exposed people to the techniques used to create misinformation, they learned to recognize them, and then they could create intellectual antibodies as a way to build resistance, much like vaccines build resistance to disease."[39]

"I love it! This is so fantastic!" Neshaki is practically dancing over the tombstone. Well done, Josette!"

"We need this in our communities too," Sofia notes. "Look at what happened round the whole question of vaccinations. Indigenous communities and families were divided in heartbreaking ways."

The Kokum Ravens begin considering future research they have to do. Down-to-earth Neshaki turned to the book they had selected: "We're supposed to be commenting on each chapter. Have you done your homework?"

"Bossy pants," Sofia breathes just under her breath. "Of course we have, Neshaki, let's get at it! I have much to say."

NOTES

1 Tomson Highway, *Laughing with the Trickster: On Sex, Death, and Accordions* (Toronto: House of Anansi Press, 2022) at 67.
2 Friedensreich Hundertwasser, quoted in *ibid* at foreword n.p.
3 "Pkols" is the Coast Salish name for the little mountain in Victoria. Its English name is Mount Douglas, after the first British Columbia premier, Sir James Douglas. "PKOLS can be translated as 'White Head' and was possibly a Songhees abbreviated version of a SENĆOŦEN name that was originally longer; it is for this reason that it is sometimes spelled with an abbreviation. The translation … has significant geological and historical implications. There is an oral history that suggests this translation … to P'KOLS being the place where glaciers last receded from Southern Vancouver Island." Lliam Hilderbrand, *Victoria and Region Green Map: A History of PKOLS (Mount Douglas)*, online: <https://crdcommunitygreenmap.ca/story/history-pkols-mount-douglas>.
4 Miriam Toews, *Women Talking* (Toronto: Alfred A. Knopf, 2018).
5 "The *Trickster* is a central figure in the myth worlds of many hunting and gathering societies. A divine figure, but deeply flawed and very human, the *Trickster* is found in myth cycles from the Americas, Africa, Australia, and Siberia ... *The Trickster* symbolizes the frailty and human qualities of the gods and their closeness to humans. These stand in pointed contrast to the omnipotent, all-knowing but distant deities that are central to the pantheons of state religions and their powerful ecclesiastical hierarchies." Richard Lee & Richard Daly, "Foragers and Others" in Richard Lee & Richard Daly, eds, *The Cambridge Encyclopedia of Hunters and Gatherers* (Cambridge: Cambridge University Press, 1999) 1 at 4–5 [footnotes omitted].
6 See for example Margaret Atwood, *The Handmaid's Tale* (Toronto: McClelland & Stewart, 1985); *The Testaments* (Toronto: McClelland & Stewart, 2019).
7 Highway, *supra* note 1.
8 For example, see the wonderful Trickster trilogy by Eden Robinson: *Return of the Trickster* (Toronto: Alfred A. Knopf, 2021); *Trickster Drift* (Toronto: Alfred A. Knopf, 2018), and *Son of a Trickster* (Toronto: Alfred A. Knopf, 2017).
9 Highway, *supra* note 1 at 70.
10 Mirjam Hirsch, "Subversive Humour: Canadian Native Playwrights' Winning Weapon of Resistance" in Drew Hayden Taylor, ed, *Me Funny* (Vancouver: Douglas & McIntyre, 2005) 99 at 109.
11 Highway, *supra* note 1 at 67.
12 *Delgamuukw* v *British Columbia*, [1997] 3 SCR 1010, 1997 CarswellBC 2358.

13 *Misdzi Yikh* v *Canada*, [2020] FCJ No. 1109, 2020 FC 1059 (motion to strike granted on the basis that the Plaintiffs' *Charter* claims were not justiciable).
14 The scope of the argument included claims of the violation of constitutional rights in ss 7 and 15 of the *Charter*, as well as the novel claim that Canada breached a duty under s 91 of the *Constitution Act, 1867* by not ensuring low GHG emissions under the "peace, order, and good government" clause. See statement of claim online: <https://raventrust.com/wp-content/uploads/2021/06/Likhtsamisyu-Statement-of-Claim-February-2020.pdf>.
15 Val Napoleon, "Demanding More from Ourselves: Indigenous Civility and Incivility" in Dimitrios Karmis & Jocelyn Maclure, eds, *Civic Freedom in an Age of Diversity* (Montreal/Kingston: McGill-Queen's University Press, 2023). Also see Val Napoleon & Hadley Friedland, "Accessing Tully" in Robert Nichols & Jakeet Singh, eds, *Freedom and Democracy in an Imperial Context: Dialogues with James Tully* (London: Routledge, 2014).
16 Highway, *supra* note 1 at 57.
17 bell hooks quoted in Rachel Loewen Walker, "Call It Misogyny" (2022) 0:0 Feminist Theory 1 at 2.
18 Barbara Smith, "Introduction to Home Girls: A Black Feminist Anthology" in Barbara Ryan, ed, *Identity Politics in the Women's Movement* (New York: New York University Press, 2001) at 146.
19 Naomi Wolf et al., "Sexism and Misogyny: What's the Difference?" *The Guardian* (17 October 2012), online: <https://www.theguardian.com/commentisfree/2012/oct/17/difference-between-sexism-and-misogyny>. Also see Loewen Walker, *supra* note 17.
20 For example, see <https://xyonline.net/sites/xyonline.net/files/The%20Male%20Privilege%20Checklist.pdf>.
21 Highway, *supra* note 1 at 166.
22 Adapted from Ronald Crelinsten, "The World of Torture: A Constructed Reality" (2003) 7 Theoretical Criminology 293 at 293.
23 Val Napoleon, "Did I Break It? Recording Indigenous (Customary) Law" (2019) 22 PER/PELJ 1 at 25.
24 John Borrows, *Canada's Indigenous Constitution* (Toronto: University of Toronto Press, 2010) at 105.
25 Val Napoleon, "An Imaginary for Our Sisters" in Jeffery Hewitt, Beverly Jacobs & Richard Moon, eds, *Indigenous Spirituality and Religious Freedom* (Toronto: University of Toronto Press, 2025).
26 Hadley Friedland, "Navigating through Narratives of Despair: Making Space for the Cree Reasonable Person in the Canadian Justice System" (2016) 67 UNB 269 at 280 and 288.
27 Val Napoleon, "Raven's Garden: A Discussion about Aboriginal Sexual Orientation and Transgender Issues" (2002) 17:2 Canadian Journal of Law and Society 149.

28 Val Napoleon, "Gitxsan Legal Personhood: Gendered" in Austin Sarat, George Pavlich & Richard Mailey, eds, *Interrupting the Legal Person* (Studies in Law, Politics, and Society, Vol 87A) (Bingley, UK: Emerald, 2022) 19.

29 Quoted by Lillian Boraks-Nemetz of the Vancouver Holocaust Education Centre, speaking at a panel titled "Reconciliation & Holocaust Remembrance: Conversations on Intergenerational Trauma and Healing in Jewish and Indigenous Communities" held at Government House, Victoria, BC, 19 January 2023.

30 For the TRC reports and calls to action, see <https://nctr.ca/about/history-of-the-trc/trc-website/>.

31 For the National Inquiry into Missing and Murdered Indigenous Women and Girls, see <https://www.mmiwg-ffada.ca/final-report/>.

32 See for example Rebecca Bychutsky, *Social Denial: An Analysis of Missing and Murdered Indigenous Women and Girls in Canada* (Master's Thesis, University of Ottawa, 2017) [unpublished]; *A Legal Analysis of Genocide*, supplementary report of the National Inquiry into Missing and Murdered Indigenous Women and Girls (Ottawa: MMIWG, 2019), online: <https://www.mmiwg-ffada.ca/wp-content/uploads/2019/06/Supplementary-Report_Genocide.pdf>; Laurence J Kirmayer, Joseph P Gone & Joshua Moses, "Rethinking Historical Trauma" (2014) 51(3) Transcultural Psychiatry 299; Leonie Pihama Paul Reynolds, Rihi Te Nana, et al,et al, "Positioning Historical Trauma Theory within Aotearoa New Zealand" (2014) 10(3) AlterNative: An International Journal of Indigenous Peoples 248 (see p 257 where state officials were very upset about comparison of Indigenous genocide with the Holocaust}; Michelle A Stanley, "Beyond Erasure: Indigenous Genocide Denial and Settler Colonialism" in John Cox, Amal Khoury & Sarah Minslow, eds, *Denial: The Final Stage of Genocide?* (London: Routledge, 2021).

33 Doris Lessing, *Prisons We Choose to Live Inside*, (New York: Harper Perennial, 1986) at 30, quoted in Val Napoleon, "Indigenous Discourse: Gender, Identity, and Community" in Ben Richardson, Shin Imai & Kent McNeil, eds, *Indigenous Peoples and the Law* (Oxford: Hart, 2009) 233 at 233.

34 *Ibid* at 150. According to Tomson Highway, the pronunciation "Cheepootaat" was the closest the Cree children's tongues could get to "Thiboudeau" because they spoke Cree as their first language, not French or English (at 145).

35 Sylvia Van Kirk, "Tracing the Fortunes of Five Founding Families of Victoria" (1997/98) no 115/116 BC Studies 149. Amelia Douglas (née Connolly) was a Cree woman from Fort Churchill married in 1828 to John Douglas, then Chief Factor (HBC) and later first governor of the Colony of British Columbia. Josette Work (née Legacé), a Coast Salish woman from

Washington, married Chief Factor (HBC) John Work in 1826. Josette is also described as Métis and as Spokane. Isabella Ross (née Mainville) was an Anishinaabe woman from the Great Lakes who married HBC fur trading clerk Charles Ross in the early 1840s. Matilda McNeill (maiden name not recorded in historical documents), a Haida woman from the Queen Charlotte Islands (Haida Gwaii), married sea Captain and HBC Chief Factor William McNeill. Neshaki McNeill (maiden name not recorded in historical documents), a Nisga'a woman from northwest British Columbia, married Captain McNeill when Matilda died. Sofia Tod (née Lolo), a Secwepemc woman from Kamloops, married Chief Trader John Tod. There is obviously much more to these women's stories than what is provided here.

36 "Kokum" means "grandmother" in Cree, and there are variations of spelling and tenses.

37 Interestingly, we are not interested in loud conversations, which we find intrusive. Rather, we want to hear those quiet conversations. We tune in to quiet voices. The best eavesdropping occurs when we have to strain a bit to catch what the voices are saying. See John Locke, *Eavesdropping: An Intimate History* (Oxford: Oxford University Press, 2010); Audrey McDermott, "Eavesdropping Actually Makes Us Better People," *Quartz* (23 August 2017), online: <https://qz.com/1035252/eavesdropping-is-your-best-bad-habit/>.

38 One of the author's relatives was called Tough Bugger Napoleon.

39 Sander van der Linden, interviewed by Bob McDonald, *Quirks and Quarks*, CBC Radio (21 January 2023).

## SOURCES CITED

Atwood, Margaret. *The Handmaid's Tale* (Toronto: McClelland & Stewart, 1985).

Atwood, Margaret. *The Testaments* (Toronto: McClelland & Stewart, 2019).

Boraks-Nemetz, Lillian. "Becoming the Enlightened Witness: Presentation to the Ben Gurion Society." Lecture delivered at the panel "Reconciliation & Holocaust Remembrance: Conversations on Intergenerational Trauma and Healing in Jewish and Indigenous Communities" Vancouver Holocaust Education Centre, 19 January 2023 [unpublished].

Borrows. John. *Canada's Indigenous Constitution* (Toronto: University of Toronto Press, 2010).

Bychutsky, Rebecca. *Social Denial: An Analysis of Missing and Murdered Indigenous Women and Girls in Canada* (Master's Thesis, University of Ottawa, 2017) [unpublished].

Canada, Truth and Reconciliation Commission of Canada. *Canada's Residential Schools: The Final Report of the Truth and Reconciliation Commission of Canada* (Montreal/Kingston: McGill-Queen's University Press, 2015).

Crelinsten, Ronald. "The World of Torture: A Constructed Reality" (2003) 7 Theoretical Criminology 293.

Friedland, Hadley. "Navigating through Narratives of Despair: Making Space for the Cree Reasonable Person in the Canadian Justice System" (2016) 67 UNB 269.

Highway, Tomson. *Laughing with the Trickster: On Sex, Death, and Accordions* (Toronto: Anansi, 2022).

Hilderbrand, Lliam. *Victoria and Region Green Map: A History of PKOLS (Mount Douglas)*. online: <https://crdcommunitygreenmap.ca/story/history-pkols-mount-douglas>.

Hirch, Mirjam. "Subversive Humour: Canadian Native Playwrights' Winning Weapon of Resistance" in Drew Hayden Taylor, ed, *Me Funny* (Vancouver: Douglas & McIntyre, 2005) 99.

Kirmayer, Laurence J, Joseph P Gone & Joshua Moses. "Rethinking Historical Trauma" (2014) 51(3) Transcultural Psychiatry 299.

Lee, Richard & Richard Daly. "Foragers and Others" in Richard Lee & Richard Daly, eds, *The Cambridge Encyclopedia of Hunters and Gatherers* (Cambridge: Cambridge University Press, 1999) 1.

Locke, John. *Eavesdropping: An Intimate History* (Oxford: Oxford University Press, 2010).

McDermott, Audrey. "Eavesdropping Actually Makes Us Better People," *Quartz* (23 August 2017), online: <https://qz.com/1035252/eavesdropping-is-your-best-bad-habit/>.

Napoleon, Val. "Demanding More from Ourselves: Indigenous Civility and Incivility" in Dimitrios Karmis & Jocelyn Maclure, eds, *Civic Freedom in an Age of Diversity: The Public Philosophy of James Tully* (Montreal/Kingston: McGill-Queen's University Press, 2023).

Napoleon, Val. "Did I Break It? Recording Indigenous (Customary) Law" (2019) 22 PER/PELJ 1.

Napoleon, Val. "Gitxsan Legal Personhood: Gendered" in Austin Sarat, George Pavlich & Richard Mailey, eds, *Interrupting the Legal Person*, Studies in Law, Politics, and Society, Vol 87A (Bingley, UK: Emerald, 2022) 19.

Napoleon, Val. "An Imaginary for Our Sisters" in Jeffery Hewitt, Beverly Jacobs & Richard Moon, eds, *Indigenous Spirituality and Religious Freedom* (Toronto: University of Toronto Press, 2015).

Napoleon, Val. "Indigenous Discourse: Gender, Identity, and Community" in Ben Richardson, Shin Imai & Kent McNeil, eds, *Indigenous Peoples and the Law* (Oxford: Hart, 2009) 233.

Napoleon, Val. "Raven's Garden: A Discussion about Aboriginal Sexual Orientation and Transgender Issues" (2002) 17:2 Cdn J Law and Soc 149.

Napoleon, Val & Hadley Friedland. "Accessing Tully" in Robert Nichols & Jakeet Singh, eds, *Freedom and Democracy in an Imperial Context: Dialogues with James Tully* (London: Routledge, 2014).

Pihama, Leonie, Paul Reynolds, Cherryl Smith, John Reid, Linda Tuhiwai Smith & Rihi Te Nana. "Positioning Historical Trauma Theory within Aotearoa New Zealand" (2014) 10(3) AlterNative 248.

Robinson, Eden. *Return of the Trickster* (Toronto: Alfred A. Knopf, 2021).

Robinson, Eden. *Son of a Trickster* (Toronto: Alfred A. Knopf, 2017).

Robinson, Eden. *Trickster Drift* (Toronto: Alfred A. Knopf, 2018).

Smith, Barbara. "Introduction to Home Girls: A Black Feminist Anthology" in Barbara Ryan, ed, *Identity Politics in the Women's Movement* (New York: New York University Press, 2001).

Stanley, Michelle A. "Beyond Erasure: Indigenous Genocide Denial and Settler Colonialism" in John Cox, Amal Khoury & Sarah Minslow, eds, *Denial: The Final Stage of Genocide?* (London: Routledge, 2021).

Toews, Miriam. *Women Talking* (Toronto: Alfred A. Knopf, 2018).

Van der Linden, Sander. Interview by Bob McDonald, *Quirks and Quarks*, CBC Radio, 21 January 2023.

Van Kirk, Sylvia. "Tracing the Fortunes of Five Founding Families of Victoria" (1997/98) 115/116 BC Studies 149.

Walker, Rachel Loewen. "Call It Misogyny" (2022) 25:1 Feminist Theory 1.

Wolf, Naomi, Julie Bindel, Nina Power, Rahila Gupta, Rhiannon Lucy Cosslett & Bidisha. "Sexism and Misogyny: What's the Difference?" *The Guardian* (17 October 2012), online: <https://www.theguardian.com/commentisfree/2012/oct/17/difference-between-sexism-and-misogyny>.

## JURISPRUDENCE

*Delgamuukw v British Columbia*, [1997]3 SCR 1010, 1997 CarswellBC 2358.

*Misdzi Yikh v Canada*, [2020]FCJ No 1109, 2020 FC 1059.

# 1 An Introduction: Indigenous Feminist Legal Studies

EMILY SNYDER

When I was a graduate student in sociology, I had the opportunity to sit in on a couple of law school courses. Law schools can be difficult spaces to inhabit – they can feel like only those officially in law programs or who are trained as lawyers belong (and even then, people can be made to feel like outsiders because of gender, sexuality, Indigeneity, race, nationhood, class, age, and ability[1]). The courses that I sat in on were taught by Val Napoleon. Napoleon pushed the boundaries of who was allowed to be in the classroom and what could be talked about. Back in 2010, she asked her students to consider what Indigenous feminist legal theory might mean and do. Napoleon has been asking important disruptive questions for some time, as we can see from her prologue to this volume.[2] When asking what Indigenous feminist legal theory might mean and do, she was asking us to think about Indigenous feminist legal analyses of *Indigenous* legal orders – of Indigenous peoples' *own* laws. There have been invaluable written (and on-the-ground) interventions by Indigenous women[3] that have interrupted and refused "gender-neutral" engagement with settler laws and how it impacts Indigenous women.[4] That scholarship, importantly, demonstrates how heteropatriarchal and settler colonial oppressions are intertwined, and how state laws work to maintain and reproduce those inequalities, for example through settler conceptualizations of gender identity, sexuality, family, property, economics, and politics. But Napoleon was asking us to do something different. She was asking us to expand the conversation, to expand how we were imagining law, and to expand what we thought feminist legal praxis was and where it happens.

When Napoleon asked that question more than a decade ago, it stuck with me. I had been studying feminism and law, and was learning about Indigenous feminisms, but as a white settler educated through lenses that normalized and naturalized settler colonial frameworks and institutions, I had neglected to consider Indigenous feminist legal frameworks and critical feminist engagement with *Indigenous* laws. As a way to engage with Napoleon's question, I wrote about Indigenous feminist legal theory by drawing on feminist legal theory, Indigenous legal theory, and Indigenous feminist theory,[5] assessing the gaps but also connections between that work. There are many ways to answer her question, and that was the particular path that I took at that time. Frameworks can be useful for understanding law, though they need to grow and change, and parts that are no longer useful should be set aside. This approach is similar to what is needed with law itself, and this work needs to be collective. Indigenous feminist legal ethics and praxis are also taken up in the everyday well beyond academic writing, and have been part of Indigenous legal orders, reasoning, and debates, even if they are not labelled as such.[6]

Much has happened in the past decade, and it is vital to reflect on what Indigenous feminist legal studies could mean and do today. There have been unprecedented changes in law school curriculum as content on Indigenous laws has increased and challenged commonly held assumptions about law in settler states.[7] That work has included the creation of the JID program at the University of Victoria, where one can complete a degree in Indigenous and Canadian laws, and the creation of an innovative research unit on Indigenous laws.[8] Scholarly and community articulations and practices of Indigenous feminisms have deepened and broadened, continuing to claim and create space in new ways and building on intergenerational Indigenous feminist activism.[9] And the realities of sexual violence faced by Indigenous women, girls, and those who are 2SLGBTQI+[10] have become increasingly present in public discourse.[11]

While consciousness of these issues has been growing, and work on Indigenous feminisms has made dynamic and provocative interventions, the field of Indigenous law (the study of Indigenous peoples' own legal orders) has yet to take up sustained engagement with Indigenous feminisms, gender, and sexuality.[12] In the prologue Napoleon asks: "What would our conversations look like in a world where Indigenous feminisms are bold and wildly on the loose and in everyone's face? Where Indigenous feminisms are the norm and not the exception?" (p 4). This collection is intended to treat Indigenous feminisms as normal, as insightful, as intellectually and practically robust, as requisite for conversations about law, and as meaningfully disruptive. In addition to the individual interventions made through each chapter, this book as a whole is intended to be an example of making critical feminist analyses normal in conversations about Indigenous laws and in deconstructions of settler laws. It should not be interpreted as a special-interest book or a text that could only be used in a gender and law course – rather, with this collection we aim to illustrate how analyses of Indigenous legal issues can change when gender is engaged *throughout*, rather than only occasionally in a chapter here and there.

## What Is Indigenous Feminist Legal Studies?

A short introduction to Indigenous feminist legal studies is provided here for readers who are new to this topic. The brief description that follows draws on relevant literature, the chapters in this collection, and conversations between some contributors regarding this introduction.[13] Indigenous feminist legal studies entails numerous theories, methodologies, methods, and pedagogical practices[14] for thinking critically about power, gender, sexuality, and Indigenous legal issues. These divergent approaches are evidenced by the chapters in this collection, by the academic work that has grown in this area,[15] and by the actions of people on the ground who leverage Indigenous feminist and queer ethics for legal change on a large scale and in everyday interactions. Within this chapter I will use the label "Indigenous feminist legal studies" (hereinafter IFLS), though readers should note that others might use different terms, including those contextually relevant to their analysis. (For example, chapter 2 by Darcy Lindberg in this collection draws on and engages with nêhiyaw law for a close analysis of gender and power.) Given the breadth and complexities of specific Indigenous legal orders, and that we are only examining IFLS in the context of Turtle Island and in relation to specific settler nation states, there is not one set answer to the question of what IFLS is, and rigid boundaries should not be put around IFLS. However, there are some central features.

An underlying assumption in IFLS is that gender and sexuality matter. Indigenous people who identify as women, as non-binary, as men, and as 2SLGBTQI+ have distinct experiences in relation to sex, gender, and sexuality.[16] Heteropatriarchy is core to the structure of settler society, and it is vital to understand how these power dynamics impact Indigenous people, communities, and laws, and how settler gender norms have been imposed on Indigenous nations through settler laws and institutions.[17] Settler colonialism and heteropatriarchy are deeply entangled social structures that have worked to create settler nations through gendered violence and oppression.[18] It is vital to recognize the complexity of gendered power dynamics experienced by Indigenous communities – understanding the imposition and impacts of settler gender norms on Indigenous societies – while also not treating Indigenous societies and gender norms as without disagreement and conflict.[19] As the conversation between Jimmy and Mack in the prologue made uncomfortably clear, Indigenous men experience male privilege alongside the complexities of facing settler colonial harms (pp 13–15). These are issues not only within universities, as Mack implored Jimmy to understand (*ibid*). Gendered power dynamics can also be experienced in relation to Indigenous governance, law, economics, health, family issues, and social representations.[20]

IFLS encourages attending to the uncomfortable and complicated ways that gender is differently experienced and to the uneven ways that Indigenous people are either empowered or constrained in relation to their gender identities, sexuality, and gender expressions. Indigenous laws and settler laws do not operate in isolation from these gendered contexts, and law can be a site through which gendered power dynamics are either reproduced or challenged. As IFLS continues to emerge in academic work, there needs to be ongoing and sustained conversations with, and reflections on, Indigenous trans, two-spirit, and queer studies, including further discussion about what Indigenous queer legal studies (including theories, methodologies, and pedagogies) might mean and do for teaching and practising Indigenous law. While it seems vital to state that IFLS should be queer, and Indigenous queer legal studies should be feminist, given the interconnected relationship between sex, gender, and sexuality, Indigenous feminist and Indigenous queer studies have their own distinct (yet deeply connected) trajectories and more work needs to be done to bring these together in relation to Indigenous law.[21]

In addition to moving beyond superficial or oversimplified conversations about gender and sexuality, IFLS needs to emphasize the importance of embracing the messiness of law and of avoiding narrow understandings of what law is.[22] Law within any society is messy, contested, and dynamic, and matters are further complicated with Indigenous legal issues by needing to account for multiple Indigenous legal orders and settler legal orders, and attending to the imbalance of power between them in settler colonial contexts.[23] IFLS engages with law through a lens that centres and validates the legitimacy of Indigenous legal orders and legal authority.[24] Indigenous laws are treated, as with all laws, as systems for managing conflict and social relations, and legal systems require ongoing work and revisions from the citizens that use them to govern their nations.[25] Legal practices and processes need to be inclusive and need to recognize the legal personhood of all gendered citizens.[26] Further, rather than narrowly conceiving law just as sets of rules,[27] IFLS embraces law as pedagogy – through law we teach, we learn, and we make meaning of intimate and social relations with the human and other-than-human worlds within which we are embedded.[28]

IFLS is deeply committed to understanding and valuing the agency and autonomy of Indigenous women and people with non-binary gender identities. Too often these perspectives and ideas are erased from, or silenced through, legal discourse, including through Indigenous legal discourse. Even within these constraining circumstances, it is vital to make visible the resistances, actions, and contributions of Indigenous citizens who identify as women and 2SLGBTQI+.[29] The issue of consent is also central to Indigenous feminist legal ethics[30] – considering consent not only in the context of specific harms, but also whether Indigenous women have consented to the legal processes being used. As this edited collection shows, IFLS turns to many sources for understanding the depth and breadth of gendered experiences with law (such as stories, oral histories, art, film, literature, Indigenous languages, reports, cases), and also recognizes that engagement with law and the material impacts of law are embodied. Differently gendered bodies carry and live those experiences in differing ways.

Indigenous feminisms are perceived by some to be about a narrowing of focus – a focus only on a segment of society (i.e., Indigenous women); however, IFLS, when understood as an analysis of gendered power relations, can broaden and deepen engagement with Indigenous laws by opening up new conversations about what is actually happening. IFLS creates space and brings in additional layers of analysis that can otherwise be ignored in mainstream legal discourse, and it instead supports a more complete and accurate legal analysis. As Hawk in Napoleon's prologue emphasized, "if people don't see or understand Indigenous feminisms, they simply have a narrower lens through which to see any Indigenous law" (p 18). It is vital that work about the experiences and realities faced by Indigenous women and people who are 2SLGBTQI+ be led by them; however, the work of learning about these issues should not fall entirely on these groups. So too is IFLS, as discussed in this collection, meant to be a resource for everyone to think about and to think with. The contributors in this collection work in different disciplines, have different community connections, are Indigenous and non-Indigenous, and have different gendered experiences. These differences enable a conversation across this collection where varying perspectives are deployed to try to better understand the complexities of Indigenous legal issues. Part of the reflexive work of thinking with IFLS includes non-Indigenous people, Indigenous men, and people who are cisgender critically reflecting on their social locations and how they will support more inclusive legal praxis that values the legal agency and knowledge of Indigenous women and people who are gender diverse.

## Outline of This Book

We come into these conversations about IFLS through stories, through engaging IFLS for addressing sexualized violence, and through analyses of the power of representations in film. These topics reflect the contributions of the authors and are certainly not meant to provide a complete portrayal of IFLS (which again, should not have rigid boundaries put around it, and which is practised by people in the everyday and not just in academic discussions). We start with stories, as both old and new stories are a valuable source of Indigenous law, and are invaluable for teaching about law.[31] We see in Napoleon's prologue how various stories can move us through time to reflect on hard truths but also the possibilities of a world where Indigenous feminisms are the norm. Bringing a critical gendered lens to the stories can expose gender bias (Darcy Lindberg's chapter 2) but can also centre the power and legal agency of Indigenous women, which may have been lost in interpretation over time (waaseyaa'sin Christina Sy's chapter 3 and Kahente Horn-Miller's chapter 4).

We then shift to critical examinations of sexual violence. Too often Indigenous women are imagined, especially in settler imaginations, only in relation to gendered colonial violence, rather than being seen as having agency and full personhood.[32] While Indigenous women are not defined by this violence, the very real and devastating impacts of sexualized violence, how the state justice system unjustly exacerbates these conditions, and how feminist legal interventions have to change, still need to be addressed (Julie Kaye and Emily Snyder's chapter 6). Turning a critical lens on laws about sexual assault through Indigenous feminist frameworks can also provide a new starting point in the formulation of laws, Indigenous or non-Indigenous, to clearly define what constitutes a sexual assault, to keep women safe, and to ensure that sexual assault is appropriately dealt with by the justice system (Sarah Deer's chapter 5).

We then turn to documentary films, which can provide a stark exposition of a gendered analysis of Indigenous women and the law.

Sometimes the hard work is done by the film, where the filmmaker brings the inherent biases to viewers' attention (Cheryl Suzack's chapter 7). Sometimes the film presents a story, and it is up to viewers to provide the critical analysis. Film provides a space to learn, analyse, and critique from a safe distance, honing the necessary skills for use in real-life situations and real law-making (Rebecca Johnston's chapter 8). As Suzack's chapter 7 shows, "film as a visual medium contributes to the reparatory goals embedded within Indigenous women's artistic practice" (p 182). We invite readers to reflect on this medium and other ways to critically engage with Indigenous feminist legal analyses that work in support of gendered legal agency, consent, and justice. The final chapter in this book (by Kim Pate and Val Napoleon) is a fictional conversation through which they hope "to generate productive ways to think about the future and about finding ways forward" in real life. We hope that this collection encourages further conversation about Indigenous feminist legal studies and Indigenous feminist legal ethics and futures.[33]

NOTES

1 See for example Tracey Lindberg, "What Do You Call an Indian Woman with a Law Degree? Nine Aboriginal Women at the University of Saskatchewan College of Law Speak Out" (1997) 9 CJWL 301; Melanie Schwartz, "Retaining Our Best: Imposter Syndrome, Cultural Safety, Complex Lives and Indigenous Student Experiences of Law School" (2018) 28:2 Legal Ed Rev 1; Mallika Balachandran, Roisin Duffy-Gideon & Hannah Gelbort, "Speak Now: Results of a One-Year Study of Women's Experiences at the University of Chicago Law School" (2019) University of Chicago Legal Forum 647; Eli Wald et al., "Looking Beyond Gender: Women's Experiences at Law School" (2012) 48:1 Tulsa L Rev 27; Elisabeth Griffiths, *The Lived Experience of Disabled Students in Law School: Present Realities and Possible Futures* (PhD Dissertation, University of Northumbria at Newcastle, 2021) [unpublished].

2 Although gender, feminism, and Indigenous laws are still underexamined, Napoleon has been writing on these issues for a long time. See for example Val Napoleon, "Aboriginal Discourse: Gender, Identity, and Community" in Benjamin J Richardson, Shin Imai & Kent McNeil, eds, *Indigenous Peoples and the Law: Comparative and Critical Perspectives* (Oxford: Hart, 2009) 233; Napoleon, "Aboriginal Self-Determination: Individual and Collective Selves" (2005) 29:2 Atlantis 31.

3 When using the term "woman" in this chapter, I understand this to include anyone who identifies as a woman.

4 This work is ongoing, though regarding earlier scholarship, see for example Patricia Monture, "The Right of Inclusion: Aboriginal Rights and/or Aboriginal Women" in Kerry Wilkins, ed, *Advancing Aboriginal Claims* (Saskatoon: Purich, 2004) 39; Sharon Donna McIvor, "Aboriginal Women Unmasked: Using Equality Litigation to Advance Women's Rights" (2004) 16:1 CJWL 106; Joyce Green, "Canaries in the Mines of Citizenship: Indian Women in Canada" (2001) 34:4 Cdn J Poli Sci 715; Patricia Monture-Angus, "Standing against Canadian Law: Naming Omissions of Race, Culture, and Gender" in Elizabeth Comack, ed, *Locating Law: Race/Class/Gender Connections* (Halifax: Fernwood, 1999) 76.

5 Emily Snyder, "Indigenous Feminist Legal Theory" (2014) 26:2 CJWL 365.

6 See for example Emily Snyder, Val Napoleon & John Borrows, "Gender and Violence: Drawing on Indigenous Legal Resources" (2015) 48:2 UBC L Rev 593.

7 See for example John Borrows, "Outsider Education: Indigenous Law and Land-Based Learning" (2016) 33 Windsor YB Access Just 1; Hanna Askew, "Learning from Bear-Walker: Indigenous Legal Orders and Intercultural Legal Education in Canadian Law Schools" (2016) 33 Windsor YB Access Just 29; Jeffrey G Hewitt, "Decolonizing and Indigenizing: Some Considerations for Law Schools" (2016) 33 Windsor YB Access Just 65.

8 For further information about the Joint Degree Program in Canadian Common Law and Indigenous Legal Orders (JD/JID) see <https://www.uvic.ca/law/admissions/jidadmissions/index.php>. For further information about the Indigenous Law Research Unit, see <https://www.uvic.ca/law/about/indigenous/indigenouslawresearchunit/index.php>. Offerings in Indigenous law, as well as research centres, are also growing at other postsecondary institutions, especially in Canada.

9 Sarah Nickel, "Introduction" in Sarah Nickel & Amanda Fehr, eds, *In Good Relation: History, Gender, and Kinship in Indigenous Feminisms* (Winnipeg: University of Manitoba Press, 2020) 1. See also Gina Starblanket, ed, *Making Space for Indigenous Feminism*, 3d ed (Winnipeg: Fernwood, 2024); Joyce Green, ed, *Making Space for Indigenous Feminism*, 2d ed (Winnipeg: Fernwood, 2017); Joanne Barker, ed, *Critically Sovereign: Indigenous Gender, Sexuality, and Feminist Studies* (Durham: Duke University Press, 2017).

10 I use "2SLGBTQI+" to refer to two-spirit, lesbian, gay, bi, trans, queer, intersex, and other identities and realities that challenge dominant norms regarding sex, gender, and sexuality. Note that authors in this collection use different terminology and explain their usage in each chapter.

11 See for example Kim Anderson, Maria Campbell & Christi Belcourt, eds, *Keetsahnak: Our Missing and Murdered Indigenous Sisters* (Edmonton: University of Alberta Press, 2018); National Inquiry into Missing and

Murdered Indigenous Women and Girls, *Reclaiming Power and Place: The Final Report of the National Inquiry into Missing and Murdered Indigenous Women and Girls*, vols 1a & 1b (Ottawa: MMIWG, 2019), online: <https://www.mmiwg-ffada.ca/wp-content/uploads/2019/06/Final_Report_Vol_1a-1.pdf> <https://www.mmiwg-ffada.ca/wp-content/uploads/2019/06/Final_Report_Vol_1b.pdf>.

12 For further discussion about this see for example Emily Snyder, "Challenges in Gendering Indigenous Legal Education: Insights from Professors Teaching about Indigenous Laws" (2019) 34:1 CJLS 33.

13 This conversation took place during a planning session for the collection, via Zoom, in the summer of 2022, and included Val Napoleon, Rebecca Johnson, Debra Mckenzie, Kahente Horn-Miller, Kim Pate, Christina Gray, Sarah Deer, Patricia Barkaskas, waaseyaa'sin Christine Sy, and Emily Snyder.

14 For a discussion on Indigenous feminist legal pedagogies, which draws on interviews with Indigenous and non-Indigenous professors working in Indigenous law, see Emily Snyder, "Indigenous Feminist Legal Pedagogies" (2021) 58:2 OHLJ 385.

15 See for example Val Napoleon, "Gitxsan Legal Personhood: Gendered" in Austin Sarat, George Pavlich & Richard Mailey, eds, *Interrupting the Legal Person,* Studies in Law, Politics, and Society, vol 87A (Bingley, UK: Emerald, 2022) 19; Sarah Deer, "Gendering Indian Law: Indigenous Feminist Legal Theory in the United States" (2019) 31:1 Yale J Law and Feminism 1; Rauna Kuokkanen, *Restructuring Relations: Indigenous Self-Determination, Governance, and Gender* (New York: Oxford University Press, 2019); Isabel Altamirano-Jiménez, "The State Is Not a Saviour: Indigenous Law, Gender and the Neoliberal State in Oaxaca" in Green, *supra* note 9, 215; Val Napoleon & Emily Snyder, "Housing on Reserve: Developing a Critical Indigenous Feminist Property Theory" in Angela Cameron, Sari Graben & Val Napoleon, eds, *Creating Indigenous Property: Power, Rights, and Relationships* (Toronto: University of Toronto Press, 2020) 41; Naomi Sayers, "Social Media and Social Change Lawyering: Influencing Change and Silencing Dissent" (2018) 169:1 Media International Australia 65.

16 See for example Nickel & Fehr, *supra* note 9; Starblanket, *supra* note 9; Green, *supra* note 9; Barker, *supra* note 9; Kai Pyle, "Reclaiming Traditional Gender Roles: A Two-Spirit Critique" in Nickel & Fehr, *supra* note 9, 109; Alex Wilson, "N'tacimowin inna nah': Our Coming In Stories" (2008) 26:3/4 Cdn Woman Studies 193; Robert Alexander Innes & Kim Anderson, eds, *Indigenous Men and Masculinities: Legacies, Identities, Regeneration* (Winnipeg: University of Manitoba Press, 2015).

17 This connection is made broadly in work on Indigenous feminisms. For a powerful discussion of these connections, see Audra Simpson, "The State

Is a Man: Theresa Spence, Loretta Saunders and the Gender of Settler Sovereignty" (2016) 19:4 Theory & Event n.p.

18 *Ibid*. See also Sarah Deer, *The Beginning and End of Rape: Confronting Sexual Violence in Native America* (Minneapolis: University of Minnesota Press, 2015).

19 See chapter 5 in this volume by Sarah Deer; Snyder, Napoleon & Borrows, *supra* note 6; Emma LaRocque, "Métis and Feminist: Ethical Reflections on Feminism, Human Rights, and Decolonization" in Joyce Green, *supra* note 9, 122; Alex Wilson, "Skirting the Issues: Indigenous Myths, Misses, and Misogyny" in Kim Anderson, Maria Campbell & Christi Belcourt, eds, *Keetsahnak: Our Missing and Murdered Indigenous Sisters* (Edmonton: University of Alberta Press, 2018) 161; Emily Snyder, *Gender, Power, and Representations of Cree Law* (Vancouver: UBC Press, 2018).

20 See for example Kuokkanen, *supra* note 15; Billie Allan & Janet Smylie, "All Our Relations: Indigenous Women's Health in Canada" in Marina Morrow, Olena Hankivsky & Colleen Varcoe, eds, *Women's Health in Canada: Challenges of Intersectionality*, 2d ed (Toronto: University of Toronto Press, 2022) 116; Starblanket, *supra* note 9; Nickel & Fehr, *supra* note 9; Green, *supra* note 9; Barker, *supra* note 9.

21 For an older discussion on queering Indigenous legal studies that is open to revision see Emily Snyder, "Queering Indigenous Legal Studies" (2015) 38:2 Dalhousie LJ 591.

22 Napoleon and Johnson, Zoom meeting, *supra* note 13.

23 See for example John Borrows, *Canada's Indigenous Constitution* (Toronto: University of Toronto Press, 2010).

24 See Indigenous Law Research Unit, "Indigenous Law 101" (2016), online: <https://ilru.ca/wp-content/uploads/2020/08/Indigenous-Law-101-With-Resources.pdf>.

25 See Borrows, *supra* note 23; Val Napoleon & Richard Overstall, "Indigenous Laws: Some Issues, Considerations and Experiences" (Paper prepared for the Centre for Indigenous Environmental Resources, 2007) [unpublished].

26 Napoleon, *supra* note 15.

27 Val Napoleon, *Ayook: Gitksan Legal Order, Law, and Legal Theory* (PhD Dissertation, University of Victoria, 2009) [unpublished] at 302–303.

28 Napoleon and Johnson, Zoom meeting, *supra* note 13.

29 Sy and Barkaskas, Zoom meeting, *supra* note 13.

30 Thank you to Heidi Kiiwetinepinesiik Stark for her earlier contributions to conversations about the importance of consent, as we gathered to discuss this collection.

31 See for example Val Napoleon & Hadley Friedland, "An Inside Job: Engaging with Indigenous Legal Traditions through Stories" (2016) 61:4 McGill LJ 725.

32 Napoleon, *supra* note 15.

33 In their work on Indigenous feminist theory and decolonizing feminist theory, Maile Arvin, Eve Tuck, and Angie Morrill discuss futurity, which works to centre futures that are created by Indigenous peoples and which destabilizes settler attempts of erasure that target Indigenous people, especially Indigenous women and people who are 2SLGBTQI+. See Arvin, Tuck & Morrill, "Decolonizing Feminism: Challenging Connections between Settler Colonialism and Heteropatriarchy" (2013) 25:1 Feminist Formations 8 at 25. Notions of futurity are central in both Indigenous feminisms and Indigenous laws, and are useful to explicitly bring together here.

## SOURCES CITED

Allan, Billie & Smylie, Janet. "All Our Relations: Indigenous Women's Health in Canada" in Marina Morrow, Olena Hankivsky & Colleen Varcoe, eds, *Women's Health in Canada: Challenges of Intersectionality*, 2d ed (Toronto: University of Toronto Press, 2022) 116.

Altamirano-Jiménez, Isabel. "The State Is Not a Saviour: Indigenous Law, Gender and the Neoliberal State in Oaxaca" in Joyce Green, ed, *Making Space for Indigenous Feminism*, 2d ed (Winnipeg: Fernwood, 2017) 215.

Anderson, Kim, Maria Campbell & Christi Belcourt, eds, *Keetsahnak: Our Missing and Murdered Indigenous Sisters* (Edmonton: University of Alberta Press, 2018).

Arvin, Maile, Eve Tuck & Angie Morrill, "Decolonizing Feminism: Challenging Connections between Settler Colonialism and Heteropatriarchy" (2013) 25:1 Feminist Formations 8.

Askew, Hanna. "Learning from Bear-Walker: Indigenous Legal Orders and Intercultural Legal Education in Canadian Law Schools" (2016) 33 Windsor YB Access Just 29.

Balachandran, Mallika, Roisin Duffy-Gideon & Hannah Gelbort. "Speak Now: Results of a One-Year Study of Women's Experiences at the University of Chicago Law School" (2019) University of Chicago Legal Forum 647.

Barker, Joanne, ed, *Critically Sovereign: Indigenous Gender, Sexuality, and Feminist Studies* (Durham: Duke University Press, 2017).

Borrows, John. *Canada's Indigenous Constitution* (Toronto: University of Toronto Press, 2010).

Borrows, John. "Outsider Education: Indigenous Law and Land-Based Learning" (2016) 33 Windsor YB Access Just 1.

Deer, Sarah. *The Beginning and End of Rape: Confronting Sexual Violence in Native America* (Minneapolis: University of Minnesota Press, 2015).

Deer, Sarah. "Gendering Indian Law: Indigenous Feminist Legal Theory in the United States" (2019) 31:1 Yale J Law and Feminism 1.

Green, Joyce. "Canaries in the Mines of Citizenship: Indian Women in Canada" (2001) 34:4 Cdn J Poli Sci 715.

Green, Joyce, ed. *Making Space for Indigenous Feminism,* 2d ed (Winnipeg: Fernwood, 2017).

Griffiths, Elisabeth. *The Lived Experience of Disabled Students in Law School: Present Realities and Possible Futures* (PhD Dissertation, University of Northumbria at Newcastle, 2021) [unpublished].

Hewitt, Jeffrey G. "Decolonizing and Indigenizing: Some Considerations for Law Schools" (2016) 33 Windsor YB Access Just 65.

Indigenous Law Research Unit. "Indigenous Law 101" (2016), online: <https://ilru.ca/wp-content/uploads/2020/08/Indigenous-Law-101-With-Resources.pdf>.

Innes, Robert Alexander & Anderson, Kim, eds, *Indigenous Men and Masculinities: Legacies, Identities, Regeneration* (Winnipeg: University of Manitoba Press, 2015).

Kuokkanen, Rauna. *Restructuring Relations: Indigenous Self-Determination, Governance, and Gender* (New York: Oxford University Press, 2019).

Lindberg, Tracey. "What Do You Call an Indian Woman with a Law Degree? Nine Aboriginal Women at the University of Saskatchewan College of Law Speak Out" (1997) 9 CJWL 301.

McIvor, Sharon Donna. "Aboriginal Women Unmasked: Using Equality Litigation to Advance Women's Rights" (2004) 16:1 CJWL 106.

Monture-Angus, Patricia. "Standing against Canadian Law: Naming Omissions of Race, Culture, and Gender" in Elizabeth Comack, ed, *Locating Law: Race/Class/Gender Connections* (Halifax: Fernwood, 1999) 76.

Monture, Patricia. "The Right of Inclusion: Aboriginal Rights and/or Aboriginal Women" in Kerry Wilkins, ed, *Advancing Aboriginal Claims* (Saskatoon: Purich, 2004) 39.

Napoleon, Val. "Aboriginal Self-Determination: Individual and Collective Selves" (2005) 29:2 Atlantis 31.

Napoleon, Val. "Aboriginal Discourse: Gender, Identity, and Community" in Benjamin J Richardson, Shin Imai & Kent McNeil, eds, *Indigenous Peoples and the Law: Comparative and Critical Perspectives* (Oxford: Hart, 2009) 233.

Napoleon, Val. *Ayook: Gitksan Legal Order, Law, and Legal Theory* (PhD Dissertation, University of Victoria, 2009) [unpublished].

Napoleon, Val. "Gitxsan Legal Personhood: Gendered" in Austin Sarat, George Pavlich & Richard Mailey, eds, *Interrupting the Legal Person,* Studies in Law, Politics, and Society, vol 87A (Bingley, UK: Emerald, 2022) 19.

Napoleon, Val & Hadley Friedland. "An Inside Job: Engaging with Indigenous Legal Traditions through Stories" (2016) 61:4 McGill LJ 725.

Napoleon, Val & Richard Overstall. "Indigenous Laws: Some Issues, Considerations and Experiences" (Paper prepared for the Centre for Indigenous Environmental Resources, 2007) [unpublished].

Napoleon, Val & Emily Snyder. "Housing on Reserve: Developing a Critical Indigenous Feminist Property Theory" in Angela Cameron, Sari Graben & Val Napoleon, eds, *Creating Indigenous Property: Power, Rights, and Relationships* (Toronto: University of Toronto Press, 2020) 41.

National Inquiry into Missing and Murdered Indigenous Women and Girls. *Reclaiming Power and Place: The Final Report of the National Inquiry into Missing and Murdered Indigenous Women and Girls,* vols 1a & 1b (Ottawa: MMIWG, 2019), online: <https://www.mmiwg-ffada.ca/wp-content/uploads/2019/06/Final_Report_Vol_1a-1.pdf> <https://www.mmiwg-ffada.ca/wp-content/uploads/2019/06/Final_Report_Vol_1b.pdf>.

Nickel, Sarah. "Introduction" in Sarah Nickel & Amanda Fehr, eds, *In Good Relation: History, Gender, and Kinship in Indigenous Feminisms* (Winnipeg: University of Manitoba Press, 2020) 1.

Nickel, Sarah & Amanda Fehr, eds. *In Good Relation: History, Gender, and Kinship in Indigenous Feminisms* (Winnipeg: University of Manitoba Press, 2020).

Pyle, Kai. "Reclaiming Traditional Gender Roles: A Two-Spirit Critique" in Sarah Nickel & Amanda Fehr, eds, *In Good Relation: History, Gender, and Kinship in Indigenous Feminisms* (Winnipeg: University of Manitoba Press, 2020) 109.

Sayers, Naomi. "Social Media and Social Change Lawyering: Influencing Change and Silencing Dissent" (2018) 169:1 Media International Australia 65.

Schwartz, Melanie. "Retaining Our Best: Imposter Syndrome, Cultural Safety, Complex Lives and Indigenous Student Experiences of Law School" (2018) 28:2 Legal Ed Rev 1.

Simpson, Audra. "The State Is a Man: Theresa Spence, Loretta Saunders and the Gender of Settler Sovereignty" (2016) 19:4 Theory & Event.

Snyder, Emily. "Indigenous Feminist Legal Theory" (2014) 26:2 CJWL 365.

Snyder, Emily. "Queering Indigenous Legal Studies" (2015) 38:2 Dalhousie LJ 591.

Snyder, Emily. *Gender, Power, and Representations of Cree Law* (Vancouver: UBC Press, 2018).

Snyder, Emily. "Challenges in Gendering Indigenous Legal Education: Insights from Professors Teaching about Indigenous Laws" (2019) 34:1 CJLS 33.

Snyder, Emily. "Indigenous Feminist Legal Pedagogies" (2021) 58:2 OHLJ 385.

Snyder, Emily, Val Napoleon & John Borrows. "Gender and Violence: Drawing on Indigenous Legal Resources" (2015) 48:2 UBC L Rev 593.

Starblanket, Gina, ed. *Making Space for Indigenous Feminism*, 3d ed (Winnipeg: Fernwood, 2024).

Wilson, Alex. "N'tacimowin inna nah': Our Coming In Stories" (2008) 26:3/4 Cdn Woman Studies 193.

Wilson, Alex. "Skirting the Issues: Indigenous Myths, Misses, and Misogyny" in Kim Anderson, Maria Campbell & Christi Belcourt, eds, *Keetsahnak: Our Missing and Murdered Indigenous Sisters* (Edmonton: University of Alberta Press, 2018) 161.

Wald, Eli et al. "Looking Beyond Gender: Women's Experiences at Law School" (2012) 48:1 Tulsa L Rev 27.

# 2 Nêhiyaw Ceremony, Gendered Protocols, and Nêhiyaw Law

DARCY LINDBERG

## Ceremony, Authority, Gender, and Law

There is an old nêhiyaw (Cree) story about Wîsahkêcâhk and the ducks. Wîsahkêcâhk is hungry so, scheming a way to capture some ducks, he gathers up some moss alongside a lakeshore where there are plenty of ducks at play. Walking closer to the lake, Wîsahkêcâhk starts singing a song. "Hey ya, hey ya. I am carrying my Shut-Eye Dance songs." Ever interested, the ducks surround Wîsahkêcâhk, wondering what he is carrying. "Why, these are my songs," Wîsahkêcâhk answers. "Then sing to us!" one of the ducks asks. Knowing the power of a secret, he answers, "No! These are new songs given to men. I cannot sing them just anywhere."

The ducks really want to hear a song. Wîsahkêcâhk proposes how. "First we must build a lodge with only one door. And when the dancing starts all those who are wanting to dance must dance with eyes shut. If there is anyone who does not want to dance the Shut-Eye Dance then leave right away!" Many ducks can't resist the mystery. So Wîsahkêcâhk entices them to move in a circle, with their eyes closed. He then says:

> Now little brothers, here in the centre I shall stand; I shall sing. When I sing, you will dance; you will close your eyes. Not until I cease singing will you open your eyes ... you will dance with all [of] your might.[1]

For those who are familiar with Wîsahkêcâhk tales, you probably know how this ends. Using the authority within the "ceremony" to his advantage he captures the ducks, one by one.

As they often do, âtayôhkêwina (original or sacred stories) involving Wîsahkêcâhk provide critical reflection on authority within law and ceremony. The story above introduces the central topic of this paper: the impacts of gendered ceremonial practices and protocols, and the role of nêhiyaw law in addressing them. As one source for critical reflection on ceremonies and law,[2] stories enable us to consider the gendered power relations within nêhiyaw law.

Hidden gendered[3] relations within Indigenous legal orders can cause or exacerbate individual and social inequalities experienced by Indigenous women and girls.[4] Indigenous women face higher levels of violence than non-Indigenous women,[5] including as victims of homicide.[6] There are also significant gaps between how Indigenous women and men experience laws surrounding marital separation.[7] Gendered laws create different outcomes in nêhiyaw social life generally for men and women. Addressing gender within law is integral to Indigenous sovereignty[8] and decolonization generally, as it loosens reliance upon Canadian state law[9] in resolving gender inequities and inequalities.[10]

In discussing the hidden gendering within nêhiyaw societies, this chapter is founded on two assumptions – that the gendered nature of some nêhiyaw ceremonial practices enables essentializations of gender to persist, and that nêhiyaw law has the ability to respond to this. To expand on the first assumption, the gendered nature of nêhiyaw ceremonies enables problematic essentializations of gender to persist in the ceremonial, social, and legal practices within nêhiyaw pimâtisiwin (Plains Cree life).[11] Specifically, originalist approaches to nêhiyaw ceremonies further entrench harmful gender stereotypes and essentializations, paralysing critical discourses. While fundamentalist beliefs on the nature of Indigenous laws underlie many areas of law,[12] critical discussions on Indigenous laws often get stifled within three areas of discourse: (1) the essentialization of women's roles in communities,[13] (2) fundamentalist positions on traditionalism,[14] and (3) reluctance to critically discuss laws sourced to sacred or natural origins.[15] These three areas of discourse can often lead to "intellectual black holes" where further theoretical or analytical work is stymied by the "idealistic rhetoric" of these concepts.[16] As Snyder, Napoleon, and Borrows state, this "rhetoric is widespread in academic texts, in discussions at conferences and workshops, in classrooms, in universities, at meetings, in the media, and in everyday conversations."[17] These "binaries of authentic/inauthentic and traditional/colonized … create intellectual black holes that have lived consequences for Indigenous peoples, especially women," as they freeze social interactions within the snapshot of these binaries.[18] This results in the persistence of systemic patriarchal structures and implicit oppressive practices within Indigenous communities. For this reason the lessons of the Shut-Eye Dance are prescient and integral – we need to be wide-eyed to the power relations presented in ceremony and other legal institutions as well.

Essentializing discourses usually conflate the role of women and girls to motherhood. Examples of this include rhetoric that talks of women as "mothers of nations" or as "backbones of our communities." As Snyder, Napoleon, and Borrows note, such rhetoric "ultimately obscures, mischaracterizes, and too narrowly frames Indigenous women's options, choices and contributions within their societies. This is particularly problematic when women's responsibilities and contributions as citizens are only framed in relation to nurturing and caring for the nation."[19]

Further, critical discourses often become flattened by assertions of tradition and the importance of upholding such traditional values. Snyder, Napoleon, and Borrows argue that "tradition is not neutral and it can be purposefully deployed in ways [that] discipline and morally police women."[20] Similar to in the harms that can come from fundamentalist positions regarding ceremony, "evocations of culture and tradition can corrosively inhibit nuanced, non-essentialized views and practices of Indigenous law."[21] The role of tradition in ceremony is especially complex, considering that much of the protocols of ceremony require some level of adherence to practices that are considered traditional. Practices sourced to sacred or natural sources are often very difficult to objectify in critical discourse. Some people simply feel uncomfortable bringing up sacred or spiritual issues, given the secular nature much of academic practice is based upon. Others believe that sacred or natural practices (like ceremony) cannot be discussed critically, due to their spiritual nature. Others may believe that such critical discourse is futile, in that sacred and natural law have no processes for change. Continued silencing of critical discussions on sacred or natural law has large consequences for both Indigenous law and gender equality. The evocation of the "sacred in law" can be employed to position these laws "beyond human challenge and understanding."[22]

The second founding assumption of this chapter is that ceremony is a part of nêhiyaw law, and as such legal theory can help redirect discourse on authority, gender, and law from paralysed and essentialized positions. Nêhiyaw law, like many other Indigenous legal orders, is best described through normative and social interactive theories of law – that is, law arises as a coordinating force in people's lives through normative practice and deliberation. Thus a normative approach to Indigenous legal ordering[23] is also supported by social interactive theories of law.[24] Law is grounded within normative practices of a community, and emerges from them to facilitate social interaction,[25] or as Lon Fuller states, "we cannot understand [positive] law unless we first obtain an understanding of what is called customary law."[26] In this sense, the primary form of all laws can be described as "customary" in nature.[27] Thus, ceremonial protocols, and by proxy the gendered assumptions and inequities they create, are not elements of tradition frozen by authority, but are social relations that are constantly adapting and changing.

The remainder of this chapter explores these two assumptions – the relational nature of law and the gendered nature of nêhiyaw ceremony – to examine how ceremonies can change and the role of legal theory in understanding the potential for change. In the following three sections I explore gendered protocols within nêhiyaw ceremonies. I then discuss originalism, authority, and how legal theory can move our discussions on ceremonial protocols away from essentialized conversations towards adaptation and change in a manner that is faithful to nêhiyaw legal process.

## Gendered Protocols

While there are many historical practices and contemporary protocols involved in nêhiyaw ceremonies that have gendered aspects to them, this chapter will focus on two in particular. First, dress protocols for both sweat lodge and pipe ceremonies stipulate that women should wear skirts during the ceremonies, often of ankle length. Second, protocols require that women refrain from partaking in pipe and sweat lodge ceremonies while they are menstruating. As protocols provide a procedural foundation for ceremony, they can also entrench practices that cause gendered inequalities.[28] Although they can be described in many different ways (including as rules, directives, procedures, custom, and laws), for consistency's sake I will use "protocol" or "rules" when discussing these two practices.

Nêhiyaw teachings and beliefs on the power and ceremony of a menstrual cycle factor significantly into the maintenance of both skirt and menstruation rules. According to some beliefs within nêhiyaw pimâtisiwin, these rules are rationalized as recognizing and honouring the life-giving force carried by women. Rules requiring skirts to be worn during ceremony are representative of this, as the skirt symbolizes the teepee or lodge, linking womanhood to the centre of the familial structure. Menstruation protocols are rooted in similar teachings. According to these beliefs, when a woman is menstruating, she is undergoing an internal cleansing ceremony, parallel to the work that occurs in the lodge. This period of cleansing has been referred to a number of different ways in nêhiyaw communities, including as "moon time,"[29] "sacred time," and a time when "(spiritual) kokums are visiting."[30] In some teachings, the connection between womanhood and the moon is a significant relation; "moon time" refers to the close link between womenhood and lunar cycles. Moon lodges (lodges held during the evenings of full moons) are an example of a practice that recognizes this connection. Moon lodge ceremonies are mostly led by women, and are mostly for women only. Similarly, in addition to the work women pipe-holders do at all times, women pipe-carriers may load their pipes for moon ceremonies during full moons. While historically there have been different characterizations of menstrual experiences within nêhiyaw communities,[31] current narratives generally characterize the protocols as honouring women and womanhood in general. It was a historical practice for women to attend their own ceremonies separate from men (and led by women ceremonial holders) during menstruation.[32] Women are asked to exclude themselves from pipe and sweat lodge ceremonies during menstruation due to beliefs that the powerful state they are in can disrupt the actions (or powers of the ceremonial holder) within some ceremonies.[33]

The power dynamics created by dress and menstruation protocols are often articulated in positive terms, couched in terms of balance and equality in ceremonial practices. Originalist approaches reinforce this positivity, often linking tradition to community cohesion and decolonization. In discourses about nêhiyaw pipe and sweat lodge ceremonies men and women are described as occupying separate halves of ceremony, each distinct but necessary for the ceremony to take part. Women's roles in this balance are often said to "occupy one half of our lodges, one half of our ceremonies, and one half of the revered positions in Indigenous societies."[34] Women have also been said to "contribut[e] to the function of [fasting] ceremon[ies]" by "occupy[ing] half the teepee."[35] Kiera Ladner would call this an example of a *gender-positive* social order.[36] In her exploration of the constitutional order of the Blackfoot Confederacy, Ladner posits that Blackfoot constitutionalism is gender positive – that while it may set out different norms and ordering for different genders, such differentiation is "not based on the subjugation, domination or oppression of women but [is] instead created in an attempt to formulate a way to live together in the best way possible."[37]

The idea of "gender-positive" balance within ceremony has been expressed by other Indigenous societies as a *duality*. This duality — "the dual unity of the feminine and masculine" that is "fundamental to the creation of the cosmos"[38] — is integral to some Indigenous feminist movements in Central America and was relied upon in reclamation of spiritual practices from the colonial effects of Catholicism.[39] In this usage, duality should not be conflated with dualism.[40] A dualism suggests a tension between genders, in that they are two contrary forces working against each other to form a balance. When one force gains the other loses, and vice versa. In contrast, a duality consists of two forces that are essential to make something whole. While each undoubtedly influences the other, the strength of one does not diminish the strength of the other, but in some beliefs enhances it.[41]

This understanding of duality can be applied to the epistemological foundations of nêhiyaw sweat and pipe ceremonies as well, as each conveys aspirations towards the maintenance of these dualities. As well as being a method to ensure safety and security, the separation of men and women into two different sides of the sweat lodge and the assignment of specific rounds of the ceremony to female relations and male relations are attempts to honour and foster the duality of the biological sexes. The pipe ceremony has a similar representation. The pipe stem is often understood to be the male aspect of the pipe, while the bowl represents the female aspect. The work of the ceremony cannot begin before the two are put together, as the pipe is not whole until then. The separation of the pipe stem and pipe bowl at the end of the ceremony is significant, as it is signals a "decentring" of the ceremonial space, and frees the relations within the ceremony to carry on outside the ceremony.

While such overt gendering in positive terms may be seen as correcting a gender-neutral positioning that allows gender to remain hidden from critique in many legal systems, this does not diminish the unequal treatment of genders in this dualistic relationship. And although there are parts of sweat lodge ceremonies that can be radically democratic and participatory, ceremonial protocols on dress and menstruation can work against (rather than reinforce) this equality work. First, within a duality, any aspect that is "gender positive" may be positive only for those who identify as heteronormatively male or female. It has been suggested that people who do not identify as cisgendered male or female experience further alienation as a result of practices where ceremonial holders are unaccustomed to dealing with (or perhaps do not acknowledge) a spectrum of gender positions. The gendered nature of pipe and sweat lodge ceremonies has caused such people to avoid taking part in the ceremonies[42] or, if they do take part, to experience shame and humiliation in their participation.[43] By its very nature, ceremonial practice based on a heteronormative duality either excludes other gender positions along the spectrum or at least causes other genders to conform towards heteronormative practices.

Further, even if some parts of pipe and sweat lodge ceremonies do realize gender positivity in some aspects, the dualistic characteristics of dress and menstruation protocols can fail to support this work. Readers will recall that a main rationale for menstruation and dress protocols is the need to maintain a balance of energy during these ceremonies; it is a teaching that the power of womanhood can be disruptive to the power of the ceremony.[44] As Janice Makokis explains, "it is believed that during [moon] time when a woman is on her natural moon cycle she possesses such power that her energy has the ability to override the men's pipe and energy during the ceremony."[45] Thus menstruating women are excluded from pipe ceremonies led by men, or from circles where men's pipes are present. While this could be interpreted as gender positive, the oppressive nature of the teaching (that women's ceremonial presence be suppressed for the benefit of the male aspect of ceremony) signals a dualism at play. The power of women is suppressed so as not to override the power of men.

The supposed gender positivity of such practices is often unrealized, as the inequality inherent in these protocols is further actualized in the treatment and expectations of women and girls outside of the ceremonies. Kim Anderson's research highlights an example of the hidden harms in gender-positive practices, via the comments of one of her research participants:

> I walked out of there, like a traditional female dancer, swaying in my skirt in the street. I felt very proud to be in a skirt as a Native woman. That's what all that symbolized, and it was really exciting. So, I really tried to observe all the practices. And some of it was my determination that this was going to be who I was, and this was what you had to adopt.
>
> It all worked fine until the day that we were supposed to sing at a feast, and lo and behold, I was on my period. And another woman in our singing group was on her period as well. So instead of going into the room and joining the circle, we stood in the middle of the room, and we were standing in the doorway, singing with them. Now already that felt kind of weird. Then we sat outside the feast room, on the floor in the stairwell the rest of the time. I remember the woman I was with didn't see this as a problem. She instructed me, kind of importantly, "Now the women have to bring us food." I felt like saying, "You're being a fool to think this is an empowering

> thing for us to do, as women, to be sitting in the stairwell outside the feast. And why is it the women have to bring us the food – so there's another bloody job for women to do? Why the hell can't the men bring us food?
>
> "So ever since then, the menstrual taboos as they are practiced right now have struck me as ... unsafe. And yet I understand how the power of giving life that it represents is so important to honor."[46]

This example highlights the complexities of ceremony's simultaneous ability to provide participants with a strong sense of belonging and at the same time create shame and marginalization. It also reveals how the protocols affect general relations between community members. As Heidi Kiiwetinepinesiik Stark points out, there is nothing within the reasoning behind menstruation protocols that prohibits men from acting as helpers – they could easily bring food to the women separated from the others due to the protocols.[47] The blending of protocol with other inequitable social norms amplifies both.

Gendered protocols can reinforce harmful misconceptions of the role of women in leadership positions as well. This dynamic is intertwined with notions of historical labour divisions within communities, where gendered divisions of labour are often linked to community governance responsibilities.[48] As Beverly Hungry Wolf describes:

> The people of the past thought it a great honour that the women should bear and rear the children, ensuring that there would be people in the future. Equally honourable was the women's work of creating the lodges that made the homes, taking them up and down when camp moved, heating them and providing the bedding and clothing for the household members. In the social life of my grandmothers, a household was judged not only by the bravery and generosity of the man, but also by the kindness and work habits of the woman.[49]

Aside from the unequal burden of labour created by these dynamics, these logics have often been used to impede the public leadership efforts of nêhiyaw women.[50] The concept of the "traditional" role of women as life-givers or the backbone of the community is sometimes interpreted as meaning they should not assume leadership positions on the front lines of their nations or communities.[51] Such beliefs in traditional gender roles and views on community leadership sometimes directly interact with the effects of menstruation protocols. An example of this surfaced in the early summer of 2015, when Kim Jonathon was named the interim chief of the Federation of Saskatchewan Indian

Nations.[52] As part of positional procedure, Chief Jonathon was presented with a headdress in a bonnet ceremony in her own community. This caused a degree of dissension, as some felt she should not be presented with the headdress based on her gender and due to beliefs rooted in the ceremonial protocols regarding menstruation.[53]

While tradition or historical practice is often used as a rationale for dress and menstruation protocols, some link them to colonial practices. Skirt protocols especially have been connected with efforts to colonize Indigenous communities. Speaking about her home community, Nêhiyaw academic Alex Wilson states: "If you talk to elders here, they can remember a time, or they tell stories of their grandparents' time, when people made their own clothes and it didn't have to do with cloth and it didn't have to do with long skirts."[54] Anishinaabe writer Leanne Simpson links skirt protocols to assimilative efforts of residential schools: "we were forced to wear skirts in residential schools, at church and in missions in order to assimilate us from being Nishnaabeg women into the ideals of settler housewives. Under colonialism the skirt has been and still is in many cases a tool of oppression."[55] While the reclamation of historical practices within Indigenous communities can address colonized methods of patriarchy,[56] such "traditional reclamation" doesn't address and further entrenches oppressive practices resident within community norms prior to colonial interruption of community practices.[57]

The important of critical discourse around skirt and menstruation protocols is heightened by a current resurgence of ceremonial practices. There are old ones still among us who remember ceremonies being prohibited by the Canadian state (like the sun dance, sweat lodge, round dance, and give-away ceremonies), and so there is a reflexive protection of ceremony as it resurges.[58] A growing number of people are returning to ceremonial practices,[59] and ceremonies are being practised in communities and institutions where they weren't before.[60] This resurgence increases the complexity for women who oppose the gendered protocols, as they can feel pride and a need to support such reclamation even as they recognize that their participation exposes them to uneven and oppressive rules.

While locating the origins of skirt protocols may be significant in critical discourses about decolonization, change should not rest upon a determination of their being a colonial or traditional practice. This line of reasoning engages in a form of essentialization regarding individual and community identity. If the adoption of new practices within a community renders those new practices (or older ones that incorporate them) "inauthentic," this creates an impossible standard for community "authenticity" and propagates stereotypical views of the authentic Indigenous person as frozen in time, bound to practices before settler contact. It fails to take into account Indigenous resiliency and agency in authoring changes in community practice, and the syncretism that is resident in many Indigenous social, economic, legal, and spiritual practices. As Lee Maracle states, if we are thinking "traditional" clothing, then we should return to men wearing loin cloths and women going topless during summer months, as her ancestors used to.[61] Nêhiyaw author Emma LaRocque acknowledges the significance of resurgent community practices such as ceremonies, yet cautions that "as women we must be circumspect in our recall of tradition," including asking "ourselves whether and to what extent tradition is liberating to us as women."[62] A blind faith in tradition in ceremony can miss the point of the ceremony entirely.

## Using Legal Theory to Make Space for Transformation

Law is a vital area that is ripe for critique because of its role in supporting continued inequitable and oppressive stereotypes and essentializations. As a social force in all societies, without critique law can seem "natural, inevitable, complete, objective and neutral."[63] Indigenous law is no exception: it is "heavily influenced by dominant social norms."[64] The harms associated with the hidden nature of gender in law are especially persistent because they are not understood until they are carefully examined.[65]

Examining the sources of Indigenous laws assists in demystifying the problematic gendered relations within nêhiyaw law. John Borrows states:

> Laws can arise whenever interpersonal interactions create expectations about proper conduct. Indigenous legal traditions develop in the same way; they can be based on supernatural declarations, naturalistic observations, positivistic proclamations, deliberative practices, or local and national customs.[66]

While laws that are sourced from positivistic, deliberative, or customary origins make easier work for our schools of theory, laws sourced from natural or sacred sources pose more difficulty for traditional lines of legal theory because of their metaphysical quality. This includes social interaction theories of law's development. As mentioned above, social interaction theorists like Fuller argue that normative coordination is a prerequisite for the creation of formal law. Sacred and natural laws challenge the premise of social interactive theories that law emerges through deliberation or contestation between members of a society, as such law involves a declaration from a source that has an authoritative influence on the social norms of a society. This is especially evident in ceremonial protocols, as they are often expressed as "original teachings" or "original law,"[67] or the product of natural divisions of gender that are cosmological in nature.[68] Further, the origins of ceremonies themselves are often viewed as gifts from sacred or natural sources. This includes pipe ceremonies,[69] sweat lodge ceremonies,[70] sun dance ceremonies, and horse dance ceremonies.[71] Originalist attitudes towards ceremonies are a barrier to transformations of nêhiyaw laws that allows harmful gender relations to persist.

In constitutional law, originalist approaches seek interpretations of constitutional and legal texts that are closest to the intentions of its original framers and drafters. While originalist interpretive methods receive (albeit critiqued) support in the United States, they are currently not a supported method in Canadian jurisprudence.[72] In particular, we should be extremely cautious in employing an interpretive ethic of originalism when engaging in law sourced from sacred, natural, or creative sources. As John Borrows states:

> Originalism privileges a "settled" view of a particular moment in the past, concluding that precise constitutional understandings are inherent within some prior declaration or experience … Originalism is often used in an exclusivist, either/or manner, prohibiting and discouraging modes of constitutional interpretation based on other grounds … Originalism generally places dispositive weight on formative historical understandings and meanings, whereas living tree constitutionalism draws guidance from history but gives it lesser weight.[73]

In terms of law based on sacred or natural instruction, an originalist approach often means relying upon ceremonial holders for the meaning of law. While there are ethical obligations that our ceremonial holders do uphold, and methods of accountability governing their use of their authority, reliance on proclamations from knowledge keepers and authoritative voices can lead to or perpetuate power imbalances, and can also leave us misinformed about which normative aspirations are actually pursuedwithin societies. Val Napoleon describes this as the danger of "mystification" of law.[74] This mystification can provide authority, or the appearance of authority, without structures of accountability. As Wîsahkêcâhk's encounter with the ducks teaches us, shutting our eyes to ceremonial processes allows ceremonial authority to be abused. One example is the current trend to regard old ones/elders as unquestionable authority figures in communities. Napoleon states that this creates an environment where elders are held up as "priest-like beings who are also sacred," seriously disrupting the balance of power and authority in communities.[75] While I hold very close the obligation to venerate our old ones as respected knowledge keepers, and to listen and attend to them in special ways (and receive so much wealth from this obligation), the knowledge they share still needs to be relational to the web of teachings throughout a community. The abuse of elder authority occurs when we take every instruction at face value and blindly follow such instructions.

The second danger is that even without any abuse of authority, charges of mysticism can obscure the reasoning processes that exist within a deeper knowledge of ceremony and cultural practices. When viewed as merely mystical, spiritual processes are given little weight in legal theory or are outright dismissed as "non-legal." Beyond creating these issues, the mystification of sacred normative practices also obscures structures internal to Indigenous communities that hold elders and ceremonial leaders accountable. Without knowledge of these internal checks on authority, external viewers see only positional authority: *an elder is an elder because they are.* This is especially problematic when legal knowledge is shared intersocietally. As nêhiyaw elders continue to be called upon to teach externally (for example, to lead ceremonies at universities and colleges), this is done at a distanced from the internal methods of legitimizing the ceremonial holder's authority. Without proper methods of translation, we are closing our eyes in ceremony, hoping the authority we give to the ceremony holder has been earned and will not be misused or abused.

Legal theory can be employed to shift discourses from an originalist approach towards the transformative potential of nêhiyaw ceremonies in addressing gendered distinctions, inequalities, and oppressions. As Lon Fuller states, "the law does not tell a [person] what [they] should do to accomplish specific ends set by the law giver; it furnishes [them] with baselines against which to organize [their] life with [their] fellows."[76] Fuller's human interaction theory rescues custom from a static view in which it is mere habit, formed from repetition, with little reasoned thought behind the action.[77]

To Fuller, customary law arises from the necessity of organization and interaction between individuals within a society. Thus, custom represents a "language of interaction" where individuals can coordinate their acts on the assumption that others will participate in the pattern.[78] Further, Fuller's theory of social interaction "avoids the dual errors of treating legal reasoning as though it were either (1) self-contained, autopoietic, generated from its own internal resources; or (2) a purely intellectual process … where the only things that are considered are prior articulations within a given normative tradition."[79]

Jeremy Webber supplements Fuller's pragmatic view of customary law by exploring possible demarcations between legal norms and other social norms, and how societies engage in this deliberation to create law from these social norms. Webber argues that it is within distinct normative contemplation and reflection that law arises:[80]

> The expressions of customary law therefore exist in an interpretive relationship with practice, mediated by other participants' interpretations and actions. That reasoning is necessarily evaluative. Participants seek to weigh the impact of past norms, judge the appropriateness or acceptability of that impact — what has proven important in previous decisions, what has proven ill-conceived —and seek to revise the norms and their application accordingly.[81]

As Elizabeth Anderson notes, Webber identifies "three levels of normative determination: the coordination of human interaction, the grammatical 'language' structure used to express norms in a legal fashion, and the debates that utilize that grammar to negotiate the resolution of a particular situation."[82] Thus, these "second and third levels operate as somewhat of a feedback loop"[83] where this process of expression of norms and contestation is "ongoing and perpetual."[84]

These three levels of normative determination are useful in analysing the development, continued expression, and contestation of ceremonial protocols. While historical gaps may obfuscate the protocol's origins (and history of practice, contestations, and changes), in the present we see the processes of the second and third levels. Contestation of the validity or relevancy of the protocols is evident in the words of certain individuals quoted above; the language used to express this contestation is a strategic force in resolving these situations. It is through this normative process that the protocols maintain within a society both their relevance and their just nature. If the practice of a norm is void of the second and third steps (a common grammar cannot be found that sets the communicative stage of the disagreement, or there is no resolution to the conflict), then the norm will lose relevancy and its legitimacy as being just.

The etymological breakdown of the word for law in *nêhiyawewin* (the Plains Nêhiyaw language) is *wiyasiwêwina,* translating as "the act of weaving."[85] This signifies a relational, egalitarian approach to law where persuasion is preferred to hierarchical coercion. Human interaction theory also allows us to view legal orders that utilize practices described as "custom" as vibrant, living, and adapting. In particular, that theory allows an interrogation of levels of normative reflection that influence these practices. This interrogation is important to legal theory's role in moving past the "intellectual black holes" discussed above. As Gerald Postema states, "implicit rules emerge over time from a process of mutual accommodation and adjustment of expectations and actions of interacting agents."[86] While some may view such conflicts in discourse as regressive or harmful, another view, which I choose to adopt, is that the consistent raising of issues with gendered protocols signifies the potential emergence of new rules. Conflict can be a necessary part of the emergence of law through interactive processes. It is regenerative. The voices of the women and girls are calling for changes; the challenging of these norms signals a healthy legal order that has maintained its ability to react to the peoples and beings it seeks to serve.

Acknowledging the ability of ceremonies to evolve and transform can lead to highly charged discussions of practices rooted in sacred or natural beliefs, as spiritual or divine law is often viewed as being connected to a creator, and thus transformation of ceremonies would be seen as violating sacred or divine instructions.[87] As I noted above, some ceremonial practices and rules are tied to beliefs that transformation would violate a fundamental balance required by these ceremonies.[88] Such a position ignores historical examples of ceremonial development and transformation. Within Nêhiyaw ceremonial practice, there are multiple examples of whole ceremonies developing in relation to the changing lives of Nêhiyaw people. The horse dance developed out of that people's evolving relationship with horses, which didn't begin until the 1700s.[89] The *Wihtigokaancimuwin* (Weetiko dance) is said to evolve from Nêhiyaw interactions with Blackfoot people,[90] which didn't occur with regularity until around 1730.[91] Thirst dance ceremonies were "adapted" into the rain dance ceremony by Plains Nêhiyaw communities as a result of the colonial prohibition of ceremonies.[92]

Moreover, ceremonial practices have undergone a long sequence of internal evolutions. Sweat lodges had to evolve during the *Indian*

*Act* prohibition of ceremonies.[93] Within the practices of some ceremonial holders, menstruation rules and the role of women generally have also been evolving.[94] Some sweat lodge holders continue to move their ceremonies away from protocols based on dress and menstruation, to reflect a transformation in the gender dynamics within both Nêhiyaw and Canadian societies.[95] The question of whether ceremony can transform and evolve is based on fundamental positions that are more normative assumption than accurate description of the history of Nêhiyaw ceremonies. A fuller dialogue would centre on the processes that have allowed for ceremonial evolution. Such a dialogue would raise important issues for future research, among them: Who is privileged with authorizing ceremonial transformations? What are the normative practices that act as barriers to a healthy evolution of ceremony? At what degree does normative fluidity become harmful to the integrity of the ceremonial practice itself?

## Conclusion: Legitimatizing Authority and Ceremony

Consideration of legal theory offers one avenue to engage in the conversation of ceremonial transformations, and specifically the aspects that cause and continue gendered inequalities and oppressions. A deeper understanding of the type of authority that we may give to sacred or natural institutions is helpful to these questions. As Val Napoleon cautions, as "laws have to be interpreted by human beings, and law is not just rules ... what are the consequences of [a] law being sacred or natural?"[96] And again: "if we believe laws are sacred, our understanding about the responsibility of human beings can become reduced to following rules."[97] Nicole Roughan has written that authority can be thought of as appearing in two forms: unilateral absolute authority and dialogic or relative authority.[98] Dialogic authority rejects absolute authority in that it is not coercive but invites the individual to investigate its claims to authority.[99] It is persuasive in nature and in this sense is relational. Again, if we think of "law as weaving," it is multiple views and experiences that give law its strength. Law is constantly reinterpreted as more experiences are added to the multitudes of strands already woven into the legal fabric of a society.

The authority of sacred or natural law rests not in the power we give institutions like ceremony, but in their ability to reflect the needs of law within society. A reference to such reflexive potential was provided where this chapter started, within our stories: our stories and teachings are full of instances of transformation, shape-shifting, and fluidity. A boy is shape-shifted into a buffalo and then back again, and finally into a rock, in order to teach of our relations to the buffalo people.[100] A prairie becomes full of hills, in order to demarcate a territory so we stop needless violence between we nêhiyawak and our Blackfoot relatives.[101] A buffalo becomes a lake that nourishes our ancestors in a time of great need.[102] The Northern Lights shape-shift above us, and transform our realities only if we do whistle and so dare. The lesson and language of transformation is all around us. *Ekosi.*

NOTES

1 This story has been reproduced in various texts, including Leonard Bloomfield, *Sacred Stories of the Sweet Grass Cree* (Ottawa: Printer to the King's Most Excellent Majesty, 1930) at 38.

2 For example, in my dissertation research I approach nêhiyaw âcimowina, or Cree stories, as a body of critical legal philosophy that characterizes legal relationships with non-human beings. See Darcy Lindberg, *Nêhiyaw Âskiy Wiyasiwêwina: Plains Cree Earth Law and Constitutional/Ecological Reconciliation* (PhD Dissertation, University of Victoria, 2020) at 200 [unpublished].

3 Acknowledging that the effects of the concepts of gender, sex, and sexuality cannot easily be separated with regard to each concept's interplay with ceremonies, this chapter focuses on the concept of gender, as conversations around gender are generally where ceremonial protocols intersect. In saying that, queering the concepts of gender, sex, and sexuality in a manner that recognizes the interconnectedness of each is one avenue towards addressing such fundamentalisms in ceremony. See Alex Wilson, "Our Coming In Stories: Cree Identity, Body Sovereignty and Gender Self-Determination" (2015) 1:1 J Global Indigeneity 1. This focus is of course not to discount the implications of fundamentalisms in Cree law on sex and sexuality within Cree lives and societies generally.

4 Emily Snyder, *Representations of Women in Cree Legal Educational Materials: An Indigenous Feminist Legal Theoretical Analysis* (PhD Dissertation, University of Alberta, 2014) at 16 [unpublished].

5 *Ibid* at 2.

6 Studies suggest that an Indigenous woman is seven times more likely to be a victim of homicide than a non-Indigenous woman. See Vivian O'Donnell and Susan Wallace, *Women in Canada: A Gender-Based Statistical Report: First Nations, Inuit and Métis Women*, Statistics Canada (2011), online: <www.statcan.gc.ca/pub/89-503-x/2010001/article/11442-eng.pdf>.

7 See Jessica Asch, Hadley Friedland & Val Napoleon, "A Toolkit for On-Reserve Matrimonial Real Property Dispute Resolution," Center for

Excellence for Matrimonial Real Property (2015), online: <https://ilru.ca/wp-content/uploads/2020/08/on-reserve-matrimonial-real-property-dispute-resolution-toolkit.pdf>; Kiera Ladner, "Gendering Decolonization, Decolonizing Gender" (Paper presented at the 80th Annual Conference of the Canadian Political Science Association, Vancouver, June 2008), online: <http://www.cpsa-acsp.ca/papers-2008/Ladner.pdf> at 6.

8 Ladner, *supra* note 7 at 10.

9 For a detailed discussion of the challenges of using state law for governance on issues related to the vulnerability and security of women and girls in Indigenous communities, see John Borrows, "Aboriginal and Treaty Rights and Violence against Women" in *Freedom and Indigenous Constitutionalism* (Toronto: University of Toronto Press, 2016) 181.

10 Ladner, *supra* note 7 at 10.

11 For a detailed exploration of this, see Darcy Lindberg, *kihcitwâw kîkway meskocipayiwin (Sacred Changes): Transforming Gendered Protocols in Nêhiyaw Ceremonies through Nêhiyaw Law* (Master's Thesis, University of Victoria Faculty of Law, 2017) [unpublished].

12 Emily Snyder, Val Napoleon & John Borrows, "Gender and Violence: Drawing on Indigenous Legal Resources" (2015) 48:2 UBC L Rev 593 at 613.

13 *Ibid* at 611.

14 *Ibid* at 609.

15 *Ibid* at 612.

16 *Ibid* at 608.

17 *Ibid*.

18 *Ibid*.

19 *Ibid* at 611.

20 *Ibid* at 618.

21 *Ibid*.

22 *Ibid* at 612.

23 For many of the reasons that a normative approach is appropriate in this examination, numerous other Indigenous legal scholars have taken similar approaches to their study of Indigenous legal orders. For example, see Val Napoleon, *Ayook: Gitksan Legal Order, Law, and Legal Theory* (PhD Dissertation, University of Victoria, 2009) [unpublished]. Napoleon argues that implicit law is made explicit through collective processes of the Gitksan peoples.

24 Lon Fuller, "Human Interaction and the Law" in Kenneth I Winston, ed, *The Principles of Social Order: Selected Essays of Lon L. Fuller*, rev ed (Portland: Hart, 2001) at 1.

25 While it is beyond the scope of this chapter, it would be interesting to study conceptions of "community" and whether that includes all beings within

*nêhiyaw pimâtisiwin* teachings, and the effect on Fuller's theory when we see that it isn't just human-to-human interaction but also human-to-animal or human-to-other-being interactions that are relevant in Nêhiyaw law-making.

26 Fuller, *supra* note 24 at 250.

27 As I will discuss below, customary law is often broadly applied to Indigenous laws due to issues of translation and outsiders' difficulty in accessing law within Indigenous communities. With improving methods, we can start to see the ongoing deliberation in some laws deemed customary.

28 Of course, nêhiyaw protocols are not simply procedural. As Mekwan Awasis states: "Following through with acts of protocol demonstrates that the one requesting information understands and respects the sacred nature of that knowledge and the laws of exchange and reciprocity that guide the process. Within this relational system of knowledge sharing, the acts of protocol themselves are equally as important as the information acquired." Mekwan Awasis as quoted in Claire Poirer, "Drawing Lines in the Museum: Plains Cree Ontology as Political Practice" (2011) 53:2 Anthropologica 291 at 294.

29 wahpimaskwasis (Little White Bear) Janice Makokis, *nehiyaw iskwew kiskinowâtasinahikewina – paminisowin namôya tipeyimisowin: Cree Women Learning Self-Determination through Sacred Teachings of the Creator* (Master's Thesis, University of Alberta, 2005) [unpublished] at 62.

30 See Reuben Quinn's teaching in Amaskwaciy History Series, "History of the Cree Language, Part 1," YouTube (9 June 2016), online: <https://www.youtube.com/watch?v=CpvuED_hJTM>.

31 Makokis, *supra* note 29 at 62.

32 *Ibid* at 112.

33 *Ibid.*

34 Tracey Lindberg, *Critical Indigenous Legal Theory* (PhD Dissertation, University of Ottawa, 2007) [unpublished] at 154.

35 Makokis, *supra* note 29 at 112.

36 Ladner, *supra* note 7 at 13.

37 *Ibid.*

38 Sylvia Marcos, "Mesoamerican Women's Indigenous Spirituality: Decolonizing Religious Beliefs" (Fall 2009) 25: 2 J of Feminist Studies in Religion 25 at 35.

39 *Ibid.*

40 *Ibid.*

41 A common refrain I hear in sweat lodge ceremonies is that the strength of women makes everything else within a community stronger.

42 Jill Alaers, "Two-Spirited People and Social Work Practice: Exploring the History of Aboriginal Gender and Sexual Diversity" (2010) 11:1 Critical Social Work 63.

43 See Drew Hayden Taylor, "The Shame of Skirt-Shaming," *Windspeaker* (2016), online: <https://www.windspeaker.com/drew-hayden-taylor/shame-skirt-shaming; Dana Wesley, *Reimagining Two-Spirit Community: Critically Centering Narratives of Urban Two-Spirit Youth* (Master's Thesis, Queen's University, 2015) at 76–77 [unpublished].

44 Makokis, *supra* note 29 at 112.

45 *Ibid*.

46 Kim Anderson, *A Recognition of Being: Reconstructing Native Womanhood* (Toronto: Second Story Press, 2000) at 265–66.

47 Author conversation with Heidi Stark, April 2017, Victoria, BC.

48 See Lindberg, *supra* note 11 at 151–53.

49 *Ibid* at 149.

50 Another common refrain I have heard from time to time: it is the men's role in communities to protect women as life givers, so they must stand behind men for this protection.

51 I have heard this especially in terms of political discussions within communities, where women leaders have been criticized for being out "in front," implying that they are putting themselves in harm's way. Notions of traditional gender roles play into these conversations, as it is sometimes said that men as "warriors" need to step in front and protect women. Aside from the overt misogyny within these sentiments, they are based on ideals of community harmony, free of gendered violence, that historically and contemporarily are not true. The high level of violence women and girls experience within our communities is indicative of this. As Val Napoleon noted in a reflection on a draft of my master's thesis: "this form of gendered nationalism provides the justification for violence against women when they fail to live up to the idealization of their role."

52 Jorge Barrera, "Feathers Ruffled after FSIN Chief Receives Headdress from Her Community," *Aboriginal Peoples Television Network* (2015), online: <https://www.aptnnews.ca/national-news/feathers-ruffled-fsin-chief-receives-headdress-community/>.

53 *Ibid*.

54 Alex Wilson, quoted in "Indigenous Ceremony at University of Winnipeg Sparks Sexism Debate," *CBC News* (22 June 2015), online: <http://www.cbc.ca/news/canada/manitoba/indigenous-ceremony-at-university-of-winnipeg-sparks-sexismdebate-1.3123568>.

55 Leanne Simpson, as cited in Taylor, *supra* note 44.

56 Patricia Monture, *Thunder in My Soul: A Mohawk Woman Speaks* (Halifax: Fernwood, 2005) at 179.

57 See Kim Anderson, "Affirmations of an Indigenous Feminist" in Cheryl Suzack et al, eds, *Indigenous Women and Feminism: Politics, Activism, Culture* (Vancouver: UBC Press, 2010) at 86–88. Further, the syncretic

nature of colonial practices with internal practices, especially within ceremony, means that reclamation of traditional practices cannot always root out patriarchal colonial oppression.

58 See generally Katherine Pettipas, *Severing the Ties That Bind: Government Repression of Indigenous Religious Ceremonies on the Prairies* (Winnipeg: University of Manitoba Press, 1994).

59 In my own experiences in working with Nêhiyaw, Stoney, and Blackfoot communities in Alberta, the last fifteen years have seen a large resurgence of sun dance/rain dance ceremonies in communities.

60 As universities engage in Indigenous ceremonial practices, there is a need to strengthen accountability measures regarding these practices, especially given that universities are generally unmoored from the accountability frameworks within Indigenous communities.

61 Maracle, as cited in Taylor, *supra* note 44.

62 Emma LaRocque, "The Colonization of a Native Woman Scholar" in Christine Miller & Patricia Chuchryk, eds, *Women of the First Nations: Power, Wisdom, and Strength* (Winnipeg: University of Manitoba Press, 1996) at 14.

63 See Lucinda Finley, "Breaking Women's Silence in Law: The Dilemma of the Gendered Nature of Legal Reasoning" (1989) 64 Notre Dame L Rev 886 at 892.

64 Snyder, Napoleon & Borrows, *supra* note 12.

65 Carolyn Korsmeyer, *Gender and Aesthetics: An Introduction* (New York: Routledge, 2004) at 3–4.

66 John Borrows, "Indigenous Legal Traditions in Canada" (Report for the Law Commission of Canada, January 2006), online: <http://publications.gc.ca/collections/collection_2008/lcc-cdc/JL2-66-2006E.pdf> at 7.

67 Nêhiyaw legal scholar Sylvia McAdam Saysewahum implies that Nêhiyaw laws, although varied in different areas now, are sourced from the same divine proclamation. See Sylvia McAdam, *Nationhood Interrupted: Revitalizing Nêhiyaw Legal Systems* (Saskatoon: Purich, 2015) at 37.

68 See Makokis, *supra* note 29 at 82–92.

69 See Mark St. Pierre & Tilda Long Soldier, *Walking in the Sacred Manner: Healers, Dreamers, and Pipe Carriers – Medicine Women of the Plains Indians* (Toronto: Simon & Schuster, 1995) at 41.

70 An origin story for sweat lodge ceremonies that I have heard from both Nêhiyaw and Anishnaabe knowledge keepers involves a young man searching to the ends of the earth for a cure for his community's people, who are overcome by a number of sicknesses. After he seeks the advice of many different animals through journeying in many different directions, finally the eagle believes he knows where the boy can find a cure. The eagle flies the

boy to the dark side of the moon, where he is met by spiritual grandmothers and grandfathers. Each mosum (grandfather) or kokum (grandmother) gives him a ceremony to help his people, and he returns to his community with seven ceremonies. One of those was the sweat lodge ceremony.

71 See the horse dance origin story (or how the Nêhiyaw acquired horses) told by Eli Pooyak from Sweetgrass Nêhiyaw Nation in Saskatchewan on 18 March 1974, Canada Plains Research Center, online: <http://ourspace.uregina.ca/bitstream/handle/10294/1610/IH-074.pdf?sequence=1>.

72 John Borrows, "(Ab)Originalism and Canada's Constitution" in *Freedom and Indigenous Constitutionalism* (Toronto: University of Toronto Press, 2016) at 130.

73 *Ibid*.

74 Val Napoleon. "Thinking about Indigenous Legal Orders" in René Provost & Colleen Sheppard, eds, *Dialogues on Human Rights and Legal Pluralism* (New York: Springer, 2013) at 6.

75 *Ibid* at 7.

76 Fuller, *supra* note 24 at 254.

77 Jeremy Webber, "The Grammar of Customary Law" 54 McGill LJ 579 at 584.

78 *Ibid*.

79 *Ibid* at 587.

80 Jeremy Webber, "Legal Pluralism and Human Agency" (2006) 44 Osgoode Hall LJ 167 at 196.

81 Webber, *supra* note 78 at 587.

82 Elizabeth Anderson, "Benevolent Grandfathers and Savage Beasts: Comparative Canadian Customary Law" (2010) 15 Appeal LJ 1 at 7–8.

83 *Ibid* at 7.

84 *Ibid* at 8.

85 Paulina R Johnson, *E-kawôtiniket 1876: Reclaiming Nêhiyaw Governance in the Territory of Maskwacîs through Wâhkôtowin (Kinship)* (PhD Dissertation, University of Western Ontario, 2017) [unpublished] at 152.

86 Gerald Postema, "Implicit Law" in Wibren van der Burg & Willem J Witteveen, eds, *Rediscovering Fuller: Essays on Implicit Law and Institutional Design* (Amsterdam: Amsterdam University Press, 1999) 255 at 258.

87 See McAdam, *supra* note 68.

88 For example, see my discussion above on protocols limiting women's participation in ceremonies while they are menstruating.

89 See John S. Milloy, *The Plains Nêhiyaw: Diplomacy and War, 1790 to 1870* (Winnipeg: University of Manitoba Press, 1990) at 24–25.

90 See Fine Day's telling of the story to David Mandelbaum. The dance involves contrary actions. According to Fine Day, it developed from an encounter with the Blackfoot while hunting buffalo. Canada Plains

Research Center (July 29), 1935, online: <http://ourspace.uregina.ca/bitstream/handle/10294/1813/IH-DM.82.pdf?sequence=1>.

91 Milloy, *supra* note 91 at 24.

92 See Pettipas, *supra* note 59 at 179–80. As the ceremonies were held in the summer when rain was much needed and often scarce on the prairies, the name change was an attempt to curry favor with local settler people. Nêhiyaw people employed settlers' mistaken belief that the ceremony's purpose was to provide rain as a way to gain allies of the ceremony during the period it was prohibited.

93 One story that is occasionally heard, though it may be apocryphal, is that to avoid detection sweats were held in houses, under kitchen tables, with rocks heated within stoves.

94 Most of the discussion around ceremonial rules has occurred via the offering of ceremonies intersocietally, for example in university settings. Pipe ceremony and sweat lodge ceremony rules are an example of this. Nêhiyaw protocols on the handling and playing of drums, for example, have similar rules of gender yet receive relatively little attention.

95 As one lodge holder shared with me, "My teacher would scold me really hard for holding lodges for men and women at the same time," as he continued to hold these non-segregated lodges.

96 Napoleon, *supra* note 75 at 6.

97 *Ibid.*

98 For a deeper look at these types of authority, see Nicole Roughan, *Authorities: Conflicts, Cooperation, and Transnational Legal Theory* (Oxford: Oxford University Press, 2013).

99 See John Cunliffe & Andrew Reeve, "Dialogic Authority" (1999) 19: 3 Oxford J of Legal Studies 453.

100 See the story of paskwaw-mostos awasis (Buffalo Child) in Neal Macleod, *Nêhiyaw Narrative Memory: From Treaties to Contemporary Times* (Saskatoon: Purich, 2007) at 21.

101 See the story of the Neutral Hills in Anne Speight, *The Shadows of the Neutrals and Open Memory's Door* (Coronation, AB: Old Timer's Centennial Book Committee, 1967) at 1–3.

102 The story of the creation of Buffalo Lake, passed on orally in my family, involved a buffalo being hunted and producing water, not blood, out of its wound. The water continued to spill out of the wound until it became the shape of a buffalo. Communities would gather at this new lake as it became a place of refuge and provided plentiful food and shelter around it.

## SOURCES CITED

Alaers, Jill. "Two-Spirited People and Social Work Practice: Exploring the History of Aboriginal Gender and Sexual Diversity" (2010) 11:1 Critical Social Work 63.

Anderson, Elizabeth. "Benevolent Grandfathers and Savage Beasts: Comparative Canadian Customary Law" (2010) 15 Appeal LJ 3.

Anderson, Kim. "Affirmations of an Indigenous Feminist" in Cheryl Suzack, Shari M. Huhndorf, Jeanne Perreault & Jean Barman, eds, *Indigenous Women and Feminism: Politics, Activism, Culture* (Vancouver: UBC Press, 2010).

Anderson, Kim. *A Recognition of Being: Reconstructing Native Womanhood* (Toronto: Second Story, 2000).

Asch, Jessica, Hadley Friedland & Val Napoleon. "A Toolkit for On-Reserve Matrimonial Real Property Dispute Resolution" (2015) Center for Excellence for Matrimonial Real Property, online: <http://coemrp.ca/wp-content/uploads/2015/12/Final-MRP-DR-Toolkit-Version-1.0.pdf>.

Barrera, Jorge. "Feathers Ruffled after FSIN Chief Receives Headdress from Her Community," *Aboriginal Peoples Television Network* (2015), online: <https://www.aptnnews.ca/national-news/feathers-ruffled-fsin-chief-receives-headdress-community/>.

Bloomfield, Leonard. *Sacred Stories of the Sweet Grass Cree* (Ottawa: Printer to the King's Most Excellent Majesty, 1930).

Borrows, John. "Aboriginal and Treaty Rights and Violence against Women" in *Freedom and Indigenous Constitutionalism* (Toronto: University of Toronto Press, 2016) 181.

Borrows, John. "(Ab)Originalism and Canada's Constitution" in *Freedom and Indigenous Constitutionalism* (Toronto: University of Toronto Press, 2016) 128.

Borrows, John. "Indigenous Legal Traditions in Canada" (Report for the Law Commission of Canada, January 2006), online: <http://publications.gc.ca/collections/collection_2008/lcc-cdc/JL2-66-2006E.pdf>.

Cunliffe, John & Andrew Reeve. "Dialogic Authority" (1999) 19:3 Oxford J of Legal Studies 453.

Day, Fine. "Telling Story." Canada Plains Research Center (29 July 1935), online: <http://ourspace.uregina.ca/bitstream/handle/10294/1813/IH-DM.82.pdf?sequence=1>.

Finley, Lucinda. "Breaking Women's Silence in Law: The Dilemma of the Gendered Nature of Legal Reasoning." 64 Notre Dame L Rev 886.

Fuller, Lon. "Human Interaction and the Law" in Kenneth I Winston, ed, *The Principles of Social Order: Selected Essays of Lon L. Fuller*, rev ed (Portland: Hart, 2001) 231.

Hayden Taylor, Drew. "The Shame of Skirt-Shaming," *Windspeaker* (2016), online: <https://windspeaker.com/drew-hayden-taylor/shame-skirt-shaming/>.

Johnson, Pauline R. *E-kawôtiniket 1876: Reclaiming Nêhiyaw Governance in the Territory of Maskwacîs through Wâhkôtowin* (Kinship) (PhD Dissertation, University of Western Ontario, 2017) [unpublished].

Korsmeyer, Carolyn. *Gender and Aesthetics: An Introduction* (New York: Routledge, 2004).

Ladner, Kiera. "Gendering Decolonization, Decolonizing Gender" (Paper delivered at the 80th Annual Conference of the Canadian Political Science Association, Vancouver, June 2008), online: <http://www.cpsa-acsp.ca/papers-2008/Ladner.pdf>.

LaRocque, Emma. "The Colonization of a Native Woman Scholar" in Christine Miller & Patricia Chuchryk, eds, *Women of the First Nations: Power, Wisdom, and Strength* (Winnipeg: University of Manitoba Press, 1996).

Lindberg, Darcy. *kihcitwâw kîkway meskocipayiwin (Sacred Changes): Transforming Gendered Protocols in Nêhiyaw Ceremonies through Nêhiyaw Law* (Master's Thesis, University of Victoria, 2017) [unpublished].

Lindberg, Darcy. *Nêhiyaw Âskiy Wiyasiwêwina: Plains Cree Earth Law and Constitutional/Ecological Reconciliation* (PhD Dissertation, University of Victoria, 2020) [unpublished].

Lindberg, Tracey. *Critical Indigenous Legal Theory* (PhD Dissertation, University of Ottawa, 2007) [unpublished].

Macleod, Neal. *Nêhiyaw Narrative Memory: From Treaties to Contemporary Times* (Saskatoon: Purich, 2007).

Makokis, Janice. *wahpimaskwasis (Little White Bear). nehiyaw iskwew kiskinowâtasinahikewina – paminisowin namôya tipeyimisowin: Cree Women Learning Self Determination through Sacred Teachings of the Creator* (Master's Thesis, University of Alberta, 2005) [unpublished].

Marcos, Sylvia. "Mesoamerican Women's Indigenous Spirituality: Decolonizing Religious Beliefs" (Fall 2009) 25: 2 J Feminist Studies in Religion 25.

McAdam, Sylvia. *Nationhood Interrupted: Revitalizing Nêhiyaw Legal Systems* (Saskatoon: Purich, 2015).

Milloy, John S. *The Plains Nêhiyaw: Diplomacy and War, 1790 to 1870* (Winnipeg: University of Manitoba Press, 1990).

Monture, Patricia. *Thunder in My Soul: A Mohawk Woman Speaks* (Halifax: Fernwood, 2005).

Napoleon, Val. *Ayook: Gitksan Legal Order, Law, and Legal Theory* (PhD Dissertation, University of Victoria, 2009) [unpublished].

Napoleon, Val. "Thinking about Indigenous Legal Orders" in René Provost & Colleen Sheppard, eds, *Dialogues on Human Rights and Legal Pluralism* (New York: Springer, 2013) 229.

O'Donnell, Vivian & Susan Wallace. *Women in Canada: A Gender-Based Statistical Report: First Nations, Inuit and Métis Women*, Statistics Canada (2011), online: www.statcan.gc.ca/pub/89-503-x/2010001/article/11442-eng.pdf>.

Pettipas, Katherine. *Severing the Ties That Bind: Government Repression of Indigenous Religious Ceremonies on the Prairies* (Winnipeg: University of Manitoba Press, 1994).

Poirer, Claire. "Drawing Lines in the Museum: Plains Cree Ontology as Political Practice" (2011) 53:2 Anthropologica 291.

Pooyak, Eli. "Telling Story: 'Horse Dance Origin,'" Canada Plains Research Center (1974), online: <http://ourspace.uregina.ca/bitstream/handle/10294/1610/IH-074.pdf?sequence=1>.

Postema, Gerald. "Implicit Law" in Willem J Witteveen & Wibren van der Burg, eds, *Rediscovering Fuller: Essays on Implicit Law and Institutional Design* (Amsterdam: Amsterdam University Press, 1999) 255.

Quinn, Reuben. "History of Nêhiyaw Language, Part 1," Amaskwaciy History Series (2015), online: <https://www.youtube.com/watch?v=CpvuED_hJTM> [YouTube video]>.

Roughan, Nicole. *Authorities: Conflicts, Cooperation, and Transnational Legal Theory* (Oxford: Oxford University Press, 2013).

Snyder, Emily. *Representations of Women in Cree Legal Educational Materials: An Indigenous Feminist Legal Theoretical Analysis* (PhD Dissertation, University of Alberta, 2014) [unpublished].

Snyder, Emily, Val Napoleon & John Borrows. "Gender and Violence: Drawing on Indigenous Legal Resources" (2015) 48:2 UBC L Rev 593.

Speight, Anne. *The Shadows of the Neutrals and Open Memory's Door* (Coronation, AB: Old Timer's Centennial Book Committee, 1967).

St. Pierre, Mark & Tilda Long Soldier. *Walking in the Sacred Manner: Healers, Dreamers, and Pipe Carriers – Medicine Women of the Plains Indians* (Toronto: Simon & Schuster, 1995).

Webber, Jeremy. "The Grammar of Customary Law" 54 McGill LJ 579.

Wesley, Dana. *Reimagining Two-Spirit Community: Critically Centering Narratives of Urban Two-Spirit Youth* (Master's Thesis, Queen's University, 2015) [unpublished].

Wilson, Alex. Quoted in "Indigenous Ceremony at University of Winnipeg Sparks Sexism Debate," *CBC News* (22 June 2015), online: <http://www.cbc.ca/news/canada/manitoba/indigenous-ceremony-at-university-of-winnipeg-sparks-sexismdebate-1.3123568>.

# 3 Understanding Indigenous Womxn's Economic Sovereignty through Story

WAASEYAA'SIN CHRISTINE SY

gizhe manidoo, please help.
– Anishinaabe womxn[1]

As an Indian woman I was free. I owned my own home, my person, the work of my hands, and my children should never forget me. I was better as an Indian woman than under white law.
– Indian woman's words[2]

It's hard to be sovereign when you cannot even feed your own children from your resources.
– Patricia Monture Angus-ban[3]

## Homefire Beginnings[4]

A long, long time ago, at the borders of winter and spring, when the cold and warm air began to mingle, a group of Anishinaabeg found themselves in a situation of starvation. Plans were afoot within the community to ceremony a young man in preparation for sending him out in search of food. In addition to being recognized for having the capacity to take on this task, this young man was also known to be loved by a young woman noted for her beauty and singing. Elsewhere in the community, there was a womxn with a young child. Having a strong sense of her personal responsibility as a parent during this time of starvation, she independently considered what she needed to do. Her idea was to also leave the community in search of food. The night before her anticipated departure, and with others who supported her, she ventured into the forest to seek guidance. Offering asemaa (tobacco) in petition to gizhe manidoo (great kind spirit/mystery), she was met with a response from ininaatig (maple tree), who instructed her to return the next day at noon. Centred in her intention, the responsibility that came with having petitioned gizhe manidoo for guidance, and receipt of the gift of creation in the form of ininaatig sounding back to her request, she returned the next day as ininaatig requested. Many members from the community accompanied her. After she had announced her return through song, ininaatig, who had been sufficiently warmed by the sun and spring air, revealed the flow of its sugary sap through scratches made in its bark by makwa (bear) and achidimo (chipmunk). In this way, Anishinaabe womxn's generative relationship with the supernatural and natural world was not only affirmed, but it also rendered sustenance for her child, herself, and her community.[5]

As this story tells, Anishinaabe peoples experienced starvation historically. Prior to colonial interference, such situations were likely due to environmental and ecological changes, and Anishinaabeg self-determined how to deal with such situations. They accounted to nobody but gizhe manidoo, the powers of the natural world, to each other within their own governance and legal systems, and presumably, in some ways, to their neighbouring nations and relations with whom they shared borderlands, kin, and social-economic ties. Colonialism and imperialism as well as globalization and global economic structures have created and imposed alternate worlds where Indigenous peoples worldwide face myriad forms of human-created precarity of life and living, including, but not limited to, starvation.[6] This precarity exists variably between Indigenous peoples within nations, communities, bands, tribes, families, and individuals. Indigenous womxn experience precarity both specifically and differently because of how these broad structures position the intersecting influence of gender, sex, bio-power, sexuality, and/or relationalities *with* being Indigenous and expressions of indigeneity.[7] The womxns' voices and sentiments that open this chapter respectively speak to experiences of struggle. As we see from the first story, such struggle includes starvation, for which help is requested from a greater power. It also includes contesting an imposed foreign legal order and problematizing the paradox of living Indigenous sovereignty within this order.[8]

These voices, gathered, illustrate that Indigenous womxn share similar struggles in their lands despite differences across history and contexts. In particular, these womxn reveal that there is a relationship between the personal/private (i.e., obtaining subsistence, having a home, having strong bonds with their children, owning the products of their labour) and the broader forces beyond the immediacy of their worlds. Each of these womxn navigated this relationship in their own way albeit presumably informed by the historical, social, and cultural values and knowledge of their relations, communities, and nations. Similarly, experiencing and witnessing comparable issues of precarity, contestation, and the paradox of living sovereign under settler colonialism, I endeavour to affirm Indigenous womxn's economic sovereignty.

A foundational premise in this discussion of critical Indigenous feminist law is that Indigenous womxn's economic sovereignty *is* Indigenous law.[9] Indigenous and allied legal scholars have been advancing this field for decades in myriad ways, including distinguishing between Indigenous and colonial justice systems, articulating Indigenous legal orders, and illuminating relevant Indigenous epistemologies, theories, and methods.[10] The latter includes mobilizing and interpreting traditional Indigenous stories through Indigenous feminist theory and application.[11] Still, some Indigenous community thinkers complicate the idea or language of "law." For instance, David Dick from the Songhees Nations in British Columbia writes, "Our ways aren't rules or laws, they're ways of living as good human beings. Rules and laws are made to be broken."[12] In another example, upon learning that her First Nation had passed a bylaw about littering, Anishinaabe Elder Carleen Elliot from Neyaashiinigmiing on Georgian Bay, Ontario, responded with "Laws are for the lawless."[13] As an Indigenous studies scholar, I enter this conversation from the multidisciplinary location of Indigenous gender studies and Anishinaabe studies, situating my contribution between critical Indigenous feminist legal studies and community ideas about law.

Since my area of study is not Indigenous law, I avoid making arguments to that end. Rather, I present developing theoretical ideas, epistemic relationships, and methods that imbricate with the subject. Further, because scholars of this field teach that Indigenous law is for everybody and are invested in diverse community engagement in its regeneration, I welcome the invitation to participate in conversations that value and understand the necessity of Indigenous feminist praxis. I also consider participating to be, in part, a responsibility. My personal agenda is to bring my subject interest of Indigenous womxn's economic sovereignty into conversation with the field of Indigenous law. My hope is that my work will assist thinkers, learners, and practitioners who have similar interests to further advance the idea of Indigenous womxn's economic sovereignty within relevant legal spheres. What I offer is an Indigenous/Anishinaabe feminist methodological approach to utilizing traditional story that may open new possibilities for this method in critical Indigenous feminist law.

To begin, I elaborate on what I mean by "Anishinaabeg womxn's economic sovereignty." Enunciating Anishinaabe feminist problematizing, I employ dibaadjimowin (the art/process of personal story) in revisiting the germinating "first-career" experience that instigated this idea.[14] I address the problem of dominating settler economies and economic relations, as well as the lack of traditional stories that affirm Anishinaabeg womxn's economic sovereignty. I do this by introducing a sugar bush story bundle where I advance an Anishinaabe feminist interpretative method. Conceiving the story bundle as a sugar bush world, I illuminate Anishinaabeg structure, governance, jurisdiction, and its presence as a place where social worlds unfold and lessons are learned. This storied world is further signified through the lens of economic sovereignty and observations about how womxn, and the female, figure in it. I remark on the potential of further contextualization, critique, and interpretation, linking the discussion back to the field of critical Indigenous feminist legal studies.

## Anishinaabe Womxn's Economic Sovereignty

Patricia Monture-Angus conceives of Indigenous sovereignty from within Indigenous nations. Situating herself as Mohawk, she states that sovereignty is

> not about "ownership" of territory in the way that Canadian politicians and lawyers would define those words. We have a Mohawk word that better describes what we mean by sovereignty and that word is 'tewatahta:wi'. It best translates to "we carry ourselves" ... [It] is about responsibilities and not just about rights ... It is the responsibility to carry ourselves; collectively as nations, as clans, as families, as well as individually, as individual Mohawk citizens, in a good way.[15]

Prompted by Monture-Angus's thinking, I consider economic sovereignty to be a nuanced aspect of Anishinaabeg sovereignty and describe it elsewhere as

> having the means, the knowledge, and the ability to sur-thrive within Anishinaabewaki in accordance with Anishinaabe ways of being. That is, through relationships with lands and waters that respect the life-force and

> intention of all beings in the natural world. Foundationally, this means the ability to procure healthy food, adequate clothing, safe housing, reliable transportation, and functional technology for self and our relations.[16]

As Anishinaabeg sovereignty endures, so too does Anishinaabeg economic sovereignty.[17]

Indigenous economic sovereignty differs from economic rights and economic citizenship. Where economic historian Robert Keller identifies economic rights as flowing from treaties between the settler state and Indigenous peoples, labour historian Chantal Norrgard states that economic citizenship involves "incorporation into the nation-state" and being "validated by settler society."[18] It is about our work, labour, and livelihood. In her investigation of Anishinaabeg seasonal labour in United States–Anishinaabeg treaty contexts, Norrgard asserts that Indigenous labour differs from the labour of citizens within a nation state. It differs because Indigenous labour is a form of Indigenous sovereignty and nationhood. Norrgard utilizes the terms "work" and "labour" "interchangeably to describe the strategies Native peoples have developed to make a living."[19] She describes livelihood as

> comprising a set of economic activities as well as the social, cultural, material, and political resources on which individuals, families, and larger social groups draw to make a living. [It] entails the social dynamics and values that shape people's economic choices and actions, and it allows us to account for indigenous labor *and* its connections to the broader social and cultural values of indigenous societies.[20]

Norrgard's articulation of livelihood opens up space for more holistic understandings of Indigenous economic practices arising from economic sovereignty. This holism is conveyed in "eshkigamigak," an Anishinaabe word for economy provided by Elder Gidigaa Migizi Doug Williams-ban that translates as "how everything comes together."[21]

Indigenous peoples' economic practices are understood as existing as a communal or familial system without distinguishing these practices across discreet differences. Further, Shalene Jobin provides a contemporary nationhood perspective that, in part, subverts and grapples with capitalist paradigms.[22] However, Indigenous peoples did act independently and in distinct groups economically, including groups signified by gender (e.g. womxn). As robust literature in Indigenous women's history reveals, Indigenous womxn have always acted as independent economic agents – in self-determined ways and through imposed structural conditions; Indigenous womxn have also always acted economically as collectives throughout various historical conditions.[23] The larger Anishinaabe feminist problematic that this discussion arises from distinguishes Indigenous economic sovereignty through gender, and in particular, through Indigenous womxn.[24] This departs from an ideal economic sovereignty that is holistically "tribal," communal, or familial, and it does so out of necessity. There are many Indigenous womxn who live in the world, for various reasons, as independent economic actors. There are many Indigenous womxn who live within systems of oppressive settler capitalist, patriarchal, or masculinist control that invisibilize, exploit, or diminish her economic sovereignty. These systems may seek to make her dependent on social-economic relations, rendering her as less-than in a hierarchy or denying her both the capability to do for herself and contribute efficaciously to the relations and communities within which she is embedded. This reality, and these conditions, are the reason I identify and elucidate the idea of "Anishinaabe womxn's economic sovereignty."

Anishinaabeg womxn's economic sovereignty has to do with Anishinaabeg womxn's labour. It also has to do with the labour of those she works with. If she has children, her labour, under certain historical contexts, includes them and any other children in her care.[25] Investigations of Indigenous womxn's labour within and across settler states help elucidate the idea of Indigenous womxn's economic sovereignty in gendered ways.[26] Research on Anishinaabeg womxn's labour, such as that of Brenda Child, Melissa Rhodes, and Alice Littlefield, support specificity.[27] Trade with other Anishinaabeg, other Indigenous nations including Métis, settlers, arrivants, and tourists to Anishinaabe home territories is also a part of being able to procure and provide. As well, trade is foundational to larger social-economic relations. These relations are, in turn, tied to political relations, governance, and relationships with land, seasons, environment, and climate. Further, it is necessary to explicate links with global economic structures, systems, or processes. For example, Sámi scholar Ruana Kuokkanen invites Indigenous scholars in global north contexts such as Canada to think about the connections between violence against Indigenous womxn and global economies.[28] Elsewhere, I have begun to query Anishinaabeg womxn's sugar bush work through a transnational Indigenous feminist lens.[29]

All Anishinaabeg have had our economic sovereignty, epistemologies, and practices eroded. Under global and settler colonial economic structures, systems, and ideologies, the means and ends of our economic well-being have been transformed. All Anishinaabeg are embedded somehow within non-Anishinaabeg economic systems, practices, and relations. While the settler economic system is closed and unjust to many, some are able to make their way or thrive within it, to some degree. Like all Indigenous peoples, there are Anishinaabeg who have the knowledge, ability, desire, and means to keep Anishinaabe land-based ways or seasonal practices and economies alive. Anishinaabeg understand that the natural world of our home-territory is a gift given to us by gizhe manidoo. We understand that there are greater beings who originally taught us how to procure and (re)produce life from the natural world in relational ways. And, as opposed to the settler liberal model of rights and responsibilities in relation to the state, many Anishinaabeg today remember that our primary exchange is one of gifts and responsibility in relation to gizhe manidoo and all of creation: we have a responsibility to live well with the gifts provided to us, which means using them and being responsible in doing so.

## Anishinaabe Feminist Problematizing: Where Are Our Stories?

Anti-indigeneity is the bedrock of settler societies. It exists everywhere. It existed between 1998 to 2006 during my first career experience as a counsellor in my territory of Anishinaabewaki. Tepid in the early years, this corrosive social dynamic became amplified after an amalgamation of counselling organizations. As one of three Anishinaabe womxn in an agency of approximately seventy white settlers, I felt very much on the margins. I was also highly motivated to engage the leadership on gendered anti-Indigenous attitudes. While I needed and wanted the job, I expected Anishinaabe womxn, including myself, to not be treated as less-than. The ideal of doing counselling work in Anishinaabe ways was not even on the radar at that time. Still, I had, and continue to have, a strong feeling that the death, the suffering, and the political impositions our people have endured and the sacrifices they have made have not been, and will not be, for nothing.

It was in the darkest moments of this threat to my social-economic well-being that my anger and indignation served me well. This struggle ignited the idea of our economic sovereignty as Indigenous womxn, as Anishinaabe womxn. In the context of "the workplace," a place shaped by settler law and history, and dominated by settlers, Indigenous peoples are normatively treated by default as economic citizens. However, Anishinaabe peoples are economically sovereign before, throughout, and after the settler workplace. For the reasons stated, I focus on Indigenous/Anishinaabe womxn's economic sovereignty. In Anishinaabeg lands, treated or otherwise, Anishinaabeg womxn have sovereignty to live an economically good life; Indigenous womxn have sovereignty to live in our lands and generate this good life. Indigenous womxn have the right to generate life from their lands and waters; to provide well for, and with, their relations; and to do so without ill treatment from non-Indigenous peoples who are there by treaty or illegal occupation. I knew Anishinaabeg womxn's economic sovereignty was rooted in our ancestral and inherited relationships with land. I knew that these relationships had been disrupted through colonial processes and settler dominance. During this time of struggle, I sought out stories to affirm our economic sovereignty as womxn. I needed them as a lifeline. I needed them to make my common-sense knowing about our sovereignty more tangible, more evidentiary.

Scanning the social-cultural life of my world at the time, I could not recall one memory or find one active story that portrayed Anishinaabeg womxn on the land as producers, providers, or overseers of material life or sustenance. We've lived in our home-territories for thousands of years, and yet there were no stories that affirmed our efficacious material or subsistence relationships with land, there were no stories about how we engaged in such relationships with and for our people. How could this be? There was a creation story about Giizhigo Ikawe (Sky Womxn), who is portrayed as a world-transitioning womb-carrier of babies, maker-of-land for her babies, and birther of babies.[30] There was also growing circulation of teachings and practices about Anishinaabeg women's spiritual relationship with water.[31] *Anishinaabeg womxn as co-maker, carrier, birther, and sustainer of human life through her body? Anishinaabeg womxn as land-maker? Anishinaabeg womxn as having spiritual relationships with water?* The profound vitality of these cultural and historical portrayals of Anishinaabe womxn cannot be overstated. However, under settler colonialism and new economic orders, there is a cavernous distance between this vitality and their meanings and how Indigenous womxn, including Anishinaabeg, are really faring socially, economically, physically, and politically, particularly in the Anthropocene and in a post-pandemic world.[32] Such depictions also do not signify Anishinaabeg womxn as makers, procurers, providers, sustainers, and organizers of subsistence or material life from the land she made, the water she has a spiritual relationship with, or the babies she carries, births, feeds from her breasts, and has responsibilities towards.

Where were the stories of Anishinaabeg womxn as knowers of, and doers with and through, the land?[33] Where were the stories of her getting, doing, providing, making, organizing, overseeing, storing, distributing? Why did I, as an Ojibway womxn, not have any of my own stories? Why did I not know how to live on our lands as my relatives and ancestors did, and in some cases still do? The dearth of living stories of this nature exponentially complicated the problem of settler colonial erosion of our economic sovereignty that I experienced in the settler workplace. Such stories are needed as lifeline-evidence; their absence within the Anishinaabe world I inhabited created a new reality. And so I met with the quintessential Indigenous feminist problem that so many Indigenous womxn are confronted with – having to contend with settler colonial cis-heteropatriarchal capitalist society and its violent imposition upon our personhood and relations within our communities and nations. Not only was Anishinaabe womxn's economic sovereignty, as generated from our land-based relations, eroded and supplanted by non-Indigenous economic systems and practices, but evidence of it was also absent within the Anishinaabe social-cultural landscape that informed my world.[34]

## Introducing A Sugar Bush Story Bundle

Although popularly circulating stories about Anishinaabeg womxn's material and subsistence-focused relationships with land were absent from my world circa 2006, through years of graduate research, and the relationships that emerged from this research, I learned that there was an abundance of information about the Anishinaabe sugar bush in historical, archival, literary, and living memory sources. This was particularly the case for cultural and visual knowledge in the form of language, songs, dance, drawings, visual art, film, photographs, and traditional stories. Most compelling was that Anishinaabeg womxn were everywhere in these sources. They figured predominantly not only as subjects but also as creators and transmitters of knowledge across generations. These sources also revealed Anishinaabe womxn as being in an active relationship with the sugar bush.

Documenting and depicting Indigenous womxn in active and generative relationships with their lands is significant for three reasons. First, the process of historical formation under settler colonialism has not only removed Indigenous womxn from her lands and waters but has reduced her to non-person status, repositioned her as structurally subordinate to mxn, and transformed her worth as arising from her relational association with mxn. These sources challenge this historical formation.[35] Second, Indigenous womxn are often erased or muted in documentation; these sources portrayed Anishinaabeg womxn as actively present. Third, where Indigenous womxn are presented in cultural or primary sources, they are often misrepresented, made marginal, or dehumanized. While some of these sources make these errors, the majority represent Anishinaabeg womxn with dignity, as central to the story, and as full, complex humans in whole relationships with the whole worlds they navigate.

The sources I focus on are traditional stories. Below I list nine published traditional sugar bush stories,[36] presented from earliest to most recently published. The exception to this is the last entry which I elaborate on in the next section. Each entry includes the title of the story and identifies the Anishinaabe source. Other details include the narrator, author, and/or translator. This information begins to reveal the genealogy and social history of these stories.

**"Mishosha; Or, The Magician and His Daughter"** (1838)
Anna Jameson from Ozhaaguscodaywayquay Susan Johnston

**"The Legend of Sap"**[37] (1887)
Mack-e-te-be-nessy Andrew J. Blackbird

**"The Bear-Maiden: An Ojibwa Folk-Tale from Lac Courte Oreille Reservation, Wisconsin"** (1902)
Albert Ernest Jencks from Pä-skiń

**"Spies: Geemootaugaedjig"** (1993)
Basil H. Johnston and Sam Ozawamick

**"Bgoji-nishinaabenhsag: Little People"** (1999)
Nmenhs Arthur McGregor

**"A Woman's Voice"** (2008)
Edward Benton-Benai

**"The Bear and Maple Sap"** (2008)
Edward Benton-Banai

**"The Anishinaabe Woman Who Married Her Brother-in-Law"** (2015)
Howard Webkamigad from Odawas at Harbour Springs, Michigan

*

**"The Tale of the Making of Maple Sugar"** (1977)
Marius Nanipowisk

Collectively, I conceive of these stories as a living sugar bush story bundle. By "living" I mean that with ongoing research and reflection, this bundle grows and becomes more complex.

Elsewhere I summarized and interpreted the stories told by Pä-skiń), Basil H. Johnston and Sam Ozawamick, and Edward Benton-Banai.[38]

Much like Emily Snyder's Indigenous feminist interpretation of the ways Cree women were, or were not, depicted in Cree legal sources,[39] I employed Anishinaabe feminist interpretations of representations of Anishinaabeg womxn, and representations of her in relationships with the natural and supernatural world involving the sugar bush. Similar to Val Napoleon's artistic approach in portraying a community-based method of engaging with story, I invited anticipated Anishinaabe readers into the interpretive process.[40] In this chapter, I expand my original selection of stories to include an additional six. I also shift the focus on representations of womxn and power in single stories to consider how a story bundle illuminates a sugar bush world where Anishinaabeg womxn are very active. This new framing allows me to ask, "*How* is the Anishinaabeg sugar bush world?" and "*How* are Anishinaabeg womxn in these worlds?"

## The Anishinaabe Sugar Bush World

First, this bundle details an Anishinaabe world whose structures include supernatural beings. Understood to impinge upon all life, these beings are acknowledged, petitioned, and communicated with. Supernatural beings are shown not only to be the creators of subsistence; they facilitate the capacity to procure and produce it. For instance, in "Mishosha" a greater power transforms the old-man magician, who gives the story its title, into a maple tree. "The Legend of Sap '' tells of a time when syrup, not sap, flowed from the maples. Nanaboozhoo, being a helper to Anishinaabeg, thought that the ease with which syrup was obtained would make sugar worthless. As a result, he diluted the syrup in the maple trees into sap, thus requiring his "nephews" to labour much more extensively to make their sugar.[41] According to Nanaboozhoo's logic, this would increase its value to his nephews in "the future time."[42] The first quote that opens this chapter contains an Anishinaabe womxn's petition of higher powers for life-sustaining help in "A Woman's Voice." Finally, Elder Nmenhs (Arthur McGregor) of Wiigwaaskingaa (White Fish River FN) tells how it was Bgojinishnaabenh'sag — little people or little wild men — who taught Anishinaabeg how to turn sap into syrup through telepathy while Anishinaabeg slept.[43]

Second, within the structure of the Anishinaabeg world, relationships exist with more-than-human beings, like the animals, plants, fish, and insects. These relationships have evolved into odoodemiwin, the clan system. This is a form of governance that emphasizes familial orders; it informs Anishinaabeg relations with each other through association with odoodem (a clan family).[44] Inherently, odoodemiwin compels and informs Anishinaabeg relations with the more-than-human world. In my reading, odoodemiwin is evident in the storied world of the sugar bush through the presence of makwa, the bear. These stories not only lend insight into how odoodemiwin operates in certain contexts, but also reveal the connections Anishinaabeg made between the more-than-human beings, the material, and the social. In "The Bear-Maiden," an ageing womxn and mxn have three daughters, the youngest of whom is nozhem (a female bear).[45] As the story unfolds, nozhem is shown to exhibit several characteristics that in modern times are understood to be exhibited by odoodem. She teaches, helps, and protects her two older human sisters when they leave their ageing parents to find work to support themselves. nozhem is also not only recognized as having the ability to restore balance in the natural world but is asked to do so by an ogiimaa (chief); on each of the three occasions her help is provided, she succeeds. Finally, she is shown to be a strategist and mediator of new social-economic worlds on behalf of her sisters. In this story, the primary item nozhem utilizes to restore balance in the natural world is maple sugar. makwa also appears in "The Bear and Maple Sap,"[46] in which during a time of starvation a young Anishinaabe mxn who is makwa odoodem is sent out by his community in search of food, and observes makwa digging up bugs from under a log and drinking sap from the maple tree. Finally, a vignette within "Spies" occurs during maple sugar season. It tells the story of an Anishinaabe mxn who returned to the sugar camp with a bear that he had hunted. His wife, an Anishinaabe medicine womxn, renders its fat through boiling. While doing so, she sees reflected in the bear fat a stranger-man spying on the camp. She discreetly tells her husband, who pretends to demonstrate how he shot the bear and instead shoots the spy, ridding the camp of this danger.

In "Spies" and "The Anishinaabe Woman Who Married her Brother-in-Law," the sugar bush during harvesting season emerges as a significant place where social worlds unfold and lessons are to be learned. The element of the supernatural is apparent in these stories as well. Womxn, as well as mxn, figure predominantly as complex, capable, fallible, and heroic characters. In one vignette from "Spies" an Anishinaabe man is portrayed as a victim of an assault by another man.[47] This assault is disrupted by his wife, who whips the man on his bare back with a rope made from hot taffy. The assailant flees and later dies. In a second vignette, a girl helps a would-be murderer to foil a treacherous plan against Anishinaabeg at their sugar bush. In "The Anishinaabe Woman Who Married her Brother-in-law" an Anishinaabeg womxn has committed moral wrongs for which she was haunted by her deceased younger sister. Her failures include marrying her brother-in-law too soon after her sister's death and doing so despite being urged not to by her parents. The story unfolds against a backdrop of cyclical sugar bush harvesting seasons, with the labour first carried out by the husband and his first wife and later by the husband and his second wife. The deceased sister haunts the living sister while she is boiling sap alone. In a panic, the living sister runs away from the sugar bush back to her village. Upon running into her lodge, she thinks she feels the ghost of her younger sister grabbing her; she trips and falls into a fire. She is removed from the fire by people in her lodge but, after telling the story of being chased by her deceased sister, she dies. Despite this womxn's supposed moral failings, she is portrayed as central in the sugar bush harvest, carrying it out independently and skilfully.

Finally, employing a decolonial method of epistemological repair through activating relationality with our neighbouring Indigenous nations, I include a published nêhiyaw (Plains Cree) story that speaks to layers of jurisdiction with the sugar bush. I include this story because nêhiyawak are bordering neighbours with Anishinaabeg. Similarities in language and kinship ties suggest similarities in stories and worldviews. More importantly, I include it because the relationships with the supernatural beings in this story coincide with living Anishinaabeg sugar bush practice. "The Tale of the Making of Maple Sugar" tells the story of how a Cree mxn named Flying Bird endeavours to harvest maple sap; his efforts are thwarted by little beings unknown to him. When he returns home and tells his wife about this problem, she says, "maimaykwaiswaq; we must move away. This is their country no matter how long we stay, we will never have any maple sugar."[48] According to Flying Bird's wife, jurisdiction of the maple sap belongs to the supernatural ones known as maimaykwaiswaq, the little people. Despite being relegated to "wife of" and being unnamed, the nêhiyaw womxn in this story embodies knowledge about sugar bush jurisdiction and acts with authority, stating that the couple need to move. Similarly, in Anishinaabe country, I know an Ojibwe womxn in the Bawating Sault Ste. Marie area who was told by a grandmother about the need to make an offering to memegwesiiyag during the sugar bush harvest. In turn, she herself practices this and teaches it.[49] Across nations, stories about maimaykwaiswaq | memegwesiiyag echo the idea of womxn holding particular knowledge, embodying and transmitting it, and materially recognizing that these supernatural ones have jurisdiction at the sugar bush during sugaring season that both supersedes Anishinaabeg relationship with this place and is mediated by Anishinaabeg womxn with humility and recognition.

Key elements of this story bundle reveal an Anishinaabeg sugar bush world, portrayed by Anishinaabeg as being structured within, and by, supernatural beings like gizhe manidoo, Nanaboozhoo, and memegwesiiyag. Recognizing the power of the more-than-human (e.g., trees that communicate, bears that teach and help) is also a part of this structure. In addition, odoodemiwan is represented through makwa and in one case nozhem. This bundle shows a world animated by and with Anishinaabe womxn and mxn and, in one story, a girl. There are non-Anishinaabeg "spies" and there is a kin-ghost. All are in relationship with each other. In some cases, the story is about how the maple tree or sap came to be or how Anishinaabeg learned about the sap or how to process it. In other cases the sugar bush, during harvesting season, is a place where Anishinaabeg sugar-making unfolds as a backdrop to other social affairs, and all of this seems likely to be activated through proper protocols with beings who have jurisdiction of this place. Transformation figures greatly in this bundle: transformation of a mxn into a maple tree, transformation of a young female bear into a young beautiful womxn, transformation of syrup into sap, taffy into a weapon, and murderous intention into life preservation.

## The Sugar Bush World and Anishinaabeg Womxn

In living settler colonial contexts where Indigenous economic sovereignty is eroded and subsumed by settler and global economic structures and economies, the patriarchal capitalist underpinnings of these systems marginalize Indigenous womxn within them. They not only deepen the disregard for her economic sovereignty but increase the barriers to her practice of it. As witnessed through my personal story, contemporary worlds are bereft of any popularized evidence of the materiality and subsistence foundations of this economic sovereignty. In her disruption to colonial historical practices of failing to include Indigenous sources in the telling of Indigenous history, Dakota scholar Waziyawatin recounts a Dakota oral history lived and embodied by her grandmother and transmitted through her maternal line.[50] Of such Indigenous stories, Waziyawatin says, "When our stories die, so will we."[51]

When I revisit the birth story for the idea of Anishinaabeg womxn's economic sovereignty, and recall the emotions of that time, I am struck by my need for and instinctual turn to story as life-line evidence. The absence of story felt like a kind of death. The power of settler colonialism around us and in our bodies, minds, spirits, and relations makes having a felt need for our stories important. This need is like a flicker of a flame, an ember. Reaching out for our stories and finding they are not there, at the ready, is significant. Looking for them, finding a tidbit, sharing the story of the search with others and their unprompted sharing of what they have come upon in their meanderings or offering up of what they have in their bundle — all of this, from the location of "I" in this case, is such an important part of Indigenous feminist method and Indigenous restoration. That our stories exist, somewhere, and can be brought together into a bundle is itself a feat. "When our stories die, so will we," but when our stories live not only do we live, but we do so in a way that is ours while simultaneously defending against the very force killing them and us. Anishinaabeg womxn's economic sovereignty, as rooted in her material relationships with the land, was an idea born of commonsense knowledge with no evidence to support it; now there is a bundle of Anishinaabe evidence that makes it tangible.

The story bundle introduced here not only provides insight into the Anishinaabe sugar bush world but shows this world to be actively animated by, or in relation with, the female, a girl, and womxn. The female bear, a clan relative, utilizes maple sugar as a tool in achieving a task for which she has been sought out, strategically facilitating security for her human sisters in doing so; womxn and a girl are the heroic medicine characters in three vignettes portraying intruders at the sugar bush during the harvest; womxn is shown to have a generative relationship with the natural world and is gifted the knowledge of sap in the maple tree whereby she, her child, and her community are able to avoid starvation; another womxn carries out the sugar bush harvest with her husband where a second womxn, her sister, is described as having the capability of carrying it out independently; and finally, womxn are shown to have knowledge about supernatural jurisdiction over the sugar bush and how to be in relationship with these beings.

There is room for further contextualization and Indigenous feminist critique of these stories. For example, it is necessary to ask what is lost in their translation into English, and to understand the translation method itself. It is also necessary to examine how they may be influenced by settler-imposed ideologies and hierarchies or class systems like patriarchy, heteronormativity, and marriage. Doing so with community members may facilitate insights about how we have been, and are, continually shaped by imposed settler ideologies about gender, sexuality, and relationality. As well, it is worth critically examining the pattern in which these stories are mostly retold and published by mxn, particularly when we consider that knowledge is power and publication is a form of generating social-economic capital. Such an inquiry will offer insight into how mxn, both settler and Anishinaabeg, engage with gender, sexuality, and relationality in the reproduction of culture, and how they see womxn in our culture and in relation to them. Finally, asking who isn't in our stories can strengthen stories and thus our communities. In the case of the stories discussed here, there is a complete lack of diversity around gender, sexuality, and relationality as well as a limited range of physical (in)abilities portrayed in seasonal labour. Engaging this limitation further will open up possibilities for retelling of the stories and for our communities.

## To Turn Sap into Syrup, You Need Fire; Syrup into Sugar, Air

Sugar-making, in Anishinaabe ways, is a highly sophisticated, laborious process with many elements, stages, and preparatory requirements. The same may be said for critical Indigenous feminist law. Both exist within a broader, deeper, and unseen paradigm of Indigenous cosmologies, ontologies, epistemologies, values, and visions for how to live well in the world. In this chapter, I take my cue from a main principle in the Indigenous feminist legal field that wants, and requires, participation from a diverse community, including non-legal scholars and practitioners. As Anishinaabe womxn who utilizes Indigenous feminist theories as necessary life-giving and life-making tools for/with Indigenous womxn who experience settler colonial (cishet) patriarchy as oppressive, life-taking, or life-diminishing, I consider contributing to the conversation a responsibility. It is also an opportunity. This chapter does not make explicit statements about critical Indigenous feminist law or legal orders. With its Indigenous/Anishinaabe feminist problematizing, method, and interpretation of a traditional story-bundle, it contributes implicitly to Indigenous, and Indigenous feminist, legal methods that utilize traditional stories. It seizes the opportunity to put forth an Indigenous feminist idea about Indigenous womxn's economic sovereignty that requires bright, tenacious, and creative minds to advance it through, with, and despite the power-institution of settler law. Another way to put this is to say that where this chapter is the fire-making process of turning sap into syrup, willing readers may opt to be the air that turns ideas herein into sugar, that is, Indigenous feminist law or legal method.

Q, Special Issue: Writing about (Writing about) American Indians 7.

## NOTES

1 This is a fictive quote distilled from the theme of a sugar bush story, "A Woman's Voice" (Edward Benton-Banai, in *Anishinaabe Almanac: Living Through the Seasons* [M'Chigeeng, ON: Kenjgewin Teg Educational

Institute, 2008] 16 at 16). In this chapter I spell "women" with an *x* to signal heterogeneity between Indigenous womxn and transformation within her/their lives as well as to signal colonial constructions and imposed meanings of womanhood upon Indigenous womxn. This applies similarly to Indigenous mxn and non-binary or transgender people. See note 1 in Sy, "Relationship with Land in Anishinaabeg Womxn's Historical Research" in Julie A Gallagher & Barbara Winslow, eds, *Reshaping Women's History: Voices of Nontraditional Women Historians* (Urbana: University of Illinois Press, 2018) 1.

2 Alice C Fletcher, "Legal Conditions of Indian Women" (Presentation to the International Council of Women, assembled by the National Woman Suffrage Association, Washington, DC, 25 March–1 April 1888) (Washington, DC: Rufus H. Darby, 1888) at 240, online: https://archive.org/details/ofinternatreport00interich/page/240/mode/2up?ref=ol&view=theater. These words convey the sentiments of Indigenous women under white law, sentiments that educator, scholar, and agent of colonization Miss Alice C Fletcher in turn conveyed and supported in her presentation to the international council.

3 Patricia Monture-Angus, *Journeying Forward, Dreaming First Nations Independence* (Winnipeg: Fernwood, 1999) at 36. ("ban" is a suffix used in Anishinaabe language to signal that the person has passed away.)

4 I am inspired by the poetic and visionary proclivities of Mushkego chapan (great grandmother) Mary Jane Metatawabin of Fort Albany First Nation, Ontario. Her use of the metaphor of "tending to our homefires" in our conversations over the years is one that keeps me grounded and alight. Permission granted to acknowledge her here.

5 Benton-Banai, *supra* note 1 at 16–23. This story weaves together and retells two stories documented by Benton-Banai. In my retelling, I've employed an Anishinaabe feminist ethic that addresses cis-heteropatriarchal power in a number of ways: it decentres the prominence of cis-het men as hunters, heroes, and primary mediators with the natural and supernatural world as well as heterosexual relationships; it corrects a misrepresentation of Anishinaabeg womxn as divesting her relationship with the natural world in order to have an Elder man mediate it; and it foregrounds Anishinaabeg womxn's agency, methods, ethics, and efficacy in identifying and solving problems through her/their whole relationships with the natural and supernatural world and her efficacy in providing for her child/ren with the support of the human, natural, and supernatural world. The inclusion of ecological knowledge with achidimo scratching the bark to access maple sap comes from Gidigaa Migizi Doug Williams-ban.

6 In elucidating patriarchy, Allan G Johnson defines structure as "the way privilege and oppression are organized through social relationships and

unequal distributions of power, rewards, opportunities, and resources." Johnson, *The Gender Knot: Unraveling Our Patriarchal Legacy* (Philadelphia: Temple University Press, 2005) at 41.

7 On foundational intersectionality see Kimberle Crenshaw, "Demarginalizing the Intersection of Race and Sex: A Black Feminist Critique of Antidiscrimination Doctrine, Feminist Theory and Antiracist Politics" (1989) 1 University of Chicago Legal Forum 139; and Crenshaw, "Mapping the Margins: Intersectionality, Identity Politics and Violence against Women of Color" (1991) 43:6 Stanford L Rev 1241. With the phrase "being Indigenous and expressions of indigeneity" I refer to political status, racialized location, subjectivity, epistemological proclivities, and identity.

8 J. Kēhaulani Kauanui conceptualizes the idea of the "paradox of sovereignty" in their monograph, elucidating how aspirations for Hawaiian liberation are intertwined with white American ideas of property title, state sovereignty, and normative gender relations and sexuality. See Kauanui, *Paradoxes of Hawaiian Sovereignty: Land, Sex, and the Colonial Politics of State Nationalism* (Durham: Duke University Press, 2018) at 3.

9 For an example of this connection, see Fletcher's full account referenced in supra note 2, including how she relays Indigenous men's contestation of how Indigenous women are treated under white law.

10 The following sources informed my thinking about Indigenous law as a non-legal scholar both inside and outside of the academy: Patricia Monture-Angus, *Thunder in My Soul: A Mohawk Woman Speaks* (Halifax: Fernwood, 1995) at 131–188 and 249–264; Rupert Ross, *Returning to the Teachings: Exploring Aboriginal Justice* (Toronto: Penguin, 1996); James Dumont, "Justice and Aboriginal Peoples" in *Aboriginal Peoples and the Justice System: Report of the National Round Table on Aboriginal Justice Issues* (Ottawa: Royal Commission on Aboriginal Peoples, 1996) 42; John Borrows, *Drawing Out Law: A Spirit's Guide* (Toronto: University of Toronto Press, 2010); and Sylvia McAdam (Saysewahum), *Nationhood Interrupted: Revitalizing nêhiyaw Legal Systems* (Saskatoon: Purlich, 2015).

11 Val Napoleon et al, *Mikomosis and the Wetiko* (Victoria: Indigenous Law Research Clinic, 2013); Val Napoleon & Hadley Friedland, "An Inside Job: Engaging with Indigenous Legal Traditions through Stories" (2016) 61:4 McGill LJ 724; Emily Snyder, *Gender, Power and Representations of Cree Law* (Vancouver: UBC Press, 2018); Emily Snyder, Val Napoleon & John Borrows, "Gender and Violence: Drawing on Indigenous Legal Resources" (2015) 48:2 UBC L Rev 593.

12 Songhees Nation, *Songhees* (Victoria: Songhees Nation, 2013) at 21.

13 Hannah Askew, "Learning from the Land: Anishinaabe Law Camp at Walpole Island First Nation," West Coast Environmental Law (15 May 2016), online: <https://wcel.org/blog/learning-land-anishinaabe-law-camp-walpole-island-first-nation>. In this blog post, Askew tells a personal story whereby she reflexively strives to understand this Elder's response.

14 "dibaadjimowad" is personal story; "story" for Anishinaabeg is a vast, complex, and sophisticated sphere of knowledge production and world-making. Other kinds of stories include creation stories and sacred stories. Sacred stories, to me, are those that are intentionally invoked within a living space in ceremonial ways for particular purposes. I refrain from describing stories here as sacred even as they may be employed that way. Instead, I describe them as "traditional."

15 Monture-Angus, *supra* note 3 at 36.

16 waaseyaa'sin Christine Sy, *Following ininaatigoog Home: Anishinaabeg Womxn iskigamiziganing* (PhD Dissertation, Trent University, 2019), 14–15 [unpublished].

17 J. Kēhaulani Kauanui, "'A Structure, Not an Event': Settler Colonialism and Enduring Indigeneity" (2016) 5:1 Lateral, online: <https://csalateral.org/issue/5-1/forum-alt-humanities-settler-colonialism-enduring-indigeneity-kauanui/>.

18 I include this in my dissertation. See Sy, *supra* note 16 at 14. See also Robert Keller, "An Economic History of Indian Treaties in the Great Lakes Region" (1978) 5:1 American Indian J 2 at 5; and Chantal Norrgard, *Seasons of Change: Labor, Treaty Rights and Ojibwe Nationhood* (Chapel Hill: University of North Carolina Press, 2014) at 10.

19 See Norrgard, *supra* note 18 at 9.

20 *Ibid.*

21 Personal communication to author, c. 2010.

22 Shalen Jobin, *Upholding Indigenous Economic Relationships: Nehiyawak Narratives* (Vancouver: UBC Press, 2022).

23 Key examples of anthologies and monographs include Brenda J Child, *Holding Our World Together: Ojibwe Women and the Survival of Community* (New York: Viking Penguin, 2012); Carol Williams, ed, *Indigenous Women and Work: From Labor to Activism* (Urbana: University of Illinois Press, 2012); Tressa Berman, *Circle of Goods: Women, Work, Welfare in a Reservation Community* (Albany: SUNY Press, 2003); and Mary Jane Logan McCallum, *Indigenous Women, Work and History: 1940–1980* (Winnipeg: University of Manitoba Press, 2014).

24 For more on the idea of an Indigenous feminist problematic as distinct, see Aileen Moreton-Robinson, "Towards an Australian Indigenous Women's Standpoint Theory: A Methodological Tool" (2013) 28:78 Australian Feminist Studies 331.

25 Christine Sy, *Indigenous Women's Work in Canada and United States, 1624–1997: A Transnational Historical Synthesis* (Master's Thesis, Trent University, 2009) at 23–27 [unpublished].

26 Ruana Kuokkanen, "Indigenous Women in Traditional Economies: The Case of Sámi Reindeer Herding" (2009) 34:3 Signs: J Women in Culture and Society 504; Kuokkanen, "Indigenous Economies, Theories of Subsistence and Women: Exploring the Social Economy Model for Indigenous Governance" (2011) 35:2 American Indian Q 215; and Williams, *supra* note 23.

27 Brenda J Child, *My Grandfather's Knocking Sticks: Ojibway Family Life and Labor on the Reservation* (St. Paul: Minnesota Historical Press Society, 2014); Child, *supra* note 23; Alice Littlefield, "Making a Living: Anishnaabe Women in Michigan's Changing Economy" in Williams, *supra* note 23 at 46; and Melissa Rohde, "Labour and Leisure in the 'Enchanted Summer Land': Anishinabe Women's Work and the Growth of Wisconsin Tourism, 1900-1940" in Williams, *supra* note 23 at 136.

28 Rauna Kuokkanen, "Globalization as Racialized, Sexualized Violence" (2008) 10:2 Int Feminist J of Politics 216.

29 Bronwyn Carlson et al., "Transnational Indigenous Feminisms: Indigenous Womxn's Boundary Crossing Cultural Productions, Resistance, & Resurgence" in Bronwyn Carlson, Tristan Kennedy & Madi Day, eds, *Global Networks of Indigeneity: Peoples, Sovereignty and Future* (Manchester: Manchester University Press, 2023).

30 As an example, see Basil Johnston, *Ojibwe Heritage* (Lincoln: University of Nebraska Press, 1976) at 11–17.

31 In this sentence I use the term "women" to suggest that these portrayals were presumed to involve women with wombs, who menstruate and have babies. I suspect that for many readers, this will be the case. However, with increased effort to decolonize understandings and expressions of gender and gender expectations, as well as sexuality and relationality, I utilize the x in womxn to disrupt normative (settler) ideas of "woman" and "womanhood" that have been imposed for hundreds of years.

32 See National Inquiry into Missing and Murdered Indigenous Women and Girls, *Reclaiming Power and Place: The Final Report of the National Inquiry into Missing and Murdered Indigenous Women and Girls* (Vancouver: Privy Council Office, 2019).

33 Nathalie Kermoal & Isabel Altamirano-Jiménez, eds, *Living on the Land: Indigenous Women's Understanding of Place* (Edmonton: Athabasca University Press, 2016). Kermoal and Altamirano-Jiménez question how patriarchy, gender, and colonialism have shaped the experience of Indigenous women as both knowers and producers of knowledge.

34 Anishinaabeg have widely varied lived experience and live in widely varied worlds. Where some Anishinaabeg womxn are raised up with relatives, with stories of relatives engaged in such land-based relations, or with cultural

knowledge or lived practice of said, many are not. I write from the location of being the daughter of a womxn who was taken away from community as a child to residential school. Thereafter, her connections to place and family as a young girl and womxn were frequently disrupted through being in a sanatorium and foster care. As a teen and young adult, my mother ultimately travelled between Winnipeg, Thunder Bay, and Sault Ste. Marie, Ontario, before settling in the latter as best she could. Aside from me and my three nêhiyaw girlfriends, who were a part of the Sixties Scoop, playing with our friends where we lived in Island Lake, Ontario, the only story about Anishinaabe womxn on the land in my memory is of seeing my mother on a hot summer day, bare-footed, walking on the dirt road towards my house.

35 For the most part, these sources also reify the gender binary and heteronormativity, thereby muting diversity in gender identity, sexuality, and family formation.

36 Anna Jameson, *Winter Studies and Summer Rambles,* vol 3 (London: Saunders and Otley, 1838) at 96; AJ Blackbird, *History of the Ottawa and Chippewa Indians of Michigan; a grammar of their language, and personal and family history of the author* (Ypsilanti, MI: The Ypsilantian Job Printing House, 1887) at 72, online: <https://babel.hathitrust.org/cgi/pt?id=loc.ark:/13960/t4zg6rr33&view=1up&seq=7>; Albert Ernest Jencks, "The Bear-Maiden: An Ojibwa Folk-Tale from Lac Courte Oreille Reservation, Wisconsin" (1902) 15:56 J of American Folklore 33; Basil H. Johnston, *Mermaids and Medicine Women: Native Myths and Legends* (Toronto: Royal Museum of Ontario, 1993) at 61; Arthur J McGregor, "Bgojinishnaabenh'sag – Little People" in Julie E Wilder & Mary E Wemigwans, eds, *Wiigwaaskingaa, "Land of Birch Trees": Ojibwe Stories* (Hobbema, AB: Blue Moon, 1999) 40; Edward Benton-Banai, *Anishinaabe Almanac: Living through the Seasons* (M'Chigeeng: Kenjgewin Teg Educational Institute, 2008) at 14; Howard Webkamigad, trans and ed, *Ottawa Stories From the Springs: anishinaabe dibaadjimowinan wodi gaa binjibaamigak wodi mookodjiwong e zhinikaadek* (East Lansing: Michigan State University Press, 2015) at 182; Marius Nanipowisk, "The Tale of the Making of Maple Sugar" in Earle H Waugh & K Dad Prithipaul, eds, *Native Religious Traditions* (Waterloo: Wilfred Laurier Press, 1977) 73.

37 This story exists embedded within a longer text, untitled. I have attributed this title to it.

38 Sy, *supra* note 16 at 134–171.

39 Snyder, *supra* note 11.

40 Napoleon et al, *supra* note 11.

41 Blackbird's telling of this story is androcentric.

42 Blackbird, *supra* note 36 at 72.

43 McGregor, *supra* note 36 at 40.

44 James Dumont, online lecture, 9 February 2022.

45 "nozhem" is defined as such by Elder Edna Manitowabi. See plaque naming Nozhem Theatre at Trent University, Peterborough, ON, in the Indigenous Studies Department.

46 "makwa" is written in accordance with Howard Webkamigad's method of writing Anishinaabemowin – that is, it is not capitalized at the beginning of a sentence. I have seen other Indigenous nations, such as syilx peoples, write their language this way as well.

47 The fact that the attack occurs while the man is sleeping and the attacker is found on top of the man with his shirt off suggests this could be a sexual assault.

48 Nanipowisk, *supra* note 36 at 72.

49 Links may be made to Elder McGregor's story about bgoji-nishnaabenhsag; however, I think doing so requires more knowledge about the nuanced differences between these supernatural ones and memegwesiiyag.

50 Angela Cavender Wilson, "Grandmother to Granddaughter: Generations of Oral History in a Dakota Family" (1996) 20:1 American Indian Q, Special Issue: Writing about (Writing about) American Indians 7. Waziyawatin, also known as Angela Cavender Wilson, changed her name legally in 2007. See Pamela Sexsmith, "Waziyatawin Appointed to Head Up Governance Program" (2008) 26:5 *Windspeaker*, online: <https://ammsa.com/publications/windspeaker/waziyatawin-appointed-head-governance-program-0>.

51 Wilson, *supra* note 49 at 13.

## SOURCES CITED

Askew, Hannah. "Learning from the Land: Anishinaabe Law Camp at Walpole Island First Nation," *West Coast Environmental Law* (15 May 2016), online: <https://wcel.org/blog/learning-land-anishinaabe-law-camp-walpole-island-first-nation>.

Benton-Banai, Edward. *Anishinaabe Almanac: Living through the Seasons* (M'Chigeeng, ON: Kenjgewin Teg Educational Institute, 2008).

Benton-Banai, Edward. "A Woman's Voice" in *Anishinaabe Almanac: Living through the Seasons.* (M'Chigeeng, ON: Kenjgewin Teg Educational Institute, 2008) 16.

Berman, Tressa. *Circle of Goods: Women, Work, Welfare in a Reservation Community* (Albany: SUNY Press, 2003).

Blackbird, AJ. *History of the Ottawa and Chippewa Indians of Michigan; a grammar of their language, and personal and family history of the author* (Ypsilanti, MI:

Ypsilantian Job Printing House, 1887), online: <https://babel.hathitrust.org/cgi/pt?id=loc.ark:/13960/t4zg6rr33&view=1up&seq=7>.

Borrows, John. *Drawing Out Law: A Spirit's Guide* (Toronto: University of Toronto Press, 2010).

Carlson, Bronwyn, Kora J-A Juanena, Yi-Chun Tricia Lin, waaseyaa'sin Christine Sy & Alex Wilson. "Transnational Indigenous Feminisms: Indigenous Womxn's Boundary Crossing Cultural Productions, Resistance, & Resurgence" in Bronwyn Carlson, Tristan Kennedy & Madi Day, eds, *Global Networks of Indigeneity: Peoples, Sovereignty and Future* (Manchester: Manchester University Press, 2023) 9.

Child, Brenda J. *Holding Our World Together: Ojibwe Women and the Survival of Community* (New York: Viking Penguin, 2012).

Child, Brenda. *My Grandfather's Knocking Sticks: Ojibway Family Life and Labor on the Reservation* (St. Paul: Minnesota Historical Press Society, 2014).

Crenshaw, Kimberle. "Demarginalizing the Intersection of Race and Sex: A Black Feminist Critique of Antidiscrimination Doctrine, Feminist Theory and Antiracist Politics" (1989) 1 University of Chicago Legal Forum 139.

Crenshaw, Kimberle. "Mapping the Margins: Intersectionality, Identity Politics and Violence against Women of Color" (1991) 43:6 Stanford L Rev 1241.

Dumont, James. "Justice and Aboriginal Peoples" in *Aboriginal Peoples and the Justice System: Report of the National Round Table on Aboriginal Justice Issues* (Ottawa: Royal Commission on Aboriginal Peoples, 1996) 42.

Fletcher, Alice C. "Legal Conditions of Indian Women" (Presentation to International Council of Women, assembled by the National Woman Suffrage Association, Washington, DC, 25 March–1 April 1888) (Washington, DC: Rufus H. Darby, 1888), online: <https://archive.org/details/ofinternatreport00interich/page/240/mode/2up?ref=ol&view=theater.>

Jameson, Anna. *Winter Studies and Summer Rambles*, vol 3 (London: Saunders and Otley, 1838).

Jencks, Albert Ernest. "The Bear-Maiden: An Ojibwa Folk-Tale from Lac Courte Oreille Reservation, Wisconsin" (1902) 15:56 J American Folklore 33.

Johnson, Allan G. *The Gender Knot: Unraveling Our Patriarchal Legacy* (Philadelphia: Temple University Press, 2005).

Johnston, Basil H. *Mermaids and Medicine Women: Native Myths and Legends* (Toronto: Royal Museum of Ontario, 1993).

Johnston, Basil H. *Ojibwe Heritage* (Lincoln: University of Nebraska Press, 1976).

Kauanui, J. Kēhaulani. *Paradoxes of Hawaiian Sovereignty: Land, Sex, and the Colonial Politics of State Nationalism* (Durham: Duke University Press, 2018).

Kauanui, J. Kēhaulani. "'A Structure, Not an Event': Settler Colonialism and Enduring Indigeneity" (2016) 5:1 *Lateral*, online: https://csalateral.org/

issue/5-1/forum-alt-humanities-settler-colonialism-enduring-indigeneity-kauanui/.

Keller, Robert. "An Economic History of Indian Treaties in the Great Lakes Region" (1978) 5:1 American Indian J2.

Kermoal, Nathalie & Isabel Altamirano-Jiménez, eds. *Living on the Land: Indigenous Women's Understanding of Place* (Edmonton: Athabasca University Press, 2016).

Kuokkanen, Ruana. "Globalization as Racialized, Sexualized Violence" (2008) 10:2 Intl Feminist J of Politics 216.

Kuokkanen, Ruana. "Indigenous Economies, Theories of Subsistence and Women: Exploring the Social Economy Model for Indigenous Governance" (2011) 35:2 American Indian Q 215.

Kuokkanen, Ruana. "Indigenous Women in Traditional Economies: The Case of Sámi Reindeer Herding" (2009) 34:3 Signs: Journal of Women in Culture and Society 504.

Littlefield, Alice. "Making a Living: Anishnaabe Women in Michigan's Changing Economy" in Carol Williams, ed, *Indigenous Women and Work: From Labor to Activism* (Urbana: University of Illinois Press, 2012) 46.

McAdam (Saysewahum), Sylvia. *Nationhood Interrupted: Revitalizing nêhiyaw Legal Systems* (Saskatoon: Purlich, 2015).

McGregor, Arthur J. "Bgojinishnaabenh'sag – Little People" in Julie E Wilder & Mary E. Wemigwans, eds, *Wiigwaaskingaa, "Land of Birch Trees": Ojibwe Stories* (Hobbema, AB: Blue Moon, 1999) 40.

Monture-Angus, Patricia. *Journeying Forward, Dreaming First Nations Independence* (Winnipeg: Fernwood, 1999).

Monture-Angus, Patricia. *Thunder in My Soul: A Mohawk Woman Speaks* (Halifax: Fernwood, 1995).

Moreton-Robinson, Aileen. "Towards an Australian Indigenous Women's Standpoint Theory: A Methodological Tool" (2013) 28:78 Australian Feminist Studies 331.

Nanipowisk, Marius. "The Tale of the Making of Maple Sugar" in Earle H Waugh & K Dad Prithipaul, eds, *Native Religious Traditions* (Waterloo: Wilfred Laurier Press, 1977) 73.

Napoleon, Val & Hadley Friedland. "An Inside Job: Engaging with Indigenous Legal Traditions through Stories" (2016) 61:4 McGill LJ 724.

Napoleon, Val, Jim Henshaw, Ken Steacy, Janine Johnston & Simon Roy. *Mikomosis and the Wetiko* (Victoria: Indigenous Law Research Clinic, 2013).

National Inquiry into Missing and Murdered Indigenous Women and Girls. *Reclaiming Power and Place: The Final Report of the National Inquiry into Missing and Murdered Indigenous Women and Girls* (Vancouver: Privy Council Office, 2019).

Norrgard Chantal. *Seasons of Change: Labor, Treaty Rights and Ojibwe Nationhood* (Chapel Hill: University of North Carolina Press, 2014).

Rohde, Melissa. "Labour and Leisure in the 'Enchanted Summer Land': Anishinabe Women's Work and the Growth of Wisconsin Tourism, 1900–1940" in Carol Williams, ed, *Indigenous Women and Work: Labor to Activism,* (Urbana: University of Illinois Press, 2012) 136.

Ross, Rupert. *Returning to the Teachings: Exploring Aboriginal Justice* (Toronto: Penguin, 1996).

Sexsmith, Pamela. "Waziyatawin Appointed to Head Up Governance Program," (2008) 26:5 *Windspeaker*, online: <https://www.ammsa.com/publications/windspeaker/waziyatawin-appointed-head-governance-program>.

Snyder, Emily. *Gender, Power and Representations of Cree Law* (Vancouver: UBC Press, 2018).

Snyder, Emily, Val Napoleon & John Borrows. "Gender and Violence: Drawing on Indigenous Legal Resources" (2015) 48:2 UBC L Rev 593.

Songhees Nation. *Songhees* (Victoria: Songhees Nation, 2013).

Sy, Christine. *Following ininaatigoog Home: Anishinaabeg Womxn iskigamiziganing* (PhD Dissertation, Trent University, 2019) [unpublished].

Sy, Christine. *Indigenous Women's Work in Canada and United States, 1624–1997: A Transnational Historical Synthesis* (Master's Thesis, Trent University, 2009). [unpublished]

Sy, Christine. "Relationship with Land in Anishinaabeg Womxn's Historical Research" in Julie A. Gallagher & Barbara Winslow, eds, *Reshaping Women's History: Voices of Nontraditional Women Historians* (Urbana: University of Illinois Press, 2018) 1.

Webkamigad, Howard, trans and ed. *Ottawa Stories from the Springs: anishinaabe dibaadjimowinan wodi gaa binjibaamigak wodi mookodjiwong e zhinikaadek* (East Lansing: Michigan State University Press, 2015).

Wilson, Angela Cavender. "Grandmother to Granddaughter: Generations of Oral History in a Dakota Family" (1996) 20:1 American Indian

# 4 Giving Voice to Jigonsaseh: A Feminine Perspective on the Haudenosaunee Legal Order

KAHENTE HORN-MILLER

In a statement posted to Facebook on 8 February 2020 calling for all Canadians to support the Wet'suwet'en in their actions against the Trans Canada Energies Coastal GasLink pipeline, Akwesasne Bear Clan mother Louise McDonald, known as Mamma Bear, used the term "mother law" to characterize the responsibilities Indigenous women have to protect the earth. Louise explains the concept in this way: "The women are forever the foundation and they're also the Supreme Law of the Land, which means there's a Mother Rite, vested in the mitochondrial DNA and in the cellular level of how a mother can transfer her genetics to her daughter and her son. So the status of who we are as Haudenosaunee follows the mother, which is a maternal order, not a paternal order. So pretty much everything that gets decided or gets set into law, the women have a big voice in it."[1]

Her use of this term inspired me to examine the Haudenosaunee legal order through a female lens to see what it might reveal and if the term was an appropriate one. My journey began in 2021 with an online message to my Uncle Loran in which I asked if there was a term that we use in our language, Kanien'ke:ha, to denote law or even the idea of a "mother law." Here is the conversation that followed:

> Hi Uncle … Is there a word/concept to describe our way of ordering ourselves to create a peaceful community?
>
> > The word that we use is "gyyanerenseragowa," which would mean the great path that has been put in place for us to follow. Whenever we have a problem we lean on those instructions. All of that is in that word.
>
> Can you break down the word components for me?
>
> > KA IEN NE, that would mean a path for us to walk. RENSERAH would mean lean up against the ways that have already been put in place. Then GOWA means big or super big. I don't think it would be appropriate to

use "mother law." What [is] usually used is "the great law." "Mother" is usually related to the earth.

Is the concept gendered?

The first two letters will tell you it's a thing, or a subject, and the thing or subject is the path.

Uncle's response is important for illustrating how the Haudenosaunee view our law, as a path to follow. The path begins with formation of the confederacy of five original nations comprised of the Kanien'kehaka (Mohawk, people of the flint), Onyota'a:ka (Oneida, people of the standing stone), Onoñda'gega (Onondaga, people of the hills), Gayogo̱hó:nǫ' (Cayuga, people of the great swamp), and Onödowa'ga:' (Seneca, people of the great hill) as articulated in the story of the Peacemaker's Journey. Elements in the story provide the foundation for the Kaienere'ko:wa, a way of peaceful coexistence based on watching what happens in nature.

The Kaienere'ko:wa is the constitution of the Haudenosaunee where the principles of justice are codified, with the fundamental principles of peace and harmony at its foundation. The Kaienere'ko:wa establishes rules for governing over matters such as adoption, emigration, relations with foreign nations, war, treason, succession, religion, laws of descent, funerals, and civil matters. As a true democratic document, it the Kaienere'ko:wa describes a process in which everyone has a voice. Peace is the ultimate goal and is accomplished by achieving substantial agreement and consensus in decision-making, since the constitution focuses on resolving community or national concerns rather than individualistic goals. It is important to consider that in this way each individual is part of a greater collective body and their every act has direct or indirect impact on the world around them. The impacts are far-reaching: involving consideration of how one's actions impact the "coming faces," children whose faces are yet under the ground.[2] This doctrine serves as the basis for understanding that a person's responsibilities go beyond the individual and are about accountability and respect for oneself and the future generations. This important principle at the heart of the Kaienere'ko:wa is also reflected in the procedures surrounding its enactment. The Thanksgiving address or Ohenton Karihwatekwen, held prior to any community gathering, is a recitation of thanks to all living things, from the smallest creatures and plants on the earth all the way up to the clouds in the sky, the moon, and the stars. The recitation reminds those gathered that they have a duty not only to uphold the way of peace, but also a responsibility to care for the natural world.

The Kaienere'ko:wa, then, is a collection of guiding principles for a peaceful life — Skennen (peace), Kasastenshera (strength), and Kahnikonriio (the good mind). Many people call this in English a *law,* which limits our understanding. The English word *law* relates to another world view communicated through the English language. If you examine the word as Uncle has provided, "kaieneserahkowa" means a way of life, a way of living in peace. While laws are legal rules that are organic, changeable, and responsive to the needs of the people, the Kaienere'ko:wa is also that. The concept of "extending the rafters" refers to the addition of new rafters to the longhouse to make room for more families. In this case, extending the rafters can also mean the addition of laws to the Kaienere'ko:wa in order to address the changing needs of the time. The ability of the Kaienere'ko:wa to grow, change, and adapt is important for understanding it in the way it was intended, as a way of peaceful coexistence.

The law of the community is grounded in the principles within the Kaienere'ko:wa and encompasses the social, spiritual, and political aspects of our traditions and culture. In this way of living, the males and females are complementary, drawing upon their gifts for the good of the clan and community. The philosophy encompassed in the Kaienere'ko:wa provides, in a sense, all the rules, thinking, and reasoning that comes out of the stories of Sky Woman, and the story of the Peacemaker's Journey.

There are biannual recitals of the story of the Peacemaker's Journey[3] performed in communities of the five nations, and one recital that is designated as confederacy-wide every four years. The recital is a moment in time when, over four days, we pause and listen to the story as it is told. It is our way of remembering the importance of maintaining peace among the nations and recalling our foundation. What is apparent at these recitals is that the role of women is minimized in the telling and in the story itself; I and other women have remarked on this fact.[4] If we are truly going to understand the Great Law that underpins the way of living in balance, then why are the voices of women not present? We are consistently told that women are the foundation of the Kaienere'ko:wa and of the Haudenosaunee, and yet our voice is not reflected in the retelling. To examine this matter further, I will foreground the story of Jigonsaseh in an effort to understand the importance of her role in the story of how the foundation of the Kaienere'ko:wacame into being. That pivotal moment is articulated in her voice.

## Sky Woman Teaches Us Kinship

> I heard three taps on the bark wall of my hut. I looked up from my mending and listened carefully. There wasn't a rustle of many feet. I could hear the birds in the trees outside. Suddenly, there was a low cough, a clearing of the throat to signal that someone was there. I put down my work and pulled back the flap to peer out.
>
> I looked to my left and to my right. At the forest edge along the trail was a young man dressed in white buckskin. I looked at him for a time, assessing the lone stranger. He looked back at me with open, clear eyes. His body was in a posture of supplication and peace as he stood with his palms open and three strings of wampum beads dangling from his outstretched hand. He carried nothing else. No weapons, no large pouch of food. He gave a silent gesture of greeting with a nod of his head and cleared his throat again and lifted the hand with the beads and began to speak: I am Dekanawidah. I come from the Wendat. I have a message I would like to share.

The Haudenosaunee origin story is depicted through the journey of Sky Woman from Sky World. She descends from the world above to begin life here on the turtle's back. She arrives pregnant and gives birth to a daughter, who later dies giving birth to twins. Sky Woman is left to raise them alone. It is through the work of her twin grandsons in creating life on earth that we learn of the balance and imbalance of the natural world. In the telling of this story we learn of how things came to be. This story forms the basis of Haudenosaunee traditions, most notably in the four major ceremonies of Midwinter, Planting, Strawberry, and Harvest.

We are reminded of the similarity of the Sky World with ours each time we recite the Ohontonkarihwatekwen, the first words. Her story teaches us the importance of kinship. Kinship is much more than what earlier anthropologists define as social convention, blood relationship, or a social procedure.[5] Among the Haudenosaunee kinship has a much deeper purpose than connecting one to one's blood relatives. Kinship lets you know what your responsibilities are, who you are accountable to, who claims you. We are accountable not only to other humans but also to the natural world. All beings and natural elements are kin.[6]

Haudenosaunee kinship is a model predicated less on the idea of biological reproduction than on relationality. The Sky Woman story is a metaphor for the importance placed on accountability as one functions within Haudenosaunee society.[7] We know that coitus is important for reproduction, but our understanding is that our children decide who their parents are as they look at us from the Sky World. When we birth our children, we recognize that they are here on earth for a time, and our responsibility is to nurture them and ensure they can enact their gifts fully in their time with us in this world. The most important aspect is that we are in relationship and how we conduct ourselves in that relationship.

In the Sky World, Sky Woman is kin with all beings. If we examine her life in the Sky World, we see she uses terms like "uncle" and "auntie" to describe close family but her relationships with the beings of that world who play a significant role in the evolution of her time there are important. When she comes through the hole under the tree and begins her fall to the earth world below, the beings look up and see her, and they begin to enact a relationship with her. She is given a platform of heron wings to stand upon. The water beings below attempt to provide her with a safe landing. The muskrat, beaver, and otter beings give their lives to bring a scoop of earth to place on the turtle being's back. That selfless act is about enacting kinship, ensuring the safety of another. Sky Woman lands and begins her life here. It is an act that defines and directs her relationship with her twin grandsons and their relations with each other and with the natural world. It is the foundation for how we are to conduct our lives according to the principles of the Kaienere'ko:wa.

The relationship of the twins is one of duality, because naturally there is always an opposing force to all things. Our four main ceremonies are where we are reminded of the relationship of these boys to each other, to their grandmother, and to the natural world. The relationships and the kinships that are formed throughout the story are always based on mutuality. This is key to understanding our legal order. We are always in relationship.

## The Structure of Society

> I watched him and listened to his words. His voice was soft and clear. He stood straight and held himself with a sense of purpose. Come inside, I said. Have something to eat and a bowl of soup. I pulled the covering back further and turned to enter. He followed me inside.
>
> A stranger at my hut was not unfamiliar. I lived along the intersection of pathways men would use to head to war. I opened my door to them. They would leave their weapons outside and take shelter.
>
> I saw myself as providing a listening ear. I heard many things in those moments. Stories of community politics, warfare. I had the power to share or not. It gave me a sense of purpose.

The structure of Haudenosaunee society has been examined extensively by anthropologists and archaeologists. In a longhouse dwelling, there were fire pits along the central corridor. The hearth is at the centre of longhouse activities and plays a central role in the symbolism of the confederacy and its philosophy, encapsulated in the Kaienere'ko:wa. Women's daily activities are centred on the hearth and are associated with the sustenance and nourishment of the family, a very important factor in the survival of the community. Women's activities also involved moving across the landscape between gathering tasks in nearby edges of the wooded areas, horticultural activities that took place in fields close to the village, and domestic tasks within the village site and the household. In the spring women gathered firewood and collected maple sap, burned and planted fields, and collected greens and berries. Summer activities were hoeing, collection and drying of berries, and tending the fields and gathering Indian hemp. In the fall women would harvest, dry crops, store them, and gather nuts along with participating in hunting and counsel. In the winter months women participated in councils and manufactured weaving mats, maintained tools, and participated in feasting and socializing.

It is widely acknowledged that the confederacy was built to symbolize a great longhouse with the Kanien'kehaka guarding the eastern door, the Seneca guarding the western door, and the Onondaga at the central fire in the middle with the Oneida and Cayuga placed at either side. The Kaienere'ko:wa describes a philosophy of mutuality and accountability that suffuses the way the nations are to relate to each other, as kin. The symbolic language used in everyday and ceremonial life is one of respect and kinship, a family. Those who are your elder female relatives are referred to as auntie, out of respect. What this tells us is that family structure, akwatsire, is a central aspect of the confederacy, and women are crucial in their role of caring for this family fire.

Men were present and played a greater role closer to the village at certain times of the year, and participated in the shared meanings associated with the hearth and food, but were less directly involved in cooking and preparation activities.[8] Although men engaged in specific tasks such as house-building, maintenance, and field clearing, men's work more often took them greater distances across the landscape to engage in hunting, trading, and warfare at various times during the spring, summer, and fall.[9] The men's activities balanced the women's to ensure that everyone was cared for

Dominant gender identity is a colonial construct.[10] In Haudenosaunee society, male and female are two categories within a wider range of differences that are not a dichotomy. In our worldview, all life forms are equal. We are a matrilineal people; this does not imply an imbalanced society where women hold more power than men. Descent is traced through the female line. Anthropological studies note that the eldest female of the clan guided the house.[11] Family life centred around the women, and so a husband moved to the home of his wife but played only a minor role in the raising of his children. The children were the responsibility of the women and men of the entire clan. A father assumed special responsibility for his sister's children. If there was a breakdown of the marriage, he took nothing and went back to the home of his mother. Instead of gender, one's role in society was and is founded in respect and accountability to the group. Reciprocity, accountability, and interdependence are foundational characteristics of our society. Men and women have different spheres of responsibility, yet women hunt and men cultivate. Roles changed based on need.

Originally, the agricultural fields were the responsibility of the women, and therefore the locations of fields and villages reflect the choices of the women. When the land became unviable, the village would move. This happened every ten or twenty years. The gendering of the landscape carries over into daily and ceremonial life. For example, the complementarity of males and females is reinforced when we dance in the longhouse ceremonies. Both men and women dance in a counter-clockwise direction, with the men in an outer ring while women dance in the inner ring. As we dance, we are reminded of the roles that each has in ensuring the survival of the community. Robert Venables examines this balanced relationship in his work "The Clearings and The Woods."[12]

## Separate but Equal

> I offered him some food and he took it gratefully. Before he sat to eat, he carefully put the wampum in a small pouch at his waist.
>
> We sat in companionable silence for a time. He ate carefully and slowly and I continued to mend my moccasins. I was the first to break the silence as he finished his food.
>
> Who are you? Why are you here? He stopped eating and looked at me over the fire. He put down his empty bowl and spoon. I have a message of peace, he said. I come from over there, indicating this with a gesture of his arm towards the east. I looked at him and replied, oh yes. I nodded for him to go on. I have a message of peace, he said. I have spent my life looking to the natural world as I try to understand why we are always at war. Why cannot we get along like the animals and plants of the natural world? I have looked to them to see what is possible.

The English word "law" evokes the idea of rules that ensure order is kept. Gendered relationships and responsibilities are inextricably connected to our Haudenosaunee legal order. As I said above, males and females are characterized as separate and equal.[13] Women have their responsibilities in raising the children, as described by Bear clan brother Kanenhariyo in a speech to a Venezuelan delegation in 2015:

> So we have laws where the women take care of our families, and they raise up the kind of people that we need to speak about things or to be our leadership. Because they have so much love for everybody, we trust them. So that's how we understand the natural way for human beings to get along – the men and the women have different jobs. The women are the ones who make sure everything works properly, so they raise up the kind of people that we need. We still remember those laws. We didn't lose our way.[14]

The equality of male and female responsibilities is felt when we dance together in the longhouse. As mentioned above, our dancing is a reminder of this relationship. Homage is paid to the important ability of a woman to carry and birth babies, which directly ties her to the power of the natural world in which everything has the power to recreate itself. That power is seen in the moment when the spark of life occurs, at the meeting of sperm and egg or the photosynthesis that takes place in the leaves on plants and trees. This special connection is recognized at our ceremonies where a song is sung for the women by the men. It is about honouring the feminine relationship women have to the natural world. It is a recognition of the life-giving force of women, as referenced by Louise McDonald when she used the term "Mother Law."

The Sky Woman story is foundational in providing the guiding philosophy in the Kaienere'ko:wa. Her fall and life here on turtle being's back teaches us about the duality of nature and our responsibilities to each other and to the natural world.[15]

The second foundational story of importance is the Peacemaker's Journey. The recitation of the story is mandated by our legal order: we are tasked to perform a recitation of this story once every four years confederacy-wide and every two years within our nations. This has been done more regularly in the years since 2015. The recitation is meant to reinvigorate it in the minds of the people and to keep it alive. We are not a written people; we are meant to remember the important stories and retell them as our way of keeping that history active in our minds. Wampum belts serve as mnemonic devices that prompt our memory of agreements, stories, and important relationships. I witnessed the reinvigoration of the great law recitals, and I noticed that women play a minor role in the event, and in some versions of the story itself. However, in examining the Peacemaker's Journey, I see that women do play an important role. The character of Jigonsaseh is central to the advancement of the Kaienere'ko:wa. She is the first to accept the way of peace offered by the Peacemaker, and the minimization of her role in the telling warrants examination.

## The Peacemaker's Journey

> I see men come down this path intent on death and destruction. No one talks of peace. They have blood in their hearts and this is the time they put those weapons down and thoughts aside to share a meal and talk of life. I have heard many stories. Many talk of dreams beyond warfare and envision life without it. No one can remember that time, the time before the wars and bloodshed. The pain has clouded our minds. We don't know how to talk to each other anymore.
>
> He listened intently. And nodded his head. Yes, he said. I have grown up and never witnessed a way of peace between the nations. But I have looked to the non-human beings of this world to see the possibilities.

The Peacemaker's Journey is a story about the formation of the Haudenosaunee, a confederacy of five original nations, Mohawk, Oneida, Onondaga, Cayuga and Seneca. (A sixth nation, the Tuscarora, joined in 1722 after migrating north from the Carolinas.) The story begins a long time ago; there is disagreement over the date that the events happened. What we do agree upon is that it originates in the land and waters where our peoples come from. Our original homelands of the Haudenosaunee territory stretched from the Genesee River in the west, through the Finger Lakes region, to the Hudson River in the east, encompassing the Eastern Woodlands. The Mohawk were originally located in the Mohawk Valley of New York State, closest to Albany and Montreal. The Oneida occupied the area around present-day Oneida County, New York. Onondaga were located in and around present-day Onondaga County, New York, south of Lake Ontario. The Cayuga occupied the area around present-day Cayuga County, New York. Seneca were located in the western part of New York State, near the Genesee River. Key landmarks in the story still exist in our territories that allow us to identify with it.

They say there was a time when the five original nations were continuously at war with each other. Life for our people was not without its bloodshed and sadness. It is said that a woman and her daughter lived away from their village. Alone in the woods. Her daughter became pregnant by the way of the spirits and gave birth to a boy. The grandmother, who was suspicious, attempted three times to kill that boy by drowning him under the ice. Each time she did this, she and her daughter would wake up in the morning and find him sleeping peacefully between them. She gave up and realized there was something special about this baby.

Raised by his mother and grandmother, the Peacemaker was born with a deep connection to the plants and animals of the natural world, and worked to develop a message of peace to bring to the original five nations. He looked to nature to understand how it was that all things could coexist. First, he developed a ceremony called the small Condolence. Represented by three strings of wampum beads, the ceremony is a symbolic clearing of the eyes, ears, and throat in order that good relations can take place. This was expanded to seventeen strings for a ceremony for a new chief that is 'raised up' into their position with a Condolence. Being condoled is about reminding the chief of the necessity of clarity, honesty, selflessness that are central to this role. Holding the title of chief is about upholding the principles of the Kaienere'ko:wa, maintaining the peace, and ensuring that everyone has a voice. Central to our governance is the consensus building process that ensures participatory democracy occurs. The Condolence ceremony enables a clear mind, open communication, and deep listening, all crucial to peace building and good governance. When the Peacemaker grew into manhood, he left in a white stone canoe and embarked on a journey to establish peace among the warring nations. The first person to accept the great peace was a woman they call Jigonsaseh, also known as the Peace Queen or Mother of All Nations.[16]

## Jigonsaseh, on the Path

The experiences and insights of Jigonsaseh, as a woman living alone and encountering the men at war, would have shaped the rest of the Peacemaker's journey. All we are told in the recitation is that her home was situated on the path to war. The warriors would leave their weapons outside the door, and she would feed them and provide a place to rest. Often it is implied that she would serve their sexual needs. I realized that her role had to be rethought and this interpretation of her part in the story recontexualized.

I know that the transcription of this story has been influenced by previous writers. Early colonial officials and anthropologists studying Haudenosaunee society and traditions would have interpreted the Peacemaker's Journey through the lens of their world view and minimized the importance of a woman like Jigonsaseh. Women in European society were viewed as property and were not held in high regard in European society and culture. To hear of a woman alone in a forest talking to a man would have been unheard of.

Recognition of Jigonsaseh and her agency in being first to accept the words of the Peacemaker is important for this examination of the Haudenosaunee legal order. Who would have taught her what to say? How to act? Given her insights? The women who raised her did, guided by the story of Sky Woman. The Peacemaker was also raised by his mother and grandmother, and interactions with them would have shaped how he himself acted, what he said, and the choices he made. I have heard many times how women bring balance to any situation. In this case, Jigonsaseh and the Peacemaker would have learned by the example of the women who raised them.

Tell me this way that you speak of. What is your vision?

He took out the shells of wampum from his pouch and held them up for me to see. I slowly put out my hand and he reached over the fire and gently put it in my outstretched palm. I brought them up to my eyes and looked at them closely, wrapping them through my fingers. Feeling their smoothness and admiring their colours. As each bead passed through my thumb and forefinger, I caressed them gently.

The purple and the white beads were placed in three unique orders. Their colours reminded me of the storm clouds in the sky when the wind pushes the dark clouds away. The clouds mixing and rolling in the sky. I continued to hold the strings as he talked, rubbing them gently with my finger.

He began to tell me the story of his birth. The insights and discoveries he had as a young child. His grandmother had tried to kill him under the ice three times. But he survived.

He talked of watching, observing nature, to see how things were in the world. He could talk to the animals and learned of their ways.

What I saw in his story was a young man who came to this world with special gifts. He was kind, compassionate, intelligent, and strong. His own people had found him strange. They ridiculed him for not participating in warfare. That was the way of men, they told him. That was what made them Wendat. They often would war with their neighbours to the south, the Kanien'kehaka. This was what made life worth living as a people.

He had understood from his mother and his grandmother the worst, the pain and the suffering of the people as a result of the constant war and bloodshed. No one would listen to each other anymore. People did not talk. The women's voices were silenced.

He had listened intently to his mother and his grandmother first as a young boy and then into his manhood. He knew how they carried their insights inside them. He understood the peace that they could bring to any situation. It was the way of the woman's mind, and he built upon that.

This way of listening intently, he understood, was one of the first things that we needed to do to build peace. But how do you quiet the mind for this to happen? Two important things needed to happen, he said. The first is to open your ears and silence the tongue.

His mother and his grandmother had told him many times as a young man to sit quietly and listen and watch. This too was something he learned from them, to open one's eyes and see clearly. To not let opinions, experiences cloud one's vision. And most important, when he sat he listened and he didn't speak until the time was right. When all talk had stopped. Then he would take a sip of water and share his insights with his grandmother and his mother. These were the first lessons he learned from them.

His grandmother had some memory of the time before. That is the way of the women, to remember. To hold the memory of the people and bring it forward. That is the gift of women, to be the memory.

With these first lessons he next began to observe nature more closely. To see the world around him with renewed vision. He observed how the plants and animals lived together in harmony. The natural order of things was done with purpose. Warfare in nature did not exist. He observed the waters sustaining the plants and animals, the natural elements working in unity to sustain life. Bugs fed on each other and the plants, and were then eaten by the birds. It was a natural cycle. It was wondrous to him, he said. Excited, with an energy in his voice. This taught me so much, he said.

As I listened I felt his excitement run through me. I wanted to know more. His words communicated such power. I began to feel renewed with hope.

He talked of finding the quahog shells and making the beads for the strings he had shared with me. Those, he said, were used as a way for him to remember what he had seen. As he made the beads and strung them, he knew he needed to determine an order that would communicate his knowledge of building peace. He knew he had to find a way to connect what he observed in nature and what he had learned from his grandmother and mother.

He said he thought about the importance of giving thanks, of ceremony in connecting the heart, mind, and body. He knew that things had to be infused with a sacredness for them to be taken seriously.

I nodded as he spoke. What he said to me made sense. It was logic.

He determined that the very first thing was for people to learn how to listen, see things clearly, and speak to each other with no harsh words.

This would be the foundation for all other things. He knew he had to then find a way for people to communicate with each other in an ordered way. In such a way that everyone had a voice. It was then he determined a way of coming to one mind, reaching consensus. What he realized was important was the way people sat, faced each other, and made eye contact. Everyone had to feel heard for a good decision to be made, which ensured that everyone acknowledged their mutual purpose. This he knew from watching his mother and grandmother speak: in order to be heard and be involved fully in the conversation, they sat face to face. Nothing was hidden. All expressions were observable. In watching them interact in this way, he saw them engage with each other in a peaceful way.

He realized that in order for things to progress and for there to be survival, the people of the warring nations needed to communicate with each other, to talk to each other. From this he determined that Kaienere'ko:wa was a message he needed to share.

I continued to listen intently as he talked. Sharing ladles of water when his voice began to crack. He would sip, pause to remember where he was, and then continue.

He had learned from his grandmother what she remembered of the old ways, the ways of the ancestors. She remembered the things they would do to bring peace among the family and community. She had explained the importance of bringing peace between the people, and of thickening one's skin so that one did not take on another's pain and suffering. He explained: I took all that my grandmother had shared with me and what I saw in the world around me and I built from that.

One day, he was ready. He left his grandmother and mother with only a small pouch of wampum strings at his side. He said he did this because he knew that the natural world contained all he would need to survive. He had carved a stone canoe. His grandmother and mother were doubtful it would float. He gently told them, if it floats, then it proves I am right. He climbed in and pushed off from the shore.

He told me of his journey from the western shore of Kanyatariio (Lake Ontario). He disembarked and began to walk. And that is how he came to my dwelling. He said to me, I am here to bring you this message of peace. This way of peace. Will you take it up? He held up the wampum strings again. Their smooth surface shone in the dim light of the lodge.

I stood up and stretched my arms, then my legs. He had been talking for quite some time. Walking in half circles on one side of the fire, I thought about what he said. I knew what warfare looked like. I had left my people to live in peace and found myself at the crossroads of war. I had taken it upon myself to provide refuge. Balance. For those men who were deter-

> mined to travel that path and shed blood. I had asked them to put their weapons down and they listened. I fed them and counselled them, realizing they only knew of war and sadness in their lifetime. I wanted to help this young man. I could see his message in my mind. In my heart I knew he was right. I knew his grandmother and mother had taught him well. That their messages came to me through him. They were my sisters. My family and I needed to listen.
>
> I walked around the fire. I put my hands on his shoulders in a gesture of balance and healing. I knew the difficulty of his task ahead and of his sacrifices to get here and share his message with me. I stroked the wampum in his hand and said, I take up this way of peace. It is a good one. I will no longer share in gossip and promote hardship here in my hut. I will only share the message of the Kaienere'ko:wa with all who pass by. In this way, we will work to bring peace to the warring nations.

As we see in this constructed narration, Jigonsaseh was the first to take up the Kaienere'ko:wa. Her reasoning is based on her knowledge as a woman who knows the ways of other women. Logically, this must have inspired the Peacemaker to continue on his mission. He met up with Haiawatha, who travelled with him. They went to the Mohawk who tested him. He offered them knowledge of this way of peace. They pointed at him. Laughed at him. Criticized him. They said: What do you know of peace? You are just a boy. The Peacemaker's Journey goes on to describe his meeting with Ayonwatha and Atotarho. The Peacemaker used the Condolence ceremony to remove the grief of Ayonwatha with the wampum shells, and asked him if he would help spread the message of peace. Ayonwatha agreed. Next, they went to Atotarho, who is described as having snakes in his hair and a crooked body, symbolizing an imbalanced mind and the effect of hate and negativity on the human body. They were without success. The Peacemaker and Ayonwatha went on to convince the other nations to take up the way of peace. When this was done, they went back to the Onondaga and spoke to Atotarho again about taking up the way of peace. They failed until all of the forty-nine men who held the titles in the confederacy sang the Hai Hai as part of the mourning rituals and won over the imbalanced mind of Atotarho. When his mind was pacified, his body straightened and the snakes were combed from his hair; he was then offered a special position in the confederacy, to watch over the central fire on behalf of the five nations. He now watches over the fire to make sure it continues to burn. He is the one who ensures the other chiefs uphold the principles of the Kaienere'ko:wa and carry out the will of the people.

## Kaienere'ko:wa (The Way of Peace)

The Kaienere'ko:wa is a manifestation of the balanced thinking that emerged from the Sky Woman story with particular focus on the twins and the Peacemaker's Story, where the ceremonies were developed to bring balance to the mind. It has three parts: the good mind, peace, and power – kahnikariio, skennen, and kasastenshera.

Kahnikariio is described as the balanced mind that comes when one has food, happiness, and healing. This comes from the ceremonies and way of living in harmony with each other, thinking of the collective and the faces still under the ground, those who are not here yet. When we put others before ourselves in all that we do, we survive as a community. Skennen or peace is achieved when we have mechanisms in the social, spiritual, and political aspects of our culture that enable us to always find an answer together by working together, doing our ceremonies, and making decisions using processes like consensus decision-making where everyone has a voice. Kasastenshera means the power and strength that comes from the people working together, making decisions together: the power of the collective. This is represented symbolically by five arrows bound together. We are stronger as a collective, thinking like a collective and acting like a collective. Women have an integral role to play in this. We are the ones who choose the chiefs by the very fact that we are the ones who raise them from birth. We also participate in making decisions together. Our voice is extremely important. It is said that women provide the balance to the process. We are recognized in the ceremonies as integral to our growth and survival as a community and a nation.

The Kaienere'ko:wa in its written form is organized into the following sections: organization of the confederacy; rights, duties, and qualification of the chiefs; the role of a Pine Tree Chief; the role of a War Chief; the roles and functions of the clans; the symbols that are used to communicate the Kaienere'ko:wa; adoptions; emigration; land title; foreigners; war; rights of the people; the installation song; protection of the house; and funerals. All of these aspects of Haudenosaunee society are interrelated like a web of knowledge. Written down, the Kaienere'ko:wa becomes a long list of rules and a formula for social, spiritual, and political organization.

The Kaienere'ko:wa does not work in an orderly proscribed way. It is much more organic. Like the natural world. It relies on human nature and common sense to be effectively understood and put into to action. In this system, the people make the decisions and the chiefs are the ones who put them into action. Women determine who becomes a chief or when someone should be adopted into the clan because they are the ones who raise the children and caretake the families. They are the ones who strengthen the family with their guidance and common sense.

Just prior to and after contact, the women's council practised alongside the men's council, at the national and confederacy levels, playing an integral role in the decision-making of the confederacy as a whole. The women also served the important function of memorizing the speeches so that when the time came for their representative to speak, the response was clear and illustrated a deep respect for the other side of the house. In these spaces, if one was able to restate what the other said almost verbatim, this meant one was listening, which displayed the important element of respect, which was necessary for effective diplomacy. Descent continues to be traced through the female line. Primacy is placed in that relationship between mother and child. The clan mother also has an important role: standing alongside the chiefs, making sure they do their duty – enacting the will of the people.

What is important is the role that women play in making this system a viable way of organizing people and keeping the peace. It is really common sense, meaning that it makes sense. It also encompasses symbolism that assists in communicating the principles of kahnikariio, skennen, and kasastenshera.

## Discussion

Jigonsaseh's presence in the historical analysis of the formation of the confederacy is not given much consideration for what it says about women in Haudenosaunee society. The fact that she was sought out as the first to accept the great peace is important in understanding the role women have in our legal order. If the Peacemaker's message was to end the wars between the nations and for the nations to embrace his philosophy, he had first to convince someone of the merits of the message, and she was the one. She had the mind to evaluate, reason, and see common sense in his words. This is a central aspect of the story that gets minimized at recitals by speakers not explaining its importance to the formation of the Haudenosaunee.

The symbolism of Jigonsaseh is just that, a symbol of women's thought.[17] Her importance lies in the fact that it was a woman who took up the peace first. There is something about her way and mind that set the path for what was to come. In representing women's thought this way in the story, our ancestors send the message that a woman's mind brings balance to any situation. The fact is that this knowledge remains. Kanenhariyo emphasized this in his speech to the Venezuelan delegation. E.F. Doxtater, in a message to me, also reinforced this responsibility as it takes place in her own home: "But we are all her! We all play those different roles. We constantly assess who is bringing healthiness into our homes, if we need protection or welcoming! Thereby we do our own micro choosing or deposing in our homes — can be partners, friends, acquaintances. Who will promote peace for me and my family and who will violate our peace?"[18] Women still do what Jigonsaseh did for the Peacemaker: we bring balance to an unbalanced situation. This is not about power, but about the ability of women to evaluate what is needed or not needed in any situation. For example, our oral history makes it known that in the times when war was an option, the women played an integral role in determining if the men would go and fight. This was recognized and written about by Sir William Johnson, who in order to get the men of the confederacy on side had to council with the women. He did this through the auspices of his wife, Molly Brant, a central woman of the confederacy at the time of the Revolutionary War.[19]

The Peacemaker's efforts to unite the warring nations were transformative. The Kaienere'ko:wa replaced anger with thinking, fear with heart and compassion, and harsh words and argument with thoughtful discussion and diplomacy. Shedding light on the Haudenosaunee legal order with a feminine outlook reveals further questions that need to be answered. However, as we have done here, bringing Jigonsaseh to life in narrative form enables us to see her importance in bringing peace and balance to the warring nations. Putting the role of the Peacemaker in the context of that balanced society gives us a new opportunity to contemplate the foundation of the confederacy and the Kaienere'ko:wa itself in a way that is reflective of that balance. Jigonsaseh is given voice.

While we may not have a mother law, per se, this concept is tied to the Kaienere'ko:wa. Using the English word 'mother' and 'law' in the same sentence recognizes the responsibilities of both men and women in creating the conditions for a peaceful and healthy society. It brings the feminine responsibilities and capabilities into dialogue with the harsh realities of an imbalanced society, encapsulated in events like the Wet'suwet'en standoff against the Trans Canada Energies Coastal Gas Link Pipeline. As illustrated, the role of Jigonsaseh in accepting the peace represents the recognition of the nature of women to bring balance and peace into any situation. Louise McDonald's use of the term Mother Law sheds light on the role of Indigenous women in caretaking the earth. Her call was a call for all women's voices to be included in the struggle for our mother.

Bringing forward the voice of Jigonsaseh opens the door to further questions and expanded thinking on the Kaienere'ko:wa from a feminine perspective and the idea of what constitutes 'law'. Without knowing our language, narrative enables one to hear her a voice and rethink the legacy of the past in a way that is more reflective of how it actually came into being, with balance. At its heart, this work illustrates that examining Indigenous legal orders through a feminine lens will have broader implications for how we understand and interpret those legal orders.

## NOTES

1 Robin Morgan, "Turning Pain into Power: An Interview with Two Mohawk Leaders in the Akwesasne Territory," *Women's Media Center News & Features* (3 November 2021), online: < <https://womensmediacenter.com/news-features/turning-pain-into-power-an-interview-with-two-mohawk-leaders-in-the-akwesasne-territory>

2 I was informed by Elder EF Doxtater and others that "Seven Generations" is an incorrect term for the principle. I will not use this term as a way of describing the philosophy of the coming faces, as this was a term developed by the Algonquin peoples and has been taken up and used incorrectly by the Haudenosaunee.

3 The Peacemaker is known as Tekanawí:ta. See "Haudenosaunee: History & Culture," online: <http://www.kahnawakelonghouse.com/index.php?mid=2>.

4 This issue was discussed in informal conversations with other women of the Haudenosaunee. Collectively we have taken note of the missing voices of our women in the events and recitation itself. This work is the first to examine and address this issue.

5 Dwight W Read, "What Is Kinship?" in R Feinberg and M Ottenheimer, eds, *The Cultural Analysis of Kinship: The Legacy of David Schneider and Its Implications for Anthropological Relativism* (Urbana: University of Illinois Press, 2001) 78 at 79.

6 See Vanessa Watts, "Indigenous Place-Thought & Agency amongst Humans and Non-humans (First Woman and Sky Woman Go On a European World Tour!)" (2013) 2:1 Decolonization: Indigeneity, Education and Society 20.

7 See Read, *supra* note 5 for an examination of the difference between kinship terminology and genealogical framing of kinship relations.

8 Kathleen M Sydoriak Allen, "Gender Dynamics, Routine Activities, and Place in Haudenosaunee Territory: An Archaeological Case Study from the Cayuga Region of Central New York State" in Sherene Baugher & Suzanne M Spencer-Wood, eds, *Archaeology and Preservation of Gendered Landscapes* (London: Palgrave MacMillan, 2010) 57 at 71.

9 *Ibid* at 62.

10 See Maria Lugones, "The Coloniality of Gender" in Livia De Souza Lima, Edith Otero Quezada & Julia Roth, eds, *Feminisms in Movement: Theories and Practices from the Americas* (New York: Columbia University Press, 2024) 35.

11 See Robert W Venables, "The Clearings and The Woods: The Haudenosaunee (Iroquois) Landscape – Gendered and Balanced" in Sherene Baugher & Suzanne M Spencer-Wood, eds, *Archaeology and Preservation of Gendered Landscapes* (London: Palgrave MacMillan, 2010) 21; John Napoleon Brinton Hewitt, "Status of Woman in Iroquois Polity before 1784" [reprint of 1932 article] in WG Spittal, ed, *Iroquois Women: An Anthology* (Ohsweken, ON: Iroqrafts, 1990) 53; Henry R Schoolcraft, *Notes on the Iroquois* [reprint of 1846 edition] (Millwood, NY: Kraus, 1975); Lewis Henry Morgan, *Houses and House-Life of the American Aborifines* (with a new introduction by Paul Bohannah) [reprint of 1881 edition] (Chicago: University of Chicago Press, 1965); Judith K Brown, "Economic Organization and the Position of Women among the Iroquois [reprint of 1970 article] in WG Spittal, ed, *Iroquois Women: An Anthology* (Ohsweken, ON: Iroqrafts, 1990) 182.

12 Venables, *supra* note 11.

13 Sydoriak Allen, *supra* note 8 at 71.

14 Kanenhariyo, speech delivered in response to Venezuelan ambassador's address in "History Is Made: Venezuelan Ambassador Visits Six Nations," *Two Row Times* (15 April 2015), online: <https://tworowtimes.com/news/history-is-made-venezuelan-ambassador-visits-six-nations/>.

15 See Kahente Horn-Miller, "What Does Indigenous Participatory Democracy Look Like? Kahnawà:Ke's Community Decision Making Process" (2013) 18:1 Rev of Constitutional Studies 111; Isabel Altamirano-Jiménez, Nathalie Kermoal & Kahente Horn-Miller, *Living on the Land: Indigenous Women's Understanding of Place* (Edmonton: University of Alberta Press, 2016); Kahente Horn-Miller, "Standing with Sky Woman: A Conversation on Cultural Fluency" in Jesse Rae Archibald-Barber, Kathleen Irwin & Moira Jean Day, eds, *Performing Turtle Island: Indigenous Theatre on the World Stage* (Regina: University of Regina Press, 2019) 51.

16 Anthony Wallace & Deborah Holler, "Reviving the Peace Queen: Revelations from Lewis Henry Morgan's Field Notes on the Tonawanda

Seneca" (2009) 5 Histories of Anthropology Annual 90; Christopher Buck, "Deganawida, the Peacemaker" in Jay Parini, ed, *American Writers: A Collection of literary Biographers* (Farmington Hills: Gale Group, 2015) 81.

17 There are those who believe that the Jigonsaseh title was passed down in families. There is debate amongst the Haudenosaunee about that. What is important to consider is her role in taking up the peace first.

18 EF Doxtater, personal communication to author (5 May 2021).

19 See Brown, *supra* note 11; Lois M Fesiter & Bonnie Pulis, "Molly Brant: Her Domestic and Poitical Roles in Eighteenth-Century New York" in Robert S Grumet, ed, *Northeastern Indian Lives, 1632–1816* (Amherst: University of Massachusetts Press, 1996) 295.

## SOURCES CITED

Altamirano-Jiménez, Isabel, Nathalie Kermoal & Kahente Horn-Miller. *Living on the Land: Indigenous Women's Understanding of Place* (Edmonton: University of Alberta Press, 2016).

Brown, Judith K. "Economic Organization and the Position of Women among the Iroquois" [reprint of 1970 article] in WG Spittal, ed, *Iroquois Women: An Anthology* (Ohsweken, ON: Iroqrafts, 1990).182.

Buck, Christopher. "Deganawida, the Peacemaker" in Jay Parini, ed, *American Writers: A Collection of Literary Biographers* (Farmington Hills: Gale Group, 2015) 81.

Fesiter, Lois M & Bonnie Pulis, "Molly Brant: Her Domestic and Political Roles in Eighteenth-Century New York" in Robert S Grumet, ed, *Northeastern Indian Lives, 1632–1816* (Amherst: University of Massachusetts Press, 1996) 295.

Hewitt, John Napoleon Brinton. "Status of Woman in Iroquois Polity before 1784" [reprint of 1932 article] in WG Spittal, ed, *Iroquois Women: An Anthology* (Ohsweken, ON: Iroqrafts, 1990) 53.

Horn-Miller, Kahente. "Standing with Sky Woman: A Conversation on Cultural Fluency" in Jesse Rae Archibald-Barber, Kathleen Irwin & Moira Jean Day, eds, *Performing Turtle Island: Indigenous Theatre on the World Stage* (Regina: University of Regina Press, 2019) 51.

Horn-Miller, Kahente. "What Does Indigenous Participatory Democracy Look Like? Kahnawà: Ke's Community Decision Making Process" (2013) 18:1 Rev Constitutional Studies 111.

Kanenhariyo, speech delivered in response to Venezuela's ambassador's address, in "History Is Made: Venezuelan Ambassador Visits Six Nations," *Two Row Times* (15 April 2015), online: <https://tworowtimes.com/news/history-is-made-venezuelan-ambassador-visits-six-nations/>.

Morgan, Lewis Henry. *Houses and House-Life of the American Aborigines* (with a new introduction by Paul Bohannah) [reprint of 1881 edition] (Chicago: University of Chicago Press, 1965).

Morgan, Robin. "Turning Pain into Power: An Interview with Two Mohawk Leaders in the Akwesasne Territory," *Women's Media Center News & Features* (3 November 2021), online:

Read, Dwight W. "What Is Kinship?" in R Feinberg and M Ottenheimer, eds, *The Cultural Analysis of Kinship: The Legacy of David Schneider and Its Implications for Anthropological Relativism* (Urbana: University of Illinois Press, 2001) 78.

Schoolcraft, Henry R. *Notes on the Iroquois* [reprint of 1846 edition] (Millwood, NY: Kraus, 1975).

Sydoriak Allen, Kathleen M. "Gender Dynamics, Routine Activities, and Place in Haudenosaunee Territory: An Archaeological Case Study from the Cayuga Region of Central New York State" in Sherene Baugher & Suzanne M Spencer-Wood, eds, *Archaeology and Preservation of Gendered Landscapes* (London: Palgrave MacMillan, 2010) 57.

Venables, Robert W. "The Clearings and The Woods: The Haudenosaunee (Iroquois) Landscape – Gendered and Balanced" in Sherene Baugher & Suzanne M Spencer-Wood, eds, *Archaeology and Preservation of Gendered Landscapes* (London: Palgrave MacMillan, 2010) 21.

Wallace, Anthony & Deborah Holler. "Reviving the Peace Queen: Revelations from Lewis Henry Morgan's Field Notes on the Tonawanda Seneca" (2009) 5 Histories of Anthropology Annual 90.

Watts, Vanessa. "Indigenous Place-Thought & Agency amongst Humans and Non-humans (First Woman and Sky Woman Go On a European World!)" (2013) 2:1 Decolonization: Indigeneity, Education and Society 20.

# 5 What If Survivors Wrote the Laws? An Indigenous Feminist Audit of Tribal Sexual Assault Laws in the United States

SARAH DEER

I remember talking to Deb[1] for hours. I was a volunteer rape crisis counsellor, and she was a Native[2] woman who had been sexually assaulted by her landlord two years earlier. She didn't call 911 or report the crime back then, and she hadn't any interest in reporting it now ("No way; not dealing with that," she said right off the bat). At the time of the assault, it didn't feel safe to report and she didn't want to lose her housing. But she called the hotline last night, and this morning we're sitting on a couch in our Centre because she wants to work through the trauma. Initially it feels awkward – partly because I'm twenty-two and she is in her forties.

We started taking long walks because she feels "stuck" in the past. She has intrusive thoughts and flashbacks to the assault, and it is interfering with work and parenting. She tried therapy last year, but she said it didn't seem to help. So she finally, as a last-ditch effort, called the local rape victim centre – just to see what we might have to offer. Mostly, she just wanted someone to talk to. And as an advocate, I'm not limited to once-a-week fifty-minute sessions.

We talked several hours that first week, mostly over the phone but sometimes in person. I remember she was really having a hard time with self-blame. She knew intellectually that she was not at fault for the sexual assault, but she was still having intrusive emotional thoughts that she could have prevented the crime. I think after an assault, many survivors want to go back in time – a time before the trauma. So our brains go to that memory, and come up with alternative, guilt-ridden scenarios.

*I shouldn't have flirted with him two days earlier…*
*I shouldn't have popped those pills that night…*
*I should've fought back harder …*

And the self-blame can reach critical levels:

*Maybe I chose not to fight back harder because I'm a stupid idiot ...*

Combine those self-blame messages with flashbacks of the actual event, and you have an untenable situation. This phenomenon used to be pathologized as "rape trauma syndrome," but that has fallen out of favour, and this form of mental anguish, at least in the United States, is categorized as post-traumatic stress disorder (PTSD) by the mental health care field. That is the same diagnosis as for combat veterans and war refugees who experience a similar mind problem – being utterly unable to think straight because your brain is literally on a loop, replaying the trauma and the corresponding emotions. And there is no easy way to turn it off. But I'm an advocate, which means I don't have to diagnose her problem by using a label or prescribing medication (indeed, either would be unethical). In my mind, then, she is a fellow Native rape survivor who wants to talk.

So we were trying to figure out ways to "snap out of it" – as she put it. She wanted to find an "off" switch. Something she could do herself, like a brain trick, to help her get the guilt to fade away. At some point, she sighed, "Maybe this wasn't really rape at all; there were so many things I could have done and so maybe I just have to live with the fact that I screwed up here. And I have to live with that."

I had just started law school, and had an idea. I said, "Let's look up the state statute on sexual assault and see what it says." She shook her head. "I'm not reporting this, I told you from the start I am not interested in a criminal case on this." I assured her that wasn't my goal. I got the sexual assault statutes from my dial-up Westlaw account and printed them out. We read it line by line together. The statutory definition of rape fit her experience like a glove. I even showed off some of my new law school skills by trying (and probably failing) to explain *mens rea* so I could help interpret the statute more carefully.

She paused.

"Wow." Another pause. "Who wrote this law again?" she asked.

I chuckled and said, "a bunch of successful white businessmen who serve in our state legislature. It's a state criminal statute. This state says that what happened to you is a *crime*. There are no exceptions here that make it okay to assault someone who was flirtatious, someone who was high, or someone who didn't fight to the death. That's the law. I know you don't want to report it, but just know – this is the public definition of rape. And while this will never go to a criminal court, you can know that he raped you.

"He raped you.

"This is what our society says."

I was super enthusiastic about this idea of helping get her brain to slow down. She could sense my energy and rolled her eyes. "Okay, I get it," she sighed. "I'll try to remember this. Even in my conservative old stupid state, the law sees me as a legit victim. Okay."

That was one of the last conversations. She said she was doing much better; just talking about it helped, she said. She was moving out of the area for a new job, and we closed our advocacy relationship, knowing that she could still reach me anytime. She sent me a really nice snail mail thank-you card from her new address.

I did hear from her several years later, when I was no longer a direct services advocate. It was a friend-of-a-friend thing that happened on social media. I saw her name and picture and recognized her, but the confidential nature of our relationship made it unethical for me to reach out to her. But a few days later, she added me as a friend. She messaged me and was so excited to be reconnected.

She was doing really well – she had just received her master's in public health and was starting a new job with a state public health agency. We caught up with kids, life, and activism. She thanked me for all the long talks we had years ago. "You really helped me," She typed. "I'm in a new place in life. Obviously I can't forget what happened, but I've stopped blaming myself every single day. That thing you did with the legal definition? I thought it was really stupid at the time, but I think it helped me. It was memorable. It had some kind of justice for me, you know? I never wanted to deal with prosecution, but it was so interesting to understand that I actually *had* a case. This was really a crime – it fit word-for-word as to what happened to me."

I'd honestly forgotten that little exercise, and I slightly cringed inside. I didn't think it was my best moment.

"I have an idea," she typed. "I know most of the survivors you work with don't report, right? But it might help other people see that what happened to [them] was a full-on violation of the law, even if they don't report, you know? I think it might help people stop blaming themselves and actually look at what society's definitions are. And it might even encourage more people to report after they read it. Anyway, thanks for that little trick."

This little trick, locked away in my brain to become useful later, was revived when I became a law professor and started thinking about tribal statutes on sexual assault. I haven't been a direct services advocate for many years; most of my time is dedicated to teaching and writing. However, I have reviewed many tribal sexual assault statutes to determine whether Native survivors could, as Deb did, rely on a similar source as a form of healing, but within their own tribal nation's legal definitions of sexual assault.

The precise legal definition of the crime of sexual assault[3] has profound implications that ripple through a community, impacting the lives of citizens for decades to come. This is particularly true for communities experiencing extremely high rates of sexual violence. If the statutory definition is too narrow, many actions that we intuitively understand as sexual assault will simply fall outside the bounds of the law – essentially legalizing many forms of sexual abuse. American rape laws, which have been notoriously difficult to reform, originally emanated from the common law of England, which narrowly defined rape as "a male engaging in forcible sexual intercourse with a female not his wife, without her consent."[4] Over the course of two hundred years, all fifty states have broadened the definition of sexual assault in a variety of ways, largely motivated by the efforts of feminist activists.[5] In this chapter, I catalogue how tribal governments define sexual assault to ascertain whether reform at the individual tribal level is warranted. In addition, I consider potential frameworks for addressing sexual assault in tribal courts in the twenty-first century by employing indigenous feminist legal theories about consent and sexual autonomy.

Most contemporary tribal criminal codes originated with the federal government's assimilative efforts to cajole tribal nations to adopt Anglo-American forms of governance.[6] Over the years, tribal nations were "encouraged" or mandated to adopt an Anglo-American criminal justice system and operate an adversarial penal system to hold perpetrators accountable.[7] As a result, many tribal criminal laws initially mirrored state (or federal) laws. These laws were not the result of a deliberative process within the tribal community but were often originally written by agents of the federal government and handed to tribal officials who then adopted the received procedural and the substantive laws wholesale. Over the years, some tribal governments have engaged in law reform efforts and changed many of the statutes to better reflect contemporary needs. However, the feminist efforts to reform sexual assault laws that swept through the state governments starting in the 1970s have largely failed to reach all tribal nations, leaving the original (and seriously outdated) rape statutes intact. Sadly, I found that many contemporary tribal sexual assault laws merely reinforce colonial tropes about the nature of sexual assault and perpetuate the oppression of Native people.

Many tribal governments have not prosecuted felony-level crimes on a regular basis, and thus the need for updating such codes may go unnoticed. There are a variety of reasons that a tribal code might still maintain the vintage language lifted from Anglo-American law, largely due to their dormancy. First, the cost is high. tribal nations retain "concurrent" or shared jurisdiction with the federal government (or state governments, in some cases) over all crimes committed by Indians (including sexual assault). As such, many tribal nations have typically not prosecuted these kinds of felony crimes in tribal court,[8] but instead have deferred prosecution in favour of letting the Anglo-American system – with its greater resources – prosecute such crimes. Investigating and prosecuting a felony can be exorbitantly expensive for a tribe; most tribal prosecutor's offices operate with few resources.

Second, due to federal law, tribal nations possess limited sentencing authority: tribal courts cannot sentence an offender to more than three years' incarceration per offence. (Until 2010, the maximum was one year.)[9] If we use the yardstick of Anglo-American criminal justice systems, a three-year sentence does not seem sufficient to truly punish the crime and deter sex offenders.[10] When laws lie dormant without any prosecutions or application in the real world, the problematic nature of the criminal definition in the tribal code may escape notice.

Third, the pervasive silence around sexual assault that permeates many tribal communities further reduces the likelihood of tribal prosecution. Sexual assault is not an easy topic to broach in some of our communities due to the long history of trauma intertwined with sexual assault. The shame that many sexual assault survivors experience can serve as an obstacle to tackling these profound violations.

In 1978, a highly criticized decision by the US Supreme Court in *Oliphant v Suquamish Indian Tribe* stripped tribal authority over non-Indians – for any crime.[11] As such, non-Indians could commit crimes on Indian reservations and escape tribal prosecution. The high declination rates from federal and state prosecutors meant that non-Indians often went unprosecuted, and tribal nations were unable to hold these perpetrators accountable. That prohibition was slightly altered by Congress through the *Violence Against Women Act* in 2013[12] and again in 2022.[13] As of 1 October 2022 tribal nations are able to prosecute both Indians and non-Indians for additional crimes, including sexual assault and sex trafficking. This change will likely lead to renewed efforts to prosecute sexual assault, and thus tribal laws on sexual assault must be closely examined to ensure that they meet the needs of the nation.

## Methodology

To determine how tribal governments define crimes that fall under the umbrella of sexual assault, I gathered as many tribal statutory definitions as possible. I ultimately ended up reviewing 216 sexual assault laws from 108 different tribal nations in the United States. Because there is no centralized database of tribal law,[14] I had to locate these codes in a variety of ways. I began with Westlaw and Lexis, which both included a small database of tribal law. I used a variety of search terms, including "rape," "sexual assault," and "sexual abuse" to find the most relevant statutes. I found a few older tribal laws on the Native American Constitution and Law Digitization Project at the University of Oklahoma (https://digital.libraries.ou.edu/law/nacl.asp). I then turned to the online National Indian Law Library (NILL), a project of the Native American Rights Fund (https://narf.org/nill/) and the Tribal Court Clearinghouse (TCC; https://www.tribal-institute.org/), a non-profit online clearing house of tribal laws established by the Tribal Law and Policy Institute. Both the NILL and the TCC have a list of federally recognized tribal nations with direct links to the official tribal government websites, where I was able to find criminal codes for some tribal nations. This entire laborious process took place over the span of several months. I included a few additional tribal laws from my personal collection, making sure to double-check that a more recent copy of the code wasn't available online. After gathering the statutes, I created a spreadsheet that allowed me to analyse the tribal rape laws by issues and topics.

There are a few limitations to this approach. First, given that there are over 570 federally recognized tribal nations, an analysis of only 108 cannot serve as a true representative sample. As such, the statutes I analysed do not necessarily represent the typical response to sexual assault – only that the statutes were accessible. I did not locate any tribal criminal codes against sexual assault for the state of Alaska (home to 229 tribal nations, the vast majority of which do not exercise criminal jurisdiction). Second, there is not an easy way to ensure that these statutes are indeed the most recent version. If I were intending to practise in a particular tribal court, I would not rely solely on an online version of the statutes – I would contact the tribal nation (either the legislative or judicial branch) to ensure that I had the most recent version. For this academic inquiry, though, I chose to rely on what is available online. Thus, what follows is a *facial* analysis of these tribal statutes (focusing on the legal text on the page), which may not reflect the current laws of any particular tribe.

This study is not intended to embarrass tribal nations or call out any particular community for having "bad" sexual assault laws. Therefore, I will discuss the statutes in the aggregate, rather than identify individual tribal nations. It is clear that many tribal laws on sexual assault were lifted directly word-for-word from older state or federal statutes, meaning that the vast majority of tribal sexual assault laws are almost certainly not the product of deliberative processes at the tribal level but are transplants from foreign (federal/state) governments. Based on my review of contemporary rape law reform at the state level, I identified several types of reform to assess whether tribal nations maintained some of this archaic language in the tribal statutes.

## Common Areas of Concern

In this section, I provide a cursory "audit" of some of the most problematic vintage Anglo-American definitions of sexual violence to determine the extent to which tribal governments still retain vestiges of outdated American substantive law (or even English common law). A minority of the tribal codes I examined still retain such problematic language, but they are worth noting here as part of basic reform needs.

### *Gender of Perpetrator and Victim*

Anglo-American common law only recognized men as perpetrators and women as victims.[15] All state governments have eliminated this restriction.[16] Only five tribal nations in this study contain this requirement. These statutes need to be repealed. This is of critical importance, particularly because of the number of Native men and boys who are victims of sexual assault,[17] as well as those who do not fall neatly into the traditional Western binary gender identity (e.g., two-spirit people).[18] Tribal law will ideally protect *all* people from sexual violence, not just cisgendered women.

### *Spousal Exemption*

A spousal exemption means that the law does not recognize that a person can commit a sexual assault against their spouse (again, emanating from Western conceptions of women as the property of men). In the mainstream American rape law reform movement, it took several decades to remove spousal exemptions from rape laws; by 2005 all fifty states had removed these exemptions.[19] In addition to outright exemptions, there are also versions of the spousal exemption that require the couple to be separated at the time of the offence. Another permutation of the spousal exemption is the requirement that there be an extremely high degree of physical force to qualify as a sexual assault, a requirement not always found in sexual assault laws outside the context of marriage. It is apparent that the spousal exemption reform effort has not reached tribal statutes. I found thirty-two tribal statutes that provide some form of explicit exemption for spouses (for at least one sexual assault statute). On the other hand, five tribal nations proactively address the issue of spousal rape through specific provisions or even a separate statute criminalizing sexual assault on a spouse. This fact may indicate that the tribal nation has done revisions to the codes it once had. I did not review domestic violence statutes, which may be applicable in the case of assault on a spouse.

*Requirement of Heterosexual Penetration*

Anglo-American rape law traditionally only recognized sexual assault when it involved penile-vaginal penetration (heterosexual intercourse). This is a corollary of the gendered laws mentioned earlier. The true "wrong" of rape in historical Anglo-American law was closely tied to women's subordination to men as well as men's ownership of women and girls, and thus the laws only recognized heterosexual intercourse as potentially criminal.[20] This common law element reflects the patriarchal society from which it emerged. As we know now, however, other forms of sexual assault can be just as dangerous, terrorizing, and humiliating as heterosexual intercourse. The harm of sexual assault comes from the violations of *sexual autonomy* wherein decisions about intimate body parts are made by a perpetrator in violation of the victim's bodily integrity. However, there is a plethora of other behaviour that can constitute sexual assault, including touching (under or through clothes), oral or anal sex, penetration by objects, and many other objectionable acts. Only twelve tribal nations still *require* penile-vaginal intercourse to establish the crime of sexual assault. Most tribal nations have laws that address penile-vaginal intercourse *and* non-penetration offences of contact such as "sexual touching" or the use of another body part or object to achieve penetration. Typically, though, the penetration offences are considered more serious than non-penetration crimes and warrant more serious punishment. Some tribal nations do not cover sexual touching at all and only cover actual penetration.

*Degrees/Gradation of Sexual Assault*

There are a variety of reasons that a government may want to have a range of "degrees" or different levels of culpability in their statutes.[21] This demarcation is usually framed by creating separate crimes, such as "rape in the first degree," "rape in the second degree," or "aggravated sexual abuse" and "sexual abuse," In this scheme, more "serious" crimes can result in more severe punishment. For example, first-degree rape may require extensive violence or be achieved through the use of a weapon, whereas second-degree rape may focus on victims who are incapacitated (intoxicated or sleeping). There are prosecutorial advantages to a range of offences from most serious to least serious, although the distinctions might not reflect the experiences of victims. Such gradations offer a more precise charge matching the behaviour as well as providing opportunities for plea bargaining. Having options for plea bargaining can be beneficial for some victims who do not want to testify in open court. Because of this, I am particularly concerned if the *only* law on the books requires an exceedingly high burden such as being required to prove victim physical resistance. If an assault does not meet these high benchmarks, then, essentially, the behaviour is lawful. Very few tribal sexual assault statutes include these limitations. Still, a total of twelve tribal nations have only *one* crime that requires proof of force and/or threats.

*Prompt Complaint*

Under American common law, a victim was typically required to report the assault within a short period of time in order to sustain a successful prosecution. This is tied to the patriarchal assumption that "true" victims immediately run to the authorities.[22] The subtext of these reporting requirements also suggests that a victim who delays reporting is lying. Victims commonly delay reporting by days, weeks, and even years, so this kind of provision serves to prevent prosecution of crimes. Typically, other crimes don't have this prompt complaint requirement – just sexual assault. Fortunately, only four tribal nations in this study retain that requirement. One tribal statute requires that a report be made within thirty days. Two tribal statutes require a report to be made within three months. A fourth tribal statute imposes the reporting timeline only on victims who are the spouse of their perpetrator: a spouse has thirty days to report a sexual assault. Given that most survivors of sexual assault do not immediately report their crimes to authorities, these limitations serve no purpose other than to limit the ability of prosecutors to make a case months or years after the assault(s).

*Intoxication*

One of the most common types of sexual assaults are those committed against people who are intoxicated or otherwise sedated.[23] Sexual assault is a crime with a close relationship to intoxication. Predators often target people who have become too high or too drunk to consent. This is particularly true in tribal context. One of the most frequent scenarios, covered to varying degrees in tribal sexual assault statutes, involves a victim who is intoxicated (by drugs and/or alcohol) and a perpetrator who uses those circumstances to their predator advantage.[24] This scenario is extremely common in the lives of Indigenous women. Unfortunately, some tribal nations only recognize intoxication incapacity if the intoxication was *involuntary* – in other words, the perpetrator intentionally caused the victim to consume drugs that incapacitate the victim. This is not the method commonly used by perpetrators. Unfortunately, if the victim is *voluntarily* intoxicated (e.g., the perpetrator waits until the victim has consumed enough drinks on the victim's own volition before making the predatory move), the law does not recognize that as true incapacity. Here is a typical example of problematic language from a tribal second-degree rape statute: "It shall be unlawful ... [to] engage in sexual intercourse with another whose power to appraise or control their conduct has been substantially impaired by the *administration* or employment of drugs or other intoxications, *without their knowledge*, and for the purpose of preventing resistance" (emphasis added). Such a statutory structure contemplates specifically involuntary intoxication (the perpetrator caused the intoxication) but does not criminalize the actions of perpetrators who take advantage of an intoxicated person who was voluntarily drinking or using drugs.

I recommend that intoxication be explicitly addressed in the statute so that tribal judges do not read incapacity-related language as referring only to mental illnesses or non-drug-induced incapacity. Of the 216 statutes:

- 45 contain language covering both involuntary and voluntary intoxication scenarios;
- 82 *only* cover involuntary intoxication;
- 31 featured sufficiently clear "without consent" language that could fairly include both types of intoxication; and
- 58 statutes did not address intoxication at all.

## Force versus Consent

In the United States, contemporary rape law reform efforts have typically focused on the question of whether to and how to define sexual assault as *non-consensual sex*.[25] The clear trend in the United States in the late twentieth century was to move from the requirement of extrinsic violence (forcible compulsion) to a definition that respects sexual autonomy by focusing on whether the victim consented to the act (no extrinsic violence or incapacity required).[26] In more recent years, a significant rift has developed within mainstream American sexual assault law regarding the correct foundational principles of consent-based sexual assault law. These twenty-first-century disputes turn on the question of whether an actor must obtain consent *before* the sexual activity (affirmative consent), or whether the onus is on the victim to protest (implied consent).[27] Mainstream feminists have taken opposite positions on these incompatible frameworks. Those who favour an affirmative consent law often argue that it is the only way to truly respect sexual autonomy.[28] Their detractors argue that the requirement of affirmative consent will unnecessarily broaden the scope of sexual assault law and intrude too deeply into the private nature of sexual behaviour.[29] Nevertheless, there seems to be some level of consensus that the use of a "consent" standard is preferable to laws requiring physical force or incapacity. The problem comes in the definition of consent. I began this analysis by looking at the extent to which tribal governments have also shifted to consent-based sexual assault laws. Building on the methodology used by Decker and Boroni in their fifty-state survey of sexual assault laws in 2012,[30] I have divided the force-versus-consent laws into three categories:

1. *True non-consent tribal nations*: These tribal nations "can convict a defendant of at least one sex offence by establishing that the victim did not consent to the sexual act. The prosecution is not required to show that the perpetrator used force or threats of force against the victim to meet the statutory requirements."[31] A typical example of language from a "true non-consent" tribal statute reads: "A person commits sexual abuse by intentionally or knowingly engaging in sexual contact with a person ... *without consent* of that person." Note that this language does not require proof of violence, threats, victim resistance or incapacity, instead relying on the standard of consent. My analysis uncovered thirty-six tribal nations that have at least one true non-consent provision – that is, there is at least *one* crime that only requires showing of lack of consent (though it is often a very low-level, less serious crime). Even the statutes that use consent as a standard still maintain force/incapacity requirements for some levels of sexual assault. Although thirty-six tribal nations codes contain consent language, nineteen of these nations do not explicitly define the term "consent," which is potentially problematic when we consider category 2.
2. *Contradictory non-consent tribal nations*: In these tribal statutes, "it may appear as though the elements of a sex offense statute are met when a victim did not affirmatively consent to the act. However,

statutory definitions of 'consent' reveal the contradictory nature of these laws. To establish a 'lack of consent' in these Tribal codes, the prosecution must show either the use of forcible compulsion *or* a victim's incapacity to consent. Requiring force or a lack of capacity to consent completely negates the purpose of including a non-consent provision."[32] There are fifteen tribal laws that can be characterized as contradictory non-consent: the word "consent" is used in the statute, but other language in the statute requires "forcible compulsion" or a victim's incapacity. Referring to state rape laws, Baker and Oberman write that "consent is rarely defined in rape statutes, and even if it is, the definition begs as many questions as does the term consent itself."[33]

3. *"Force" tribal codes*. This category includes tribal nations that have *at least one* sex offence that requires showing "forcible compulsion" or "incapacity to consent." A typical force-based definition requires that the actor "compel another to submit to sexual intercourse by force or by the threat of imminent death, serious bodily injury, extreme pain, or kidnapping." This is an extremely high standard to meet, and does not match the reality of most types of sexual assault seen on reservations today. I identified nineteen tribal nations that do not mention the word "consent" (or a synonym) at all. In addition, thirty-eight tribal nations still have at least one sex crime that requires a showing force or incapacity. There is high variation among "force" tribal nations. Some make it almost impossible to prove a sexual assault crime beyond a reasonable doubt. Decker and Baroni included two types of state statutes under the "force state" designation: (1) states that allowed both force and incapacity/intoxication to be independent pathways towards convicting a perpetrator, and (2) one state that permitted *only* force as the pathway towards convicting a perpetrator. In my review of the language of force tribal nations, I noticed a higher degree of variation that requires additional analysis. Some tribal statutes *require* proof that force was used (and did not provide for an alternate pathway to conviction in cases of victim incapacity or intoxication). Other statutes allowed force *or* incapacity/intoxication to suffice to achieve a conviction.

I also noted several tribal statutes that have extremely heightened requirements with no contemporary state law analogue. These tribal statutes require a victim's *physical resistance* to be overcome by force; otherwise, no crime has been committed. To be sure, many of these statutes have additional pathways to conviction, including incapacity/intoxication. I also found some statutes that *hinted* at a resistance requirement but did not feature language to the effect of "victim's resistance is overcome by force." Instead, these statutes contain language indicating that the prosecutor may need to address the possibility of the victim's resistance (or lack thereof) as they seek a conviction. These particular force statutes use the subjunctive tense to indicate not that force-overcoming-resistance is a requirement, but rather that the nature of the threat of force or type of force employed would cause a victim to decide that physical resistance would not be worth the effort. Here is one example: "It shall be unlawful to ... [c]ompel another to submit to sexual intercourse by any threat *that would prevent resistance* by a person of ordinary resolution" (emphasis added). Oftentimes this provision would appear in second-degree rape, but not first-degree. Finally, I noticed some statutes, mostly sexual touching statutes, did not require force per se, but also were plainly not consent-based statutes. Frequently these statutes used antiquated language that I decided supported neither a true non-consent designation nor a force designation of any type. Specifically, many of these statutes referred to contact that the perpetrator knows "is offensive to the other person." The other pathways to conviction, if any, were the typical incapacity and/or intoxication provisions.

Ultimately, the tribal statutes fell into the following categories: 40 true non-consent; 21 contradictory non-consent; 117 force statutes (plus 26 statutes that did not cover force but spoke only to the victim's incapacity). Overall, then, in my study of 108 tribal nations, there are 39 that have at least one true non-consent statute, while the remaining 69 do not have any such statute.

Based on my work with Native survivors as well as this review of tribal codes, I contend that (re)defining sexual assault as a consent-based crime will better serve tribal nations, even for those that do not have an adversarial criminal process. Tribal nations are in a unique position to develop an elevated legal approach to sexual assault that will facilitate a more comprehensive victim-centred approach to criminal law. As for the debate between affirmative consent and implied consent, I maintain that these questions desperately need Indigenous feminist legal input. Perhaps Indigenous feminists are in the best position to draw out these important themes about why and how consent can be centralized in a contemporary tribal court setting.

## Reform

I argue that tribal nations should consider broadening the legal definition of sexual assault where possible and relevant. This would involve, among other reforms, eliminating any language, even non-binding language, suggesting or requiring victim resistance. More broadly, tribal nations may need to wrestle with the question of whether affirmative consent is a good fit for the nation. Ideally, tribal nations should recognize the sexual autonomy of each person in its jurisdiction by deploying Indigenous feminist legal theory as a tool. What do today's Native people have to say about sexual autonomy and the harms of non-consensual sex? Answering this question requires feminist inquiry unique to tribal cultures.

*Reliance on Traditional (Customary) Law*

In the United States, there is a movement to re-envision a statutory scheme that is connected in some way to tribal common law or tribal traditional law. In some tribal "choice of law" statutes, judges and justices of tribal nations are required to look to "tribal traditions" in the event that the tribal code is silent or ambiguous. This approach must be carefully considered in the context of contemporary laws against sexual assault. As Napoleon and others have pointed out, questions about what "tradition" or "traditional values" can contribute to contemporary tribal laws are fraught.[34] There are variety of ways to try to ascertain how tribal nations responded to sexual assault "prior to colonization." Some scholars have suggested that sexual assault was once a rare crime – at least for some tribal nations.[35] Some tribal culture-bearers have encouraged a reclamation of non-violence as a traditional tenet, and it has become common for many tribal anti-violence programs to proclaim "violence is not traditional" in awareness materials.[36]

However, Emily Snyder, Val Napoleon, and John Borrows have correctly reminded us that we must be cautious about claiming a romanticized past as a tool to address contemporary gendered violence.[37] "Culture" can be "hijacked" by those who intend to reinforce male dominance.[38] Thus, I tread carefully with this approach, aware that culture "can be a source for the abuse of power, as much as it can be a force for liberation when examined in real world terms."[39]

Cree/Metis scholar Emma LaRoque reminds us:

> As women we must be circumspect in our recall of tradition. We must ask ourselves whether and to what extent tradition is liberating us as women. We must ask ourselves wherein lie our sources of empowerment. We know enough about human history that we cannot assume that all Aboriginal traditions universally respected and honoured women. (And is

> "respect" and "honour" all that we can ask for?) It should not be assumed, even those original societies that were structured along matriarchal lines, that matriarchies necessarily prevented men from oppressing women ... As Native women, we are faced with very difficult and painful choices, but, nonetheless, we are challenged to change, create, and embrace "traditions" consistent with contemporary and international human rights standards.[40]

Thus, it is important not to rely solely on "traditional" concepts when crafting a societally relevant *contemporary* tribal statute. Even if we assume that rape was once a very rare crime, this is certainly not the case today. Over fifty per cent of Native women in the United States will experience sexual assault in their lifetime.[41] So merely referencing a romanticized past cannot necessarily grant us wisdom in responding to this current crisis. In order to draft better specific statutory language, we need contemporary voices and perspectives to help us change this reality. In her important essay about traditional tribal law, Christine Zuni Cruz (Isleta Pueblo) asks, "Do our written laws even make room to help our people resolve the underlying problems in a way that restores their self-dignity and self-worth so that the individual is reminded of their connection to the greater community?"[42] To answer this question in the affirmative means that we listen to those most affected by the laws – survivors.

### *Indigenous Feminist Perspectives on the Nature of Sexual Assault*

In this section I consider how Indigenous feminisms can cultivate and refine definitions of sexual assault that are relevant and meaningful in the contemporary tribal setting. In so doing, I explore how Indigenous people talk and write about the nature of sexual assault, and then consider how such wrongful acts might be inform tribal statutory law. I seek answers to the question posed by Snyder, Napoleon, and Borrows: "How might we begin thinking about violence against Indigenous women through the frame of Indigenous law?"[43]

At the outset, it is important to understand that there is not and will not be "one" Indigenous feminist approach to rape. As with feminisms more generally, Indigenous feminists may express unique perspectives on crime depending on their own culture, language, and experiences. Rather than determining the best tribal code for all, I explore the types of questions that Indigenous feminists may develop in order to begin or continue important tribal-centric reform effort. I argue that we should turn to contemporary Indigenous feminists and consider how they describe the harm of rape and the need to respond. While not all of the voices featured below emanate from self-identified Indigenous feminists, the perspectives they bring offer cogent ideas that could foster an Indigenous feminist dialogue. Reformers need to think critically about what kind of sexual assault law reforms are needed. Athabascan scholar Dian Million writes, "we are rightly campaigning to put laws in place to enhance our chances of safety, and to seek justice for ourselves and our families. We are not safe because our societies, our local communities, or the Nation-states are not safe."[44] I'm particularly interested in how Indigenous women and two-spirit survivors talk and write about sexual assault – and how they articulate the harm they experienced to help craft language that will hold perpetrators accountable. The voices of two-spirit and Native LGBTQ voices must be centralized in this process because we know that sexual violence is unfortunately far too common for these folks as well.[45] I've gathered a few passages to stimulate discussion. For example, Tewa elder Vickie Downey reminds us: "Women have to be recognized. The words of women have to be recognized. The women will come out. It might be prophesied or doesn't have to be prophesied, but the feeling is so strong that the women will come out and voice their feelings. Whether people want to hear it or not, it's going to come because it's meant to be. It's that time."[46]

Cree elder Ruth Morin was interviewed by Kim Anderson for her book *A Recognition of Being*. Regarding contemporary problems, she noted that "we don't have built-in ways to pass along the teachings about sex." But she does suggest a framework for such discussions: "Viewing ourselves with a sense of sacredness is vital: "How would you view one who has tampered with that sacredness? … Would you tend to view a single abusive act of this nature differently than a molestation that takes place over several years? Viewing oneself as a sacred being has implications for healing. It has implications for prevention as well, for sacred beings do not act in this manner toward other sacred beings."[47]

Employing this principle as a starting point for contemporary sexual assault law, we might use such an insight to think about the how tribal law should define rape. How might we ensure that tribal sexual assault laws are consistent with the principle of sacredness? Is a reference to "sacredness" too closely tied to spiritual or religious beliefs? Does it provide ideas as to the appropriate kind of response to perpetrators? Should the government response be different for a one-time occurrence as opposed to a serial offender? The right answers may differ by community.

Rachel Flowers' (Leeyq'sun) recent powerful essay *Refusal to Forgive: Indigenous Women's Love and Rage* offered the following wisdom on Indigenous women's bodies as the site of gendered violence:

> While Indigenous women's bodies are described as targets of gendered colonial violence, it is critical not to lose sight that we are also legal and political actors. [Lee] Maracle's grandmother taught her that, "In the end, granddaughter, our body is the only house we will ever truly own. It is the one thing we truly own ... What is more, in the end, command of it will only amount to the sacred right of choice." Here she is explaining the "the absolute right to be cherished and the absolute freedom to govern our love's expression" but, to my mind, she is also speaking to the right to choose who receives our love, who we allow to enter our house, our village, and our world.[48]

Leanne Betasamosake Simpson (Alderville First Nation) is both eloquent and bold about her position on sexual violence:

> Let me be clear, from within Nishnaabewin, the decisions about how I use my body, my mind, my sexuality, my spirituality, and the relationships I'm embedded in are my decision and no one else's. The regulation of my body, my brain, and my sexuality are attacks on my body as a political order, my nationhood, and my freedom, regardless of intent. I do not consent to have my freedom restricted by those who believe they know best for me and my body. I refuse.[49]

Other indigenous authors have made connections between tribal sovereignty and bodily autonomy, such as Ashley Noel Mack and Tiara R. Na'puti, who write, "Sovereign bodies enact self-determination by making decisions about how to keep their bodies safe from violence, defining and identifying relationships and sexualities, and making decisions about their land, resources, and lives."[50] Audrey Shenandoah reminds us that sovereignty is not just about governing: "Sovereignty is the ability to carry out your own direction."[51] Tłaliłila'ogwa scholar Sarah Hunt encourages us to deepen "our understanding of what self-determination means at the bodily level."[52]

Clear themes emerge from these passages: bodily integrity, sexual autonomy, and self-determination. These are certainly not the building blocks for historical American rape law. So perhaps, by writing a victim-centred sexual assault law, the survivors within a community could come together to conceptualize new ways to articulate expectations for what behaviour constitutes sexual assault. For example, how should "bodily integrity" be defined in tribal law? Do survivors in the community have thoughts about the question of affirmative consent and implicit consent? If yes, we should be listening to them.

## Examples of Victim-Centred Tribal Laws

In my review of the tribal codes, I came across a variety of tribal statutes where it is clear that the drafters have engaged with some sort of contemporary reform efforts around issues of consent. I share these examples as possible starting points for stimulating discussion. For example, consent is explicitly defined in several tribal codes. Examples follow:

- "Consent" means that at the time of the act of sexual intercourse or sexual contact there are actual words or conduct indicating freely given agreement to have sexual intercourse or sexual contact.
- "Consent" means a voluntary, uncoerced manifestation of a present agreement to perform a particular sex act with the defendant.
- "Consent" means the knowing and voluntary agreement of two or more individuals, each of whom is sixteen years of age or older and otherwise capable of understanding the nature and consequences of such agreement, to commit some act.

I am not suggesting that any of these examples are the correct or best language for tribal nations, but they may provide a springboard for discussion. If these types of definitions resonate with community members, such language could serve as a starting point in drafting new definitions.

### *Legislative Intent*

Another contemporary development found in tribal sexual assault laws is to provide preamble language or purpose to make clear the legislative intent. These provisions could be relied upon by prosecutors and tribal judges when interpreting statutory language. I identified a handful of tribal nations whose codes contain helpful preamble language that clearly establishes the legislative intent in passing the laws. For instance:

> The purpose of this chapter is: 1) To proscribe sexual conduct that causes or threatens substantial harm to individuals residing within [tribal jurisdiction]; 2) To give fair warning of proscribed conduct and its related sentencing upon conviction; and 3) To promote public safety through deterrence based on conviction and proper sentencing.

Another tribal nation takes clear ownership of the crisis as follows:

> Only the informed [tribal nation] and its families can stop sexual abuse among its people. The laws and legal system are tools assisting the community in this effort. The purposes of the Chapter shall be as follows: (1) to assist in protecting the community from sexual assault and abuse, especially our precious children and other vulnerable individuals; (2) to provide offenders and their families with a resource for accountability, penance and restitution for their harmful actions; and (3) to promote healing for individuals, families and the community who have been impacted by these offenses. This includes rehabilitative treatment for offenders.

**Alternatives to the Criminal Justice System**

In this section, I return to the question of whether the Western law-and-order system (and contemporary tribal criminal law) is the answer to the rates of high violence against Native people. While sexual assault in Indian country remains largely unprosecuted, we must counter that knowledge with an understanding that Native women and two-spirit people are over-criminalized themselves.[53] Many Indigenous feminists are rightly concerned about the assimilation of Western law and order, penal systems that focus on incarceration and punishment as the best response to criminal behaviour.[54] Expanding the definition of any crime raises concern, particularly when the tribal government has adopted an assimilated criminal justice system.[55]

Christine Zuni Cruz reminds us that "not every sovereign act undertaken by an indigenous Nation necessarily promotes the sovereignty of the people."[56] While this chapter has focused on Anglo-American–style statutes, many tribal nations continue to practise pre-colonial methods of dispute resolution, and some tribal nations have recently revitalized less adversarial responses to crime. I contend that statutory reform is an *exercise* by which a community can begin to determine, for itself, how harm and wrong are defined. Even if the tribal nation offers (or prefers) alternatives to Anglo-American adversarial justice, the project of *defining* consent and sexual assault can still serve justice in the end, because the harm described in the law is officially acknowledged by the tribal government.[57] Even in traditional dispute resolution, I suggest that we should be concerned with crafting at least some bright-line definitions of sexual assault to demarcate the difference between acceptable and unacceptable behaviour.[58] Thus, even tribal nations that do not intend to begin prosecuting sexual assault (in the Western sense) can still benefit from drafting or revising a tribal definition of sexual assault.

**Areas for Future Study**

While this cursory survey of tribal codes may be useful for some efforts, there is much more work to be done. Tribal legislatures may wish to review related tribal statutes to ensure that victims receive adequate legal protection and that there are procedural protections for victims. For example, survivors of sexual assault may fear that their confidential mental health or advocacy records could be subpoenaed by defence attorneys. A tribal statute or court rule may be necessary in order to protect this information. Tribal governments may wish to consider offering a procedural mechanism for bringing an expert witness to testify about common responses to sexual assault. A tribal community might want to ponder how it will respond to minors who commit acts of sexual assault[59] or special issues regarding Elder victims.[60] Tribal judges may wish to review their jury instructions to ensure they do not contain any "cautionary" directives in sexual assault cases. (Before widespread reform, the Anglo-American system often cautioned juries that testimony of victims should be viewed sceptically.) Perhaps most important is to consider whether the tribal nation has a "rape shield statute" that prohibits the use of the victim's sexual past to impeach her credibility.

During the course of analysing the laws, I became aware of several other issues that compel additional inquiry. When reviewing the sexual assault laws, I often came across clear prohibitions on consensual sodomy, which criminalizes two-spirit (Native LGBTQ+) people for simply *existing*. I hope to launch another audit looking more closely at such provisions. While there are intellectual disagreements among some scholars about the colonial roots of heteronormativity, we must face the contemporary fact that many tribal communities espouse homophobic or transphobic principles that have no place in a contemporary anti-rape regime.[61]

There are other topics that need exploration. For example, I did not explore how tribal nations currently characterize prostitution, survival sex, or sex trafficking, or the issue of missing and murdered Indigenous women, but in in passing, I noticed that many tribal nation in my sample outlaw prostitution, with penalties for "sellers." The terminology around "consent" will be perhaps even more important in this genre of law. Sarah Hunt provide some specific guidance on these questions: "Efforts to address human trafficking must simultaneously distinguish between adult sex work, trafficking, sexual exploitation, and a range of violent offences, while acknowledging the colonial roots that link various forms of abuse and marginalization emerging within ongoing colonial relations."[62]

## Conclusion

It is clear that many tribal statutes need reform if they are to be applicable to a wide variety of victims and circumstances in the contemporary setting. Across the globe, it is important to remember that tribal statutory reform is not where the efforts stop. Changing the wording of a statute does not address other obstacles on the ground, such as victim-blaming by the community or legal system. "Even in countries with developed sexual offences legislation and strong women's movements, impunity for rape continues."[63] Passing a new statute does not guarantee that law enforcement officers and prosecutors will be compelled to prosecute any particular case.

This is precisely the reason that anti-rape efforts must begin within community conversations. The language that Indigenous people use to talk about sexual violence is both legal language and political language. In order to address the unacceptable rates of sexual assault against Native people, this language is imperative – without these voices, we will be unable to craft statutes, rules, and expectations that meet the needs of victims. If our people are truly "sacred," then we should not make the process of holding accountable those who sexually victimize them so unnecessarily onerous.

This brings me back to my prologue. My friend Deb found solace and comfort after understanding that the state law recognized and acknowledged the context of her own experience with sexual assault. While she decided not to pursue justice through the criminal system, the statute itself was still meaningful to her. Whether a sexual assault definition is intended to apply in tribal courts or is used as an anchor for discussing sexual assault in non-legal spaces, it should reflect the needs of survivors from the community. Opening up the dialogue about consent and autonomy is critical to the future well-being of Indigenous people.

ACKNOWLEDGMENT

I thank my research assistants, Lydia Jensen and Kevin C Barnett.

NOTES

1 Pseudonym. This story is based on true events, but multiple facts have been changed to ensure the woman's anonymity. I also spoke to the woman herself, and she was comfortable with my retelling for this purpose.

2 In the United States, Indigenous people are more often referred to as "Native," "Native American," "American Indian," or "Indian." In American law, "Federal Indian Law" is most often used to describe federal laws that impact tribal nations. In addition, "Indian Country" is a legal term of art in the United States, referring to reservations and other land bases that are held in trust by the federal government. I will use "Indigenous" when referring to perspectives from Canada, where that term is more common.

3 While "rape" was the word used in original American common law, there are a variety of other terms used by governments when defining sex crimes, including "sexual assault," "sexual abuse," and "sexual battery." In this chapter, I will primarily use the term "sexual assault" to encompass a wide range of illegal sexual behaviour. Individual survivors often choose the term that is more accurate to them, and that may differ from legal language.

4 Constance Backhouse & Lorna Schoenroth, "A Comparative Study of Canadian and American Rape Law" (1984) 7 Can-US LJ 173 at 174.

5 Susan Caringella, *Addressing Rape Reform in Law and Practice* (New York: Columbia University Press, 2009); Cassia Spohn & Julie Horney, *Rape Law Reform* (New York: Springer, 1992)

6 William J Lawrence, "Tribal Injustice: The Red Lake Court of Indian Offenses" (1972) 48:4 North Dakota L Rev 639 at 640; Laurence French, "Law Enforcement in Indian Country" (2005) 18:1 Crim Justice Stud 69; Lisa J Bond-Maupin, "Who Made the Code in the First Place?: Delinquency and Justice in an American Indian Community" (1996) 25:2 Crime, L Soc Chang 133, online: <http://link.springer.com/10.1007/BF00389751>; Robert D Cooter & Wolfgang Fikentscher, "American Indian Law Codes: Pragmatic Law and Tribal Identity" (2008) 56 Am J Comp L 29.

7 Russel Lawrence Barsh & J Youngblood Henderson, "Tribal Courts, the Model Code, and the Police Idea in American Indian Policy" (1976) 40:1 L Contemp Probl 25.

8 Amber Halldin, "Restoring the Victim and the Community: A Look at the Tribal Response to Sexual Violence Committed by Non-Indians in Indian Country through Non-Criminal Approaches" (2008) 84 N D L Rev 1 at 8.

9 *Tribal Law and Order Act*, 25 U.S.C. § 1302(b) – Offenses subject to greater than 1-year imprisonment or a fine greater than $5,000.

10 Average sentence length for sex offenses in the USA is ten to eighteen years. See Danielle Kaeble, *Time Served in State Prison, 2018* (US Dept of Justice, Office of Justice Programs, Bureau of Justice Statistics, 2021) at 4.
11 *Oliphant v Suquamish Indian Tribe,* 435 US 191 (1978).
12 *Violence against Women Reauthorization Act of 2013,* S 1312, 115th Congress (2013).
13 *Violence against Women Reauthorization Act of 2022,* S 3623, 117th Congress (2022).
14 Bonnie Shucha, "'Whatever Tribal Precedent There May Be': The (Un) Availability of Tribal Law" (2014) 106:2 L Library J 199; Cooter & Fikentscher, *supra* note 6.
15 Spohn & Horney, *supra* note 5 at 21–22; Lynn Hecht Schafran & Jillian Weinberger, "Impressive Progress alongside Persistent Problems: Rape Law, Policy and Practice In the United States" in Nicole Westmarland & Geetanjali Gangoli, eds, *International Approaches to Rape* (Bristol: Policy, 2012) 193; Estelle B Freedman, *Redefining Rape: Sexual Violence in the Era of Suffrage and Segregation* (Cambridge, MA: Harvard University Press, 2013) at 274.
16 Caringella, *supra* note 5 at 18.
17 Larry Echohawk & Tessa Meyer Santiago, "What Indian Tribes Can Do to Combat Child Sexual Abuse" 4:1 (2003) 4 Tribal LJ 1.
18 One study concluded that 85 per cent of two-spirit women have been sexually assaulted: Keren Lehavot, Karina L Walters & Jane M Simoni, "Abuse, Mastery, and Health among Lesbian, Bisexual, and Two-Spirit American Indian and Alaska Native Women" (2009) 15:3 Cult Divers Ethn Minor Psychol 275, online: <http://doi.apa.org/getdoi.cfm?doi=10.1037/a0013458>; Jessica HL Elm et al, "'I'm in This World for a Reason': Resilience and Recovery among American Indian and Alaska Native Two-Spirit Women" (2016) 20:3–4 J Lesbian Stud 352.
19 Schafran & Weinberger, *supra* note 15 at 193.
20 Diane M Daane, "Rape Law Reform: How Far Have We Come?" (1988) 68:2 Prison J 3 at 4.
21 Katharine K Baker & Michelle Oberman, "Women's Sexual Agency and the Law of Rape in the 21st Century" (2016) Stud L Polit Soc 63 at 69–70.
22 Caringella, *supra* note 5 at 204.
23 Debra Kaysen et al, "Incapacitated Rape and Alcohol Use: A Prospective Analysis" (2006) 31:10 Addict Behav 1820 at 1827.
24 Margo L Nightingale, "Judicial Attitudes and Differential Treatment: Native Women in Sexual Assault Cases" (1991) 23:1 Ottawa L Rev 71; Becky Farley, "A Perpetrator's Paradise: Outdated Sexual Assault Statutes Provide Minimal Protection to Survivors Who Are Victimized in Common Sexual Assault Scenarios" (2017) 17:2 Wyoming L Rev 315.

25 Caroline Davidson, "Rape In Context: Lessons for the United States from the International Criminal Court" (2018) 39 Cardozo L Rev 1191.

26 Catherine O Jacquet, *The Injustices of Rape: How Activists Responded to Sexual Violence, 1950–1980* (Chapel Hill: University of North Carolina Press, 2019) at 31.

27 Michelle J Anderson, "Negotiating Sex" (2005) 78 South Calif L Rev 101 at 104–105.

28 John Decker & Peter Baroni, "'No' Still Means 'Yes': The Failure of the 'Non-Consent' Reform Movement in American Rape and Sexual Assault Law" (2012) 101:4 J Crim L 1081; Caringella, *supra* note 5 at 4–5.

29 Janet Halley, "The Move to Affirmative Consent" (2016) 42:1 Signs: J Women in Culture and Society 257.

30 Decker & Baroni, *supra* note 28.

31 *Ibid* at 1084.

32 *Ibid* at 1085.

33 Baker & Oberman, *supra* note 21 at 64.

34 Val Napoleon & Hadley Friedland, "Indigenous Legal Traditions: Roots to Renaissance" in Markus D Dubber and Tatjana Hornle, eds, *Oxford Handbook of Criminal Law* (Oxford University Press, 2015) 225.

35 See, e.g., Lisa M Poupart, "The Familiar Face of Genocide: Internalized Oppression among American Indians" (2003) 18:2 Hypatia A J Fem Philos 86 at 91: "According to the oral traditions within our tribal communities, it is understood that prior to mass Euro-American invasion and influence, violence was virtually nonexistent in traditional Indian families and communities."

36 A few summers ago, a friend who had just driven across the Muscogee reservation and seen several "violence is not traditional" billboards asked me a very honest, direct question. "But what if it was?"

37 Emily Snyder, Val Napoleon & John Borrows, "Gender and Violence: Drawing on Indigenous Legal Resources" (2015) 48:2 UBC L Review 593 at 594.

38 *Ibid* at 595.

39 *Ibid*.

40 Emma LaRocque, "The Colonization of a Native Woman Scholar" in Christine Miller and Patricia Chuchryk, eds, *Women of the First Nations: Power, Wisdom and Strength* (Winnipeg: University of Manitoba Press, 1996) 11 at 14.

41 André B Rosay, "Violence against American Indian and Alaska Native Women and Men" (2016) 277 NIJ 38 at 39.

42 Christine Zuni-Cruz, "Tribal Law as Indigenous Social Reality and Separate Consciousness [Re]Incorporating Customs and Traditions into Tribal Law" (2001) 1:1 Tribal LJ 1 at 21.

43 Snyder, Napoleon & Borrows, *supra* note 37 at 596.
44 Dian Million, *Therapeutic Nations: Healing in an Age of Indigenous Human Rights* (Arizona: University of Arizona Press, 2013) at 177.
45 Hilary N Weaver, *Trauma and Resilience in the Lives of Contemporary Native Americans* (Milton Park: Routledge, 2019) at 78–79.
46 Vickie Downey, "Tewa Tesuque Pueblo" in Steve Wall, ed, *Wisdom's Daughters: Conversations with Women Elders of Native America* (New York: HarperCollins, 1993) at 12–13.
47 Kim Anderson, *A Recognition of Being*, 2nd ed (London: Women's Press, 2016) at 177–178.
48 Rachel Flowers, "Refusal to Forgive: Indigenous Women's Love and Rage" (2015) 4:2 Decolonization Indig Educ Soc 32 at 41.
49 Leanne Betasamosake Simpson, *As We Have Always Done: Indigenous Freedom through Radical Resistance* (Minneapolis: University of Minnesota Press, 2017) at 114.
50 Ashley Noel Mack & Tiara Na'puti, "'Our Bodies Are Not Terra Nullius': Building a Decolonial Feminist Resistance to Gendered Violence" (2019) 42:3 Women's Studies in Communication 347 at 359.
51 Wilma Mankiller, *Every Day is a Good Day: Reflections by Contemporary Indigenous Women,* memorial ed (Arvada, CO: Fulcrum, 2011) at 93.
52 Sarah Hunt, "Decolonizing the Roots of Rape Culture: Reflections on Consent, Sexual Violence and University Campuses" (Paper delivered at "The Power of Our Collective Voices: Changing the Conversation on Sexual Violence at Post-Secondary Institutions," Musqueam Territories, 30 September 2016) [unpublished] at 8.
53 Gillian Balfour, "Falling Between the Cracks of Retributive and Restorative Justice: The Victimization and Punishment of Aboriginal Women" (2008) 3:2 Fem Criminol 101, online: <http://journals.sagepub.com/doi/10.1177/1557085108317551>.
54 Ross, Luana, "Settler Colonialism and the Legislating of Criminality" (2016) 40:1 Am Indian Cult Res J 1.
55 Mack & Na'puti, *supra* note 50 at 364; Eileen M Luna-Firebaugh, "Incarcerating Ourselves: Tribal Jails and Corrections" (2003) 83:1 Prison J 51, online: <http://tpj.sagepub.com/cgi/doi/10.1177/0032885502250384>.
56 Zuni-Cruz, *supra* note 42 at 3.
57 "Rape reform legislation does not provide a total solution to the problem[;] it should be enacted since it will, at the very least, establish a strong public policy in support of the rape victim." Jacquet, *supra* note 26 at 183.
58 "Unless the law is prepared to abandon rape as a crime, it must always be concerned with how to draw bright lines demarcating the difference between permissible and impermissible sexual conduct." Baker & Oberman, *supra* note 21 at 68.

59 Clare E Lyon, "Alternative Methods For Sentencing Youthful Offenders: Using Traditional Tribal Methods as a Model" (2006) 4:Winter Ave Maria L Rev 211.
60 Justin Seigler, "Injustice in Indian Country: The Need for a Serious Response to Native American Elder Abuse" (2012) 19 Elder LJ 415.
61 Brian Joseph Gilley, "Native Sexual Inequalities: American Indian Cultural Conservative Homophobia and the Problem of Tradition" (2010) 13:1 Sexualities 47.
62 Sarah Hunt, "Representing Colonial Violence: Trafficking, Sex Work, and the Violence of Law" (2016) 37:2 Atlantis Crit Stud in Gender, Cult & Soc Justice 25.
63 Nicole Westmarland & Geetanjali Gangoli, *International Approaches to Rape* (Bristol: Policy, 2012) at 1–11.

## SOURCES CITED

Anderson, Kim. *A Recognition of Being*, 2nd ed (London: Women's Press, 2016).

Anderson, Michelle J. "Negotiating Sex" (2005) 78 South Calif L Rev 101.

Backhouse, Constance & Lorna Schoenroth. "A Comparative Study of Canadian and American Rape Law" (1984) 7 Can-US LJ 173.

Baker, Katharine K & Michelle Oberman. "Women's Sexual Agency and the Law of Rape in the 21st Century" (2016) Stud L Polit Soc 63.

Balfour, Gillian. "Falling between the Cracks of Retributive and Restorative Justice: The Victimization and Punishment of Aboriginal Women" (2008) 3:2 Fem Criminol 101.

Barsh, Russel Lawrence & J Youngblood Henderson. "Tribal Courts, the Model Code, and the Police Idea in American Indian Policy" (1976) 40:1 L Contemp Probl 25.

Bond-Maupin, Lisa J. "Who Made the Code in the First Place?: Delinquency and Justice in an American Indian Community" (1996) 25:2 Crime, Law Soc Chang 133.

Caringella, Susan. *Addressing Rape Reform in Law and Practice* (New York: Columbia University Press, 2009).

Cooter, Robert D & Wolfgang Fikentscher. "American Indian Law Codes: Pragmatic Law and Tribal Identity" (2008) 56 Am J Comp Law 29.

Daane, Diane M. "Rape Law Reform: How Far Have We Come?" (1988) 68:2 Prison J 3.

Davidson, Caroline. "Rape in Context: Lessons for the United States from the International Criminal Court" (2018) 39 Cardozo L Rev 1191.

Decker, John & Peter Baroni. "'No' Still Means 'Yes': The Failure of the 'Non-Consent' Reform Movement in American Rape and Sexual Assault Law" (2012) 101:4 J Crim L 1081.

Downey, Vickie. "Tewa Tesuque Pueblo" in Steve Wall, ed, *Wisdom's Daughters: Conversations with Women Elders of Native America* (New York: HarperCollins, 1993) 3.

Echohawk, Larry & Tessa Meyer Santiago. "What Indian Tribes Can Do to Combat Child Sexual Abuse" 4:1 (2003) 4 Tribal Law J 1.

Elm, Jessica HL, Jordan P Lewis, Karina L Walters & Jen M Self. "'I'm in This World for a Reason': Resilience and Recovery among American Indian and Alaska Native Two-Spirit Women" (2016) 20:3–4 J Lesbian Stud 352.

Farley, Becky. "A Perpetrator's Paradise: Outdated Sexual Assault Statutes Provide Minimal Protection to Survivors Who Are Victimized in Common Sexual Assault Scenarios" (2017) 17:2 Wyoming L Rev 315.

Flowers, Rachel. "Refusal to Forgive: Indigenous Women's Love and Rage" (2015) 4:2 Decolonization Indig Educ Soc 32.

Freedman, Estelle B. *Redefining Rape: Sexual Violence in the Era of Suffrage and Segregation* (Cambridge, MA: Harvard University Press, 2013).

French, Laurence. "Law Enforcement in Indian Country" (2005) 18:1 Crim J Stud 69.

Gilley, Brian Joseph. "Native Sexual Inequalities: American Indian Cultural Conservative Homophobia and the Problem of Tradition" (2010) 13:1 Sexualities 47.

Halldin, Amber. "Restoring the Victim and the Community: A Look at the Tribal Response to Sexual Violence Committed by Non-Indians in Indian Country through Non-Criminal Approaches" (2008) 84 N D L Rev 1.

Hunt, Sarah. "Decolonizing the Roots of Rape Culture: Reflections on Consent, Sexual Violence and University Campuses" (Paper delivered at "The Power of Our Collective Voices: Changing the Conversation on Sexual Violence at Post-Secondary Institutions," Musqueam Territories, 30 September 2016) [unpublished].

Hunt, Sarah. "Representing Colonial Violence: Trafficking, Sex Work, and the Violence of Law" (2016) 37:2 Atlantis Crit Stud in Gender, Cult & Soc Justice 25.

Jacquet, Catherine O. *The Injustices of Rape: How Activists Responded to Sexual Violence, 1950–1980* (Chapel Hill: University of North Carolina Press, 2019).

Kaeble, Danielle. *Time Served in State Prison, 2018* (US Dept of Justice, Office of Justice Programs, Bureau of Justice Statistics, 2021).

Kaysen, Debra, Clayton Neighbors, Joel Martell, Nicole Fossos & Mary E. Larimer. "Incapacitated Rape and Alcohol Use: A Prospective Analysis" (2006) 31:10 Addict Behav 1820.

LaRocque, Emma. "The Colonization of a Native Woman Scholar" in Christine Miller and Patricia Chuchryk, eds, *Women of the First Nations: Power, Wisdom and Strength* (Winnipeg: University of Manitoba Press, 1996) 11.

Lawrence, William J. "Tribal Injustice: The Red Lake Court of Indian Offenses" (1972) 48:4 North Dakota L Rev 639.

Lehavot, Keren, Karina L Walters & Jane M Simoni. "Abuse, Mastery, and Health among Lesbian, Bisexual, and Two-Spirit American Indian and Alaska Native Women" (2009) 15:3 Cult Divers Ethn Minor Psychol 275.

Luana, Ross. "Settler Colonialism and the Legislating of Criminality" (2016) 40:1 Am Indian Cult Res J 1.

Luna-Firebaugh, Eileen M. "Incarcerating Ourselves: Tribal Jails and Corrections" (2003) 83:1 Prison J 51.

Mack, Ashley Noel & Tiara Na'puti. "'Our Bodies Are Not Terra Nullius': Building a Decolonial Feminist Resistance to Gendered Violence" (2019) 42:3 Women's Studies in Communication 347.

Mankiller, Wilma. *Every Day Is a Good Day: Reflections By Contemporary Indigenous Women*, memorial ed (Arvada, CO: Fulcrum, 2011).

Million, Dian. *Therapeutic Nations: Healing in an Age of Indigenous Human Rights* (Tucson: University of Arizona Press, 2013).

Napoleon, Val & Hadley Friedland. "Indigenous Legal Traditions: Roots to Renaissance" in Markus D Dubber and Tatjana Hornle, eds, *Oxford Handbook of Criminal Law* (Oxford University Press, 2015) 225.

Nightingale, Margo L. "Judicial Attitudes and Differential Treatment: Native Women in Sexual Assault Cases" (1991) 23:1 Ottawa L Rev 71.

Poupart, Lisa M. "The Familiar Face of Genocide: Internalized Oppression among American Indians" (2003) 18:2 Hypatia: A J Fem Philos 86.

Rosay, André B. "Violence against American Indian and Alaska Native Women and Men" (2016) 277 NIJ 38.

Schafran, Lynn Hecht & Jillian Weinberger. "Impressive Progress alongside Persistent Problems: Rape Law, Policy and Practice in the United States" in Nicole Westmarland & Geetanjali Gangoli, eds, *International Approaches to Rape* (Bristol: Policy, 2012) 193.

Shucha, Bonnie. "'Whatever Tribal Precedent There May Be': The (Un) Availability of Tribal Law" (2014) 106:2 L Library J 199.

Simpson, Leanne Betasamosake. *As We Have Always Done: Indigenous Freedom through Radical Resistance* (Minneapolis: University of Minnesota Press, 2017).

Snyder, Emily, Val Napoleon & John Borrows. "Gender and Violence: Drawing on Indigenous Legal Resources" (2015) 48:2 UBC L Review 593.

Spohn, Cassia & Julie Horney. *Rape Law Reform* (New York: Springer, 1992).

Weaver, Hilary N. *Trauma and Resilience in the Lives of Contemporary Native Americans* (Milton Park: Routledge, 2019).

Westmarland, Nicole & Geetanjali Gangoli. *International Approaches to Rape* (Bristol: Policy, 2012).

Zuni-Cruz, Christine. "Tribal Law as Indigenous Social Reality and Separate Consciousness [Re]Incorporating Customs and Traditions into Tribal Law" (2001) 1:1 Tribal LJ 1.

JURISPRUDENCE

*Oliphant v Suquamish Indian Tribe*, 435 US 191 (1978).

LEGISLATION

*Tribal Law and Order Act*, 25 USC § 1302(b).
*Violence against Women Reauthorization Act of 2013*, S 1312, 115th Congress (2013).
*Violence against Women Reauthorization Act of 2022*, S 3623, 117th Congress (2022).

# 6 Deliberating Feminist Legal Strategies

JULIE KAYE AND EMILY SNYDER

Public discourse about the disproportionate violence experienced by Indigenous women in Canada continues to increase, including naming the ongoing crisis of missing and murdered Indigenous women, girls, trans, and two-spirit persons a "genocide."[1] In spite of growing awareness, there has been resistance to the recommendations of the National Inquiry into Missing and Murdered Indigenous Women and Girls, and many anti-violence efforts and state legal interventions continue to engage superficially in analyses of settler colonialism, including failing to closely examine how it is gendered.[2] This chapter considers this problem through a discussion about feminist legal strategies in the context of the *R v Barton*[3] case that initially acquitted Bradley Barton, a white settler, in the violent 2011 death of Cindy Gladue, an Indigenous woman connected to her Cree and Métis communities. In writing Cindy Gladue's name in this article, we hold deepest respect for her spirit and her loved ones. Her mother stated: "She's still human … She still has a name."[4] We recognize that, at the time of writing this chapter, her family continued to endure the pain of having "her honour, her spirit and her dignity dragged through yet another legal proceeding" when Barton was convicted of killing Cindy Gladue at a 2021 retrial but then appealed the decision (his appeal was rejected by the Alberta Court of Appeal).[5] The work of addressing gendered colonial violence and holding the criminal legal system to account is of extreme importance. Horrific acts of dehumanization took place in the initial *R v Barton* trial. As Beverly Jacobs states, "this was the first time in the history of any court proceeding that a woman's most private parts were displayed as evidence in a public courtroom. The spirit of the murder victim cannot rest until this is over. Her family cannot rest until this is over."[6]

This chapter takes up a small portion of this work of challenging gendered colonial violence by exploring the limitations and possibilities of feminist legal interventions that are focused on Indigenous legal issues, and examines these in the context of settler colonialism. Much of what has been written specifically about *R v Barton* appears in blogs and news stories,[7] with a variety of approaches taken, though with a core of insightful pieces by Indigenous women.[8] A public awareness booklet was also created by an informal working group composed of Indigenous women from the Institute for the Advancement of Aboriginal Women (IAAW), members of the family of the deceased, community-engaged academics, and leaders of Indigenous communities and organizations.[9] There is also a small body of academic work that has examined this case,[10] and here we add to that discussion through a consideration of feminist legal intervention strategies.

This case was a matter of significant national attention whereby Cindy Gladue's dignity and humanity were violated in a way that did not afford her the full protection of the law. As the Supreme Court concluded, "the criminal justice system … let her down – indeed, it let us all down."[11] There is much analysis to be done in relation to the case and findings at the Supreme Court in 2019, as well as the subsequent retrial and dismissed appeal. In this chapter, we will examine only the initial trial, as well as the original appeals and the feminist legal strategies employed by the Women's Legal Education and Action Fund (LEAF) and IAAW at the Alberta Court of Appeal and the Supreme Court of Canada.[12] We focus on these earlier proceedings to encourage analyses and discussion about more effective feminist legal interventions. IAAW and LEAF were the sole interveners at the Alberta Court of Appeal.[13] They were joined by a number of intervenors at the Supreme Court of Canada, where the role IAAW and LEAF played at the Alberta Court of Appeal was brought into question.[14] We specifically explore the role of IAAW and LEAF given their interventions at both the Court of Appeal and Supreme Court. Of note, the Supreme Court specifically took up the role of interveners in its hearing of Barton's appeal. Secondarily, we also reflect on the existing, albeit small, body of feminist legal scholarship on this case to analyse feminist legal strategies in settler colonial contexts.

Both LEAF and IAAW have made invaluable interventions in fighting injustices, in this case and beyond. Our intention here is to honour those efforts while also raising difficult questions about some of the impediments that need to be considered in future interventions. Feminist legal strategies have the potential for critical disruption, but they can also be limited in effecting transformative changes necessary to challenge ongoing settler colonial gendered violence that creates and reinforces conditions of white settler supremacy and hegemonic masculinities. As Audra Simpson clearly states, "Canada requires the death and 'disappearance' of Indigenous women in order to secure its sovereignty."[15] Gendered colonial violence has been, and continues to be, *central* to settler colonialism. The Canadian legal system has also been, and continues to be, a *core* mechanism of authorizing and operationalizing settler colonialism, including its concomitant heteropatriarchal violence.

There are important questions that have been and can continue to be raised about this case.[16] In this chapter, we focus on the following question: What happens if feminist legal strategies intending to *challenge* settler colonial gendered violence end up *reproducing* such colonial imperatives? Although feminist legal praxis offers a site of liberation for many, it too often upholds settler conditions by relying on state institutions that work to sustain colonial gendered violence. Intimately connected to this problem is the invisibilization of Indigenous laws.[17] While Indigenous feminisms played an essential role in the LEAF and IAAW intervention, we argue that so long as Indigenous legal orders have a peripheral status in the criminal justice system, *and* in feminist legal scholarship, there is limited space to move beyond recognition efforts to Indigenize such processes, thereby eliding possibilities of meaningful change.

The absence of Indigenous laws becomes particularly apparent when considering the joint intervention of LEAF and IAAW at the Alberta Court of Appeal because it represents an intersectional effort to unite Indigenous feminist anti-violence organizing with feminist legal strategies. In spite of intersectional grounding, the intervention highlights the ongoing structural decentring of Indigenous laws. It is noteworthy that Cree and Métis law were later incorporated into the IAAW and LEAF factum at the Supreme Court of Canada.[18] However, the inclusion of Indigenous law within the context of colonial constraint imposed by the settler legal system created a form of recognition of Indigenous laws without being able to adequately disrupt the settler system itself. As we discuss in this chapter, there are constraints placed upon feminist legal interveners by the courts, which limit the depth of feminist legal strategies in this case. At the same time, such constraints cannot excuse the inability of feminist legal strategies to take Indigenous law seriously. As we also discuss, for too long feminist legal studies has not meaningfully dealt with its own settler origins and the ways that the field is shaped by settler colonialism. There is an ongoing need for those working in feminist legal studies, ourselves included, to engage in discussion about decolonial feminist praxis that could untether the "justice system" from its settler colonial core and could alter the structural and material conditions in which gendered colonial violence is rooted. We make these arguments as white feminist settler scholars who aim to reflect on and centre decolonial feminist frameworks in our work. Julie was also research advisor for IAAW during the joint interventions at both the Court of Appeal and Supreme Court.

We begin by briefly discussing the theoretical approach underpinning our analysis. We then provide background information and analysis of the *R v Barton* case and, subsequently, the intervention from LEAF and IAAW at the Alberta Court of Appeal and Supreme Court of Canada. It is noteworthy that the purpose of this chapter is not to engage in a substantive analysis of Canadian law nor Cree and Métis law; rather, our focus is a broader critical reflection on feminist legal strategies and some of the specific challenges such strategies faced in the context of this case.

## Theorizing Settler Colonial Gendered Violence in the Context of Feminist Legal Strategies

There are many different approaches that scholars and activists take in trying to understand, explain, and challenge violence against Indigenous women and girls.[19] Yet often academics, practitioners, decision-makers, and everyday citizens have failed to take seriously calls from Indigenous feminist scholars and activists to understand the inseparable relationship between colonialism and heteropatriarchy.[20] As a field, feminist legal studies utilizes a variety of theoretical, methodological, and pedagogical approaches, but in many ways is also relatively homogeneous. As Patricia Monture, Twila L. Perry, and Rakhi Ruparelia argue, feminist legal studies is still very state centred and is dominated by white settler feminist politics.[21] The deep structural aspects of settler colonialism, and the ways that law functions as one of the key sites of reproduction, are often not well acknowledged in feminist legal studies. Certainly many understand that sexism, racism, and colonialism can be perpetuated via state law, but very often the response to these issues is to call for legal reform, diversity or cultural competency training of judges and lawyers, or more sophisticated legal strategies. Such approaches have challenged discrimination;[22] however, they can also leave settler colonial structures relatively intact.

While intersectionality is generally embraced in feminist legal discourse, it is not as well embraced in action and has not fundamentally disrupted or radically transformed the field away from settler-centred politics. As Glen Coulthard explains, settler colonialism "is a relationship where power – in this case, interrelated discursive and nondiscursive facets of economic, gendered, racial, and state power – has been structured into a relatively secure or sedimented set of hierarchical social relations that continue to facilitate the *dispossession* of Indigenous peoples of their lands and self-determining authority."[23] Taking Indigenous agency, knowledge, laws, and governance seriously requires a radical altering of feminist legal studies. There is a need to shift away from conceptualizations that treat intersectionality as being about identity categories, to understanding how structures of oppression and violence are entangled and how deeply settler colonial law is committed to maintaining that entanglement.

Indigenous feminist legal theory challenges settler privileging of state laws and the omission of Indigenous laws in feminist legal studies. It challenges the too-common privileging of masculinized knowledge and experience, the universalizing of male legal subjectivity, and the omission of Indigenous feminist perspectives in Indigenous law.[24] An Indigenous feminist legal framework brings an understanding that Indigenous laws can be used to challenge gendered violence but can also be interpreted and practised in ways that perpetuate it.[25] Inuit legal scholar Gordon Christie notes of Indigenous legal theory that it can be taken up to provide critiques of settler laws or to theorize and engage Indigenous legal orders.[26] Some have approached Indigenous feminist legal theory as a framework for engaging with Indigenous law,[27] gendered violence,[28] and gendered analysis of federal Indian law and tribal law (in the United States).[29] Our approach here expands on this work alongside theorizing settler colonialism.

The ongoing violence perpetrated by the criminal legal system is a continuation of colonial systems of dispossession and harm, reproduced through multiple and interconnected forms of systemic, material, and physical violence.[30] Drawing on settler colonial theorizing about the politics of recognition and the invisibilizing dynamics of settler colonialism, and arguing that the settler colonial state continues to treat Indigenous women's bodies as *humanitas nullius* (as people to be emptied of their humanity), Julie Kaye notes that the treatment of Cindy Gladue in *R v Barton* cannot be separated from the enactment of Canadian criminal law rooted in colonial gendered violence.[31] In this context of reconciliation as recognition, the criminal justice system reproduces structural and material forms of domination through an ongoing erasure of self-determination and sovereignty. It is this approach that we expand on here in conversation with Indigenous feminist legal studies to encourage dialogue in feminist legal studies about the complexities of using settler laws given their historical and ongoing function to render Indigenous laws, agency, and resistance absent – particularly Indigenous women and queer people's legal subjectivity, agency, and resistance.

## Background: *R v Barton*

In *R v Barton*, Cindy Gladue was described as a thirty-six-year-old Cree and Métis woman who bled to death as a result of a severe wound that Barton admittedly inflicted to her vaginal wall. To her family, "she was part of the lifeblood of our family: our daughter, mother, sister, cousin, niece. And she was so very loved by us all."[32] Yet throughout the police investigation and trial she was dehumanized, referred to as "the Native girl" and "the prostitute," including by the Crown prosecutor.[33] This framing of the case aligns with what Tracey Lindberg, Priscilla Campeau, and Maria Campbell identify as "a layering of judicial supremacy and the construction and destruction of Indigenous womanhoods … an *absence of discussion about who we really are*."[34]

In June 2011, Barton was charged with first degree murder under Section 235(1) of the Criminal Code,[35] which includes the lesser offence of unlawful act manslaughter. The former charge required the Crown to prove that he intended to kill the victim or knew he was causing her bodily harm likely to cause her death, while the latter required evidentiary proof of her death occurring in the context of a sexual assault. The initial trial was heard by Justice Rob Graesser and a jury composed of primarily men, and no jurors who identified as being Indigenous[36] – at the Court of Queen's Bench of Alberta from 17 February 2015 until 18 March 2015.[37] Uncontested at trial was the fact that Cindy Gladue bled to death in Barton's hotel room as the result of a severe wound inflicted by Barton to her vaginal wall.[38]

In an effort to prove a first degree murder charge, the Crown sought to demonstrate that Barton intentionally killed Cindy Gladue. The Crown theorized that she died as a result of a wound inflicted by a knife or sharp object. They attained expert testimony from Dr. Jones demonstrating Cindy Gladue's level of intoxication, with a blood alcohol content described as "four times the legal limit,"[39] and evidence from Dr. Dowling, the assistant chief medical examiner in Edmonton. After conducting an autopsy on 23 June 2011, Dr. Dowling "preserved a portion of the deceased's pelvic region."[40] Arguing that the tissue (a portion of Cindy Gladue's vagina) is "real evidence" – relevant and material to the trial proceedings – the Crown sought to have the "preserved tissue" shown to the jury.[41]

Following Barton's acquittal, mass outrage mobilized in response to the verdict, the violation of Cindy Gladue's body by the court, and the violation of Indigenous rights and protocols for caring for the dead.[42] Although the actions of the Crown were purportedly an effort to prove Barton's guilt, it was this evidence that seemingly enabled doubt to enter the minds of the jury. Although the defence opposed the admission of this evidence on the basis that it would have a prejudicial effect on the jury, it was this evidentiary point that ultimately framed the defence's theory.

The defence's argument emphasized depictions of Barton as an innocent "common man," an important characterization given the agreed-upon fact that Barton had inflicted the wound that led to Cindy Gladue's death, and portrayed Cindy Gladue as "the prostitute," two characterizations that we discuss further in the next section. The central theory of the defence rested on the testimony of Barton, who claimed the wound occurred by "unforeseeable" accident. As the instructions to the jury detail, this defence was "based on his experience of some 26 hours earlier where they had similar sexual activity and his interactions with her on the night in question."[43]

On 18 March 2015 Barton was acquitted by a jury on charges of first-degree murder and manslaughter in the death of Cindy Gladue.[44] That verdict was overturned on appeal to the Alberta Court of Appeal. Barton appealed to the Supreme Court of Canada, where a retrial on the charge of manslaughter was ordered. In 2021 Barton was convicted of killing Cindy Gladue during a sexual assault and sentenced to twelve and a half years in prison. Barton then appealed that decision, and in 2024 the Alberta Court of Appeal rejected his appeal.

## Feminist Legal Intervention by LEAF and IAAW

Following the initial acquittal, the Alberta Crown filed a notice of appeal on 1 April 2015. The Crown's application was premised on errors in law and, particularly, on erroneous and misleading instructions to the jury with respect to motive, manslaughter, and consent on a previous occasion as support for a finding of honest but mistaken belief in consent. The available grounds for the Crown's appeal were restricted to those provided for in the Criminal Code; thus they could not include the errors made by the Crown prosecutors in this trial and so fail to address the violations of protocols and violence towards Cindy Gladue's body and dignity.

In response to the errors of the court as a whole – including the instructions of the judge and the actions of the Crown and the defence – a feminist legal intervention was formed. Given the important role of an Indigenous women–led organization (IAAW) in the collaborative intervention of LEAF and IAAW, some might consider it an Indigenous feminist legal intervention. We argue, however, that the rules guiding the interveners' involvement in the criminal legal system restrict the intervention to instances of recognition that, importantly, are able to create some change within the system, but cannot produce the needed unsettling of the system as a whole that would accompany taking Indigenous laws seriously.

On 24 February 2016 LEAF and IAAW sought joint leave to intervene in the appeal of *R v Barton* in a motion heard before Alberta Court of Appeal Justice Berger. The interveners' factum submitted that

> the trial Court made two errors regarding the material issue of Cindy Gladue's alleged consent to sexual activity with the Respondent. First, the Court below admitted evidence of Ms. Gladue's sexual history, including her engagement in sexual activity in exchange for payment, that risked distracting the jury from the step-by-step analysis of subjective consent to sexual activity that is required by Canadian law. Second, the Court failed to inform the jury that consent to a given form of sexual touching does not extend to the use of any conceivable degree of force by one's sexual partner.[45]

The interveners argued that the trial Court uncritically admitted "irrelevant and prejudicial information" that was coupled with an inaccurate charge to the jury about the Canadian law of consent.[46] Together, these formed the errors in law the interveners sought to address:

- whether it is always incumbent on a trial judge to require an application to be made under s. 276 of the *Criminal Code* before allowing introduction into evidence of a sexual assault complainant's sexual history; and
- whether or not consent to a specific sexual activity is also consent, in law, to any degree of force a sexual partner uses while performing that activity.[47]

Notably, interveners' submissions are limited to addressing issues raised in the submitted grounds of appeal. As was stated at the motion to intervene hearing, the point of such interventions is "to be of assistance in the development of [Canadian] law."[48] Thus, notwithstanding the significant contributions such interventions have made to clarify Canadian law and ensure increased gender equality under the law, they pre-emptively erase space for Indigenous legal intervention that would necessarily go beyond the particulars of the trial court rooted in a colonial legal system. Indigenous feminism can only be added to such interventions, rather than such interventions being rooted, in their core, in Indigenous feminisms and in Indigenous law. Indigenous feminism, as Cheryl Suzack has explained elsewhere, "aspires to an intersectional framework that not only conceptualizes social justice as a goal of community empowerment, but also explains how gender relations matter to Indigenous emancipation and tribal sovereignty practice."[49]

The interveners were initially represented by Khullar and McLeod, who argued at the motion hearing that the intervention was in line with principles relating to intervening, including no rule against intervening nor against intervening in criminal cases. They further argued that the interveners would bring a different perspective to the court than could be provided by the Crown or the defence. Moreover, they suggested that the interveners were able to bring guidance to the public, which is essential to uphold the public nature of the court.

The defence, represented by Bottos, opposed the intervention, arguing that the interveners would bolster one side and go even further than the Crown in their arguments. Bottos argued that cases about constitutional issues are more likely to grant intervener status, while such interventions in criminal cases are considered a rarity. He argued that the prevailing view of the Alberta Court of Appeal is that the court "should be slow to do so." The defence indicated the intervention could derail the appeal hearing and bring the appeal into something far different, raising concern that it would become a "judicial inquiry," a concern that we analyse in detail in the following section. The defence further argued at this time that the defendant should not have to face a retrial based on the failings of the Crown in the initial trial, and that an intervention risked going further than the arguments put forward by the Crown, which risked opening a third route to conviction. In particular, the defence maintained that the grounds of reaching a manslaughter verdict were agreed upon by the Crown. According to Bottos, "eight times the Crown said only two routes to manslaughter": being too incapacitated to consent, and if Mr. Barton intended to cause bodily harm. The defence suggested that the interveners' argument opens a third possible route: that of objective foreseeable bodily harm, which the Crown did not raise at trial and should therefore be considered prejudicial. At the same time, it was noted that the obligation rests with the trial court to get justice right, even if both of the parties of the court do not. In such instances, onus rests on the trial judge. These arguments became a central focus of the subsequent appeal at the Supreme Court of Canada in which the majority decision called for the retrial of Barton on the lesser charge of manslaughter.

On 8 March 2016 Justice Berger granted LEAF and IAAW leave to intervene limited to a written submission: "I see no prejudice to the respondent, provided that the submissions of the interveners are confined to the proposed joint factum."[50] The appeal was heard on 6 September 2016. The LEAF and IAAW joint-intervener factum argued that the trial judge erred by failing to properly instruct the jury on the law of consent, and further erred in failing to apply the available legal protections intended to protect sexual assault victims in the trial process. The intervention took place within a context of systemic constraint imposed by the colonial system of criminal justice in Canada.

## Feminist Legal Interventions and Colonial Imperatives

In this section, we turn to further discussing the case, as well as analysing tensions with feminist legal interventions. We examine how feminist legal strategies can work to challenge gendered violence but can also uncomfortably and problematically uphold settler colonial imperatives that sustain hegemonic masculinities and institutions that are part of the structures of gendered colonial violence. Although our focus is the Canadian legal system, this institution is just one part of a broader arrangement of institutions that work to uphold settler colonialism. What is especially compelling about the legal system, though, is the way that it has the power of force behind it – that people can be literally locked away or be "set free." These settler laws of force, as Val Napoleon and Hadley Friedland have emphasized, have been attributed ultimate authority by settlers, undermining the ability of Indigenous legal orders to be acted on and practised in full.[51]

This section of the chapter raises more questions than it answers, as we hope to draw out constraints, contradictions, and possibilities that are under-discussed in feminist legal strategies. We first examine the issue that state law has operated, and continues to operate, as a male colonial system and that while feminist legal interveners have done an excellent job in showing how male privilege is upheld through the law, how settler colonialism is upheld is not as well addressed. Second, we discuss a problem with identification: that Indigenous laws are often not treated as law and are often treated as incapable of dealing with gendered violence, resulting in both state courts and feminist legal interveners overlooking the important legal tools available in Indigenous law. Lastly, we raise questions about whether state laws can safely and effectively have a role to play in relation to colonial gendered violence.

### *State Law as a White Heteropatriarchal Colonial System*

Feminist legal scholars have long identified that state law is a heteropatriarchal institution. Indigenous feminist scholars of law have further demonstrated that heteropatriarchy does not operate in isolation of colonialism and that state law is, to its core, a colonial institution[52] that is a mechanism that constrains Indigenous agency. For example, Lindberg, Campeau, and Campbell have noted that in sexual assault cases, "Indigenous women's lives have become irrelevant [in Canadian law], once by the people who harmed them, and again through their erasure by the judiciary."[53] Such dehumanizing further erases space for Indigenous legal agency, and as Napoleon has argued, the legal personhood of Indigenous women who have experienced violence is further denigrated when their "rights" are considered only in relation to settler laws, rather than also understanding their legal personhood within Indigenous laws.[54] All of this is not to suggest that Cindy Gladue and Indigenous women in general would automatically be treated perfectly in Indigenous legal orders, but that state law as a colonial heteropatriarchal institution was unable to read her humanity during the trial. At the same time, state law permitted and encouraged the humanization of Barton, who was given exceptions that are not permitted for a sexual assault victim. In the context of settler colonialism, he is "more legally cognizable to the judiciary" than the woman he killed.[55]

As noted, the defence portrayed Barton as a "common man" – a victim of circumstance. Bottos remarked to the jury:

> You've heard the Crown's theory based largely on Crown's experts, okay? … How about we get back to some reality? How about we address really what this man did and what he did not do? To do that, it's not just theory, it's just a common man in a very tough predicament, and I kindly ask you to hear him out.[56]

The "common man" trope is particularly noteworthy given the settler colonial legal system, which is premised on justice for the white, common man. The usage of this rhetoric works to depict Barton as relatable or at least as one for whom the jury should extend understanding. He is portrayed as sharing a universal experience as someone who is "just a man" and who is going through something difficult. While Bottos imagines his approach – and the court – as objective, his argument highlights a legal institution that is meant to work for white male settlers in the guise of being for everyone.

Barton is afforded exemptions that are rarely afforded to individuals victimized by sexual assault, such as challenges with recalling an event because of drinking. In Bottos's plea to the jury, he argues:

> I'm asking you to pay attention to him and appreciate him for who he is, as just a man who's going to try to tell what he recalls. *This just may happen to be – in fact I'm going to suggest to you – this will be the hardest couple of days of his life.* He's going to have to tell you about hiring Cindy Gladue. He's going to have to tell you about having sex with Cindy Gladue. He's going to have to tell you that he cheated on his wife. He's going to have to tell you about what he did and did not do. He's going to have to tell you about the panic and why he went away for 18 minutes. Okay? All of that is stuff that nobody would really want to admit to and therefore *is very hard to do for human beings*. But when you take the stand here, you tell the truth, the whole truth, and nothing but the truth. That's why, well, you take oaths, he'll take an oath … He's also going to be burdened with the fact that these events took place three years and eight months ago … Furthermore, some of these details will be recalled while he was actually drinking beer, okay? And it's hard to remember things from that long ago, and it's even harder when you're drinking. So all I'm asking you to do is understand the context.[57]

As this excerpt suggests, the jury is being asked in this instance to humanize Barton by referencing the difficulty he faces, and does so by dehumanizing Cindy Gladue – whose very relation to Barton in the context of sexualized labour is stigmatized and deemed shameful. Thus, while Cindy Gladue is represented and stereotyped as "the prostitute," Barton is portrayed as warranting the jury's concern for having to undergo the difficult work of disclosing having had extramarital sex with the stigmatized figure (i.e., "the prostitute"). Great care was taken to ensure white innocence was maintained, including framing Barton as the one who was harmed by the burden and inconvenience of the trial process, while Cindy Gladue was stigmatized, dehumanized, and depicted as deviant. Many argued that such dehumanization enabled the court to justify consideration of a portion of her pelvic region as evidence.[58]

What remains concealed in this plea of the defence is that stigmatizing portrayals of Indigenous women as "prostitutes" are a pivotal part of the nation-building narratives in Canada and in corresponding notions of purity and whiteness.[59] As Lindberg, Campeau, and Campbell emphasize of sexual assault cases against Indigenous women more generally, "the power to make decisions about what is central to a case and what is not is a power that contains both the potential of recognition and critical inclusion and of stereotyping and erasure."[60] This erasure of agency is highlighted by Napoleon's comment on *R v Barton*, which states that "Cindy Gladue was a legal agent and a person according to Cree and Métis law. She made the best decisions she could within the constraints of the power relations she was both within and a part of."[61] By suggesting the difficulty faced by Barton was having to openly express his interactions with *a person* dehumanized as "the prostitute," the defence and Court relied on engrained stereotypes about Indigenous women and about individuals who trade and sell sexual services. These stereotypes too often lead to the erasure of legal rights afforded to sex workers in cases of sexual assault.

In the broader context of settler colonial Canada, much like the jury here, we are intended to read Barton's experience through the well-established social script of the innocent white male settler. White male settler sexuality is constructed in a way that relies on entitlement to women's bodies – particularly Indigenous women's bodies as a part of settler conquest.[62] With these scripts in mind, we are intended to feel that Barton was justified in his actions, but to also feel sorry for him as being led astray from his wife (and white purity) by a racialized (impure) Indigenous woman and bearing the shame of having to disclose this narrative to his largely white male peers. Although this is not the context Mr. Bottos is directly referring to in his statement "all I'm asking you to do is understand the context," it is certainly how such statements must be read in the context of a settler colonial trial held for a white man in the death of an Indigenous woman.

Feminist legal strategies, including the collaborative Indigenous and feminist joint intervention, certainly drew attention to the ways that sexism, racism, and colonialism shaped the initial outcome in this case. Drawing on precedent set out by the Supreme Court of Canada regarding widespread systemic racism within the criminal justice system, the interveners argued that the trial court's characterizations of Cindy Gladue "invited the application of sexist and racist myths and stereotypes and may well have tainted the jury's evaluation of the evidence."[63] It is evident that the interveners approached the state legal system as an institution and mechanism that works to perpetuate gendered colonial violence. Yet interventions are also limited in many ways, as they ultimately must argue that the way forward is to improve the state legal system to be less racist, sexist, and colonial. In turn, that system's inherent role in maintaining these underlying root causes of violence goes unaddressed.

This tension of standing against gendered colonial violence while also naturalizing state law and invisibilizing Indigenous law is similarly found in some of the interventions in feminist legal studies. Doenmez, for instance, provides a thoughtful analysis of the violence against Cindy Gladue by bringing together Teju Cole's notion of the unmournable body and Judith Butler's work on ungrievable lives, to analyse the criminalization of Indigenous women generally and sex work specifically, yet she does not address the possibility of Indigenous laws and legal responses to the case.[64] This issue is commonly found in calls for cultural competency training that declares there is a need for broader contextual information that can be used in state courts, and call for settlers to do a better job at providing resources and including Indigenous people in Canadian society. What is often not said is how capitalism and state law are intertwined so as to ensure Indigenous dispossession from land and legal, political, and educational sovereignty, and how Indigenous women and people who are 2SLGBTQI+ experience these harms disproportionately. "Cultural competence" might be perceived as a nod to Indigenous law; however, as discussed further below, speaking about cultural competence is not the same as speaking directly about Indigenous law.

By considering feminist legal strategies in the wider context of settler colonialism and the production of state law as a colonial system upholding the priorities of white heteropatriarchy, we raise a number of questions required to uncover a decolonial praxis of intervention: How might the conversation and practice of law shift if feminist legal strategies were to move away from discussing only state law in relation to the practice of law? What constraints and possibilities exist in doing so, and how can these be engaged by feminist legal strategies, in conversation with Indigenous feminists and Indigenous legal practitioners and theorists?

*What Constitutes Law?*

In a 2015 news story, Edmonton journalist Paula Simons wrote the following:

> Is this justice for Cindy Gladue – poor, addicted, aboriginal, who died in a tub stained with her own blood? No wonder people want to protest. But the Crown and the courts can't be hostage to community outrage. Any future appeal of the Barton verdict can't be based on public anger or political pressure. It can only be based on the law.[65]

While reinforcing a stigmatizing portrayal, Simons also depicts "community outrage" as political and thus not part of law. She negates the reality that law is inherently political, and fails to comprehend that legal obligations are to a broader community (a public) and that community (public) outrage is a call for legal accountability. Second, she treats protestors (which we argue would be primarily perceived as Indigenous people, and secondarily as feminist) as overly emotional and therefore illogical, holding the "objective" state justice system "hostage" from being able to do its (more) important work. Third, she centres state law as *the* form of law that exists, and as the ultimate authority in what should happen next with the case.

These views of Simon's are part of a settler legal common sense wherein Indigenous law is too often perceived to not exist and individuals facing and resisting systemic colonial violence are dismissed in the name of political outrage.[66] With this approach, Indigenous peoples are treated as lawless or as having only custom, tradition, or culture. While Indigenous law includes customary law (so too does Canadian law), John Borrows explains that there are many additional sources of law in Indigenous legal orders, including deliberative law, positivistic law, natural law, and sacred law.[67] Napoleon and others have noted that treating Indigenous law as only custom treats Indigenous peoples as unthinkingly following rules from the past rather than as legal agents who draw on and reason with law and act together in the doing of law.[68] Indigenous law is also intimately connected with tradition and culture (as is Canadian law), but too frequently law gets lost in these discussions. Napoleon and Friedland emphasize that Indigenous "legal traditions encompass far more than just rules for conduct. They include formal laws and informal laws, worldviews, aspirations, pedagogies, processes and practices."[69] Friedland suggests that there is a need to shift from general discussions about culture to specific conversations about Indigenous laws and legal principles.[70] It is imperative to approach Indigenous law "seriously as *law*," as Napoleon and Friedland insist.[71]

The problem of Indigenous law not being taken seriously as law can be seen in the intervention both from the courts and in how the intervention was initially constructed. At the Alberta Court of Appeal, the defence raised similar concerns to those expressed by Simons: that the intervention could derail the appeal hearing and turn the appeal into a "judicial inquiry."

As noted above, LEAF-IAAW faced significant constraints. Justice Berger noted that social scientific evidence should be excluded as it risked diverting the focus from law to an inquiry. Khullar counter-argued that the interveners were merely seeking leave to intervene in the nature of twenty minutes of oral arguments and the submission of a factum; she conceded that social scientific evidence would not be included. Although perhaps strategic in ensuring the motion to intervene was successful, the limitation of social scientific evidence invisibilizes the context in which the court operates and reinforces troubling ideas about law as something that can be discussed separate from social context. This disconnect is not only an impossibility, as social norms shape how laws are articulated and interpreted, but it also works to remove important contextual information about gendered and racialized attitudes towards sexual assault, sex work, and the broader problem of gendered colonial violence and state complicity in violence against Indigenous women that are central in this case.

The message from Justice Berger, then, was to make *legal* arguments. We suggest that in outlining this expectation, Justice Berger was asking for *state legal* arguments in particular – an intervention that highlighted an interpretation of state laws from within the context of the state legal system. Connected to the conflation of Indigenous law with custom, tradition, and/or culture is the placing of Indigenous law under the realm of "social science." Although Indigenous law was not directly cited in the restrictions placed on the interveners, it is problematic that such a limitation discouraged the incorporation of Indigenous law in the interveners' arguments. This further reinforces the settler legal common sense of state laws as "hard" law and other forms of law as "soft" law and more about social and cultural norms.

Even if LEAF and IAAW initially wanted to include Indigenous law in their joint factum, it would not have been possible to do so as they were constrained by the instructions from Justice Berger to focus on state law. Such an argument, however, works to reinforce this problem of Indigenous law not being treated as law. One might ask why legal arguments drawing on Cree and Métis law were not submitted either solely or alongside the other arguments about state law made by the interveners. Given the restrictions guiding the interveners' actions, it is possible that the inclusion of Cree and Métis *legal* arguments may not have been seen as viable or as something that the court would accept. However, this also raises broader issues about the role of feminist legal strategies in challenging not only gendered violence but also settler colonial violence and erasures.

At Barton's appeal to the Supreme Court of Canada, the IAAW-LEAF interveners did incorporate Cree and Métis legal principles into their joint factum. Their statement of argument initiates with a section on "Wahkohtowin." They argue:

> In Nehiyawak (Cree) and Métis legal traditions, the doctrine of "wahkohtowin" refers to the "responsibilities and reciprocal obligations" we hold in relation to one another. The guiding legal principle of such

> inter-relatedness emphasizes that judicial processes, decisions, and actions have relational sources and consequences … The principle of *wahkohtowin* counteracts any impulse to artificially isolate this case from systemic discrimination within the justice system simply because the defendant is not the subject of this discrimination.[72]

Although this intervention speaks to Indigenous law in a way that could be interpreted as radical within the context of the Supreme Court, it remains restricted and predominately symbolic in its inclusion. In particular, Indigenous law is imagined in relation to social context – employed to contextualize the case as part of a broader form of systemic discrimination. We live in a society with multiple legal orders, and the appeal should not be based, as Simons suggests, only on "the law"; or if it was to be based on just one legal approach, then arguably a decolonial feminist legal strategy would contend that it should be based on the Indigenous laws of the territory or in line with the wishes of the Indigenous people involved.[73]

Of note, at the Supreme Court Jean Teillet's intervention on behalf of Women of the Métis Nation put to record the "violent indignity" and stark violation of human rights that occurred when a portion of Cindy Gladue's body was brought into the court as evidence at the initial trial. In her oral submission, Teillet highlighted the "unconscious" and "unacknowledged" nature of how prejudice operates within the administration of justice:[74]

> I wish to focus on one issue … and that is what the state did to Cindy Gladue during the trial process. And I am saying this because it really needs to be said and, believe me, five years ago I would never have thought we needed to say this. But, it needs to be said that the dismemberment of an Indigenous woman's body and the use of it as evidence in a trial was an assault by the state on an Indigenous woman and it has shocked the consciousness of the country and I say it has brought this system of justice into disrepute … Cindy Gladue's body, Indigenous women's bodies, our bodies in whole or in part, are not the price of justice.[75]

Nonetheless, at the Alberta Court of Appeal Justice Berger and council for the defence, Crown, and interveners all sought to avoid transforming the court into a "political theatre" based on the faulty premise that Canadian courts are apolitical, thereby invisibilizing the overt state violation of an Indigenous woman, the basic human rights of the deceased, and Indigenous legal orders on caring for the dead.

We recognize that there is perhaps too much at stake in trying to make Indigenous legal arguments in a case such as the appeal of *R v Barton*. The constraints imposed by the settler legal system on feminist and Indigenous legal interventions need to be acknowledged and challenged. What also concerns us, though, is what is at stake when feminist legal strategies do not fully engage (or even engage at all) with Indigenous laws, and what the implications are when this problem is not openly discussed. We contend that in the context of settler colonial courts, there are more limitations faced by feminist legal interventions in praxis than there are on academic feminist legal interventions (though the two are not disconnected), and it is troubling how commonly state laws are challenged in feminist legal studies *at the same time that they are naturalized*.

We wonder what feminist legal strategies would look like if feminist legal practitioners and scholars were more knowledgeable about Indigenous laws (ourselves included). We wonder about how feminist legal scholars can learn about Indigenous legal orders, what the legitimate processes are within a legal order, who would be appropriate to reach out to, and how to do this in a way that upholds Indigenous feminisms as well as Indigenous legal agency and sovereignty rather than burdening Indigenous people with having to teach settlers about Indigenous laws. It is also important to further consider the insights from Napoleon and Friedland that Indigenous laws not be romanticized, dichotomized, and defined as distinct from state laws – "reduced to over-simplified, idealized foils to critique state criminal justice systems within academic literature," as such an approach "does not allow us the intellectual room to imagine Indigenous laws beyond a symbolic resistance to colonialism."[76]

Part of the invisibilization of Indigenous laws and Indigenous women and girls' legal agency also involves the idea that Indigenous laws cannot or should not be used in situations of gendered violence. Indigenous laws are also often mischaracterized as potentially harmful to women or as working perfectly for Indigenous women (under the auspices of gender balance). All of these stereotypes about Indigenous laws impact their usability and undermine the complexities of law and gender in Indigenous people's lives and communities.[77] The idea that Indigenous laws should not be used because they are inherently sexist/dangerous stems from gendered racialized ideas about Indigenous masculinity,[78] but can also stem from a concern about the ways that sexism could operate in and through Indigenous legal interpretations and practices.[79] These critiques come from very different places. In drawing on Indigenous feminist legal theory, we take an approach here that

Indigenous laws are gendered: Indigenous law is embedded in social relations, which includes gendered power relations that can shape Indigenous legal practices, and this was a reality to contend with in the past as well as the present.[80] Rather than using this understanding of Indigenous laws as gendered to ignore or disregard Indigenous law (state laws also have this challenge of gendered power dynamics, yet state laws are not ignored), we approach Indigenous law, as Snyder, Napoleon, and Borrows have argued, as containing important resources for also challenging gendered oppression.[81]

*Should Feminist Legal Interveners Stop Using State Legal Institutions?*

By arguing that Indigenous law needs to be centred in feminist legal interventions, and by cautioning against state laws as reproducing colonial imperatives, we do not mean to suggest that state law should never be engaged. There are many reasons why people might use state law, an approach that attempts to draw on state and Indigenous laws, or only Indigenous legal responses. Regarding the use of state law, people might perceive that law to be more viable, given the power and authority granted to the Canadian legal system by settlers. State laws also might be the only option, even if one fundamentally disagrees with the imposition of settler laws and is troubled by the ways that oppression operates through them. Because the full ability to act on Indigenous laws and legal responses is undermined and denied by settler laws,[82] Indigenous laws might not be perceived as useful. Further, it should not be assumed that because someone is Indigenous they will want to use Indigenous law. The complex reasons that Indigenous people may or may not engage with Indigenous law, and the agency of families of missing and murdered Indigenous women and girls, needs to be respected. It is also pertinent to consider that some Indigenous legal practitioners and scholars might not want to work with feminist legal practitioners and scholars, given serious concerns about feminism as a settler politic that centres and works largely for white settler women. It would be vital, then, to consider how Indigenous feminist legal practices and strategies could shape and inform critically gendered approaches to Indigenous law and decolonial feminist politics.

At the same time, a decolonial transformation of the criminal justice system necessitates some forms of refusal and a centring of Indigenous legal orders to address the reproduction of a criminal justice system founded on the erasure of Indigenous people, especially Indigenous women, and that continues to reproduce widespread colonial gender violence and disproportionate criminalization of Indigenous women.

Carceral feminist practices are clearly limited when it comes to decolonial praxis, yet intersectional feminist legal interventions that move beyond such carceral approaches have also been unable to offer a transformative decolonial contribution. The issues and the questions that arise from centring Indigenous laws remain unaddressed. In instances of feminist legal interventions, we suggest that this is so partly because feminist legal strategies are both constrained by settler colonialism and heavily influenced by settlers who naturalize state laws and invisibilize or tokenize Indigenous laws in their approaches. If feminist legal studies took up decolonizing praxis, it is possible that such work could more meaningfully add to the ongoing efforts by Indigenous communities to challenge and undermine the constraints and falsehoods deployed by the Canadian legal system.

The treatment of Cindy Gladue and her family by the criminal justice system points to the reproduction of a system that was working in the very ways it was designed to – by proclaiming itself to be *the* legitimate authority in Indigenous territories while dehumanizing an Indigenous woman, state justice perpetuates masculinized settler colonial systems that reproduce the contexts in which colonial gendered violence occurs. Feminist legal interventions have tried to challenge this problem, but many of these approaches have themselves simultaneously reproduced settler colonial logics.

## Conclusion

LEAF's involvement in legal interventions has consistently aimed to advance equality in Canada.[83] Such interventions have shaped Canadian sexual assault laws and conceptions of consent.[84] Clearly, feminist legal interventions have provided important disruptions that have challenged practices of gendered violence and changed the criminal justice system in Canada. At the same time, as our analysis of the *R v Barton* case demonstrates, such interventions, while providing an important site of resistance, have been unable to unsettle the justice system to its core. As Maile Arvin, Eve Tuck, and Angie Morrill emphasize in their work on decolonizing feminism: "This is not to deny that the pursuit of civil rights within the nation-states that claim authority over Indigenous peoples is important and often vitally necessary, but simply to encourage ideas of social change and social justice that do not *only* look to the models of governance and community that settler nation-states are founded on."[85] As we challenge ourselves to think differently about feminist legal interventions, so too has LEAF noted the need for change, stating on their website that "LEAF recognizes the inherent limitations of Canadian colonial law in achieving justice for Indigenous women, girls, and 2SLGBTQQIA persons – and will take steps to better understand our relationship with the diverse Indigenous legal traditions that exist across Turtle Island."[86]

This chapter does not claim to advance an understanding of Cree and Métis law, how to use them, or what might be said about the intervention into *R v Barton* within different legal orders, although it is certainly clear that Cindy Gladue's body would not have been treated in Cree or Métis law as it was in state law. As Christa Big Canoe argues, for example, "in any other context this could be seen as desecration of her remains, but in this judicial process it was called preservation of evidence. It is simply horrific. It appears that the court did not contemplate Cindy's dignity, death rites, or any indigenous perspective on caring for the dead."[87] Moreover, as Napoleon illustrates, it is vital to understand Indigenous women's legal personhood as also residing in Indigenous laws.[88] While some praised the Supreme Court decision[89] for condemning the use of racist and sexist stereotypes about Indigenous women and calling on the courts to take account of the treatment of Indigenous persons within its trial processes, the court did not take up the erasure of Indigenous laws. As a statement by the IAAW and LEAF joint intervention suggests, the decision "in no way erases the anger, humiliation, and dehumanization of the lower court for the barbaric treatment of her body or the violation of Indigenous laws in caring for the deceased ... condemning stereotypes is important, but it cannot account for the level of violence Indigenous women experience in this system. We must continue to work together to dismantle the racism, sexism, and systemic discrimination perpetuated by the criminal legal system."[90]

The important analysis of Indigenous legal principles, reasoning, evidence, and decision-making in relation to cases of gendered violence against Indigenous women should be guided by practitioners of Indigenous law through direct engagement with Indigenous women, girls, trans, and two spirit+ persons, and communities most affected by the decisions made under these laws. Our discussion aims to spur further analysis of how feminist legal strategies can acknowledge the settler colonial constraints of the Canadian legal system while also finding ways to meaningfully challenge the ongoing invisibilization of Indigenous law and inform a decolonial feminist praxis of intervention. Although our analysis focused specifically on the case of *R v Barton* and the criminal justice system's dehumanizing treatment of Cindy Gladue and her family, this analysis raises issues that need to be discussed in relation to feminist legal strategies more widely.

NOTES

1 National Inquiry into Missing and Murdered Indigenous Women and Girls, *Reclaiming Power and Place: The Final Report of the National Inquiry into Missing and Murdered Indigenous Women and Girls* (2019) [MMIWG], online: <https://www.mmiwg-ffada.ca/final-report/>. The Supplementary Report of the MMIWG is entitled *A Legal Analysis of Genocide* (2019), online: <https://www.mmiwg-ffada.ca/wp-content/uploads/2019/06/Supplementary-Report_Genocide.pdf>.

2 See Eve Tuck & K Wayne Yang, "Decolonization Is Not a Metaphor" (2012) 1:1 Decolonization: Indigeneity, Education & Society 1; Glen Coulthard, *Red Skin, White Masks: Rejecting the Colonial Politics of Recognition* (Minneapolis: University of Minnesota Press, 2014); Audra Simpson, "The Chief's Two Bodies: Theresa Spence and the Gender of Settler Sovereignty: Unsettling Conversations" (Keynote delivered at Critical Race and Anti-Colonial Studies Conference, Edmonton, 4 November 2014), online: <https://vimeo.com/110948627>.

3 2019 SCC 33 (CanLII), [2019] 2 SCR 579. [*R v Barton*].

4 Katherine Blaze Carlson, "More than a Tragic Headline: Cindy Gladue Dreamt of a Happy Life," *Globe and Mail* (15 May 2015), online: <https://www.theglobeandmail.com/news/national/the-death-and-life-of-cindy-gladue/article24455472/>.

5 Madeline Smith, "Cindy Gladue's Family Reaffirms Her Dignity as Killer's Appeal Rescheduled," *Edmonton Journal* (6 January 2023), online: <https://shorturl.at/4fm9Q>; *R v Barton*, 2024 ABCA 34.

6 Beverly Jacobs, "Outrage of Injustice, Vaginas on Display: *R* v *Barton*" (2020) 3:1 J Crim and Forensic Studies 1.

7 We are not focusing on news stories because an analysis of media representations is beyond the conversation that we can address here. For a discussion about media representations of violence against Indigenous women, see Kristen Gilchrist, "'Newsworthy' Victims? Exploring Differences in Canadian Local Press Coverage of Missing/Murdered Aboriginal and White Women" (2010) 10:4 Feminist Media Studies 373. For specific analyses of media related to the case we are examining, see Brook Madigan, Natalie Snow & Arsala Khan, "#JusticeforCindy: a content analysis of legacy and social media" (2025) 23:2 Journal of Ethnicity in Criminal Justice 118; Kyllie Cripps, "Media constructions of Indigenous women in sexual assault cases: reflections from Australia and Canada" (2021) 33:3 Current Issues in Criminal Justice 300.

8 See Naomi Sayers, "#CindyGladue: I Want to Think about Ways that Do Not Rely on the Criminal (In)Justice System to Feel Safe," *kwetoday: fierce indigenous feminism* (26 March 2015), online (blog): <https://kwetoday.

com/2015/03/26/cindygladue-i-want-to-think-about-ways-that-do-not-rely-on-the-criminal-injustice-system-to-feel-safe/>; Tracey Lindberg, "Violence against Indigenous women and the Case of Cindy Gladue," *Rabble* (30 March 2015), online (blog): <http://rabble.ca/blogs/bloggers/views-expressed/2015/03/violence-against-indigenous-women-and-case-cindy-gladue>; Erica Violet Lee, "For Cindy, For Ourselves: Healing in the Context of Colonial Gender Violence," *Moontime Warrior* (2 April 2015), online (blog): <https://moontimewarrior.com/2015/04/02/for-cindy-for-ourselves-healing-in-the-context-of-colonial-gender-violence/>; Christa Big Canoe, "Cindy Gladue Suffered Her Last Indignity at Murder Trial," *CBC News* (2 April 2015), online: <https://www.cbc.ca/news/indigenous/cindy-gladue-suffered-her-last-indignity-at-murder-trial-1.3019500>; Sarah Hunt & Naomi Sayers, "Cindy Gladue Case Sends a Chilling Message to Indigenous Women" *Globe and Mail* (25 March 2015), online: <https://www.theglobeandmail.com/opinion/cindy-gladue-case-sends-a-chilling-message-to-indigenous-women/article23609986/>.

9 Working Group Seeking Justice for Cindy Gladue, *Our Breaking Point: Canada's Violation of Rights in Life and Death* (community-based resource book) (2016), online: <https://justiceforcindygladue.files.wordpress.com/2016/08/ourbreakingpoint-cindygladue.pdf>.

10 Sherene H Razack, "Gendering Disposability" (2016) 28:2 Cdn J Women and the Law 285; Caroline Fidan Tyler Doenmez, "The Unmournable Body of Cindy Gladue: On Corporeal Integrity and Grievability" in DM Lavell-Harvard & J Brant, eds, *Forever Loved: Exposing the Hidden Crises of Missing and Murdered Indigenous Women and Girls in Canada* (Brantford, ON: Demeter, 2016) 111; Emma Cunliffe, "Far from Equal: Indigeneity, Gender and Reasonable Doubt in *R* v *Barton*" (Paper delivered at the 2019 Canadian Law and Society Association annual conference, Vancouver, 3 June 2019) [unpublished]; Cunliffe, "Gendered Racial Violence: *R v Barton* and the Death of Cindy Gladue" (Centre for Feminist Legal Studies lecture series, delivered at Peter A Allard School of Law, UBC, 8 March 2016), online: <https://mediasitemob1.mediagroup.ubc.ca/Mediasite/Play/51124fe74ce64bd29f8b4fedcf938b8d1d>; Julie Kaye, "Reconciliation in the Context of Settler-Colonial Gender Violence: 'How Do We Reconcile with an Abuser?'" (2016) 53:4 Canadian Rev Sociology 461. Our focus is on earlier feminist scholarship and interventions; however, we acknowledge additional work that includes analyses of *R v Barton* has been published, see Rashmee Singh & Dawn Moore, "Bare death: femicide, forensics and the necropolitics of the corpse" in Marie-Andrée Jacob & Anna Kirkland, eds, *Research Handbook on Socio-Legal Studies of Medicine and Law*, vol 808 (Northampton, MA: Edward Elgar, 2020) 287; Janine Benedet, "The Role

of Motive in Sexual Assault Trials" (2022) 34:2 Cdn J Women and the Law 331.

11 *R v Barton, supra* note 3 at para 210.

12 *R v Barton,* 2013 ABQB 673; *R v Barton,* 2015 ABQB 159; *R v Barton,* 2016 ABCA 68; *R v Barton,* 2017 ABCA 216; *R v Barton,* 2019 SCC 33; *R v Barton* (2016), ABCA 68 (Factum of the Interveners: Institute for the Advancement of Aboriginal Women and the Women's Legal Education and Action Fund), online: <https://www.leaf.ca/wp-content/uploads/2016/05/2016-05-02-final-LEAF-IAAW-factum-R-v-Barton-ABCA.pdf>; *R v Barton* (2019), SCC 33 (Factum of the Interveners: Institute for the Advancement of Aboriginal Women and the Women's Legal Education and Action Fund), online: <https://www.scc-csc.ca/WebDocuments-DocumentsWeb/37769/FM100_Intervener_LEAF.pdf>. In our analysis, we analyzed the *R v Barton* trial transcripts, the transcripts from the Alberta Court of Appeal and the appeal at the Supreme Court of Canada, notes taken during the appeal proceedings, as well as the factums submitted by LEAF and IAAW.

13 *R v Barton,* 2016 ABCA 68; *R v Barton,* 2017 ABCA 216; *R v Barton* (2016), ABCA 68 (Factum of the Interveners: Institute for the Advancement of Aboriginal Women and the Women's Legal Education and Action Fund), *supra* note 12.

14 *R v Barton* (2019), SCC 33 (Factum of the Interveners: Institute for the Advancement of Aboriginal Women and the Women's Legal Education and Action Fund) *supra* note 12.

15 Audra Simpson, "The State Is a Man: Theresa Spence, Loretta Saunders and the Gender of Settler Sovereignty" in Sunera Thobani, ed, *Coloniality and Racial (In)Justice in the University* (Toronto: University of Toronto Press, 2022) 136 at 136.

16 See Big Canoe, *supra* note 8; Blaze Carlson, *supra* note 4; Hunt & Sayers, *supra* note 8; Julie Kaye, "Justice for Cindy Gladue Demands an Appeal of Recent Verdict, Knowledge Mobilization in Area of Sex Work, Violence against Indigenous Women, Colonial Gender Violence," *Edmonton Journal* (26 March 2015), online: <https://edmontonjournal.com/opinion/opinion-justice-for-cindy-gladue-demands-an-appeal-of-recent-verdict>; Josephine Savarese, "Challenging Colonial Norms and Attending to Presencing in Stories of Missing and Murdered Indigenous Women" (2017) 29:1 Cdn J Women and the Law 157; Doenmez, *supra* note 10 at 111; Razack, *supra* note 10; Cunliffe, *supra* note 10.

17 "Indigenous law" here refers to Indigenous peoples' own legal orders and systems (e.g., Cree law), whereas "Aboriginal law" refers to state laws about Indigenous people.

18 *R* v *Barton, supra* note 3 at 33.

19 See Amnesty International, Canada, *Stolen Sisters: A Human Rights Response to Discrimination and Violence against Indigenous Women in Canada* (2004), online: <https://www.amnesty.ca/sites/amnesty/files/amr200032004enstolensisters.pdf>; Cindy Holmes, Sarah Hunt & Amy Piedalue, "Violence, Colonialism, and Space: Towards a Decolonizing Dialogue" (2014) 14:2 ACME: An International E-Journal for Critical Geographies 539; RCMP, *Missing and Murdered Aboriginal Women: A National Operational Overview* (2014), online: <http://www.rcmp-grc.gc.ca/en/missing-and-murdered-aboriginal-women-national-operational-overview>; Sarah Deer, *The Beginning and End of Rape: Confronting Sexual Violence in Native America* (Minneapolis: University of Minnesota Press, 2015); Amber Dean, *Remembering Vancouver's Disappeared Women: Settler Colonialism and the Difficulty of Inheritance* (Toronto: University of Toronto Press, 2015); Kim Anderson, Maria Campbell & Christi Belcourt, eds, *Keetsahnak: Our Missing and Murdered Indigenous Sisters* (Edmonton: University of Alberta Press, 2018); Legal Strategy Coalition on Violence Against Indigenous Women, "Ongoing Systemic Inequalities and Violence against Indigenous Women in Canada" (discussion paper presented to UN Special Rapporteur on Violence against Women, Its Causes and Consequences, 20 April 2018), online: <https://www.amnesty.ca/sites/amnesty/files/LSC%20Discussion%20Paper%20to%20Special%20Rapporteur%20-%20Final.pdf>; MMIWG, *supra* note 1.

20 See Jennifer Nez Denetdale, "Chairmen, Presidents, and Princesses: The Navajo Nation, Gender, and the Politics of Tradition" (2006) 21:1 Wicazo Sa Rev 9; Simpson, *supra* note 15; Deer, *supra* note 19.

21 Patricia Monture, "The Right of Inclusion: Aboriginal Rights and/or Aboriginal Women?" in Kerry Wilkins, ed, *Advancing Aboriginal Claims* (Saskatoon: Purich, 2004) 39; Twila L. Perry, "Family Law, Feminist Legal Theory, and the Problem of Racial Hierarchy" in Martha Albertson Fineman, ed, *Transcending the Boundaries of Law: Generations of Feminism and Legal Theory* (New York: Routledge, 2011) 243; Rakhi Ruparelia, "Legal Feminism and the Post-Racism Fantasy" (2016) 26:1 Cdn J Women and the Law 81; Emily Snyder, "Indigenous Feminist Legal Theory" (2014) 26:2 Cdn J Women and the Law 365.

22 See Manitoba Public Inquiry into the Administration of Justice and Aboriginal People, *Report of the Aboriginal Justice Inquiry of Manitoba: The Justice System and Aboriginal People* (Winnipeg: Government of Manitoba, 1999); British Columbia Missing Women Commission of Inquiry, *Forsaken: The Report of the Missing Women Commission of Inquiry* (Victoria: Government of British Columbia, 2012), online: <http://www.missingwomeninquiry.ca/wp-content/uploads/2010/10/Forsaken-ES-web-RGB.pdf>; Institute for the Advancement of

Aboriginal Women (IAAW) and the Women's Legal Education and Action Fund (LEAF), *IAAW–LEAF Joint Submission to the Independent Review of Circumstances Surrounding the Treatment of "Angela Cardinal" in* R. v. Blanchard (15 October 2017), online: <https://www.leaf.ca/wp-content/uploads/2018/02/Cardinal-Inquiry-IAAW-and-LEAF-Final-Submission-Oct-15.pdf>.

23 Coulthard, *supra* note 2 at 6.

24 See Snyder, *supra* note 21. Naomi Sayers has since written about this concept, extending the analysis to include questions about sex work: Sayers, "Doing/Undoing Justice: Violence through Colonial Law," *kwetoday: fierce indigenous feminism* (6 July 2016), online (blog): <https://kwetoday.com/2016/07/06/doingundoing-justice-violence-through-colonial-law/>.

25 Emily Snyder, *Gender, Power, and Representations of Cree Law* (Vancouver: UBC Press, 2018); Emily Snyder, Val Napoleon & John Borrows, "Gender and Violence: Drawing on Indigenous Legal Resources" (2015) 48:2 UBC L Rev 593.

26 Gordon Christie, "Indigenous Legal Theory: Some Initial Considerations" in Benjamin J Richardson, Shin Imai & Kent McNeil, eds, *Indigenous Peoples and the Law: Comparative and Critical Perspectives* (Oxford: Hart, 2009) 195. Indigenous legal theory can be used to examine both Indigenous and state laws together. See Tracey Lindberg, Priscilla Campeau & Maria Campbell, "Indigenous Women and Sexual Assault in Canada," in Elizabeth Sheehy, ed, *Sexual Assault in Canada: Law, Legal Practice and Women's Activism* (Ottawa: University of Ottawa Press, 2012) 87; John Borrows, *Freedom and Indigenous Constitutionalism* (Toronto: University of Toronto Press, 2016); Borrows, *Canada's Indigenous Constitution* (Toronto: University of Toronto Press, 2010).

27 Snyder, *supra* note 21.

28 Snyder, Napoleon & Borrows, *supra* note 25.

29 Sarah Deer, "(En)Gendering Indian Law: Indigenous Feminist Legal Theory in the United States" (2019) 31:1 Yale J Law and Feminism 1.

30 Sunera Thobani, *Exalted Subjects: Studies in the Making of Race and Nation in Canada* (Toronto: University of Toronto Press, 2007); Tuck and Yang, *supra* note 2; Simpson, *supra* note 2;" Coulthard, *supra* note 2. In relation to this case, see Kaye, *supra* note 10.

31 Kaye, *supra* note 10. Thobani explains "'as was the case with the deployment of the concept of *terra nullius* to claim European legal entitlement over territories emptied of Aboriginal presence, a corresponding *humanitus nullius* was deployed … to empty Native peoples of their human status'" (quoted in Kaye, *supra* note 10 at 462). See also Thobani, *supra* note 30 at 50.

32 "Statement from the Family of Cindy Gladue" (read at Holding Space for Cindy Gladue Teach-In, Wahkohtowin Law and Governance Lodge, University of Alberta, 5 January 2023).

33 *Barton* (2016), ABCA 68 (Factum of the Interveners: Institute for the Advancement of Aboriginal Women and the Women's Legal Education and Action Fund), *supra* note 12.

34 Lindberg, Campeau & Campbell, *supra* note 26 at 108.

35 *Criminal Code*, RSC 1985, c C-46.

36 Regarding Indigenous representation on the jury, Will Willier identified that one person was Asian and one person was Black. None were Indigenous. See Kim Wheeler, "Cindy Gladue Case: Not Guilty Verdict Prompts Rallies Calling for Appeal," CBC News (31 March 2015), online: <https://www.cbc.ca/news/indigenous/cindy-gladue-case-not-guilty-verdict-prompts-rallies-calling-for-appeal-1.3016603>.

37 *R v Barton*, 2015 ABQB 159.

38 *Ibid* at 50. Instructions to the Jury Delivered by Mr. Justice R.A. Graesser, 17 March 2015. The jury charge indicates that the eleven-centimetre wound was the most significant wound, but it was not the only wound to her vaginal wall.

39 *Ibid* at 15.

40 *Ibid* at 737.

41 *Ibid* at 105.

42 At the time of writing, this violation continues as this portion of Cindy Gladue's body remains in evidence.

43 *R v Barton*, 2015 ABQB 159 at 1761.

44 *Ibid* at 673.

45 IAAW/LEAF Barton Factum 2016, *supra* note 12 at 1.

46 *Ibid* at 1–2.

47 *Ibid*.

48 This section relies on notes taken by Julie Kaye at the court proceedings on 24 February 2016.

49 Cheryl Suzack, *Indigenous Women's Writing and the Cultural Study of Law* (Toronto: University of Toronto Press, 2017) at 12.

50 *R v Barton* 2016 ABCA 68 (Can II).

51 Val Napoleon & Hadley Friedland, "Indigenous Legal Traditions: Roots to Renaissance" in Markus D Dubber and Tatjana Hörnle, eds, *The Oxford Handbook on Criminal Law* (Oxford: Oxford University Press, 2014) 225. Regarding our point that there are few options but to use Canadian law, we acknowledge that with criminal law, no one engages state law by choice. We contend, though, that Indigenous people *should* have a choice to not have state legal mechanisms imposed on them, given the existence

of Indigenous legal orders and the distinct and inherent legal rights of Indigenous peoples to use and draw on those legal orders.

52 See Patricia Monture-Angus, *Thunder in my Soul* (Halifax: Fernwood, 1995); Irene Watson, "Aboriginal Women's Laws and Lives: How Might We Keep Growing the Law?" (2007) 26:1 Australian Feminist LJ 95; Deer, *supra* note 19.

53 Lindberg, Campeau & Campbell, *supra* note 26 at 108.

54 Val Napoleon, "Gitxsan Legal Personhood: Gendered" in Austin Sarat, George Pavlich & Richard Mailey, eds, *Interrupting the Legal Person*, Studies in Law, Politics, and Society, vol 87A (Bingley, UK: Emerald, 2022) 19.

55 Lindberg, Campeau & Campbell, *supra* note 26 at 103.

56 *R v Barton*, 2015 ABQB 159 at 1086.

57 *Ibid* at 1085, emphasis added.

58 See Doenmez, *supra* note 10; Razack, *supra* note 10; Big Canoe, *supra* note 8; Hunt and Sayers, *supra* note 8.

59 Lesley Erickson, *Westward Bound: Sex Violence, the Law, and the Making of a Settler Society* (Vancouver: University of British Columbia Press, 2011).

60 Lindberg, Campeau & Campbell, *supra* note 26 at 108.

61 Napoleon, *supra* note 54 at 12.

62 Doenmez, *supra* note 10 at 117–118.

63 *R v Barton* 2016 (Factum of Interveners: IAAW/LEAF) *supra* note 12 at 19.

64 Doenmez, *supra* note 10.

65 Paula Simons, "Public Outrage over Cindy Gladue Verdict No Legal Basis for Appeal," *Edmonton Journal* (31 March 2015), online: <https://edmontonjournal.com/news/local-news/simons-public-outrage-over-cindy-gladue-verdict-no-legal-basis-for-appeal>.

66 Mark Rifkin writes of "settler common sense" that "the phrase suggests the ways the legal and political structures that enable non-Native access to Indigenous territories come to be lived as given, as simply the unmarked, generic conditions of possibility for occupancy, association, history, and personhood." Rifkin, "Settler Common Sense" (2013) 3:3–4 Settler Colonial Studies 322. We use the phrase "settler legal common sense" to emphasize the naturalization of settler laws and to stress that this "common sense" is based on a male settler subject.

67 See Borrows, *Freedom and Indigenous Constitutionalism*, *supra* note 26.

68 Val Napoleon, "Creating Space for the Project of Indigenous Law within Political Science" (Paper delivered at the Canadian Political Science Association 84th annual conference, Edmonton, 15 June 2012) [unpublished].

69 Napoleon & Friedland, *supra* note 51 at 230–231.
70 Hadley Friedland, "Reflective Frameworks: Methods for Accessing, Understanding and Applying Indigenous Laws" (2012) 11:1 Indigenous LJ 29.
71 Napoleon & Friedland, *supra* note 51 at 240.
72 *R v Barton* (2019), SCC 33 (Factum of the Interveners: Institute for the Advancement of Aboriginal Women and the Women's Legal Education and Action Fund), *supra* note 12 at 1–2.
73 See also Borrows, *Freedom and Indigenous Constitutionalism, supra* note 26 on gender and Indigenous laws as treaty rights.
74 Citing L'HeureuxDubé J in *R* v *Osolin*, [1993] SCJ No 135; [1993] 4 SCR 595, online: <https://scc-csc.lexum.com/scc-csc/scc-csc/en/item/1092/index.do>.
75 Jean Teillet, oral submission to the SCC on behalf of the Women of the Métis Nation. See Factum of the Intervener of Women of the Métis Nation, online: <https://www.scc-csc.ca/WebDocuments-DocumentsWeb/37769/FM150_Women-Metis_Intervener.pdf>.
76 Napoleon & Friedland, *supra* note 51 at 239.
77 Snyder, *supra* note 25.
78 For a discussion of stereotypes about Indigenous men, see Sam McKegney, "Warriors, Healers, Lovers, and Leaders: Colonial Impositions on Indigenous Male Roles and Responsibilities" in Jason A. Laker, ed, *Canadian Perspectives on Men and Masculinities* (Oxford: Oxford University Press, 2012) 241.
79 See Sarah Deer, "Decolonizing Rape Law: A Native Feminist Synthesis of Safety and Sovereignty" (2009) 24:2 Wicazo Sa Rev 149.
80 See Snyder, Napoleon & Borrows, *supra* note 25.
81 *Ibid.*
82 Napoleon & Friedland, *supra* note 51.
83 LEAF, "Our Work," online: <https://www.leaf.ca/our-work/>. Accessed 19 May 2025.
84 For example, *R v Ewanchuck,* [1999] 1 SCR 330 that replaced the standard of consent to only "yes means yes"; *R v Darrach,* [2000] 2 SCR 443 that ensured sexual history cannot be used to imply consent in sexual assault cases; *R v JA,* [2011] SCR 440 that necessitates active, ongoing consent to sexual activity.
85 Maile Arvin, Eve Tuck & Angie Morrill, "Decolonizing Feminism: Challenging Connection between Settler Colonialism and Heteropatriarchy" (2013) 25:1 Feminist Formations 16.
86 LEAF, "Issue Area: Indigenous Rights and Law," online: <https://www.leaf.ca/issue-area/indigenous-rights-and-aboriginal-law/> (accessed 19 May 2025).

87 Big Canoe quoted in Working Group Seeking Justice for Cindy Gladue, *supra* note 9 at 14.
88 Napoleon, *supra* note 54.
89 *R v Barton*, 2019 SCC 33.
90 LEAF, Case News, "IAAW and LEAF React to the Supreme Court of Canada Judgment in R v Barton," online: <https://www.leaf.ca/iaaw-and-leaf-react-to-the-supreme-court-of-canada-judgment-in-r-v-barton/> [accessed 24 May 2019].

## SOURCES CITED

Amnesty International, Canada. *Stolen Sisters: A Human Rights Response to Discrimination and Violence against Indigenous Women in Canada* (2004), online: <https://www.amnesty.ca/sites/amnesty/files/amr200032004enstolensisters.pdf>.

Anderson, Kim, Maria Campbell & Christi Belcourt, eds, *Keetsahnak: Our Missing and Murdered Indigenous Sisters* (Edmonton: University of Alberta Press, 2018).

Arvin, Maile, Eve Tuck & Angie Morrill. "Decolonizing Feminism: Challenging Connection between Settler Colonialism and Heteropatriarchy" (2013) 25:1 Feminist Formations 16.

Benedet, Janine. "The Role of Motive in Sexual Assault Trials" (2022) 34:2 Cdn J Women and the Law 331.

Big Canoe, Christa. "Cindy Gladue Suffered Her Last Indignity at Murder Trial," *CBC News* (2 April 2015), online: <https://www.cbc.ca/news/indigenous/cindy-gladue-suffered-her-last-indignity-at-murder-trial-1.3019500>.

Blaze Carlson, Katherine. "More than a Tragic Headline: Cindy Gladue Dreamt of a Happy Life," *Globe and Mail* (15 May 2015), online: <https://www.theglobeandmail.com/news/national/the-death-and-life-of-cindy-gladue/article24455472/>.

Borrows, John. *Canada's Indigenous Constitution* (Toronto: University of Toronto Press, 2010).

Borrows, John. *Freedom and Indigenous Constitutionalism* (Toronto: University of Toronto Press, 2016).

British Columbia Missing Women Commission of Inquiry. *Forsaken: The Report of the Missing Women Commission of Inquiry* (Victoria: Government of British Columbia, 2012), online: <http://www.missingwomeninquiry.ca/wp-content/uploads/2010/10/Forsaken-ES-web-RGB.pdf>.

Christie, Gordon. "Indigenous Legal Theory: Some Initial Considerations" in Benjamin J Richardson, Shin Imai & Kent McNeil, eds, *Indigenous Peoples and the Law: Comparative and Critical Perspectives* (Oxford: Hart, 2009) 195.

Coulthard, Glen. *Red Skin, White Masks: Rejecting the Colonial Politics of Recognition* (Minneapolis: University of Minnesota Press, 2014).

Cripps, Kyllie. "Media Constructions of Indigenous Women in Sexual Assault Cases: Reflections from Australia and Canada" (2021) 33:3 Current Issues in Criminal Justice 300.

Cunliffe, Emma. "Far from Equal: Indigeneity, Gender and Reasonable Doubt in R v Barton" (Paper delivered at the 2019 Canadian Law and Society Association annual conference, Vancouver, 3 June 2019) [unpublished].

Cunliffe, Emma. "Gendered Racial Violence: *R v Barton* and the Death of Cindy Gladue" (Centre for Feminist Legal Studies lecture series, delivered at Peter A Allard School of Law, UBC, 8 March 2016), online: <https://allard.ubc.ca/sites/default/files/2020-06/CFLS%20Lectures%202015-2016.pdf>.

Dean, Amber. *Remembering Vancouver's Disappeared Women: Settler Colonialism and the Difficulty of Inheritance* (Toronto: University of Toronto Press, 2015).

Deer, Sarah. "Decolonizing Rape Law: A Native Feminist Synthesis of Safety and Sovereignty" (2009) 24:2 Wicazo Sa Rev 149.

Deer, Sarah. *The Beginning and End of Rape: Confronting Sexual Violence in Native America* (Minneapolis: University of Minnesota Press, 2015).

Deer, Sarah. "(En)Gendering Indian Law: Indigenous Feminist Legal Theory in the United States" (2019) 31:1 Yale J Law and Feminism 1.

Doenmez, Caroline Fidan Tyler. "The Unmournable Body of Cindy Gladue: On Corporeal Integrity and Grievability" in DM Lavell-Harvard & J Brant, eds, *Forever Loved: Exposing the Hidden Crises of Missing and Murdered Indigenous Women and Girls in Canada* (Brantford, ON: Demeter, 2016) 111.

Erickson, Lesley. *Westward Bound: Sex Violence, the Law, and the Making of a Settler Society* (Vancouver: University of British Columbia Press, 2011).

Friedland, Hadley. "Reflective Frameworks: Methods for Accessing, Understanding and Applying Indigenous Laws" (2012) 11:1 *Indigenous LJ* 29.

Gilchrist, Kristen. "'Newsworthy' Victims? Exploring Differences in Canadian Local Press Coverage of Missing/Murdered Aboriginal and White Women" (2010) 10:4 Feminist Media Studies 373.

Gladue Family. "Statement from the Family of Cindy Gladue" (read at Holding Space for Cindy Gladue Teach-In, Wahkohtowin Law and Governance Lodge, University of Alberta, Edmonton, 5 January 2023).

Holmes, Cindy, Sarah Hunt & Amy Piedalue. "Violence, Colonialism, and Space: Towards a Decolonizing Dialogue" (2014) 14:2 ACME: An International E-Journal for Critical Geographies 539.

Hunt, Sarah & Naomi Sayers. "Cindy Gladue Case Sends a Chilling Message to Indigenous Women," *Globe and Mail* (25 March 2015), online: <https://www.theglobeandmail.com/opinion/cindy-gladue-case-sends-a-chilling-message-to-indigenous-women/article23609986/>.

Institute for the Advancement of Aboriginal Women (IAAW) and the Women's Legal Education and Action Fund (LEAF). *IAAW–LEAF Joint Submission to the Independent Review of Circumstances Surrounding the Treatment of "Angela Cardinal" in* R. v. Blanchard (15 October 2017), online: <https://www.leaf.ca/wp-content/uploads/2018/02/Cardinal-Inquiry-IAAW-and-LEAF-Final-Submission-Oct-15.pdf>.

Jacobs, Beverly. "Outrage of Injustice, Vaginas on Display: *R v Barton*" (2020) 3:1 J Crim and Forensic Studies 1.

Kaye, Julie. "Justice for Cindy Gladue Demands an Appeal of Recent Verdict, Knowledge Mobilization in Area of Sex Work, Violence against Indigenous Women, Colonial Gender Violence," *Edmonton Journal* (26 March 2015), online: <https://edmontonjournal.com/opinion/opinion-justice-for-cindy-gladue-demands-an-appeal-of-recent-verdict>.

Kaye, Julie. "Reconciliation in the Context of Settler-Colonial Gender Violence: 'How Do We Reconcile with an Abuser?'" (2016) 53:4 Cdn Rev Sociology 461.

LEAF. "IAAW and LEAF React to the Supreme Court of Canada Judgment in R v Barton," online: https://www.leaf.ca/iaaw-and-leaf-react-to-the-supreme-court-of-canada-judgment-in-r-v-barton/ [accessed 24 May 2019].

LEAF. "Issue Area: Indigenous Rights and Law," online: < https://www.leaf.ca/issue-area/indigenous-rights-and-aboriginal-law/> [accessed 19 May 2015].

LEAF. "Our Work," online: < https://www.leaf.ca/our-work/> [accessed 19 May 2025].

Lee, Erica Violet. "For Cindy, For Ourselves: Healing in the Context of Colonial Gender Violence," *Moontime Warrior* (2 April 2015), online (blog): <https://moontimewarrior.com/2015/04/02/for-cindy-for-ourselves-healing-in-the-context-of-colonial-gender-violence/>.

Legal Strategy Coalition on Violence Against Indigenous Women (LSC). "Ongoing Systemic Inequalities and Violence against Indigenous Women in Canada" (discussion paper presented to UN Special Rapporteur on Violence against Women, Its Causes and Consequences, 20 April 2018), online: <https://www.amnesty.ca/sites/amnesty/files/LSC %20Discussion%20Paper%20to%20Special%20Rapporteur%20-%20Final.pdf>.

Lindberg, Tracey. "Violence against Indigenous Women and the Case of Cindy Gladue," *Rabble* (30 March 2015), online (blog): <http://rabble.ca/blogs/bloggers/views-expressed/2015/03/violence-against-indigenous-women-and-case-cindy-gladue>.

Lindberg, Tracey, Priscilla Campeau & Maria Campbell. "Indigenous Women and Sexual Assault in Canada" in Elizabeth Sheehy, ed, *Sexual Assault in Canada: Law, Legal Practice and Women's Activism* (Ottawa: University of Ottawa Press, 2012) 87.

Madigan, Brook, Natalie Snow & Arsala Khan. "#JusticeforCindy: A Content Analysis of Legacy and Social Media" (2025) 23:2 J Ethnicity in Criminal Justice 118.

Manitoba Public Inquiry into the Administration of Justice and Aboriginal People. *Report of the Aboriginal Justice Inquiry of Manitoba: The Justice System and Aboriginal People* (Winnipeg: Government of Manitoba, 1991).

McKegney, Sam. "Warriors, Healers, Lovers, and Leaders: Colonial Impositions on Indigenous Male Roles and Responsibilities" in Jason A. Laker, ed, *Canadian Perspectives on Men and Masculinities* (Oxford: Oxford University Press, 2012) 241.

Monture, Patricia. "The Right of Inclusion: Aboriginal Rights and/or Aboriginal Women?" in Kerry Wilkins, ed, *Advancing Aboriginal Claims* (Saskatoon: Purich, 2004) 39.

Monture-Angus, Patricia. *Thunder in my Soul* (Halifax: Fernwood, 1995).

Napoleon, Val. "Creating Space for the Project of Indigenous Law within Political Science" (Paper delivered at the Canadian Political Science Association 84th annual conference, University of Alberta, Edmonton, AB, 15 June 2012) [unpublished].

Napoleon, Val. "Gitxsan Legal Personhood: Gendered" in Austin Sarat, George Pavlich & Richard Mailey, eds, *Interrupting the Legal Person*, Studies in Law, Politics, and Society, vol 87A (Bingley, UK: Emerald, 2022) 19.

Napoleon, Val & Hadley Friedland. "Indigenous Legal Traditions: Roots to Renaissance" in Markus D Dubber and Tatjana Hörnle, eds, *The Oxford Handbook on Criminal Law* (Oxford: Oxford University Press, 2014) 225.

National Inquiry into Missing and Murdered Indigenous Women and Girls. *Reclaiming Power and Place: The Final Report of the National Inquiry into Missing and Murdered Indigenous Women and Girls* (Ottawa: MMIWG, 2019), online: <https://www.mmiwg-ffada.ca/final-report/>.

National Inquiry into Missing and Murdered Indigenous Women and Girls. *Supplementary Report of the MMIWG: A Legal Analysis of Genocide*, (2019), online: <https://www.mmiwg-ffada.ca/wp-content/uploads/2019/06/Supplementary-Report_Genocide.pdf>.

Nez Denetdale, Jennifer. "Chairmen, Presidents, and Princesses: The Navajo Nation, Gender, and the Politics of Tradition" (2006) 21:1 Wicazo Sa Rev 9.

Perry, Twila L. "Family Law, Feminist Legal Theory, and the Problem of Racial Hierarchy" in Martha Albertson Fineman, ed, *Transcending the Boundaries of Law: Generations of Feminism and Legal Theory* (New York: Routledge, 2011) 243.

Razack, Sherene H. "Gendering Disposability" (2016) 28:2 Cdn J Women and the Law 285.

RCMP. *Missing and Murdered Aboriginal Women: A National Operational Overview* (2014), online: <http://www.rcmp-grc.gc.ca/en/missing-and-murdered-aboriginal-women-national-operational-overview>.

Rifkin, Mark. "Settler Common Sense" (2013) 3:3–4 Settler Colonial Studies 322.

Ruparelia, Rakhi. "Legal Feminism and the Post-Racism Fantasy" (2016) 26:1 Cdn J Women and the Law 81.

Savarese, Josephine. "Challenging Colonial Norms and Attending to Presencing in Stories of Missing and Murdered Indigenous Women" (2017) 29:1 Cdn J Women and the Law 157.

Sayers, Naomi. "#CindyGladue: I Want to Think about Ways that Do Not Rely on the Criminal (In)Justice System to Feel Safe," *kwetoday: fierce indigenous feminism* (26 March 2015), online (blog): <https://kwetoday.com/2015/03/26/cindygladue-i-want-to-think-about-ways-that-do-not-rely-on-the-criminal-injustice-system-to-feel-safe/>.

Sayers, Naomi. "Doing/Undoing Justice: Violence through Colonial Law," *kwetoday: fierce indigenous feminism* (6 July 2016), online (blog): <https://kwetoday.com/2016/07/06/doingundoing-justice-violence-through-colonial-law/>.

Simons, Paula. "Public Outrage over Cindy Gladue Verdict No Legal Basis for Appeal," *Edmonton Journal* (31 March 2015), online: <https://edmontonjournal.com/news/local-news/simons-public-outrage-over-cindy-gladue-verdict-no-legal-basis-for-appeal>.

Simpson, Audra. "The Chief's Two Bodies: Theresa Spence and the Gender of Settler Sovereignty: Unsettling Conversations" (Keynote delivered at Critical Race and Anti-Colonial Studies Conference, Edmonton, 4 November 2014), online: <https://vimeo.com/110948627>.

Simpson, Audra. "The State Is a Man: Theresa Spence, Loretta Saunders and the Gender of Settler Sovereignty" in Sunera Thobani, ed, *Coloniality and Racial (In) Justice in the University* (Toronto: University of Toronto Press, 2022) 136.

Singh, Rashmee & Dawn Moore. "Bare Death: Femicide, Forensics and the Necropolitics of the Corpse," in Marie-Andrée Jacob & Anna Kirkland, eds, *Research Handbook on Socio-Legal Studies of Medicine and Law,* vol 808 (Northampton, MA: Edward Elgar, 2020) 287.

Smith, Madeline, "Cindy Gladue's Family Reaffirms Her Dignity as Killer's Appeal Rescheduled," *Edmonton Journal* (6 January 2023), online: <https://edmontonjournal.com/news/local-news/cindy-gladues-family-reaffirms-her-dignity-as-killers-appeal-rescheduled/wcm/4c9f15ab-94dd-4930-8c23-ec5d9971c530/amp/?fbclid=IwAR2kPqgmmaLrnJ0FXaxSUH3AWkH4O-rR0EuVDyKDu8ALTIeUxOPhpa-cElw>.

Snyder, Emily. "Indigenous Feminist Legal Theory" (2014) 26:2 Cdn J Women and the Law 365.
Snyder, Emily. *Gender, Power, and Representations of Cree Law* (Vancouver: UBC Press, Snyder, 2018).
Snyder, Emily, Val Napoleon & John Borrows. "Gender and Violence: Drawing on Indigenous Legal Resources" (2015) 48:2 UBC L Rev 593.
Suzack, Cheryl. *Indigenous Women's Writing and the Cultural Study of Law* (Toronto: University of Toronto Press, 2017).
Thobani, Sunera. *Exalted Subjects: Studies in the Making of Race and Nation in Canada* (Toronto: University of Toronto Press, 2007).
Tuck, Eve & K Wayne Yang. "Decolonization Is Not a Metaphor" (2012) 1:1 Decolonization: Indigeneity, Education & Society 1.
Watson, Irene. "Aboriginal Women's Laws and Lives: How Might We Keep Growing the Law?" (2007) 26:1 *Australian Feminist LJ* 95.
Wheeler, Kim. "Cindy Gladue Case: Not Guilty Verdict Prompts Rallies Calling for Appeal,", *CBC News* (31 March 2015), online: <https://www.cbc.ca/news/indigenous/cindy-gladue-case-not-guilty-verdict-prompts-rallies-calling-for-appeal-1.3016603>.
Working Group Seeking Justice for Cindy Gladue. *Our Breaking Point: Canada's Violation of Rights in Life and Death* (community-based resource book) (2016), online: <https://justiceforcindygladue.files.wordpress.com/2016/08/ourbreakingpoint-cindygladue.pdf>.

## LEGISLATION

*Criminal Code*, RSC 1985, c C-46.

## JURISPRUDENCE

*R v Barton*, 2024 ABCA 34.
*R v Barton*, 2019 SCC 33, [2019]2 SCR 579.
*R v Barton*, 2016 ABCA 68.
*R v Darrach*, [2000]2 SCR 443.
*R v Ewanchuck*, [1999]1 SCR 330.
*R v JA*, [2011]SCR 440.
*R v Barton* (2019), SCC 33 (Factum of the Intervener: Women of the Métis Nation), online: <https://www.scc-csc.ca/WebDocuments-DocumentsWeb/37769/FM150_Women-Metis_Intervener.pdf>.
*R v Barton* (2019), SCC 33 (Factum of the Interveners: Institute for the Advancement of Aboriginal Women and the Women's Legal

Education and Action Fund), online: <https://www.scc-csc.ca/WebDocuments-DocumentsWeb/37769/FM100_Intervener_LEAF.pdf>.

*R v Barton* (2016), ABCA 68 (Factum of the Interveners: Institute for the Advancement of Aboriginal Women and the Women's Legal Education and Action Fund), online: <https://www.leaf.ca/wp-content/uploads/2016/05/2016-05-02-final-LEAF-IAAW-factum-R-v-Barton-ABCA.pdf>.

# 7 Visualizing Violence against Indigenous Women: Documentary Film as Disruption in *Finding Dawn* and *American Outrage*

CHERYL SUZACK

In October 2001 the Institute for the Advancement of Aboriginal Women (IAAW)[1] presented its inaugural social justice award to Detective Freeman Taylor, a non-Indigenous member of the Edmonton Police Service who had been instrumental in arresting the man responsible for the vicious assault and death of Ms. Joyce Cardinal.[2] The institute honoured the officer for his role in pursuing the case over a seven-year period during which time he continued to track the lone suspect, leading to an arrest.[3] The institute's founder, Ms. Muriel Stanley Venne, presented the award, praising Detective Taylor for "solving one of the murders"[4] involving missing and murdered Indigenous women, and drawing attention to the leadership role Indigenous women's organizations had taken to protect Indigenous women's human rights and to establish alternative forms of community justice and social repair. "Here was a man who solved one of the murders," Ms. Stanley Venne observed. "We, as the Aboriginal women's organization, have to honour and encourage the dedication of this officer in the Edmonton Police Service."[5]

The IAAW awards,[6] like other public events and memorials associated with violence against Indigenous women,[7] have become an important part of the transitional justice landscape in settler colonial countries, such as Canada and the United States, that have not undergone regime reconstruction in their relations with Indigenous peoples. Increasingly recognized as part of a truth commission's or national inquiry's "world-building character"[8] and truth-gathering mandate,[9] public memorials, art installations, Indigenous women's storywork,[10] social media networking,[11] and "commemorative sit-ins"[12] represent strategies by Indigenous women that create reparatory justice mechanisms and hold settler colonial states accountable for Indigenous women's suffering by making plausible through art new forms of gender justice practice. In adapting artistic media to further community repair, their public performances highlight artistic approaches within multiple social sites, reclaiming these spaces for political intervention through which to grant status to individuals who have been deprived of their human rights, while publicly acknowledging victims' social value, dignity, and respect in the aftermath of trauma, loss, and broken social relationships that countless Indigenous peoples suffer as a consequence of gender violence. Through aesthetic practices that focus on Indigenous women, their families, and a wider community affected by violence, Indigenous women use artistic media to create community connections and overcome the "gap" that exists between "court-ordered reparations" and "broad ... segments of society," making visible a "whole universe of victims" deserving of "reparation[s]" that cannot be fulfilled by "court judgements."[13]

Métis visual artist and curator Christie Belcourt explains the broad ability of artistic justice practices to enact reconciliation in the wake of gender violence. Speaking about her installation "Walking with Our Sisters," an exhibit of moccasin vamps crafted to honour and recognize missing and murdered Indigenous women, she observes about the exhibit: "It's commemoration, it's ceremony, it's an honouring, it's art, it's community taking action, it's a way to demonstrate we care."[14] Anishinaabe artist Jamie Black's REDress Project evolved out of similar concerns about social responsibility and community repair.[15] The multidisciplinary artist and founder of the REDress project installed red dresses in public spaces to overcome Indigenous women's absence and bring recognition to Indigenous women as the lifeblood of the community.[16] Black notes that stories about missing and murdered Indigenous women inspired her to create the exhibit as a way to convey "grief" and "feelings of connectedness to fellow Indigenous women."[17] When the installation opened at the Smithsonian Institution in 2019 to mark Women's History Month, Washington journalist Alicia Ault drew a strong link between the epidemic of missing and murdered Indigenous women in Canada and the prevalence of missing and murdered American Indian and Alaska Native women in the United States. Ault noted the epidemic of violence against Indigenous women evident in data by the Urban Indian Health Institute that recorded 5,712 missing women and girls in 2016, with projections that the numbers may be much higher due to under-reporting among tribal communities. Reflecting on the impact of Black's installation, in its capacity to reach a transnational audience and to heighten awareness about the incidence of sexual violence that Indigenous women suffer from, Ault observed,

"[The] dresses are haunting and evocative. One can easily imagine a woman who once inhabited each garment."[18]

Ault's response to the installation's powerful message in reviving Indigenous women's presence at the same time as it registers their loss encapsulates one of the central dilemmas associated with violence against Indigenous women in settler colonial countries. Although the issue has been squarely within the public eye, having been brought to national and international attention by state and non-state actors,[19] its treatment by settler colonial countries remains indifferent at best, leading to local and international criticism directed at both Canada and the United States for objectifying Indigenous women's suffering through a "frozen gaze on victimization,"[20] in the case of Canada, and for inaction in disregarding Indigenous women as "invisible victims," in the case of the United States.[21] Ault's comments show how Black's installation creates a transnational platform of collective struggle; on the one hand, this platform recognizes the problem's international dimensions as an issue specific to Indigenous women in settler colonial countries; on the other hand, it concretizes an injustice that requires international attention in order to transcend a state's inadequate attention to the issue.[22] Indigenous women's artistic practices are important because they represent Indigenous women's local and transnational agency in overcoming these silencing practices. They convey Indigenous women's perspectives and experiences of violence, reinforcing public awareness that colonial gender violence represents a national and transnational issue, and they recast the issue of violence against Indigenous women in the political and cultural terms set by Indigenous women and their families. Indigenous women's artistic forms thus directly engage colonial-legal and gendered social realities. By interrupting the settler-state's monopoly in using legal practices to dictate how sexual violence is "written" and how it is "socially [understood],"[23] these practices establish new political methods from which to bring attention to overlooked dimensions of this issue, defining colonial gender violence as the pervasive social harm it represents – as a barrier to Indigenous women's security, as an obstacle to their social standing and political legitimacy, and as an infringement of their social, cultural, and political well-being.

In this chapter, I explore the issue of colonial gender violence as it is portrayed in documentary films produced by and about Indigenous women to show how film as a visual medium contributes to the reparatory goals embedded within Indigenous women's artistic practice. *Finding Dawn*[24] from Canada, a film that uses personal narrative and documentary filmmaking techniques to highlight the relationship between colonial legal violence and missing and murdered Indigenous women, and *American Outrage*[25] from the United States, which records the decades-long legal battle of Western Shoshone Elders Mary and Carrie Dann to stop United States' officials from violating their rights to graze their livestock on Western Shoshone ancestral lands, provide visual access to the vulnerability within settler colonial countries that Indigenous women are subject to. Underscoring what happens to Indigenous women when they are rendered landless by the institutions of state violence or denied the legal agency to stand against land dispossession, the films demonstrate the global character of colonial-legal violence in its capacity to unhinge the normative political, legal, and ethical orders that link together practices of living with land sovereignty and that ensure Indigenous women's security and survival. Formed in response to deprivation, these practices are best described as "regimes of living"[26] to signal how state power is unbound from social or political constraints in raced and gendered spaces. The films portray these sites to illustrate colonial state power's heterogeneity and local affects as it structures "common problems of living"[27] for Indigenous women. As records of Indigenous women's dispossession, the films invite audiences to see the intersections of race and gender violence that are embedded in Indigenous women's survival strategies. In their reach to document the failure of human rights protection through their portrayal of Indigenous women's struggles, the films illuminate Indigenous women's precarious and contingent lives, demonstrating the violence of state security forces in responding to the problem of missing and murdered Indigenous women in Canada, and in opposing Indigenous land defence in the United States. Each film shows how the apparatus of state power situates Indigenous women as "bodies to be acted on,"[28] in ways that align Indigenous women in settler colonial countries with Indigenous women globally, highlighting the state violence that is at the nexus of race and gender violations to which Indigenous women are subject within these countries. In representing violence against Indigenous women as state authorized, the films demonstrate the capacities of Indigenous women artists' transnational agency to clarify the situation of colonial gender violence as an issue "neglected [by] … global agendas."[29]

### Settler Colonial Nation States and Indigenous Women's Agency: Documentary Film's Capacity to Intervene Locally

Despite calls by Indigenous women and human rights actors for settler colonial countries, such as Canada and the United States, to enact laws that protect Indigenous women,[30] Indigenous women's voices remain muted within international legal fora due to the position accorded these countries on the international stage. Regarded by international human rights bodies as "First World societies," with "pacified" state status, Canada and the United States benefit from an international "self-image" that views them as "homogeneous, cohesive, and egalitarian."[31] This status redirects attention from Indigenous women as "excluded populations," occupying sites of legal and social "peripheralization,"[32] to policies that support state-centred practices that represent violence against Indigenous women on the state's own terms: either as "distinctive [to Indigenous] women's experience," thereby allowing the issue to be narrowed as an idiosyncratic problem, or incidental to broader state matters, enabling it to be "factored out of the international legal process."[33]

Feminist human rights scholars argue that the "categorization" of an issue on intersectional political grounds is fundamental to its local and international reception, its capacity to express a complex and "messy reality," and its acceptance by women across different identity statuses and varied lived experiences, all of which are necessary to building women's consensus, their political organizing, and transnational connections.[34] Feminist intersectionality helps to define and clarify an issue's empowerment goals through principles that heighten attention to features of a problem "that other methods overlook."[35] Indigenous women require feminist international recognition and intersectional analysis against which to compare their local experiences because, increasingly, international law represents "a last resort" when their "human rights are violated by the representatives of their states" and their "demands for justice go unresolved by their national justice systems."[36] Because documentary film provides access to "real-life dilemmas from the perspective of the excluded,"[37] it focuses attention on systemic features Indigenous women confront as women and as Indigenous people, furthering recognition of common areas of race and gender experience and struggle, and distinguishing colonial gender violence as a category requiring legal standing in its own right. Documentary film's access to direct representation also builds a foundation for a collective agency that "transforms … cultures of violence" within states.[38] Through its capacity for comparative critical scrutiny and critique, film dramatizes the "conditions in which violence is experienced … and responses to such violence are negotiated."[39] Feminist human rights scholars remind us that international legal activism was essential to according sexual violence in war its recognition as a gender-based crime and crime against humanity.[40] This recognition led to direct legal consequences and international censure of offending states.[41] As Katherine Franke observes, "It now goes without saying – largely because important legal authorities have said it – that the kind of harm caused by this sort of sexual violence is normatively and legally on a par with the kinds of harm that men have traditionally suffered in war and in grossly unjust societies."[42]

To require Canada and the United States to be accountable to the voices of Indigenous women speaking to their experiences of a state's "grossly unjust" practices supports the call by international agencies for Indigenous women to be more visible at the international level. Although sexual violence against Indigenous women has been condemned in Canada as a "deliberate … genocide"[43] and in the United States as an "Indian rape epidemic,"[44] its colonial dimensions are often overlooked, and few opportunities exist for Indigenous women to participate internationally to convey direct knowledge about how they experience sexual violence as a colonial process, as a personal violation, as a systemic harm, and as an effect of ongoing dispossession. In reviewing the issue of Indigenous women's international status, the UN Permanent Forum on Indigenous Issues found that Indigenous women were poorly represented, had limited opportunities to participate in its institutional structures, few resources to carry out advocacy work, and poor visibility in making "the right to live free from violence" urgent among the forum's priorities.[45] The report found that "silos" exist among "gender justice advocates,"[46] impeding visibility and political voice, and obscuring recognition of how race and gender violence intersect within settler colonial countries in ways that prevent recognition of colonial gender violence as a human rights issue.

Documentary films by and about Indigenous women are an important resource for showing these connections. Since its adoption by Human Rights Watch to portray "social and political issues," documentary film has become an effective "tool for the promotion of human rights."[47] Its political appeal and broad cultural impact[48] arise from its mode of "non-neutral" storytelling.[49] Using visual images that convey the immediacy of the "human face" and techniques that "mak[e] the viewer feel immersively, physically, [and] haptically what it is like to live in that space,"[50] documentary film associated with human rights protection emphasizes "issues of representation germane to … a human rights context," informing viewers about "threats to individual freedom and dignity" while also conveying to audiences the "power of the human spirit and intellect to prevail."[51] As a narrative form, human rights documentaries craft stories and visual records that align film's representational features to the goal of helping the viewer "'read' truth" into situations of violation.[52] Because the "truth" that films convey appears through "delegitimized forms in human rights theory – oral narratives, environmental activism, visual texts, [and] ephemeral performances"[53] – documentary film raises the issue of representation as a fundamental concern associated with its message in advancing human rights. Two of its most important features are its disruption of a state's official narrative that "crafts victims in the perpetrators' own image"[54] and its capacity to expose state tactics in rewriting the past using "heroic rhetoric" to move beyond periods of conflict and atrocity.[55] Filmmaker Joshua Oppenheimer aligns documentary film's transitional justice impact with its ability to heighten awareness of "the power of perpetrators" over "survivors" in the films he produced chronicling the mass murders in Indonesia that brought to power President Suharto.[56] In speaking about his task in making the films, he asks, "What does the lack of truth and reconciliation, the lack of transitional justice, the ongoing power of the perpetrators do to the survivors?"[57] In providing an answer – that it permits states to "sugarcoat the unspeakable" and to retroactively "justify … violence"[58] – Oppenheimer distills documentary film's capacity to connect the political with the visual as a crucial source for bearing witness to state violence and mass atrocity from the victim's point of view.

Highlighting how legal processes and visual records may be adapted to conceptualize colonial gender violence from the victims' point of view, *Finding Dawn* and *American Outrage* participate in human rights work by using victim-centred storytelling techniques to show how Indigenous women are objectified through state violence. The films use family photographs, personal interviews, oral narratives, and visual reconstructions of legal events to signal their human rights documentary methods, and to illuminate visual media's capacity to interrupt the state's authority in determining how violence against Indigenous women is understood, restoring to Indigenous women the presence and selfhood that violence has destroyed. By giving Indigenous women access through film to sources of authority and self-representation that exist beyond the courtroom, the films advance Indigenous women's rights by preventing the state from using legal mechanisms to eclipse their social and political agency. The sections that follow highlight the artistic and narrative strategies that both films use to bring national and international attention to Indigenous women's experiences of colonial gender violence by both portraying and condemning its prevalence and neglect.

## The Condition of "Being Marginal:" Christine Welsh's *Finding Dawn*

Métis filmmaker Christine Welsh uses a human rights lens to analyse the issue of colonial gender violence by figuring settler colonial law as an extractive industry that amplifies violence against Indigenous women. Foregrounding her standpoint as an Indigenous woman struggling to understand and "put a human face to what happened to so many of [her] sisters,"[59] Welsh highlights the human voice as central to understanding the issue of missing and murdered Indigenous women, even as she implicates the issue in extractive technologies and state legal practices that play a role in silencing Indigenous women through their practices of dispossession. The film's opening sequence and narration by Welsh frame these overlapping insights. As the camera shifts between indistinct visual imagery – a darkened city street, a woman standing in the rain, a police vehicle and hotel sign that are juxtaposed to generate a sense of distance and defamiliarization – viewers are confronted by a set of photographs and names that register women identified on Vancouver's "Missing and Murdered Women's List." As viewers search the list of faces and names to restore a sense of the familiar, Welsh's camera thwarts recognition by shifting its focus away from the images, interrupting the visual focus to ask, "What is it about numbers? What do they tell us? Do they help us understand? One woman goes missing, then another, then another, for a long time only those who know and love them pay attention until the numbers start to add up."[60] By panning back from the photographs and preventing recognition, Welsh distinguishes the problem of sexual violence as an issue of visibility bound up in access to state modes and technologies of representation. As the photographs fade from view, Welsh shifts attention to the cases of missing and murdered Indigenous women that mark a monumental legal event, unparalleled in Canadian history, in the form of "the biggest serial murder investigation in Canadian history,"[61] an investigation that begins locally on a farm just outside of Vancouver (Figure 7.1).

Figure 7.1 The Pickton farm and site of forensic investigation into the remains of at least twenty-three women.

The issue of colonial gender violence, for Welsh, is intersected by power, visibility, and scale. As Indigenous women retreat from view, law enforcement officials and their representatives claim visual authority and public space. Sexual violence is thus bound up with colonial violence through the extractive technologies of state law and its forensic practices. Viewers are jarred into this realization by the sudden and dramatic images of bulldozers, conveyer belts, and equipment that delves into the earth to extract evidence of Indigenous women's bodies (Figures 7.2 and 7.3).

Welsh's voiceover explains the significance of the images: "For two years, hundreds of forensic investigators sift through tons of earth and debris from the farm, searching for traces of missing women. Murder charges are laid against the owner of the farm. First two, then seven, then fifteen. Then, in February 2004, the twenty-third woman is identified from DNA found in the earth taken from the farm" (@: 39). The desecration of the earth that Welsh portrays serves as a synecdoche that stands in for and amplifies the destruction of Indigenous women's bodies. As Welsh walks around the investigation site, we observe with her the transformation of the land into isolated piles of rubble and debris. When she asks in relation to Dawn Crey, the twenty-third woman iden-

Figure 7.2 An excavator arm digging into the earth searching for DNA evidence dehumanizes the work of recovering the remains of missing women and serves as a power metaphor for the normalization and destruction of Indigenous women's bodies.

tified by recovered DNA, "who was she, and how did we lose her," she forces us to reflect on how we have also lost our way, how we have become complacent in the destruction of the earth, how we have become bystanders in the desecration of Indigenous women's lives and bodies. Welsh's marking of the site by placing a ceremonial rose and sacred sage on the metal barricade represents an act of atonement that undoes our complacency (Figure 7.4), a redemptive gesture on the part of the filmmaker to recognize and honour Indigenous women's lives that exceed our understanding, women who are withheld from us through sociopolitical legal frameworks that obscure their humanity and normalize their losses in numbers and rubble, Indigenous women, like Dawn, who receive no legal justice because forensic investigators are unable to compile enough DNA evidence from soil samples to permit prosecutors to charge the farm's owner with her disappearance and murder.[62] When Welsh in this way interrupts with ceremonial Indigenous medicines the Canadian state's "forensic narration"[63] in its search for evidence and truth, she atones for the earth's desecration and violence against Indigenous women that settler colonial legal technologies enact by making both Indigenous women and the land vulnerable to government-authorized forms of extraction.

The intersecting themes of injustice, visibility, and scale that introduce the film's focus on sexual violence empower the filmmaker's insights to establish Indigenous women as peripheral to the settler colonial state

Figure 7.3 A bulldozer sorting earth for evidence of women's DNA represents again the inhuman dimensions of this atrocity.

and to show how their peripheralization is both direct and ongoing. Through interviews with Dawn's siblings, Ernie and Lorraine Crey, Welsh turns our view away from the state's forensic investigation that fails to establish an evidentiary truth about what happened to Dawn towards personal narratives, interviews, and photographs that help to restore her presence. In a canny modelling of how truth commissions and commissions of inquiry ought to carry out their tasks, the film shifts us deeper into the Canadian landscape through Welsh's travels to Chilliwack to meet with Dawn's family on their traditional territory. As we travel closer to her family and the immediacy of her life story, we also move closer through the film to the sites of social deprivation that constituted Dawn's life, her personal struggles, and the survival strategies she used to manage her life on the streets. Dawn's siblings describe her devastation following her father's death, her mother's loss of custody of Dawn and her siblings,[64] and Dawn's absence of Indigenous connections through the state's out-adoption policies. By emphasizing the vulnerability, poverty, and addiction that Dawn falls victim to following her move to Vancouver after her release from foster

Figure 7.4 Welsh places a rose and sage, one of four Indigenous medicines, on the metal barricade in an act of atonement recognizing and honouring Indigenous women's lives.

care,[65] the film links the state's extractive industries with state policies towards Indigenous peoples that displace Dawn from her Sto:lo roots to the streets of Vancouver as one of many "powerless" Indigenous women living in the city's Downtown Eastside (DTES).[66] When the film intercuts images that shift between a photograph of Dawn standing in bright detail against the mountains of the Fraser Valley to urban images of where she was last seen on the corner of Hastings and Main, the film's movement reflects Dawn's displacement by inscribing in viewers a sense of disorientation. Signalled by the interlaced camera shifts and the missing details of Dawn's life story, the film captures the experience of abandonment and lack of care that Dawn experienced. Welsh uses images of Vancouver's annual Women's Memorial March held on Valentine's Day to restore our disquiet, easing viewers into an event that honours all women who have disappeared or been murdered from the DTES, so that not only are we apprised of the systemic dimensions of the problem of missing and murdered women for one neighbourhood in Canada, we are also brought into a collective mode of being in community with members who struggle for the issue's recognition. As hundreds of people gather to march in support, and daughters testify about what it means to be mothers of children whose grandmother is listed on

Figure 7.5 A rose and sage mark the site where Indigenous women go missing from the streets of Vancouver.

the "Missing and Murdered Women's List," an organizer explains the difficult task of being the first line of access for families arriving to the neighbourhood looking for their loved ones. The film's visual sequence focuses on Dawn's family walking with other family members, survivors, and participants through the streets amid drumming and singing. The ceremonial connection contrasts with the opening depiction of conveyor belts sifting through the earth, highlighting the difference between the indignity of state forensic practices destroying the earth in the search for evidence of women's bodies, and local organizers' actions honouring women through Indigenous forms of ceremony and remembrance. When Welsh lays a second garland of sacred cedar, sage, and a rose at the site (Figure 7.5), her gesture connects the Pickton farm where she marked the investigator's fence to Vancouver's streets from which Indigenous and non-Indigenous women were taken, and to the spirit of a Coast Salish woman whose remains were found at the corner of Hastings and Main fifteen years earlier and whose death originated the first march.[67] Welsh's actions establish a visual and collective spirit of reconciliation premised in Indigenous forms of remembrance that connect these disparate locations across time and space through the filmmaker's act that recalls the actions of the Coast Salish woman's family who enacted a cleansing ceremony where her remains were found.[68] The scenes represent Indigenous artistic practice and transitional justice as multifaceted and multidirectional, moving back in time to prior losses resonating with and amplifying present-day harms, and flowing forward from the land, the people, and the spiritual world through Indigenous ceremonies that restore broken relations brought about by violence against Indigenous women.

Because Welsh uses images of land and loss to represent the issue of violence against Indigenous women, the film inscribes the recognition that violence within settler colonial countries remains an ongoing feature of Indigenous peoples' lives. When Welsh remarks in an opening frame while looking at the Pickton farm through a chain link fence, now empty of forensic researchers, "There is nothing left now at the farm to tell us what really happened here,"[69] she prompts our awareness that Canada's governing relations with Indigenous peoples, like those of other settler colonial states, have disfigured the land through extractive industries by emptying out Indigenous lifeways so that the people and the land are no longer recognizable as what they once were, as sites and practices of human habitation. Scholars working on the problem of "advanced marginality"[70] among peripheralized peoples have turned their attention to the situation of Indigenous peoples deprived of land and cultural practices.[71] They argue that Indigenous peoples without state recognition and land bases increasingly occupy "territories of exclusion" within Western locations where they are subject to "extreme poverty and social destitution."[72] Resembling studies confronting the appalling forms of violence against Indigenous peoples in these countries,[73] Welsh's film associates the vulnerability of Indigenous women to colonial gender violence within Canada's urban centres with other global locations that have "more than [their] share of homelessness, drug addiction, prostitution, and crime."[74] It is an important feature of Welsh's documentary that it provides a visual record of these connections, helping us to see these locations within Canada, even as Canada's domestic and international self-image withholds them from our view.[75]

As the film expands on the implications of the loss of Indigenous women and the loss of land, Welsh assembles through interviews in Terrace, BC, a site of loss and violence located along the infamous "Trail of Tears," a stretch of the Yellowhead Highway that runs across Western Canada connecting northern communities between Prince George and Prince Rupert in British Columbia. Known locally and nationally as a place where Indigenous women disappear, it is also depicted as a site of social and economic deprivation through Canada's interests in resource extraction in remote locations.[76] "Many women living along the Highway experience poverty, unemployment and inadequate education opportunities," scholars maintain, "leading to social marginalization and increased risk of violence."[77]

For Welsh, the highway makes visible how extractive industries in the form of tourism, government roads, and logging activities have altered the land and undermined Indigenous women's safety. As the film pans "big rigs" and vehicles that pass Welsh's car, the images associate changes to the land with changes to Indigenous women's status and their susceptibility to violence by residents who exploit Indigenous women's hitch-hiking practices in these remote places. Welsh's voice-over explains that since the 1990s eight Indigenous women have disappeared or been killed along the highway's route. In an interview with local radio host Lynne Terbasket, the film underscores how colonial laws have altered local knowledge about the land, drawing a direct correlation between settler colonial intrusion, land jurisdiction, and the safety risks and physical consequences for Indigenous women. In recounting a failed search to find a missing community member, Lynne explains how Indigenous women have been dispossessed of their knowledge, authority, and community practices. "The Pacific Northwest," Lynne observes, "our terrain is, is like wrinkled-up old skin, and it's just bumpy and hilly and the mountains are huge, and there's so many cut blocks and clear cuts and roads that go into the mountains, deep into the mountains. And you know, it's impossible to search every road, it's impossible to search every gully and every ditch because it's so huge. You know, it's a big place and so that's, that's how our search ended. It snowed and we couldn't look anymore."[78] Lynne emphasizes that the land the community once knew, with knowledge that would have aided their search, has been altered by colonial extraction. The searchers cannot track the land and its many hiding places in the ways they once could, nor can they protect young women, like missing community member Ramona Wilson, because they no longer retain jurisdiction over the land. The loss of Indigenous land title is intimately bound up with the loss of the community's capacity to protect Indigenous women, and by extension, the community's land dispossession is intimately bound up with the family's and community's loss of Ramona Wilson.

Indigenous women's losses and their peripheral status to the Canadian nation state represent two of the most powerful insights that the film conveys in demonstrating that not all citizens are treated equally, and some are more unequal than others, especially when it comes to triggering police protection. In a report published by Human Rights

Watch on abusive policing and the Canadian state's treatment of Indigenous women and girls, Meghan Rhoad observes that members of the Human Rights Watch research team "were struck ... by the high levels of fear of police among the women interviewed, levels of fear that Human Rights Watch normally finds in communities in post-conflict or post-transition countries such as Iraq where security forces have played an integral role in state abuses and enforcement of authoritarian policies."[79] The report highlights Canada's human rights failures using on-site interviews, visits, and forensic documentary reporting, methods that Welsh uses as she strives to "put a human face to what's happened to so many of her sisters." The film's narrative strategies are comparable to Human Rights Watch's reporting, as it documents conditions of mistrust and police anger and inflexibility when questioned by family members, illuminating each family's inability to break down officials' indifference by disclosing that their loved ones are missing. The film assembles these testimonies and experiences, exposing the systemic, pervasive, and callous ways in which Indigenous people are treated by legal actors and the Canadian state. For Ramona Wilson's family in northern British Columbia and Daleen Bosse's parents in Saskatoon, police indifference is a source of grief that amplifies their suffering. From interviews with Janice Acoose and Fay Blaney, who speak about their experiences as women surviving "violence," "abuse," and "life on the streets,"[80] Welsh depicts their struggles to overcome state and community antipathy. Film's capacity to depict the human spirit's struggle in the face of adversity is a characteristic of documentary filmmaking associated with human rights work, leading to affirmations of film's capacity to convey both "hope and optimism."[81] But if we turn towards hope without also engaging in political action, we risk apathy as viewers in requiring the filmmaker and documentary form to undertake political work that as audience members we must undertake ourselves. Welsh's film aptly anticipates this problem.

Through her interviews with Fay Blaney, Welsh highlights Blaney's work in her community to prevent the "gang rape of young Indigenous girls," as a community member who has herself been subjected to sexual violence and whose mother fled from the community to escape it. The film's representation of Fay's suffering is portrayed in complex visual and narrative ways: as the daughter of a woman suffering from sexual assault in her community, as a woman who has overcome sexual assault, and as a survivor who must work among the perpetrators of abuse with other survivors. In showing these overlapping and intergenerational effects, Welsh demonstrates the complexity of the problem and aligns Canada's indifference with countries whose track record on the protection of Indigenous women's rights are damning.[82] The film invites critical scrutiny of Canada's treatment of Indigenous women at the international level by demonstrating the issue's complexity in ways that interrupt and challenge violence against Indigenous women in its local and political nation state framing.[83]

In showing how sexual violence represents an extension of colonial violence that is intergenerational in its effects, *Finding Dawn* traces conditions of marginality and dispossession linking sexual violence to other losses Indigenous communities have suffered through the state's deliberate peripheralization of Indigenous women's voices and their experiences. In its sustained attention to constructing a visual record that restores solidarity and collectivity among Indigenous communities, the film works to overcome Indigenous women's political isolation and the localization of sexual violence as an individual or random issue. The film thus alters situations of indignity and remoteness that Indigenous women suffer from within the colonial nation state, according women through documentary film a medium expressing their collective struggle that gives voice to their experiences in ways that recentre their experiences as the starting point for addressing sexual violence and achieving social recognition about the pervasive impacts on families of this issue. In the next section, I shift to an exploration of the documentary *American Outrage* to illustrate how its visual representation furthers a justice-seeking objective through its juxtaposition of the Dann Sisters' legal struggles with the narration of their legal knowledge based in spiritual sources and their relationship to the land. Comparatively with Welsh's film, the visual and narrative record the film constructs challenges the legal injustice the Danns suffer at the hands of Western legal frameworks.

## The Dann Sisters' Litigation: Colonial Gender Violence in the Protection of Shoshone Homelands

When the case of *Mary and Carrie Dann v United States*[84] appeared before the Inter-American Commission on Human Rights, an international body comprised of member states from the Americas, whose principal function is to promote and protect human rights against their infringement by domestic governments,[85] the case brought international attention to the struggle by Mary and Carrie Dann to secure a legal mechanism that could prevent the United States from interfering with their ownership, use, and occupancy of their traditional Western Shoshone homelands. Members of the Western Shoshone Nation, Mary and Carrie Dann resided on a ranch in the rural community of Crescent Valley,

Nevada, where they and their ancestors lived and worked the land in accordance with their rights as Western Shoshone peoples since time immemorial. Title to their land is unextinguished and their occupancy is uninterrupted. As signatories to the Treaty of Ruby Valley, a treaty of peace and friendship signed in 1863 between the Western Shoshone and the United States,[86] they hold aboriginal title to and occupy a territory known as the "Dann lands," an area that includes not only the ranch on which they live but also the rangelands and other property "principally [located] in the state of Nevada."[87] Through their traditional Indigenous practices, they and their extended family use these lands to meet their subsistence needs. They harvest customary food sources, engage in ranching practices, and augment their economic base by selling "livestock, goods, and produce to neighboring Western Shoshone and to [non-Indigenous people]."[88]

Since 1951, the Danns were forced to court by the United States and its agents on eight occasions in order to protect their rights from its trespass actions, and to restrain the government from enacting and threatening further violence against them. These threats and violations include issuing civil and criminal penalty notices, levying fines for the use of their traditional lands, confiscating and auctioning off their livestock, imposing barriers to their use and access to sacred sites, preventing the gathering of their subsistence foods, and authorizing private mining companies and military activities on traditional Western lands that "threaten … the environment and destroy … available resources."[89] As petitioners before the Inter-American Commission, they urged the court to enact "precautionary measures"[90] to stop further "aggressive government action"[91] by the state that threatened their "economic and cultural survival" due to its "impounding [of their] property,"[92] and to halt its passage of legislation in the form of a Nevada public land bill and a distribution bill. These bills would dispose of "public" land, including "land used and occupied by the Danns," by "selling it in open bidding to mining, ranching and other private interests," and would "authorize the distribution of … funds awarded by the [Indian Claims Commission, ICC] but never accepted by the Western Shoshone people."[93] These funds are a source of contestation among the Western Shoshone Nation, as they represent compensation by the United States for prior land takings that were litigated through the ICC process and that the government and courts assert extinguished the Shoshone peoples' collective aboriginal title. In the original petition, the petitioners[94] claimed that the state's actions infringed the Dann sisters' rights under Articles II, III, VI, XIV, XVIII, and XXIII of the *American Declaration of the Rights and Duties of Man*,[95] to which the United States is a signatory, by interfering with their right to equality before the law, their right to religious freedom and worship, their right to family and its protection, the right to work and fair remuneration, their right to a fair trial, and their right to property.[96]

The Inter-American Commission found in favour of the Dann's petition insofar as it concluded that "the State failed to ensure the Danns' right to property under conditions of equality contrary to Articles II, XVIII and XXIII of the *American Declaration* in connection with their claims to property rights in the Western Shoshone ancestral lands."[97] It judged that the United States violated the Danns' "special protection[s] as indigenous peoples" by engaging in discriminatory practices that reflected larger patterns of mistreatment "suffered by indigenous peoples,"[98] and it censured the state for its treatment of the Dann sisters, emphasizing the state's larger and more invidious practices of "racial discrimination."[99] These practices included land takings that were litigated through the domestic courts without adequate consultation with Western Shoshone peoples and without mechanisms that recognized a "valid public purpose" or "fair market value of the property taken";[100] "imped[ing] the ability of the Danns to continue to occupy and use the lands in question"[101] by appropriating Western Shoshone ancestral territories as public lands that were "lost" by the "Danns and other Western Shoshone as a result of … [gradual] encroachment by non-Native Americans";[102] and upholding a date of extinguishment of Western Shoshone title that "d[id] not bear any relevant connection to the issue of whether and to what extent all or part of Western Shoshone title in their traditional lands, including that of the Danns, may [continue to] subsist."[103] In finding that the state had violated their due process rights, the commission ordered the state to "provide Mary and Carrie Dann with an effective remedy … to ensure respect for [their] rights to property … in connection with their claims to property rights in the Western Shoshone ancestral lands," and to "review its laws, procedures and practices to ensure that the property rights of indigenous persons are determined in accordance with the rights established under the American Declaration."[104] When the United States refused to act on the commission's decision by "reject[ing] the … report in its entirety," by making "public" its preliminary findings prior to the commission's official release,[105] and by "seizing," "confiscating," and "auctioning off" more than 225 head of cattle on the "Danns' ancestral lands" through the actions of the US Bureau of Land Management and forty armed federal agents, the Danns asked the UN's Committee for the Elimination of Racial Discrimination (CERD) to act under its early warning and urgent action procedure on the situation of the Western Shoshone Indigenous people.

In its report, CERD urged the United States to "freeze any plans to privatize Western Shoshone ancestral lands to multinational extractive industries and energy developers," to "desist from all activities planned and/or conducted on [Western Shoshone] ancestral lands," and to "stop imposing grazing fees, trespass, and collection notices, horse and livestock impoundments, restrictions on hunting, fishing and gathering, as well as arrests ... inflicted on Western Shoshone while using their ancestral lands."[106] To this date, the United States has failed to act on these findings. It refuses to recognize the ownership of "the land that the Danns assert is actually part of the ancestral or traditional lands of the Western Shoshone Nation,"[107] forcing members to attempt to secure their land rights through continuous appeals to the federal government through the domestic court system.[108]

The Dann sisters' petition before the Inter-American Commission on Human Rights and their application to the United Nations represent appeals to legal forums that demonstrate Indigenous peoples' "unfree status." This status persists despite the recognition by domestic and international courts that Indigenous peoples' pre-existing land rights and political sovereignty precede a state's governing authority, and a state is duty bound by its international obligations to protect these rights. The dilemma that Indigenous peoples confront is that they must petition within state legal systems that require them to alter their lifeways and epistemologies in order to conform to paradigms of "judicial redress"[109] that fit within a nation state's domestic and internal legal frameworks. Under the internationalizing reach of human rights instruments, these forums emerge as "due process" protections against the state when it threatens to deprive citizens of "life, liberty, property, or ... equal protection of the laws."[110] Should Indigenous claimants fail to fit within these models, they forfeit redress. As Stephen Best and Saidiya Hartmann explain, "If [victims] fail in their attempt to achieve redress, it will be due not to the nation's failure to recognize historical wrongs, but, curiously, to their own negligence."[111] Indigenous peoples are confronted by a critical impasse: if they do not enact their claims through domestic laws, they lose their access to justice-serving mechanisms. Domestic and international laws thus practise tangible and intangible forms of dispossession that extend beyond the loss of culture and land that these international systems are designed to protect.

In complex ways, the Dann sisters' litigation fits within and belies this observation. For more than thirty years, they struggled to secure Western legal recognition that their land rights can be neither bought nor sold. Their legal claims turn on distinguishing intangible elements of their Native title that do not conform to Western legal systems and are unrepresented by them. In their efforts to defend themselves from colonial-legal violation, their actions to protect Shoshone lands demonstrate the ways in which judicial procedures enact what Alyosha Goldstein describes as a "torturous articulation of juridical reason and multi-scalar distribution of political and legal authority [that] reinforce[s] colonial rule even when appearing to challenge it."[112] Taking critical distance from the law's attempts to incorporate Western Shoshone land sovereignty and political liberty into Western legal systems and thereby expand colonial law's reach, the Dann sisters have asserted alternative paradigms of law and justice that contest Western legal systems even as they show how these systems fail to legitimate their Indigenous laws and world view. The documentary film *American Outrage* illuminates these objectives.

## *American Outrage*: "Honouring the Truth, Protecting the Creator's Law"

*American Outrage* explores interlocking themes concerning Western Shoshone land rights, settler colonial law, Indigenous land defence, and social justice. It analyses these issues in order to expose how settler colonial law claims its legitimacy, how it achieves its meaning-making function, and how it defends and authorizes its use of violence against Indigenous peoples. Centred on the experiences of Mary and Carrie Dann and their relationship to Western Shoshone traditional practices, the film deploys the cinematic gaze to bring the viewer into familiarity and proximity with the sisters as they undertake to live on and protect their land, drawing viewers' awareness to the acts of stewardship and land dependence that are inextricably interlinked for the sisters. Stewardship and interdependence provide the foundation in Western Shoshone law from which the Dann sisters launch their legal struggle against the United States in protesting its land grants that permitted settlers to "gradually encroach" into their territory, its authorizing of mining activities that destroy the land and water table, and its empowerment of government agents who harass and attack the Danns and their relatives as they stand against the Bureau of Land Management (BLM) and government agents. Connected through Carrie Dann's centring logic of the Creator's will and the Treaty of Ruby Valley, the Danns' act of protest founded in the Creator's law and Western Shoshone legal obligations provides the plot device that builds towards the story the film tells about the Danns' success in securing the United Nations' condemnation of their treatment by the United States.

Figure 7.6 A ceremonial round dance by the Western Shoshone people carried out in honour of their spiritual relationship to the land.

The film's opening scenes convey the spiritual and ancestral laws that motivate the Danns' actions as they depict the Western Shoshone people's ceremonial dance (Figure 7.6) and Western Shoshone Elder Corbin Harney's ceremonial drumming (Figure 7.7) that set the stage for the documentary's overarching theme: that the Western Shoshone spiritual relationship to the land can neither be bought nor sold and that the Western Shoshone people can no more enter into an agreement to market the land under threat of the United States' legal actions and violence than they can live without the earth, water, air, and sun. Carrie's voice-over asserts these philosophical principles that bind the people to Mother Earth. As the camera focuses on the ritual that forms the ceremonial opening for the film, Carrie's honouring of the Creator becomes the guide for the sisters' actions that the documentary records. These are the essential legal relations that Carrie enacts through the prayers and ceremony that introduce their story and the relations that motivate their defence of their land. Land stewardship is thus a right and an obligation: the Western Shoshone endure through the will of the Creator,

Figure 7.7 Elder Corbin Harney singing and drumming.

who gives and represents life; no life can exist without this spiritual relationship. Paradoxically, as the film demonstrates, these are the very relations that are under threat from United States interests that seek to "privatize Western Shoshone ancestral lands [through] their transfer to multinational extractive industries and energy developers."[113] The struggle that the Dann sisters take up is one of protecting this sacred duty and obligation. When the Danns speak on behalf of Western Shoshone land rights, they also speak on behalf of the land. As the film's interlaced pictures demonstrate, the land represents the site for the "irreparable harms threatened by massive land projects … [that] will be visited most directly on the plaintiffs."[114]

When the Danns speak for the land, they also voice through Western Shoshone culture and tradition a defence on behalf of inanimate objects and lives that cannot speak for themselves. The camera pans back to the range, the mountains, and the slate-grey sky to present the viewer with the magnificent landscape in its awe-inspiring insolation and lonely beauty. The mountains stand in tribute to the Creator's presence, even as the Dann sisters stand against the invading forces represented by the United States government. In one respect, the land's remoteness appears to represent metaphorically the Western Shoshone sisters' isolation. The director aligns these parallel images to establish the unequal power relations that organize several violent encounters between the Danns and the BLM that initiate the struggle over obedience to competing legal authorities. The set-up is deliberately reminiscent of other colonial encounters that viewers are invited to draw parallels with. We recall, for example, literary resemblances in the lonely and isolated figure of Robinson Crusoe interrupted by a footprint representing an unknown and unwelcome "colonial other." The camera's point of view in *American Outrage*, however, is deliberately reversed. The occupants are Indigenous, and the invaders are BLM government officials. The film narrates and provides a visual record to this hostile encounter. As Mary Dann overseas her land, she is confronted by a visitor, an "uninvited guest," who refuses her hospitality and accosts her with the accusation that she is trespassing. Neither outwitted by the intruder nor intimidated by his verbal attack, Mary invites him in, offering him hospitality, which he refuses. She then counters his authority by replying that she will not leave her land to discuss his charge or to recognize his authority as a BLM agent. Moreover, in response to his attack, Mary turns to her own sources of legal authority that empower her obligations – a map that indicates her territory, one that is in her family's possession, and Indigenous knowledge of Indigenous-to-Indigenous relations to which she is bound. As she declares for the camera, the map not only authorizes her place on the land as a rightful claim; it also encompasses other forms of legal obligations that precede the arrival of the BLM agent as an "uninvited guest." Had she stepped further in one direction, she explains, she would be trespassing on Paiute land. Her concern for that act of trespass and prior relationship thwarts the authority of the US claim through the invocation of Indigenous understandings of history, time, and succession, that is, an understanding of time and relationships that exists outside of the legal consciousness that the BLM agent seeks to impose. Moreover, these legal relations hold her to a bond of loyalty, duty, and obligation that recognizes and affirms Western Shoshone sovereign relations with other Indigenous nations. "I should have said you're the one whose trespassing," she recalls, indicating her recognition that his accusation is premised in a violent discursive act that seeks to erase her sovereign presence and obligation to prior Indigenous laws. More importantly, she shows no hesitation in communicating her knowledge that should she find herself trespassing on Paiute land she would be "violating" and potentially "offending" Paiute sovereignty. Her demeanour suggests, however, that Western

Shoshone relations recognize these obligations, which are not premised on violent and dispossessive legal orders but on relations of peace and friendship that the Treaty of Ruby Valley establishes between the Western Shoshone Nation and the United States, a legal relationship that takes on wider connotations as a continuation of treaty rights that were already existing among Indigenous peoples, relations that continue to exist between the Western Shoshone and Paiute Nations. As viewers, we understand that Mary's actions are both legally bound and legally motivated in ways that precede and pre-empt the United States' invading legal presence.

### "I Have the Right to Protect My Livestock," or, How the United States "Resolves Matters Administratively"

If we use law to establish the "political behaviour" of states that can serve as "a locus for its collective memory,"[115] then we are able to uncover and make known aspects of legal reasoning that a state adopts to govern its behaviour, protect its interests, and safeguard its authority. Within this decision-making matrix, as Rebecca Johnson explains, are legal stories about "women's political agency, sexual agency, reproductive agency, financial agency, and more" (see chapter 8), stories that, as Johnson contends, tend to "flatten and erase" the state's construction of Indigenous women's law-governed condition. We are also invited by Indigenous-feminist legal storytelling to speculate on state measures that find no representation in these archives. The Dann sisters' experiences of physical harm as a form of colonial gender violence constitutes one of these measures. As images from the film depict, Carrie acts on her rights to protect her livestock because she is bound by that duty through her commitments to the Creator's laws. Western Shoshone jurisdiction and the Creator's laws empower her acts. When she tries to enter the grain elevator to protect the livestock from being impounded, her actions elicit restraining force by the state and its agents (Figure 7.8). The camera captures the tense and aggressive manner in which she is impeded by the BLM. It also shows how the state establishes its authority by protecting and enacting its monopoly on violence.[116] Carrie cannot free herself from the agent's grasp, and she cannot strike back to prevent the agent's physical assault on her. In a second confrontation when the family gathers to protect their livestock, we see why. Clifford Dann's actions, in setting fire to himself to protect their property, elicit the charge of assaulting an officer, and he is subjected to nine months in prison and a five thousand dollar fine, although he himself is covered

Figure 7.8 Carrie Dann being restrained by private security agents as she tries to protect her livestock.

in blood, confined by handcuffs by BLM agents, and suffering from burns to most of his body (Figure 7.9).

## "The Search for Laws Founded in Justice and Humanity"

Laws founded in justice and humanity represent, for Vine Deloria, Jr., the highest achievement of legal principles because they strive to affect the "lives of ordinary people."[117] These laws, he explains, "must have something to do with the emotional feelings of justice, … [they] must speak to our basic humanity, and … [they] must give us common-sense directions as to what behaviour and beliefs are right and wrong."[118] Carrie Dann's respect for the CERD decision by the United Nations demonstrates her understanding that Western Shoshone laws intersect with domestic and international law because her own laws are built on these basic moral principles. Her triumphant voice emerges powerfully in footage when she speaks before the UN and in the celebration held with her legal representative sug-

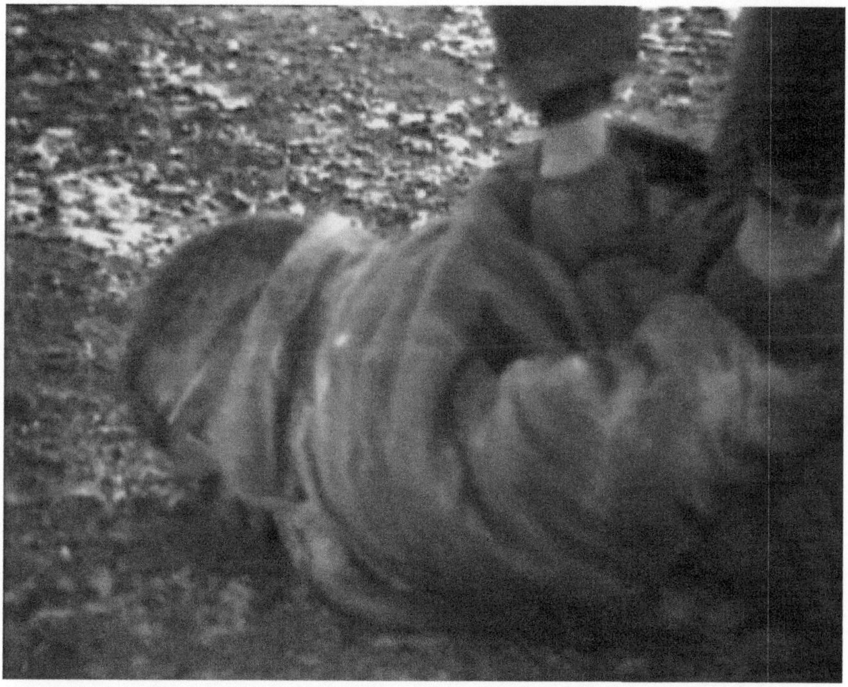

Figure 7.9 Clifford Dann lies face down in the snow pinned by private security agents.

gesting that the outcome of their petition is the source of her joy. In this regard, the linear approach of documentary and its drive towards cinematic closure impede our recollection of her commitment to Western Shoshone law. At a number of points in the documentary, she reiterates the Western Shoshone peoples' obligations to the Creator. She condemns the colonial interests that break this law by degrading the land and proposing to "sell" it for commercial interests. In images reminiscent of Welsh's clips of the Pickton farm's post-forensic extraction (Figure 7.10), *American Outrage* shows viewers Western Shoshone ancestral lands that have been violated by resource extraction. Carrie refuses to better her situation at the expense of Western Shoshone claims, as neither she nor Mary agrees to accept US offers to settle that improve their access to range land. As the film portrays, they are not fighting to protect their self-interest but rather fighting for Western Shoshone land rights and title.

Figure 7.10 Image of an open-pit cyanide heat-bleach mine demonstrates the environmental damage to the land by open-pit mining.

Documentary film directed towards narrative closure obscures these important facts that demonstrate the principles, ethics, and legal reasoning that inform gendered opposition to resource extraction, land violation, and violence against Indigenous women and their communities.

## Conclusion: Documentary Film and Human Rights

Reflecting on the power of international organizations in the struggle to end violence against Indigenous women, Sarah Deer notes the political necessity and human impact of their international reach: "[Amnesty report] *Maze of Injustice,*" she observes, "was invaluable … [it] provided a human face for the stark, dehumanizing statistics that had been released eight years earlier by the Department of Justice. The pictures and personal stories in the report raised the profile of the crisis and captured the attention of national news media, such as the *New York Times*. Suddenly, things began to move quickly."[119] As Deer explains, the human story is a powerful story, one that can lead to concrete change. Hearing the voices of

Indigenous women through mainstream news media, international reports, and domestic law highlights the power of direct speech to raise political consciousness and further local action. The documentary films *Finding Dawn* and *American Outrage* advance this agenda. Placing tremendous weight on the stories Indigenous women tell, on the power of Indigenous women's experiences to help us comprehend gender injustice, and on the capacity for Indigenous women's suffering to move audiences towards the defence and protection of those women's human rights, the films portray the meaning of colonial gender violence in its micro-details and local experience while urging us to decode the pervasive ways in which the state's use of legal violence structures all aspects of Indigenous women's lives. In privileging Indigenous women's voices, the films authenticate multiple forms of storytelling "transfer,"[120] building a human rights literacy specific to Indigenous women and permitting audiences to understand colonial gender violence by "look[ing] [collectively] to … women's stories for guidance."[121] As an artistic practice working against the authority of state-authorized representations, these films by and about Indigenous women provide another source from which to build a platform so that Indigenous women may speak to their experiences of colonial gender violations and have a voice in these struggles.[122]

## NOTES

1 The IAAW is a non-profit organization dedicated to supporting and advancing Indigenous women. It recognizes their contributions to society through a broad mandate that includes addressing gender discrimination, identifying and promoting women's participation in policy development and decision-making, celebrating women's achievements, and establishing networks for the exchange of information and experience. Two of its priorities are the promotion and advancement of Indigenous women's human rights, and leadership initiatives that focus on economic, social, cultural, and political issues at the state and international levels that impact Indigenous women and their communities. See online: Institute for the Advancement of Aboriginal Women, "About Us," <https://iaaw.ca/about-us/> (last visited 21 May 2025). The institute was founded in 1994 by award-winning human rights activist Muriel Stanley Venne to provide legal support to Indigenous women by lessening the "vulnerability" and "unconscionable suffering" they were subject to without access to legal resources and representation. See online:

"Muriel Stanley Venne" (29 March 2013), <https://albertalabourhistory.org/wp-content/uploads/2018/04/2013032801-2013032802-Stanley-Venne-Muriel-r-WG-cor-AF-1.pdf.>

2 Press coverage described the case as the city of Edmonton's "most horrific murder," and noted the "weeping" of Ms. Cardinal's relatives in the courtroom during sentencing as they listened to the appalling details of the crime; see "Edmonton Petty Thief Turned Killer Gets Life for City's Most Horrific Murder," *Canadian Press* (30 March 2001). Police admitted during the investigation that they were "stumped in their search" for Ms. Cardinal's killer, proposing that it might be a "stranger" who had attacked the "small, shy woman" in such a "brutal fashion," when after several months of working exclusively on the case they had "run out of leads"; see "Killing Stumps Police," *Winnipeg Free Press* (3 April 1994).

3 Todd Christopher Elliott pled guilty to second-degree murder and was sentenced to life in prison without parole for fifteen years. *Canadian Press, supra* note 2.

4 Inna Dansereau, "Detective Receives Social Justice Award" (2001) 8.2 Alberta Sweetgrass 8, online: <https://ammsa.com/publications/alberta-sweetgrass/detective-receives-social-justice-award>.

5 *Ibid.*

6 The IAAW's "Esquao Awards" honour Indigenous women by recognizing and celebrating their exceptional achievement. "Esquao" represents a "stylized version for the Cree word for woman" ("Esquao Awards Overview," <https://iaaw.ca/program/esquao-awards/>) and counters the racialized and sexualized slur used to denigrate women. Ms. Venne explains that she envisaged the award when she learned about a young Indigenous girl who was crying after being called the denigrating name. The IAAW Awards also include youth leadership programming to build confidence and skills among young women ("Esquao Youth Leadership Development Program," <https://iaaw.ca/program/esquao-youth-and-adult-leadership-development/> ).

7 *Keetsahnak: Our Missing and Murdered Indigenous Sisters*, a collection edited and contributed to by Kim Anderson, Maria Campbell, and Christi Belcourt (Edmonton: University of Alberta Press, 2018), provides an overview of many of these ceremonies and the principles that inform the gatherings. The work contains contributions by Belcourt; Laura Harjo, Jenell Navarro, and Kimberly Robertson as well as Ann Marie Livingston and Sarah Hunt; and the epilogue presents a discursive form of commemorative justice through the dialogic voices of the participants. Karyn Recollet theorizes commemorative artistic practices as reparatory forms of "decolonial love" that build social activism and pedagogical sites of resistance in "Glyphing Decolonial Love through Urban Flash

Mobbing and *Walking with Our Sisters*" (2015) 45(1) Curriculum Inquiry 129. Tracy Bear explains that ceremonies, such as "Walking with Our Sisters," honour missing and murdered Indigenous women by building sites of "relational accountability" that enact the "concept of otcinawin," a Cree word that designates "a type of natural justice," holding people accountable to their relations; see Tracy Bear, "Walking with Our Sisters: An Art Installation Centered in Ceremony" (2014) 3: 1–2 Aboriginal Policy Studies 223 at 229.

8 Commissions of inquiry and truth commissions increasingly incorporate art's "world-building character" by recognizing the role artistic practices play in truth-gathering. Robert Cover's influential essay "Violence and the Word" examines the "world-building character of interpretive commitments to law" that cultural activities express; see (1986) 95.8 Yale LJ 1601. For three examples, see the artwork commissioned by the Missing and Murdered Indigenous Women Inquiry, online at National Inquiry into Missing and Murdered Indigenous Women and Girls, "Protocols, Symbols and Ceremonies," <https://www.mmiwg-ffada.ca/protocols-symbols-and-ceremonies/>; the artistic submissions incorporated into the Truth and Reconciliation Commission of Canada, online at the National Centre for Truth and Reconciliation, "Exhibits," <https://nctr.ca/exhibits/>; and the photo essay included by Human Rights Watch in its report – see Meghan Rhoad, *Those Who Take Us Away: Abusive Policing and Failures in Protection of Indigenous Women and Girls in Northern British Columbia, Canada* (New York: Human Rights Watch, 2013) at 88, online: <https://www.hrw.org/report/2013/02/13/those-who-take-us-away/abusive-policing-and-failures-protection-indigenous-women>.

9 Anne Orford observes that "the commissioning of truths is one means by which institutions of transitional justice attempt to narrate or make plausible the movement from one regime to another"; see "Commissioning the Truth" (2006) 15.3 Columbia J Gender and Law 851 at 881.

10 "Indigenous storywork," theorized by Jo-Ann Archibald, conceptualizes "how a story fits within a people's belief system" (26) and how "cultural knowledge, traditions, and healing" lessen the impact of colonization by enacting power to "bring storied life back to [Indigenous peoples]" (139). Storywork principles are holistic, incorporating "heart, mind, body, and spirit" (143), and land based, requiring integration between the "traditional location for telling stories" and the participant's active engagement with the laws, duties, and principles associated with the territory on which the stories are told and that they impart (71); see *Indigenous Storywork: Educating the Heart, Mind, Body, and Spirit* (Vancouver: UBC Press, 2008).

11 See Kaitlyn Watson, "Missing and Murdered Indigenous Women: The Role of Grassroots Organizations and Social Media in Education" (2018–2019) 33:1–2 Cdn Woman Studies 204, wherein Watson explains the use of social media to circulate the political campaign, for example, "#AmINext," a media event launched by Holly Jarrett, the cousin of Loretta Saunders, an Inuit university student murdered by two individuals whom she met while subletting her apartment. Jarrett's Twitter hashtag became a national movement, with Indigenous women asking angrily "#AmINext" and others protesting, "#ImNotNext" (208).

12 Kim Anderson, Maria Campbell, and Christi Belcourt, in "Epilogue: Sitting In with Sisters," describe the meetings held at the Ontario Federation of Indian Friendship Centre as an accompaniment to "Walking with Our Sisters," an installation organized to commemorate, honour, and educate the public about violence against Indigenous women. See Anderson, Campbell & Belcourt, *supra* note 7.

13 See Lisa Magarrell, "Reparations for Massive or Widespread Human Rights Violations: Sorting Out Claims for Reparations and the Struggle for Social Justice" (2003) 22 Windsor Yearbook of Access to Justice 85 at 86, 90. As a means of overcoming the social fragmentation caused by Ms. Cardinal's death, the IAAW event included several restorative justice practices: the bestowal of an award, the presentation of a Métis sash, and a formal robing ceremony. At the conclusion of the formal event in accordance with the ceremonies, a receiving line was formed by Indigenous women who waited to embrace and thank Detective Taylor for his dedication to the case. The receiving line was a spontaneous act that had the effect of reshaping the audience into a social collective joined in its appreciation and respect for Detective Taylor and for the Cardinal family. The description of this practice and intent is based on my recall of the event.

14 Anderson, Campbell & Belcourt, *supra* note 7 at xi.

15 Black's installation inspired the founding of Red Dress Day on May 5th to honour missing and murdered Indigenous women. Commemorative events include rallies and ceremonies that broaden the concern over violence against Indigenous women to include issues of disproportionate victimization, intimate partner violence, and over-representation in incarceration (Amnesty International Canada, "Red Dress Day 2025" https://amnesty.ca/red-dress-day/).

16 See Elizabeth Brulé, "The REDress Project: Casting an Indigenous Feminist Worldview on Sexual Violence Prevention and Education Programs in Ontario's Universities" (2018) 12:2 Studies in Social Justice 337. Brulé describes the project as "an aesthetic response to over 1,000 unresolved cases of missing and murdered Indigenous women, girls,

transgender and twospirit persons" (338). Its installations appeared across Canada at several venues and "land-based spaces," including the Canadian Museum of Human Rights (338).

17 Quoted in Alicia Ault, "These Haunting Red Dresses Memorialize Murdered and Missing Indigenous Women" (19 March 2019) *Smithsonian Magazine*, online: <https://www.smithsonianmag.com/smithsonian-institution/these-haunting-red-dresses-memorialize-murdered-and-missing-indigenous-women-180971730/>.

18 *Ibid.*

19 Among the many scholars and international organizations that have condemned state inaction in regard to violence against Indigenous women, see Rauna Kuokkanen, "Indigenous Women's Rights and International Law: Challenges of the UN Declaration on the Rights of Indigenous Peoples" in Corinne Lennox & Damien Short, eds, *Handbook on Indigenous Peoples' Rights* (London: Routledge, 2016) 275; Kuokkanen, "Self-Determination and Indigenous Women's Rights at the Intersection of International Human Rights" (2012) 34:1 Human Rights Q 225; Ryan Devreskracht, "House Republicans Add Insult To Native Women's Injury" (2014) 3 U Miami Race & Soc Just L Rev 1 1, online: <http://repository.law.miami.edu/umrsjlr/vol3/iss1/3>. These scholars underscore the legal and feminist implications associated with state inaction. Indigenous artists have also been joined in their censure by scholars and legal actors who have described the impasse in the following ways: as an "epidemic" and a "disturbing phenomenon": James Anaya quoted in Susana Mas, "UN Aboriginal Envoy Says Canada Is Facing a 'Crisis,'" *CBC News* (16 October 2013), online: <https://www.cbc.ca/news/politics/un-aboriginal-envoy-says-canada-is-facing-a-crisis-1.2054682>; as a "national disgrace": Augie Fleras, "Finding Dawn" (2010) 26:1 Visual Anthropology Rev 47 at 47, cited in Allison Hargreaves, "*Finding Dawn* and Missing Women in Canada: Story-Based Methods in Antiviolence Research and Remembrance" (2015) 27:3 Studies in American Indian Literatures 82 at 96; as a "genocide": *Reclaiming Power and Place: The Final Report of the National Inquiry into Missing and Murdered Indigenous Women and Girls* (Ottawa: MMIWG, 2019), online: <https://www.loc.gov/item/lcwaN0028038/> [MMIWG]; and as a "severe problem": James Anaya in United Nations General Assembly, "Report of the Special Rapporteur on the Rights of Indigenous Peoples" (Human Rights Council, 2014) at 11, online: <http://unsr.jamesanaya.org>.

20 Josephine L. Savarese, "Challenging Colonial Norms and Attending to Presencing in Stories of Missing and Murdered Indigenous Women" (2017) 29:1 Cdn J Women and the Law 157at 178.

21 Lena Campagna, "Invisible Victims: American Indian Women and Adolescent Involvement in the Domestic Sex Trade" (2016) 40:1 American Indian Culture and Res J 47 at 47. Campagna notes that the state's lack of attention to the issue of American Indian women's experiences of "colonial sexual exploitation" (50) led researchers to characterize Indigenous women as "invisible victims" (47).

22 Among the many artistic and literary voices associated with portraying violence against Indigenous women, the most haunting voice belongs to Marilyn Dumont in her poem "Helen Betty Osborne" (online: <https://www.poetryfoundation.org/poems/147310/helen-betty-osborne>), a lament memorializing the poet's grief and struggle to understand the senseless abduction and murder in 1971 of Ms. Osborne, a high school student from Norway House Indian Reserve, whose death and the betrayal of public trust that erupted over a sixteen-year period as police worked to resolve the case amassed decades of grief on the part of Ms. Osborne's family and the wider Indigenous community. A fuller account of these events is provided by the *Report of the Aboriginal Justice Inquiry of Manitoba* (Winnipeg: Government of Manitoba, 1991), online: <http://www.ajic.mb.ca/volumell/chapter1.html>.

23 Ruti G. Teitel, *Transitional Justice* (Oxford: Oxford University Press, 2002) at 20.

24 Christine Welsh [executive producer], *Finding Dawn* (Canada: National Film Board of Canada, 2006).

25 Beth Gage & George Gage [directors], *American Outrage* (Onley, PA: Gage and Gage Productions, 2008).

26 Stephen J. Collier & Andrew Lakoff, "On Regimes of Living" in Aihwa Ong & Stephen J Collier, eds, *Global Assemblages: Technology, Politics, and Ethics as Anthropological Problems* (Hoboken: Wiley & Sons, 2008) 22 at 35.

27 *Ibid.*

28 Denise Ferreira da Silva, "No-Bodies: Law, Raciality and Violence" (2009) 18:2 Griffith L Rev 212 at 231; da Silva, "The Banalization of Racial Events" (2017) 20:1 Theory & Event 61 at 64.

29 Inderpal Grewal, "'Women's Rights as Human Rights': Feminist Practices, Global Feminism, and Human Rights Regimes in Transnationality" (1999) 3:3 Citizenship Studies 337 at 339, citing Charlotte Bunch, "Transforming Human Rights from a Feminist Perspective" in JS Peters & Andrea Wolper, eds, *Women's Rights, Human Rights: International Feminist Perspectives* (New York: Routledge, 1995) 11.

30 See Sarah Deer, *The Beginning and End of Rape: Confronting Sexual Violence in Native America* (Minneapolis: University of Minnesota Press, 2015); Kuokkanen, *supra* note 18; and Dubravka Šimonović,

*Report of the Special Rapporteur on Violence against Women, Its Causes and Consequences* (United Nations General Assembly, 24 June–12 July 2019) A/HRC/41/42/Add.I.

31 Loic JD Wacquant, "The Rise of Advanced Marginality: Notes on Its Nature and Implications" (1996) 39:2 Acta Sociologica 121 at 121. Kirsten Manley-Casimir characterizes the "myth of Canada" held by the international community as regarding Canada as a "neutrally situated peacemaker," despite a history of "colonial injustice" in its relations with Indigenous communities; see "Creating Space for Indigenous Storytelling in Courts" (2012) 27.2 Cdn J Law and Society 231 at 231.

32 Wacquant, *supra* note 30 at 123.

33 Hilary Charlesworth, Christine Chinkin & Shelley Wright, "Feminist Approaches to International Law" (1991) 85:4 American J Int L 613 at 616. The Women's Legal Education and Action Fund observes that more than seven hundred recommendations in fifty-eight reports over two decades have failed to be implemented by Canada, notwithstanding the interventions of a coalition of actors from First Nations' Family Services, lawyers, scholars, and members of the Union of British Columbia Indian Chiefs calling for measures; see "Viewpoint 39-5: Hundreds of Recommendations Go Unimplemented" (May 2015) 39:5 *LawNow*, online: <https://ca.vlex.com/vid/viewpoint-39-5-hundreds-693882749>. An open letter by more than fifteen hundred academics attempted to shame the Canadian government into implementing the MMIWI recommendations; see Jaime Pashagumskum, "1,500 Academics Prod Feds to Move on MMIWG Action Plan," *APTN National News* (3 September 2020), online: <https://www.aptnnews.ca/national-news/1500-academics-prod-feds-to-move-on-mmiwg-action-plan/>. Community leaders and members critical of the MMIWIG Inquiry's shortcomings joined together to urge the government not to provide more time and money to the inquiry in light of its delays and trauma-inducing impact on families and grass-roots community members; see "An Open Letter Calling for the Refusal of the MMIWG Inquiry Extension Request," Letter to the Editor, *Manitoulin Expositor* (11 April 2008), online: <https://www.manitoulin.com/an-open-letter-calling-for-the-refusal-of-the-mmiwg-inquiry-extension-request/>.

34 Mariana Prandini Assis, "Violence against Women as a Translocal Category in the Jurisprudence of the Inter-American Court of Human Rights" (2017) 8:2 Rev. Direito e Práxis 1507 at 1515.

35 Genevieve Renard Painter, "Thinking Past Rights: Towards Feminist Theories of Reparations" (2012) 20 Windsor Yearbook of Access to Justice 1 at 2.

36 Rosalva Aída Hernádez Castillo, "Between Community Justice and International Litigation: The Case of Inés Fernández before the Inter-

American Court" in Rachel Seider, ed, *Demanding Justice and Security: Indigenous Women and Legal Pluralities* (New Brunswick, NJ: Rutgers University Press, 2017) 29 at 30–31.

37 *Ibid*, fn at 34.

38 Julie Kaye, "Reconciliation in the Context of Settler-Colonial Gender Violence: 'How Do We Reconcile with an Abuser?'" (November 2016) 53:4 Cdn Rev Soc 461 at 463.

39 *Ibid*.

40 Katherine M. Franke, "Gendered Subjects of Transitional Justice" (2006) 15:3 Columbia J Gender and Law 813 at 817; Julieta Lemaitre & Kristin Bergtora Sandvik, "Beyond Sexual Violence in Transitional Justice: Political Insecurity as a Gendered Harm" (2014) 22 Feminist Legal Studies 243 at 244.

41 Violence against Indigenous women has been characterized as a continuation of war by other means; see Beverly Jacobs, "There Has Been a War against Indigenous Women since Colonization: Former NWAC President," *APTN National News* (23 September 2014), online: <https://www.aptnnews.ca/national-news/war-indigenous-women-since-colonization-former-nwac-president/>; Genevieve M. LeMay, "The Cycles of Violence against Native Women: An Analysis of Colonialism, Historical Legislation and the Violence Against Women Reauthorization Act of 2013" (2018) 12.1 PSU McNair Scholars Online J, article 1, online: <https://pdxscholar.library.pdx.edu/cgi/viewcontent.cgi?article=1177&context=mcnair>; and Veldon Coburn, "Why Are the Deaths of Indigenous Women and Girls Ungrievable?" *Policy Options Magazine* (11 June 2019), online: <https://policyoptions.irpp.org/magazines/june-2019/why-are-the-deaths-of-indigenous-women-and-girls-ungrievable/>. Although this view presents an important framing of the issue, especially in recasting how violence against Indigenous women is understood and represented by settler colonial countries, it is an area of debate that I do not take up here.

42 Franke, *supra* note 39 at 820.

43 Justin Ling, "Canada Reckons with Genocide," *Foreign Policy* (24 June 2019), online: <https://foreignpolicy.com/2019/06/24/canada-reckons-with-genocide-inquiry-missing-murdered-indigenous-women-girls/>, citing MMIWG, *supra* note 18.

44 Devreskracht, *supra* note 19 at 10.

45 United Nations Population Fund, "Recommendations of the UN Permanent Forum on Indigenous Issues Regarding Sexual and Reproductive Health and Rights & Gender-Based Violence: Progress and Challenges, Executive Summary" (2018) at 2, online: <https://www.unfpa.org/featured-publication/recommendations-un-permanent-forum-indigenous-issues-regarding-sexual-and>. The report's executive

summary finds that "only 15.5 per cent of all recommendations make explicit reference to the situation of indigenous women or girls, and /or gender equality" (2) and that the priority of the forum seems to be advancing "indigenous diplomacy" (2).

46 Alma Luz Beltrán Y Puga et al, "Gender Justice in the Americas: A Transnational Dialogue on Sexuality, Violence, Reproduction, and Human Rights (2011) 65:3 U of Miami L Rev 751 at 757.

47 Sonia Tascón, "Considering Human Rights Films, Representation, and Ethics: Whose Face?" (2012) 34:3 Human Rights Q 864 at 865; Alexandra Schultheis Moore, "Film after Atrocity: An Interview with Joshua Oppenheimer" in Sophia A. McClennen & Alexandra Schultheis Moore, eds, *The Routledge Companion to Literature and Human Rights* (London: Routledge, 2016) 480. Tascón argues that human rights films and festivals work through practices of subversion by directing our attention to issues not previously considered by legal frameworks and by focusing on topics that have not been widely discussed and disseminated beyond the immediate community aware of the human rights violation; see Tascón, *Human Rights Film Festivals: Activism in Context* (Houndmills, UK: Palgrave Macmillan, 2015) 209.

48 Tascón, "Considering Human Rights Films," *supra* note 47, notes that human rights film festivals have arisen globally since Human Rights Watch's inaugural international festival held in London in the late 1980s (864).

49 *Ibid* at 865.

50 Moore, *supra* note 47 at 481.

51 Tascón, "Considering Human Rights Films," *supra* note 47 at 866–867.

52 *Ibid* at 870. Jessica Silbey engages with film as a "silent witness" (25) to truth used in legal practices supporting parties' claims that the only "story to be believed was the one the video told" (25): "Cross-Examining Film" (2008) 8:1 U of Maryland LJ of Race, Religion, Gender & Class 17. Silbey's analysis of the US Supreme Court's use of a police officer's dash-cam footage in *Scott v Harris* directs our attention to how film's bias may be deployed for different ends, but her overall concern is to debunk the prevailing idea accepted by the US Supreme Court that film represents a true "depiction of reality" (17). All films are biased in their form, meaning, and techniques, Silbey notes, and therefore they all "tell more than one story and less than the whole story" (34). They gain their visual impact and persuasive force from their capacity to "conjure" and "exploit" the idea that they "show … the whole story" (43). Rather than setting aside documentary sources, such as film, as having no legal value, Silbey argues that because there is no unbiased access provided by film, legal actors require techniques for analysing and deploying visual forms,

that is, they require instruction in their use as testimony and evidence because video and film have become important parts of the legal texts relied on by courts.

53 Hanna Musiol, "Sites of Human Rights Theory" in Sophia McClennan & Alexandra Schultheis Moore, eds, *The Routledge Companion to Literature and Human Rights* (London: Routledge, 2015) 389 at 394.

54 Moore, *supra* note 47 at 482.

55 *Ibid* at 484.

56 *Ibid* at 480.

57 *Ibid* at 481.

58 *Ibid* at 484.

59 Welsh, *supra* note 23 at 2:47.

60 *Ibid* at :39.

61 *Ibid* at :47.

62 As we learn in subsequent interviews with Lorraine Crey, Dawn's sister, Dawn's case is not among those that prosecutors proceed with in laying murder charges for twenty-six of the sixty-seven women missing from Vancouver's DTES. Legal justice and closure are not possible despite the enormous financial costs of bringing the case against the owner of the farm, Robert Pickton, to trial. Reports released by the *Canadian Press* indicate that the province's guilty verdict cost British Columbia $102 million, with the RCMP investigation running to $70 million to secure second-degree murder convictions for the murder of six women (*Canadian Press*, "Serial Killer," online: <https://www.upi.com/Top_News/World-News/2010/11/16/Canada-serial-killer-case-cost-102M/47011289942064/>). The expense associated with the investigation draws into sharp contrast Dawn's brother's comments that the missing women were poor and lacked social power to motivate police help when reports of missing women were brought forward by family members.

63 Johanne Helbo Bøndergaard, *Forensic Memory: Literature after Testimony* (Cham, Switzerland: Palgrave Macmillan, 2017) at 167.

64 Welsh's film leaves her audience to draw conclusions as to why the Crey children were taken from their mother. Other Indigenous artists provide clues. In writing about his personal experience of residential schooling, Basil Johnston in *Indian School Days* (Toronto: Key Porter, 1988) identifies widowed women, single women, and grandmother-headed households as family units targeted by the Indian Agent (8, 19). In her important and sensitive analysis of *Finding Dawn*, Hargreaves, *supra* note 18 at 83, argues that, through family narratives, Welsh invites the audience's attention to the intergenerational impacts of colonial gender violence as indicative of "an ongoing history of gendered racism" represented by residential schooling and foster care, the gendered and racialized dimensions of

which are expressed directly through Dawn's inability to reconnect with her Sto:lo heritage. Shari Huhndorf, in "Scenes from the Fringe: Gendered Violence and the Geographies of Indigenous Feminism" underscores the direct link between "colonial policies of dispossession," artistic media, and "the racial dimensions of the murders [that] escaped public notice" to assert that even as "the social invisibility of Native people obscures the challenges that Indigeneity poses to the political order, so too does it conceal the violence that ensues from dispossession" (564): "Scenes from the Fringe" (Spring 2021) 46.3 Signs: Journal of Women in Culture and Society 535. Dispossession in its multiple forms and implications, as these scholars note, represents an important sub-text to the film's focus on searching for answers and legal accountability.

65 Hargreaves, *supra* note 18 at 85, aptly describes these institutional disparities and life struggles as "gendered violence[s] of colonial origin." Huhndorf, *supra* note 63 at 535, observes that the state's depiction of deprivation "naturalize[s] the violence that occurs in impoverished neighborhoods, attributing it to the degeneracy of the inhabitants."

66 Welsh, *supra* note 23, at 13:14.

67 *Ibid* at 15:35.

68 *Ibid*.

69 *Ibid* at 2:36.

70 Wacquant, *supra* note 30 at 122.

71 Lucas Bessire, "The Rise of Indigenous Hypermarginality: Native Culture as a Neoliberal Politics of Life" (2014) 55:3 Current Anthropology 276 at 286.

72 Wacquant, *supra* note 30 at 123.

73 See Lemaitre and Sandvik, *supra* note 39 at 258; João Biehl, "Vita: Life in a Zone of Social Abandonment" (2001) 68:1 Social Text 131 at 134; and Bessire, *supra* note 70 at 279.

74 Welsh, supra note 23 at 3:02.

75 Katherena Vermette's novel *The Break* (Toronto: Anansi, 2016) depicts these conditions through her protagonist Phoenix's life story and the impoverishment and violence that other characters are subject to. Ling, *supra* note 42, draws similar conclusions. See also Canada, *National Inquiry into Missing and Murdered Indigenous Women and Girls: A Legal Analysis of Genocide: Supplementary Report of the National Inquiry* (Vancouver: Privy Council Office, 2019). I note here my discomfort with citing in an approving way Sherene Razack's "Gendering Disposability" (2016) 28:2 Cdn J Women and the Law 285 at 286, because I find her use for scholarly reasons of details citing the Crown's use of Cindy Gladue's body for legal reasons equally violating. I share with Ann-Marie Livingston and Sarah Hunt the view that lawyers and researchers

revictimize Indigenous women when they use excessive details to condemn the state's actions without understanding the impact of these details on a victim's family members and the wider Indigenous community involved by their concern for and solidarity with Indigenous women. Ann-Marie (one of the daughters featured in Welsh's film) argues that, as the daughter of a missing Indigenous woman, she can be heard on behalf of her mother, Elsie, in ways that her mother was never granted an audience; see "Honouring Elsie: Was She Just a Dream?" in *Keetsahnak, supra* note 7, 45 at 59. It is an indication of the achievement of Welsh's film and her human rights work that she accords respect to Indigenous women as victims without eroding their dignity and that the film, in linking colonial gender violence to Indigenous women's bodies, does not deploy violence against Indigenous women to describe the actions of perpetrators who commit violence against Indigenous women. Vermette's novel takes up a similar form of dignity-granting status for victims through her characterization of Elsie's story in *The Break*.

76 For a moving account of this issue, see Helen Knott's *In My Own Moccasins: A Memoir of Resilience* (Regina: University of Regina Press, 2020). Knott's work with Amnesty International connecting Indigenous women's insecurity and resource extraction, and the honour accorded her by the Nobel Women's Initiative as a peace activist protecting Indigenous women's bodies and land (<https://nobelwomensinitiative.org/meet-helen-knott-canada/>), demonstrate the multilayered ways that Indigenous women mobilize against colonial, gender, and land violence.

77 Katherine Morton, "Hitchhiking and Missing and Murdered Indigenous Women: A Critical Discourse Analysis of Billboards on the Highway of Tears" (2016) 41:3 Cdn J of Sociology 299 at 304.

78 Welsh, *supra* note 23 at 31:53.

79 Rhoad, *supra* note 8.

80 Augie Fleras, "Finding Dawn, Directed by Christine Welsh" (2010) 26:1 Visual Anthropology Rev 47 at 47.

81 *Ibid*; see also Tascón, "Considering Human Rights Films," *supra* note 46.

82 Lemaitre and Sandvik, *supra* note 39 at 246.

83 The situation of Indigenous women and girls and the inadequate protection of their human rights by the Canadian state are noted by Special Rapporteur Dubravka Šimonović during her visit to Canada in April 2018. The statistics indicate the high rate of violence in which Indigenous women and girls are three times more likely to be victimized by violent crime and six times more likely to be the victim of homicide, despite being 5 per cent of the population: "Report of the Special Rapporteur on Violence Against Women, Its Causes and Consequences," United Nations General Assembly (2019, 24 June–12 July) A/HRC/41/42/Add.I., 3. These statistics stand out

in the general context of statements that open the report and that comment on Canada's "long-standing record of support at the United Nations for issues relating to violence against women" (3). The starting point for the report's condemnation of Canada's failure to engage with violence against Indigenous women and girls is the country's compliance with rather than its infringement of Indigenous women's human rights, through its failure to act to protect Indigenous women. The wider perception among Indigenous women at the state level – that international representatives fail to understand – is that their local experiences as Indigenous peoples are representative of colonial gender violence cross-hatching all aspects of their lives. Local situations require greater attention by international actors to underscore the context of settler-state injustice in their reporting, yet Indigenous women's voices are rarely included in these reports. The local online campaign by Indigenous women asking "Am I next?" highlighted this absence as it called attention to the state's indifference to the prevalence of missing and murdered Indigenous women: see Connie Walker, "Indigenous Women Ask "Am I Next" to Raise Awareness about Missing and Murdered," *CBC News* (5 September 2014), online: <https://www.cbc.ca/news/indigenous/indigenous-women-ask-am-i-next-to-raise-awareness-about-missing-and-murdered-1.2757295>. Ms. Šimonović's report, like those of other international human rights bodies, uses the standpoint of the state rather than Indigenous women's experiences as the entry point to the report, thereby permitting the state's implication in a legacy of injustice and dispossession to subtend rather than launch her inquiry into Indigenous women's status as dispossessed Indigenous peoples subject to colonial gender violence.

84 *Mary and Carrie Dann v United States*, (2002) Case 11.140, Report No 75/02, Inter-Am CHR Doc 5 rev 1 at 860 [*Mary and Carrie Dann*].

85 Organization of American States, Inter-American Commission on Human Rights, "What Is the IACHR?," online: <https://www.oas.org/en/IACHR/jsForm/?File=/en/iachr/mandate/what.asp>; Amy S Dwyer, "The Inter-American Court of Human Rights: Towards Establishing an Effective Regional Contentious Jurisdiction" (1990) 13:1 Boston College Int and Comp L Rev 127 at 129.

86 Organization of American States, Inter-American Commission on Human Rights, Report No 99/99, Case 11.140, Mary and Carrie Dann United States (1999 September 27) at para 4. Commissioners Robert Goldman, chair, and Claudio Grossman did not participate in the discussion and decision of this report, pursuant to Article 19(2)(a) of the commission's regulations [Inter-American Comm on Human Rights Report].

87 *Mary and Carrie Dann*, *supra* note 84 at para 36.

88 *Ibid* at para 38.

89 *Ibid* at para 60.
90 *Ibid* at para 14.
91 *Ibid* at para 16.
92 *Ibid*.
93 *Ibid* at para 23.
94 Steven M Tullberg and Robert T Coulter of the Indian Law Resource Center presented the petition on behalf of the Dann sisters.
95 *American Declaration of the Rights and Duties of Man*, 2 May 1948, Inter-American Commission on Human Rights, online: <https://www.refworld.org/docid/3ae6b3710.html>.
96 Inter-American Comm on Human Rights Report, *supra* note 85 at para 8.
97 *Mary and Carrie Dann, supra* note 84 at 172.
98 *Ibid* at para 54.
99 *Ibid* at paras 54 and 58.
100 *Ibid* at para 55.
101 *Ibid* at para 49.
102 *Ibid* at para 82.
103 *Ibid* at para 144.
104 Organization of American States, Inter-American Commission on Human Rights, Report No 113/01, Case No 11.140, Mary and Carrie Dann United States (15 October 2001) at paras 148.1 & 2. These recommendations were reiterated by the commission in its conclusion at *Mary and Carrie Dann, supra* note 84, para 173: 1, 2.
105 Organization of American States, Inter-American Commission on Human Rights, Mary and Carrie Dann v United States, Case 11.140, Report No 75/02., Doc 5 rev 1 (2002), para 148.
106 United Nations, Committee for the Elimination of Racial Discrimination, "Early Warning and Action Procedure Decision 1 (68), United States of America," CERD/USA/DEC/1, 11 April 2006, para 10 [CERD].
107 Robert Coulter, private communication, 13 November 2017 (communication on file with author).
108 See "Western Shoshone," James E. Rogers College of Law, University of Arizona, online: <https://law.arizona.edu/western-shoshone>.
109 Stephen Best & Saidiya Hartman, "Fugitive Justice" (2005 Fall) 92:1 *Representations* (2005) 1 at 8.
110 *Ibid*.
111 *Ibid*.
112 Alyosha Goldstein, "Where the Nation Takes Place: Proprietary Regimes, Antistatism, and U.S. Settler Colonialism" (2008 Fall) 107:4 South Atlantic Q 833 at 842. The Dann sisters were also forced to fend off the United States' use of racial classifications that it deployed to undermine their political status as members of the Western Shoshone people, classifications

that sought to call into question their political standing and deprive them of their land. In response to the Bureau of Land Management's claim that they were trespassing on "public lands" by grazing their cattle and horses on the open range, they challenged the BLM to prove in court that the lands belonged to the federal government and not to them. The trespass charge brought by the state initiated the court proceedings through which the Danns used the Western legal system to defend Western Shoshone land rights before the domestic court system, the Supreme Court of the United States, and the United Nations. The state opposed their claims to ownership and possession before both the Inter-American Commission and the United Nations by arguing that the Danns' complaint with regard to the Indian Claims Commission's proceedings represented a dispute among members about the status of the tribe's "single governing authority" (US Department of State, CERD Annex II, 23 April 2007, para 9, online: <https://2009-2017.state.gov/j/drl/rls/cerd_report/83406.htm>), rather than their recognition that the ICC decision would be taken up by domestic courts under the "erroneous view that loss of possession results in extinguishment of Indian title": John D O'Connell, "Constructive Conquests in the Courts: A Legal History of the Western Shoshon [*sic*] Lands Struggle – 1861 to 1991" (2002) 42:4 Natural Resources J 765 at 775, fn 33. How the Danns understood these implications is unexplained by the court records. Yet the way in which they grasped the micro-analytics of power and legal relations from within their Western Shoshone traditions has wider implications for their claim. These tribal claims contribute in important ways to Indigenous law in its capacity to provide a standpoint from which to define and defend Indigenous sovereignty for both domestic and international law relations and for Indigenous women's legal empowerment as tribal actors enacting and protecting tribal sovereignty. For Indigenous-feminist legal scholarship enacting these goals, see Sarah Deer & Mary Kathryn Nagle, "Return to Worcester: Dollar General and the Restoration of Tribal Jurisdiction to Protect Native Women and Children" (2018) 41:1 Harv Women's LJ 179.

113 CERD, *supra* note 105 at para 7.

114 US Court of Appeals, 9th Circuit, *South Fork Band v DOI* (2009), No 09-15230 at 15823, 15840.

115 Jane L Curry, "When an Authoritarian State Victimizes the Nation: Transitional Justice, Collective Memory, and Political Divides" (2007) 37:1 Int J Sociology 58 at 58.

116 The state's capacity to use violence to preserve and protect its monopoly on law and justice in both law-making and law-preserving forms is aptly explored by Walter Benjamin in "Critique of Violence" in Marcus Bullock & Michael Jennings, eds, *Walter Benjamin: Selected Writings,*

*Volume 1, 1913–1926* (Cambridge, MA: Harvard University Press, 1996) 236 at 242, 243. The systematic application of legal reasoning and legal consequences through the mechanism of violence is analysed by Robert Cover's "Violence and the Word," *supra* note 8. These foundational essays redirect our understanding of the relationship between law and violence in the creation of normative universes, a body of scholarship that is too voluminous to cite here.

117 Vine Deloria, Jr, "Laws Founded in Justice and Humanity: Reflections on the Content and Character of Federal Indian Law" (1989) 31:2 Arizona L Rev 203 at 204.

118 *Ibid.*

119 Deer, *supra* note 29 at 100.

120 Shannon Speed, "Representations of Violence: (Re)Telling Indigenous Women's Stories and the Politics of Knowledge Production" in Chris Anderson & Jean M O'Brien, eds, *Sources and Methods in Indigenous Studies* (London: Routledge, 2017) at 181.

121 *Ibid* at 182.

122 I am indebted to Debra Mckenzie and Jennifer Henderson for comments and suggestions that greatly improved the clarity and coherence of this chapter and to the editors of the collection for intellectual support and community throughout the writing process.

## JURISPRUDENCE

*Mary and Carrie Dann v United States*, (2002) Case 11.140, Report No 75/02, Inter-Am CHR Doc 5 rev 1 at 860.

*Mary and Carrie Dann v United States*, US Court of Appeals, 9th Circuit, *South Fork Band v DOI* (2009), No 09-15230.

## OTHER SOURCES

Amnesty International Canada. "Red Dress Day," online: <https://amnesty.ca/red-dress-day/>.

Anaya, James. "Report of the Special Rapporteur on the Rights of Indigenous Peoples" (Human Rights Council, 2014), online: <http://unsr.jamesanaya.org>.

Anderson, Kim Maria Campbell & Christi Belcourt (eds). *Keetsahnak: Our Missing and Murdered Indigenous Sisters* (Edmonton: University of Alberta Press, 2018).

Archibald, Jo-Ann. *Indigenous Storywork: Educating the Heart, Mind, Body, and Spirit* (Vancouver: UBC Press, 2008).

Assis, Mariana Prandini. "Violence against Women as a Translocal Category in the Jurisprudence of the Inter-American Court of Human Rights" (2017) 8:2 Rev. Direito e Práxis 1507.

Ault, Alicia. "These Haunting Red Dresses Memorialize Murdered and Missing Indigenous Women." *Smithsonian Magazine* (19 March 2019), online: <https://www.smithsonianmag.com/smithsonian-institution/these-haunting-red-dresses-memorialize-murdered-and-missing-indigenous-women-180971730/>.

Bear, Tracy. "Walking with Our Sisters: An Art Installation Centered in Ceremony" (2014) 3:1–2 Aboriginal Policy Studies 223.

Benjamin, Walter. "Critique of Violence" in Marcus Bullock & Michael Jennings, eds, *Walter Benjamin: Selected Writings, Volume 1, 1913–1926* (Cambridge, MA: Harvard University Press, 1996) 236.

Bessire, Lucas. "The Rise of Indigenous Hypermarginality: Native Culture as a Neoliberal Politics of Life" (2014) 55:3 Current Anthropology 276.

Best, Stephen & Saidiya Hartman. "Fugitive Justice" (2005 Fall) 92:1 Representations 1.

Biehl, Joao. "Vita: Life in a Zone of Social Abandonment" (2001) 68:1 Social Text 131.

Bøndergaard, Johanne Helbo. *Forensic Memory: Literature after Testimony* (Cham, Switzerland: Palgrave Macmillan, 2017).

Brulé, Elizabeth. "The REDdress Project: Casting an Indigenous Feminist Worldview on Sexual Violence Prevention and Education Programs in Ontario's Universities" (2018) 12:2 Studies in Social Justice 337.

Bunch, Charlotte. "Transforming Human Rights from a Feminist Perspective" in JS Peters & Andrea Wolper, eds, *Women's Rights, Human Rights: International Feminist Perspectives* (New York: Routledge, 1995) 11.

Campagna, Lena. "Invisible Victims: American Indian Women and Adolescent Involvement in the Domestic Sex Trade" (2016) 40:1 American Indian Culture and Res J 47.

Canadian Press. "Edmonton Petty Thief Turned Killer Gets Life for City's Most Horrific Murder" (30 March 2001).

Canadian Press. "Serial Killer," online: <https://www.upi.com/Top_News/World-News/2010/11/16/Canada-serial-killer-case-cost-102M/47011289942064/>.

Castillo, Rosalva Aída Hernádez. "Between Community Justice and International Litigation: The Case of Inés Fernández before the Inter-American Court" in Rachel Seider, ed, *Demanding Justice and Security: Indigenous Women and Legal Pluralities* (New Brunswick, NJ: Rutgers University Press, 2017).

Charlesworth, Hilary, Christine Chinkin & Shelley Wright. "Feminist Approaches to International Law" (1991) 85:4 American J Int L 613.

Coburn, Veldon. "Why Are the Deaths of Indigenous Women and Girls Ungrievable?" *Policy Options Magazine* (11 June 2019), online: <https://policyoptions.irpp.org/magazines/june-2019/why-are-the-deaths-of-indigenous-women-and-girls-ungrievable/>.

Collier, Stephen J. & Andrew Lakoff. "On Regimes of Living" in Aihwa Ong & Stephen J Collier, eds, *Global Assemblages: Technology, Politics, and Ethics as Anthropological Problems* (Hoboken: Wiley & Sons, 2008) 22.

Cover, Robert. "Violence and the Word" (1986) 95:8 Yale LJ 1601.

Curry, Jane L. "When an Authoritarian State Victimizes the Nation: Transitional Justice, Collective Memory, and Political Divides" (2007) 37:1 Int J Sociology 58.

Dansereau, Inna. "Detective Receives Social Justice Award" (2001) 8.2 Alberta Sweetgrass 8, online:<https://ammsa.com/publications/alberta-sweetgrass/detective-receives-social-justice-award>.

da Silva, Denise Ferreira. "The Banalization of Racial Events" (2017) 20:1 Theory & Event 61.

da Silva, Inna. "No-Bodies: Law, Raciality and Violence" (2009) 18:2 Griffith L Rev 212.

Deer, Sarah & Mary Kathryn Nagle. *The Beginning and End of Rape: Confronting Sexual Violence in Native America* (Minneapolis: University of Minnesota Press, 2015).

Deer, Sarah & Mary Kathryn Nagle. "Return to Worcester: Dollar General and the Restoration of Tribal Jurisdiction to Protect Native Women and Children" (2018) 41:1 Harv Women's LJ 179.

Deloria, Vine Jr. "Laws Founded in Justice and Humanity: Reflections on the Content and Character of Federal Indian Law" (1989) 31:2 Arizona L Rev 203.

Devreskracht, Ryan. "House Republicans Add Insult to Native Women's Injury" (2014) 3 U Miami Race & Soc Just L Rev 1, online: http://repository.law.miami.edu/umrsjlr/vol3/iss1/3/.

Dumont, Marilyn. "Helen Betty Osborne," online: <https://www.poetryfoundation.org/poems/147310/helen-betty-osborne>.

Dwyer, Amy S. "The Inter-American Court of Human Rights: Towards Establishing an Effective Regional Contentious Jurisdiction" (1990) 13:1 Boston College Int and Comp L Rev 127.

Esquao: Institute for the Advancement of Aboriginal Women. "Esquao Awards," online: <https://iaaw.ca/program/esquao-awards/>.

Esquao: Institute for the Advancement of Aboriginal Women. "Esquao Youth Leadership Development Program," online: <https://iaaw.ca/program/esquao-youth-and-adult-leadership-development/>.

Fleras, Augie. "Finding Dawn, Directed by Christine Welsh" (2010) 26:1 Visual Anthropology Rev 47, online: <https://doi.org/10.1111/j.1548-7458.2010.01053.x>.

Franke, Katherine M. "Gendered Subjects of Transitional Justice" (2006) 15:3 Columbia J Gender and Law 813.

Gage, Beth & George Gage [directors]. *American Outrage* (Onley, PA: Gage and Gage Productions, 2008).

Gereluk, Winston. "Muriel Stanley-Venne: #1. Interview" (29 March 2013), Alberta Labour History Institute, online: <https://albertalabourhistory.org/wp-content/uploads/2018/04/2013032801-2013032802-Stanley-Venne-Muriel-r-WG-cor-AF-1.pdf>.

Goldstein, Alyosha. "Where the Nation Takes Place: Proprietary Regimes, Antistatism, and U.S. Settler Colonialism" (2008 Fall) 107:4 South Atlantic Q 833.

Government of Manitoba. *Report of the Aboriginal Justice Inquiry of Manitoba* (Winnipeg: Government of Manitoba, 1991), online: <http://www.ajic.mb.ca/volumell/chapter1.html>.

Grewal, Inderpal. "'Women's Rights as Human Rights': Feminist Practices, Global Feminism, and Human Rights Regimes in Transnationality" (1999) 3:3 Citizenship Studies 337.

Hargreaves, Allison. "*Finding Dawn* and Missing Women in Canada: Story-Based Methods in Antiviolence Research and Remembrance" (2015) 27:53 Studies in American Indian Literatures 82.

Huhndorf, Shari. "Scenes from the Fringe: Gendered Violence and the Geographies of Indigenous Feminism" (Spring 2021) 46.3 Signs: Journal of Women in Culture and Society 535.

Institute for the Advancement of Aboriginal Women. "About Us," online: <https://iaaw.ca/about-us/>.

Inter-American Commission on Human Rights. *American Declaration of the Rights and Duties of Man*, 2 May 1948, online: <https://www.refworld.org/docid/3ae6b3710.html>.

Jacobs, Beverly. "There Has Been a War against Indigenous Women since Colonization: Former NWAC President," *APTN National News* (23 September 2014), online: <https://www.aptnnews.ca/national-news/war-indigenous-women-since-colonization-former-nwac-president/>.

Johnston, Basil. *Indian School Days* (Toronto: Key Porter, 1988).

Kaye, Julie. "Reconciliation in the Context of Settler-Colonial Gender Violence: 'How Do We Reconcile with an Abuser?'" (November 2016) 53:4 Cdn Rev Soc 461.

Knott, Helen. *In My Own Moccasins: A Memoir of Resilience* (Regina: University of Regina Press, 2020).

Kuokkanen, Rauna. "Indigenous Women's Rights and International Law: Challenges of the UN Declaration on the Rights of Indigenous Peoples" in Corinne Lennox & Damien Short, eds, *Handbook on Indigenous Peoples' Rights* (London: Routledge, 2016) 275.

Kuokkanen, Rauna. "Self-Determination and Indigenous Women's Rights at the Intersection of International Human Rights" (2012) 34:1 Human Rights Q 225.

Lemaitre, Julieta & Kristin Bergtora Sandvik. "Beyond Sexual Violence in Transitional Justice: Political Insecurity as a Gendered Harm" (2014) 22 Feminist Legal Studies 243.

LeMay, Genevieve M. "The Cycles of Violence against Native Women: An Analysis of Colonialism, Historical Legislation and the Violence Against Women Reauthorization Act of 2013" (2018) 12.1 PSU McNair Scholars Online J, article 1, online: <https://pdxscholar.library.pdx.edu/cgi/viewcontent.cgi?article=1177&context=mcnair>.

Ling, Justin. "Canada Reckons with Genocide," *Foreign Policy* (24 June 2019), online: <https://foreignpolicy.com/2019/06/24/canada-reckons-with-genocide-inquiry-missing-murdered-indigenous-women-girls/>.

Livingston, Ann-Marie & Sarah Hunt. "Honouring Elsie: Was She Just a Dream?" in Anderson, Kim, Maria Campbell & Christi Belcourt, eds, *Keetsahnak: Our Missing and Murdered Indigenous Sisters* (Edmonton: University of Alberta Press, 2018) 45.

Magarrell, Lisa. "Reparations for Massive or Widespread Human Rights Violations: Sorting Out Claims for Reparations and the Struggle for Social Justice" (2003) 22 Windsor Yearbook of Access to Justice 85.

Manley-Casimir Kirsten. "Creating Space for Indigenous Storytelling in Courts" (2012) 27.2 Cdn J Law and Society 231.

Mas, Susana. "UN Aboriginal Envoy Says Canada Is Facing a 'Crisis,'" CBC News (16 October 2013), online: <https://www.cbc.ca/news/politics/un-aboriginal-envoy-says-canada-is-facing-a-crisis-1.2054682>.

Moore, Alexandra Schultheis. "Film after Atrocity: An Interview with Joshua Oppenheimer" in Sophia A. McClennen & Alexandra Schultheis Moore, eds, *The Routledge Companion to Literature and Human Rights* (London: Routledge, 2016) 480.

Morton, Katherine. "Hitchhiking and Missing and Murdered Indigenous Women: A Critical Discourse Analysis of Billboards on the Highway of Tears" (2016) 41:3 Cdn J of Sociology 299.

Musiol, Hanna. "Sites of Human Rights Theory" in Sophia McClennan & Alexandra Schultheis Moore, eds, *The Routledge Companion to Literature and Human Rights* (London: Routledge, 2016) 389.

National Centre for Truth and Reconciliation. "Exhibits," online: <https://nctr.ca/exhibits/>.

National Inquiry into Missing and Murdered Indigenous Women and Girls. *A Legal Analysis of Genocide: Supplementary Report of the National Inquiry* (Vancouver: Privy Council Office, 2019), online: <https://www.mmiwg-ffada.ca/wp-content/uploads/2019/06/Supplementary-Report_Genocide.pdf>.

National Inquiry into Missing and Murdered Indigenous Women and Girls. "Protocols, Symbols and Ceremonies," online: <https://www.mmiwg-ffada.ca/protocols-symbols-and-ceremonies/>.

National Inquiry into Missing and Murdered Indigenous Women and Girls. *Reclaiming Power and Place: The Final Report of the National Inquiry into Missing and Murdered Indigenous Women and Girls* (Ottawa: MMIWG, 2019), online: <https://www.loc.gov/item/lcwaN0028038/>.

O'Connell, John D. "Constructive Conquests in the Courts: A Legal History of the Western Shoshon [*sic*] Lands Struggle – 1861 to 1991" (2002) 42:4 Natural Resources J 765.

"An Open Letter Calling for the Refusal of the MMIWG Inquiry Extension Request" (letter to the editor), *Manitoulin Expositor* (11 April 2008), online: <https://www.manitoulin.com/an-open-letter-calling-for-the-refusal-of-the-mmiwg-inquiry-extension-request/.>

Orford, Anne. "Commissioning the Truth" (2006) 15.3 Columbia J Gender and Law 851.

Organization of American States, Inter-American Commission on Human Rights. "What Is the IACHR?" online: <https://www.oas.org/en/IACHR/jsForm/?File=/en/iachr/mandate/what.asp>.

Painter, Genevieve Renard. "Thinking Past Rights: Towards Feminist Theories of Reparations" (2012) 20 Windsor Yearbook of Access to Justice 1.

Pashagumskum, Jaime."1,500 Academics Prod Feds to Move on MMIWG Action Plan," *APTN National News* (3 September 2020), online: <https://www.aptnnews.ca/national-news/1500-academics-prod-feds-to-move-on-mmiwg-action-plan/>.

Puga, Alma Luz Beltrán Y, et al. "Gender Justice in the Americas: A Transnational Dialogue on Sexuality, Violence, Reproduction, and Human Rights (2011) 65:3 U of Miami L Rev 751.

Razack, Sherene. "Gendering Disposability" (2016) 28:2 Cdn J Women and the Law 285.

Recollet, Karyn. "Glyphing Decolonial Love through Urban Flash Mobbing and *Walking with Our Sisters*" (2015) 45(1) Curriculum Inquiry 129.

Rhoad, Meghan. *Those Who Take Us Away: Abusive Policing and Failures in Protection of Indigenous Women and Girls in Northern British Columbia, Canada* (New York: Human Rights Watch, 2013).

Savarese, Josephine L. "Challenging Colonial Norms and Attending to Presencing in Stories of Missing and Murdered Indigenous Women" (2017) 29:1 Cdn J Women and the Law 157.

Silbey, Jessica. "Cross-Examining Film" (2008) 8:1 U of Maryland LJ of Race, Religion, Gender & Class 17.

Šimonović, Dubravka. *Report of the Special Rapporteur on Violence against Women, Its Causes and Consequences*, United Nations General Assembly (24 June–12 July 2019) A/HRC/41/42/Add.I, 3.

Speed, Shannon. "Representations of Violence: (Re)Telling Indigenous Women's Stories and the Politics of Knowledge Production" in Chris

Anderson & Jean M O'Brien, eds, *Sources and Methods in Indigenous Studies* (London: Routledge, 2017).

Tascón, Sonia. "Considering Human Rights Films, Representation, and Ethics: Whose Face?" (2012) 34:3 Human Rights Q 864.

Tascón, Sonia. *Human Rights Film Festivals: Activism in Context* (Houndmills, UK: Palgrave Macmillan, 2015).

Teitel, Ruti G. *Transitional Justice* (Oxford: Oxford University Press, 2002).

United Nations, Committee for the Elimination of Racial Discrimination (CERD). "Early Warning and Action Procedure Decision 1 (68), United States of America," CERD/USA/DEC/1, 11 April 2006, para 10.

United Nations Population Fund. "Recommendations of the UN Permanent Forum on Indigenous Issues Regarding Sexual and Reproductive Health and Rights & Gender-Based Violence: Progress and Challenges, Executive Summary" (2018), online: <https://www.unfpa.org/featured-publication/recommendations-un-permanent-forum-indigenous-issues-regarding-sexual-and>.

University of Arizona, James E. Rogers College of Law. "Western Shoshone," online: <https://law.arizona.edu/western-shoshone>.

Vermette, Katherena. *The Break* (Toronto: Anansi, 2016).

Wacquant, Loic JD. "The Rise of Advanced Marginality: Notes on Its Nature and Implications" (1996) 39:2 Acta Sociologica 121.

Walker, Connie. "Indigenous Women Ask 'Am I Next' to Raise Awareness about Missing and Murdered," *CBC News* (5 September 2014), online:<https://www.cbc.ca/news/indigenous/indigenous-women-ask-am-i-next-to-raise-awareness-about-missing-and-murdered-1.2757295>.

Watson, Kaitlyn. "Missing and Murdered Indigenous Women: The Role of Grassroots Organizations and Social Media in Education" (2018–19) 33:1 2 Cdn Woman Studies 204.

Welsh, Christine [executive producer]. *Finding Dawn* (Canada: National Film Board of Canada, 2006).

Women's Legal Education and Action Fund. "Viewpoint 39-5: Hundreds of Recommendations Go Unimplemented" (May 2015) 39:5 *LawNow*, online: <https://ca.vlex.com/vid/viewpoint-39-5-hundreds-693882749>.

# 8 Sovereign Refusals: Spending Time with Apak in *The Journals of Knud Rasmussen*

REBECCA JOHNSON

We are born into and live our lives in storied worlds. Stories can open us up to worlds of possibility. They can also describe our worlds in ways that foreclose possibility, deny opportunities, and justify violence. They can invite us to accept a given vision of "what is," and they can invite us to participate in reimagining and transforming the world. The stories we are told, and that we tell in return, provide us with maps and blueprints for making sense of ourselves and others.[1]

For feminist legal scholars (in the common law world in which I live) there is a long history of attending to the stories that law tells about women. In those stories, legislators and courts have opined on women's political agency, sexual agency, reproductive agency, financial agency, and more. Are women persons with political voice?[2] Do women have the right to make their own decisions about reproduction?[3] About conditions of employment that do not reduce them to their sexuality, or their reproductive possibility?[4] About the use of force to defend themselves from intimate partners?[5] About access to property in marriage and divorce?[6] About admission to educational institutions, or professions?[7] About serving in combat positions in the armed forces?[8]

In too many of these stories, women's experience is flattened. It is perhaps in the nature of judicial decision-making that outcomes are generally binary: a case will be won or lost, a person jailed or freed, an injury compensated or not, a child remains with a parent or is placed in foster case. But it is not inevitable that law's account of women should be similarly binary. Too often, legal storytelling leans in the direction of simple stories, in which gender is binary and women are described in flat and unidimensional terms: sometimes as valiant or self-sacrificing or on a pedestal; frequently in the role of victim or vixen or villain. Legal conflicts about trans, non-binary and Two-Spirited bodies often describe bright lines between "male" and "female" lives, pressing people to comply with persisting cisgender expectations. The roles available to women are further differentially distributed based on race, class, and able-bodiedness. In these flattened contexts, it is difficult to see and discuss the gendered dimensions of experience that are shared, and those that are not.

This flattening of narrative possibility is particularly visible in law's account of Indigenous women's lives and bodies. In these stories, women may emerge as land defenders or water defenders, placing their bodies in the path of development (or extractive industry). More frequently, Indigenous women appear to us in law's stories as criminals, or as failed mothers, or as the murdered and missing. Such stories describe narrow conditions for flourishing, sustaining a "reality" in which Indigenous women are denied access to social and economic resources, are offered a circumscribed range of opportunities, and are subjected to heightened levels of social, economic, and physical violence.[9] As Val Napoleon argues, it is all too rare for Indigenous women to appear as sovereign[10] bodies, who make deliberate and hard-thought-through choices in the context of socially constructed spaces of danger, lawlessness, and erasure.[11]

Stories are, as Louis Bird reminds us, "tools for thinking."[12] In this paper, I take up a story that engages with Indigenous critical feminist legal thought, and centres Indigenous women's bodily sovereignty. I do so as a non-Indigenous feminist legal scholar who is a white, cisgender female, relatively neurotypical, relatively able-bodied, and the mother of two. I am conscious of the important questions of ethics that are sometimes raised in the context of non-Indigenous scholars doing this work, as well as of the "they/us" binaries that persist in my own voice and thinking. I am also conscious of the imperative for non-Indigenous scholars to understand themselves as fully implicated in this work, and thus to take up the invitation to lean with humility into stories of greater complexity, stories that invite a rethinking of the question "Who are we to each other?"[13] In what follows, I want to follow a path of "refusal." Let me move forward by sharing three snapshots – three moments that shape the discussion to follow.

### Snapshot 1: The Hunger Strike of Theresa Spence

In a 2022 workshop I attended at the University of Victoria, Julianna Hu Pegues invited participants into an extended conversation about Audra Simpson's 2016 article "The State Is a Man." In that piece, Audra Simpson drew attention to the body of Attapiskawat Chief Theresa Spence, who in 2014 engaged in a highly publicized hunger strike as form of protest against the dire conditions of living in her community, demanding a conversation with Prime Minister Steven Harper.[14] As Simpson notes, the mainstream media responded to Theresa Spence's protest with a vicious campaign of body shaming and mockery, denying the politics in her activity, as if outraged by her refusal to die. Simpson invites us to think about Spence's protest as a very specific kind of political sovereign activity, one in which Spence was not demonstrating a desire to die but was rather making visible a political reality and demanding a political response. Simpson invites us to think about the Chief's *two bodies*, both the physical and the political. In particular, she invites us to think of Theresa Spence's body – an Indigenous female body that enacts a series of "refusals" – as a political order, as an enactment of sovereignty.[15] I was left with questions about how to better read this Indigenous woman's acts of refusal. What was I to make of the combined refusal to eat and refusal to die? What was I to make of refusals linking women's bodies with obligations across time and space, obligations touching on the conditions of not simply surviving but also thriving (what Christine Sy refers to in chapter 3 as "sur-thriving"). What could such refusals teach about the relationship between ideas and practices? As I understood both Audra Simpson and Julianna Hu Pegues, they were inviting us not simply to read Theresa Spence differently, but to consider the productive power of attending more generally to Indigenous women's enactments of sovereignty, often performed in spaces of dissent, and with all the political entanglements of colonial contexts. I left the workshop wondering about my own place in this conversation; how might non-Indigenous scholars better enter into expanded practices of reading Indigenous women's actions – of reading them through the lenses of critical legal feminism, attentive to practices of dissent and refusal, practices rooted in women's bodily sovereignty?

**Snapshot 2: The Students on the Stairs**

My mind fluttered back to the early spring of 2018, where questions about Indigenous people's bodies were very much in the news. The Alberta Court of Appeal had recently reversed the acquittal of Bradley Barton for the killing of Cindy Gladue.[16] The case would be going to the Supreme Court of Canada, but much of the conversation about guilt or innocence was taking a back seat to conversations about the ways that Cindy Gladue's personhood had been erased, both through how she was spoken of in the court decisions and through decisions to admit parts of her body as evidence. With this erasure of Indigenous personhood[17] floating like an oil slick on top of the water, the news

Figure 8.1 The students on the stairs. (Photo by Rebecca Johnson, with the permission of the students)

feeds continued to generate information about two more high-profile trials dealing with the killing of young Indigenous people. Within weeks of each other, Gerald Stanley was acquitted for the killing of Colton Boushie and Raymond Cormier was acquitted in the killing of Tina Fontaine. Following a weekend of rallies and protests, I arrive at the law school Monday morning to see that each of the sidewalks leading to the law school doors are covered with strings of text in vibrant chalk colours. I look more carefully at the ground and see, written in chalk, "25.2% of men in prison are Indigenous, 36.1% are women." I see also "No Justice – No Reconciliation," "MMIWG," and the names of Colten Boushie, Tina Fontaine, Cindy Gladue, Neil Stonechild, Helen Betty Osborne, Paul Alphonse, and more. I look at the words written around me and think to myself that it must be our students, bringing the protest back from the streets to the law school, where it belongs! Good for them! I pull out my camera, to take photos of the sidewalks. As I open the door to enter the law school, camera in hand, I notice that there also appear to be posters up on the walls just waiting for their photo-moment. I walk in, excited to talk to someone about this amazing piece of activism, and I am stopped in my tracks. Stopped cold. Because now I know who is responsible. Yes. It is our Indigenous law students. There they are, putting the finishing touches on their protest, attaching the last few signs to the wall. But there will be no conversation. They have covered their mouths with duct tape. They sit on the stairs in silence, blanketed (see Figure 8.1). They offer no words. They offer their silence. I am silenced in return.

I reflected on the law students' response to the court judgements regarding the deaths of both Tina Fontaine and Colton Boushie: sitting on the stairs of the law school, mouths covered with duct tape, their bodies holding space as silent witnesses.[18] They did not withdraw from public space; rather, they have placed themselves in the central location of transit. They did not block movement; people could pass. The students made themselves hypervisible, but neither in the classroom nor the library nor the lounge. They chose the spaces of entry and transit, the spaces through which people move on their way to somewhere else. The deaths that summer of Indigenous men, women, children demanded an analysis apt for the work of critical Indigenous legal feminisms, work that took up the many threads of gender, colonialism, property, urban and rural spaces of unsafety, work, play, parenting, economy, joy, despair, and more. But how to begin those conversations in the face of unbearable grief? Their "refusal" made visible the ways that legal talk was failing to produce change. Theirs was a refusal to provide more words. It was a way of saying, "We have said enough. It is your turn to make sense of this. You cannot expect us to carry your grief in the space of our own grief."

There are important questions raised both by the media excoriation of Theresa Spence and by the political refusal of the law students to speak in the face of the law's response to Colton Boushie's and Tina Fontaine's deaths. Both snapshots situate us in contexts where we are engaged in "witnessing" of a certain kind, where we are sitting with the bones of the dead, and in the company of those who live past those moments. The very real questions about ethical responsiveness are further heightened in the context of non-Indigenous engagements with Indigenous critical theory. This is not a question of who is or is not allowed (or indeed required) to speak, but of struggling over ways to do this, conscious of the need for non-Indigenous Canadian society to participate in the work of re-storying. These questions of voice and conversation were ones that resonated with challenges of pedagogy in a third moment.

## Snapshot 3: Difficult Stories in the Classroom

More than two decades ago now, in my first years of teaching, I was assigned to teach a course called "Feminist Legal Advocacy." The course name had recently been changed from "Women and the Law," which was also at the time a new introduction to law school course offerings.[19] The name change was a way of acknowledging the need to not simply theorize the status of women, but to claim the politics in the term "feminism." We worked with case law, legislation, facta (the legal arguments), and secondary literature to engage with cases about sexual orientation, childcare, taxation, sexual harassment, and sexual violence. The students were engaged and engaging, the material was powerful. And yet, time and time again I was left reflecting on the ways that class members (me included) engaged in critique of either the named plaintiffs (or indeed, their lawyers) in ways that felt incomplete (and perhaps even wrong). The courtroom contexts produced an extreme flattening and erasure of women's experiences.[20] And for Indigenous women this flattening was even more extreme.[21]

In the classroom, engagement with "the real" often brought us to a stop. Occasionally, in response to readings, students would share their own stories of having experienced violence or abuse. While this was sometimes powerful, it often came with the risk that those stories could not be easily pulled back, and students were left feeling vulnerable. In the face of those stories, other students were cautious about speaking for fear of doing damage, worrying (or not considering) that some questions were invasive or judgmental in ways that would cause distress to students who had lived through similar experiences. At times it was difficult to get to critical questions without students worrying that their opinions would do harm to the person who had spoken of their own truth. Other times, students would get trapped in conversations that were "evidentiary" in some way: looking for changes in ways that were judgmental (i.e., if only you had dressed differently, you chose to have children, what were you thinking, you made your bed and will have to lie in it). Where the conversation had to engage with the material body of a colleague in the room (or a real person in the court report), we got stuck. It felt as if we had been high-centred by fears and conflicts about "the truth." It became very difficult to deepen conversations, because the weight of "the real" became paralysing.

The following semester, I was assigned to teach "Critical Approaches to Law." Because I was told I could shape it how I wished, I decided to take a law and film approach, using a syllabus put together by one of my friends from grad school, Orit Kamir. The subtitle of her planned class was "Women and Law in Popular Cultural Narratives," and that fit the bill perfectly.[22] Teaching the two courses back to back was a surprise; questions of gender, violence, choice, agency, and autonomy were the taproots for both classes, but something very different happened in the two classrooms. Most notably, in the law and film course students appeared to have an easier time taking seriously the complexity of women's engagements with "the real" when working with the distance made possible through fiction. I began to appreciate how film would let us pick up a complicated gendered story in ways that invited conversation. In film, we could more easily both see and feel the experience of our fictional characters and could also see the structures of power constraining them within the imagined world of film. We could more easily share different views about how we experienced the film and its stories and characters without being trapped in the shroud of "the truth" or of doing more direct harm to each other through our critiques and questions.

I began to better appreciate the power of Indigenous storywork.[23] In many Indigenous legal orders, there are important storied legal resources that not only speak in complicated ways to history (i.e., stories carry important histories) but also work to create the context through which important human problems and recurrent social/political/economic situations can be articulated. In this volume, Darcy Lindberg (chapter 2), Christine Sy (chapter 3), and Kahente Horn-Miller (chapter 4) draw on these histories. I focus here on stories told through film – the cultural storytelling genre of our time.[24] Film – cinematic storytelling – is a valuable resource for critical Indigenous legal feminism, as it offers a path of indirection that can enable people to work through contemporary challenges in less politically charged contexts.[25] As Cheryl Suzack argues (chapter 7 in this volume), some of those challenges have been powerfully taken up in the context of Indigenous documentary filmmaking.[26] In this chapter, I turn to fiction to explore the world of the actual and the possible. Film provides the right balance of proximity and distance to facilitate critical work on hard questions. It enables us to occupy a site of the imaginary, without getting stuck in complicated practices of engagement with the real.[27] Put another way, in the filmic context there are important questions about the ways truth and fiction are held together in narrative form. One might speak of, for example, both truthful fictions and fictional truths, particularly in the context of the documentary film-making traditions.[28]

To step momentarily into questions of method, there is power in film's ability to invite us into its fictional world, in ways that enable us to temporarily inhabit the characters. In film, as in literature, one is given an open invitation to occupy the central characters – to do this outside the space of appropriation and to do so in ways that clearly make visible that one is occupying a position, and is invited to do so not only in a narrative way but in a way that makes arguments about the felt, seen, and heard environments.[29] Because film always is an invitation to feel, it gives us a site not to determine "what is," but to share with each other observations about the experience of stepping into those stories, to ask what might be learned about ourselves. Film invites us to bring our whole selves (Indigenous and non-Indigenous alike) to the cinematic experience, but also invites us to imagine ourselves into other subject positions in ways that can extend our capacity to understand other expressions of sovereignty. This is one powerful way to work at the intersection of encounters across difference.

Let us move, then, in the direction of one particular film, to see how we might work with it to think through the challenges in the three snapshots above. The film I have chosen here takes up questions about the relationship of Inuit and colonial legal orders through the restaging of a set of encounters between the Danish explorer Knud Rasmussen and the family of the great Inuk shaman Avva.

### *The Journals of Knud Rasmussen*

*The Journals of Knud Rasmussen* (2006) is the second film in what is commonly referred to as the Isuma Trilogy (the other two films are *Atanarjuat: The Fast Runner* and *Before Tomorrow*).[30] The film is produced by Igloolik Isuma Productions, co-founded by Zacharias Kunuk and Norman Cohn and one of the best-known Indigenous film companies in the world.[31] Their movies, written entirely in Inuktitut, invite the viewer into a fully Inuit life world. Their movies are well known for producing strong feelings of immediacy and presence. Part of this is the result of using video as a format rather than film, and part of it is linked to shooting choices – viewers are placed in ways that allow them to occupy many different subject positions, and to be in close proximity to the action.[32] Their films also enact an Inuit temporality – the action does not move as quickly, so viewers are held in a space that invites a longer engagement with what is seen and heard.[33]

The script for this film draws from the journals of Danish ethnographer Knud Rasmussen, who in the 1920s travelled across the circumpolar region, hunting out stories and encounters with Inuktitut-speaking peoples of the Arctic. This period of time was characterized by anthropological encounters of various sorts, sometimes responding to or amplifying societal beliefs about the need to preserve vanishing

(Indigenous) cultures. Franz Boas, James Teit, Diamond Jenness, and Marius Barbeau were all active during these years.[34] It was also a time that gave birth to the anthropological docudrama in the form of Robert Flaherty's *Nanook of the North* (1922).

Knud Rasmussen, while influenced by the salvage anthropological winds of his time, also occupied a unique place. He was a specific kind of insider/outsider: he was of mixed blood, looking like a Dane but with an Inuk grandmother. Because of the time Rasmussen had spent living on the land with his grandmother, a Greenlander who spoke only Inuktitut, he had linguistic fluency and the skills needed for living in the Arctic. This enabled him to do a particularly nuanced kind of ethnographic work. With some training in opera, he was also attentive to music and poetry, and included Inuit music and song in his writings.[35] His travels across the North resulted in a collection of ten volumes entitled *The Fifth Thule Expedition*. In volume 7, *The Intellectual Culture of the Iglulik Eskimos*, Rasmussen includes accounts of his encounters with the great shaman Avva and his family.

Zacharias Kunuk and Norman Cohn drew on extracts from Rasmussen's journals to construct the original screenplay for the film, but then also shifted angles to tell those stories from inside a reimagined Inuit perspective.[36] The result is a film that is located on the borders of fact and fiction, speaking to and through historical figures and characters who are filtered through many lenses: through the eyes of Knud Rasmussen, then into the Kunuk/Cohn screenplay, then through the voices and improvisations of the actors, and then through the editing process, into the completed film.

Here is a short summary of what is a complex cinematic text. The film begins with a staging of the encounter between Rasmussen's expeditionary team and the extended family of the shaman Avva. Rasmussen not only asks the Inuit to share song and stories about their beliefs, but also asks them if they would be willing to take his colleagues up to Igloolik: Rasmussen is taking a side voyage, and they plan to meet up later. Avva agrees, and Rasmussen leaves (and he is thus largely absent throughout the film that is given his name). His colleagues, however, remain behind with the Inuit, and the viewers enter fully into the life of the community. Many of the stories Rasmussen sought are indeed shared with the viewer, often with words taken directly from the journals, and filmed in ways that create the feeling that the audience is being directly addressed (in a quasi-documentary way). Avva himself tells us the story of his birth, of the many rules his mother had to follow to ensure his survival, of specific taboos about foods that shamans can or cannot eat, how he came to have his spirit helpers. He tells us how his spirit helpers abandoned him during a period of despair following the death of his son, as well as how they eventually returned to him. Orulu, Avva's wife, shares the story of her life, including her experience of being a neglected orphan, of being welcomed into a new community, and of celebrations and abundance of food, joy, and song. We spend time also with Avva and Orulu's two children, their son Natar and daughter Apak. Apak, like her father, has shamanic powers and can speak with spirits. She is, we are told by other characters, "too beautiful to be safe": following the murder of Apak's second husband, she was given a new husband in order to prevent further bloodshed between two families. We also enter into the lives of Rasmussen's colleagues, Peter Freuchen and Therkel Mathiassen, as they spend time with the community, sharing in conversation, games, food, and song. A visit from Apak's first sweetheart Nuqallaq (who had been chased away by Avva when Nuqallaq chose to follow the ways of the white people) makes visible that there are increasing rifts emerging between Inuit communities who follow the traditional ways and those that have taken up new, Christian beliefs. These rifts lie behind Avva's reluctance to visit Igloolik. But as the film continues, the weather becomes increasingly bad, the hunts are unsuccessful, and stores of both food and oil begin to run out. At the end of the film, the group arrives in Igloolik on the verge of starvation. There, we learn that Umik, a former shaman turned evangelical Christian, has converted the whole community to Christianity. He also controls all the food resources and will not share food with Avva and his family unless they first agree to eat a sacrament of foods that are taboo for a shaman, which would rupture the relationships between a shaman and their spirit helpers. In the final scenes of the film, with his family starving, and in the face of this forced choice, Avva walks across the snow to where three people are standing, seemingly waiting for him. He thanks them for all the help they have given him over his life and tells them he has unfortunately had to choose another path, and thus must send them away. The three do not move, but begin weeping. Avva yells at them to leave now. They turn and walk away, weeping and wailing as they go, turning occasionally to look back at him. Avva stands watching for a moment longer and then turns away, walking in the other direction.

## Focusing on the Father, or Focusing on the Daughter?

My friend Ruth Buchanan and I watched this film when it was first released and spent many hours talking and thinking through our shared responses to this film. One piece of the puzzle is that we had been so struck by the soundscape of the film, and the ways it seemed to invite us as viewers into a space of shared singing, games, and laughter. Even where we didn't quite understand everything we were hearing or seeing, we nonetheless felt as if we had been invited into the film, much in the way that Rasmussen's colleagues had been invited in. But there was also a gutting sense of loss at the end, when Avva sends his spirit helpers away (and when we realized for the first time that those helpers had been visible to us throughout the whole film). I felt somewhat slammed in the gut by the ending, as I struggled to reprocess the film, to place those spirits more solidly as a part of the community throughout. I felt their loss deeply.

But this too is only a starting point, because much of the power of working with film rests in the conversations one can have with others about different experiences of the film. At one point, Ruth and I found ourselves in a conversation with our friend Hadley Friedland about the film. We were struggling, we told her, with how to write about the film. We were unsure how to talk about the end of the film without "spoiling it" by revealing that the spirit helpers had been there all along. Hadley told us in return about her experience of the film. She had watched it with her Cree partner Ken McDonald (of the Aseniwuche Winewak Nation), and reported that Ken had seen from the beginning that there were spirit helpers present in the film. He had not been surprised by the ending in the way that Ruth and I were. The big questions for him were not about the shaman and his spirit helpers, but about the relationship between father and daughter. Ken was more curious about how the two of them negotiated her moments of what might be called "wilful refusal." In light of his comments, I found myself returning to the film, thinking less about my non-Inuk surprise at what seemed unfamiliar to me (the relationship to the more-than-human) and ready to engage with the film's invitation to explore questions of embodied sovereignty in Apak's social and political refusals.

## Spending Time with a Storied Character

As we turn our attention to Apak, we might first acknowledge the messiness of the encounter. We cannot settle with certainty any claims about who she "is." The character of Apak is at the same time both historical and fictional. There is of course an actual historical Apak, but she takes partial form in the stories told by her or of her in Rasmussen's journals. We have yet a third Apak constructed in the film's screenplay, and a fourth Apak brought to life in the acting of Leah Angutimarik, and then a fifth version woven through the framing, filming, and editing choices of the Isuma team. All of these are shadows that interact, all of them constructions, or fragments, or moments of conversation. In significant measure, we are exploring Indigenous women's refusals and bodily sovereignty in the context of an Inuk character whose stories are being shaped by men in the world around her (her father, her husband, Rasmussen, and Kunuk/Cohn). And yet, the film offers us a way to move into the space of story, drawing on these "fragments" or "storied moments" to do the hard work of asking about Indigenous women's bodily sovereignty, asking about acts of agency and resistance in the context of lives entangled in structures of gender and power. My goal in this reading is to watch and describe, drawing on the insights and theorizing of critical Indigenous legal feminisms, to speak to and of what I see in these shadow encounters and moments of speaking across time and genre to the spirit of Apak.

Focusing on stories as tools for thinking, let us return to the film to centre Apak and her various bodies (both the traces in the text and the cinematically imagined Apak). In the film, she performs a number of important refusals, laying a claim to sovereignty over her choices, even if those choices are limited or constrained by the larger political and social order in which she is entangled. These entanglements involve the structures of colonization, but also involve gendered relations of power within the Inuit legal order that structures and nourishes the shape of her life.[37] Let us focus on three places where specific refusals invite us to consider her sovereignty and the politics of her choices. The first of these involves the shaping of her story: she refuses to tell a simple narrative, claiming the right to narrate in a way that links her story to the stories of many. The second of these involves autonomy over her sexual/embodied desires: she refuses to have her sexual desires be determined by others. The third refusal involves questions of voice and food: she refuses to have her voice controlled by others, and refuses to place taboo or principle above her desires for life.

## Shaping the Story: Claiming the Right to Narrate a Complex Story

The film begins with text telling us that we are in "The Arctic, 1912." As viewers, we are positioned in the role of photographer, about to take a group photo. Before us are a number of Inuit in a warmly lit interior space, organizing themselves and objects around them in preparation for the photo shoot. As they settle into place, the movement of the characters is stilled, as the image changes tone, shifting towards the black and white of what has become a photo. The camera slowly zooms in on the young woman in the centre of the photo (Figure 8.2). At this

Figure 8.2 Apak positioned to narrate the story (screenshot, *Journals of Knud Rasmussen*, 2:08).

point, we begin to hear the voice of an old woman, connecting herself as narrator to the image of this young woman. She tells us: "I am called Usarak, though I was called Apak at the time of the story."

The next shot takes us back into a scene drenched with full colour and action, as we see Apak sitting with an accordion in her hands, smiling and laughing as she attempts to play. The setting indicates that she is inside the ship of the famous Captain George Cormer, with other Inuit. The voice over continues:

> When I was still Apak, my father was the famous Iglulik shaman, Avva, who, with my mother Orulu, both passed away many years ago. I was thirteen years old when I saw my first White Man. Those days I was travelling with Nuqallaq, my first sweetheart. I saw my first white man at the age of thirteen, when I was travelling with my first sweetheart, Nuqallaq. Even then he was already working for the whites.

In this beginning then, we are first invited to imagine ourselves listening through the voice of Usarak/Apak, a woman who had lived at the centre of big events. Among them, we know that her first sweetheart, Nuqallaq, would later be charged with murder in one of the first big show trials of the North.[38] A flood of visual images sweeps past us as she speaks, now documenting some of these big events. We see a map of syllabics (which enabled the translation of English into Inukti-

Figure 8.3 DVD cover for *The Journals of Knud Rasmussen*.

tut, and the spread of Inuktitut bibles in the North). We see her uncle Evaluarjuk tracing out the letters to pronounce his own name. Two men sing together before a gramophone of sorts that seems to be recording their voices on wax cylinders, with the others listening in pleasure. In a tight close-up, we see her sweetheart Nuqallaq light a pipe, which is clearly a trade item, given the layering of its wood body and crafted metal bowl. It appears to be filled with tobacco, which would also have been a trade good. The visual frames here have all the markers of the Isuma style (creating a strong feeling of immediacy and presence). Though we see no white characters, all the objects in the frame show us that Apak and her community have encountered them: the syllabarium, a lead pencil, a gramophone that is clearly recording a song onto a scroll, the pipe that Nuqallaq is smoking.

A number of threads draw us in immediately and offer us a first refusal. In some ways, it is a refusal of the very shaping of the film itself: the title of the film points us to Knud Rasmussen, suggesting that it is his story; the image on the DVD cover features a close-up shot of Avva, suggesting instead that it is his story (Figure 8.3). And yet, the first voice we hear is that of Apak. She refuses a singular focus on the two men, by inserting herself right into the beginning. If this is a story of Knud Rasmussen or of Avva, it is a story that *she* will tell. It is a woman's voice narrating the story for us. It is a woman's story we will hear, or at least the framing of a story from the position of a woman.

In this framing, our narrator also claims all her names, both the one she carries with age and the name of her youth. We are placed into a stream of temporal movement. She also requires us to see that this story is one shaped by intersocietal contact right from the beginning. We see it in her invocation of her first sweetheart, making visible that the tensions between ways of living will impact even intimate relationships. Naming him as her "first" sweetheart also brings us to begin thinking about the many people to whom one might give their heart or self over their lifetime. This again suggests to us that it is her story we are hearing, and we have the insight of age reflecting back on the story. In these next five minutes, the visuals that accompany her narrative include a storm of fragments gathering together characters, music, syllabics, contact, traders, ships, and more. Each of these fragments is laden with history and possibility. Each would open itself up to another conversation. But she does not explain them for us. The fragments are left for us to make sense of. She stands at the centre of these experiences and claims her place as witness or participant in all that follows, but she does not explain. Significantly, this narrative voice almost immediate goes quiet; we never again hear her interpret the events that follow, or interject to explain. The work of making sense of all that happens is left to the viewer. Let us turn then to the next site of refusal, one linked to her sexuality.

## Sovereignty in Sexual Choosing

As Usarak/Apak stops speaking, the screen goes dark, and we are given an intertitle to indicate we are positioned "10 years later." In the next scene, there is a radical shift of both point of view and tone. We have followed our narrator directly into her sexual life. For the next one and a half minutes we are pulled into an intense sexual encounter, one filmed in a very non-conventional fashion. Sound is central to the scene, which relies on the rhythmic, air-filled guttural throat-singing of Inuk artist Tanya Tagak.[39] The colour is bled out of the scene, so it is filmed in a palette of bright light and shifting shadow, distorted and partial, with extreme and splintered close-ups of various body parts in motion, coming in and out of focus: a close-up of Apak's mouth, of a hand covering a breast, a close-up of a facial tattoo, of a woman's hand on the back of a man's head, of hair sliding over a cheek, of a hand with a wedding ring visible, across the frame. All of this comes in and out of focus, constantly returning to extreme close-ups of Apak's face.

While there is extreme intimacy in the scene, the viewers are denied anything in the nature of the conventional voyeuristic gaze (male or otherwise). The scene situates us at the centre of Apak's sexual pleasure but with a very interesting form of what **feels** simultaneously like proximity and distance. We are taken into an intimate frame that gives us close-ups of her face, centring her experience. We do have some shots that imply the male subject position (a male hand on her breast), but which also show her as active (her hand on a male chest). The scene takes us less in the direction of seeing than it focuses our attention on sound and energy. The colour choice (drained of colour) and the time frame between shots also disrupt the sense of "business as usual" in the portrayal of female pleasure.

The scene is then suddenly interrupted by what is audibly a man's derisive laughter. This laughter pulls both Apak and us (as viewers) out of the scene, which snaps back into colour. Apak is situated as fully present in the now, pulling up her clothes around her, as the camera zooms out, revealing that we are inside an igloo, furs spread around. We can see no male partner with her on the furs, but only an old man, fully clothed in white skins and sitting on a chair close by, the flames of the qulliq (the stone lamp proving warmth and light to the space) flickering beside him. He turns his head towards her; a mocking look on his face as his eyes slide over her partially naked body.

There is a tight close-up on his face as he laughs at her, saying, "Why always make love to a dead person instead of living?" As his mocking laughter continues, the film returns us to the framing of the previous shot. This time, though she is positioned in the same spot and the qulliq continues to burn, the chair is empty. We can no longer see the old man, but his mocking laughter continues to echo as the camera now switches to a tight close-up on her face. She continues to keep her eyes focused on the spot where the man was, a look of defiance on her face (Figure 8.4).

As viewers, we are held in this view as she remains direct in her gaze, as his laughter fades out. We know now that one of the spirit helpers has been watching her. She finally speaks, saying, "Asshole." She then turns to pull her parka back up over her head.

This scene enables us to see the fragility of the barrier between the physical and more-than-human worlds. If we have been told that her father is a great shaman, we see that she too has some connection with the spirit world. Further, we are not just told this but are *shown* it. While one might agree that the movie does not definitively answer the question of whether she is "remembering, dreaming, hallucinating or making actual contact,"[40] the cinematic choices do lean in the direction of

Figure 8.4 Apak's refusal to be shamed (screenshot, *Journals of Knud Rasmussen*, 5:53).

inviting us to accept the possibility of actual contact. We are positioned to see both her sexual partner (we are shown splinters of her hands on his head, her face on his chest, his hands on her breasts) and the voyeuristic old man who seeks to shame her for her choices.

Spending time looking at the shot, I find it interesting that the tight focus on her face means we are focused on the details of her facial responses, and not on the nakedness of her body (which was more visible in the earlier scene). The framing keeps our focus on her response to the challenge of her choice. Because the man also is visible in one frame and not in another, we are left to grapple with the question of the two men present and yet invisible in the space: the dead man she finds her pleasure with and the man who watches. She seems unperturbed, not fearful or ashamed. As viewers, we come to know that she has been required to marry again in order to disrupt a blood feud. But she insists on choosing sex with the husband who was killed and not the one she has been required to accept. She insists on her own pleasure. Further, in calling the spirit helper an asshole, she not only refuses to be shamed by him but names his judgmental and voyeuristic behaviour for what it is.

It is also interesting that in the very next scene, Apak is once again in the company of others, in a large ice house. We see her carrying a baby in the hood of her amauti (parka); she is cutting small pieces of meat and feeding it to the baby. We are treated to a lovely close-up of this baby babbling and playing with its fingers. And so, her moment of sexual choosing is immediately followed by one that centres relationships to children and others. This is followed with a scene of Apak playing games with a group of young children. Her husband walks past, saying, "Stop playing with the children." Again, we have a man telling her what to do, in this case, asserting that her parenting is an inappropriate form of play. And her sticking her tongue out behind his back signals her lack of submission or obedience. If this marriage was arranged to avoid bloodshed, it is not one of her desiring, and she continues to indicate this through her refusal to enter fully into the relations. That her choices are clear to all leads her father to say to her, "You should be warmer to your husband." And so, to this point, three male characters have intervened to correct her in her choices of sexual or parenting pleasures. She rejects the direction of all three.

## Refusing to Speak, Choosing to Eat

Let us look, finally, at the ending of the film, to see what might be learned from spending time with her refusals related to speaking and eating. Recall that the group (Avva's family and the Norwegian explorers) arrives in Igloolik on the verge of starvation. As viewers, at this point in the film we have already witnessed several occasions where Apak, with her own powerful connections to the spirit world, seems to have had visions of what is ahead, visions in which we have heard the sorrowful wailing of voices. They arrive in Igloolik and are greeted by the priest Umik, whose offers of food and help are contingent on Avva's family singing new songs, offering new prayers, and eating taboo foods. Avva declines the offer. Avva's family hold their own ceremony to connect to the spirit world to uncover any possible violations and see if they can draw on their own traditions to seek liberation from the bad luck that has denied them any other access to food. In this scene, Evaluarjuk the shaman calls out that he sees something that looks like human tissue, hidden away. In response, Apak acknowledges that she had a miscarriage earlier that year, and sought to hide the evidence of it rather than follow the taboos. Her family state that this was a wrong, but also say, "let her be free of it." They then conclude that all possible harms have been made visible, determine there is nothing else left to be done, and begin to exit the igloo. But Avva stops them, calling to Apak: "Wait. We're not finished yet."

The conversation that follows is framed so that we have Apak in the far-right foreground of the shot, in profile, facing the left of the screen. Avva is sitting beside her, also in profile, towards the middle of the

Figure 8.5 Apak's refusal to say more (screenshot, *Journals of Knud Rasmussen*, 1:32).

frame, facing to the left but twisted slightly in Apak's direction. In the lower-left-third of the shot, we have one of the spirit helpers, facing us directly, so that both Avva and Apak are positioned between us and the spirit helper, as we watch together the interaction between father and daughter (Figure 8.5). Avva continues to interrogate his daughter, and each of his phrases is followed by silence from her, with her continued gaze focused across the scene rather than into his eyes.

"What are you not telling? You see something ahead of us. Tell it now. What do you see?" After maintaining her silence after each demand, she finally responds while continuing to keep her eyes straight ahead, not looking at him: "I see everything. Whatever more I could say it would not help now." Her father responds, with his voice beginning to rise in volume: "Even now you disobey me. You, who sees the spirit world as I do. Do you want to see me weak like this?" Finally, she turns slightly and responds, "No. I want you to eat, father, and live." To his expression of frustration, she continues, "It's not my fight, father. I don't have your strength. I just want you to eat. And live."

And so she has made clear both that she will not say what she has seen, and that she is separating herself from the beliefs and values that her father holds. His voice increasingly angry, he says, "You want to eat? You betray me for some food?" He understands her refusal, and we are witness to the costs she is required to bear for asserting her own desires. Here, her brother Natar intervenes in her support, interjecting to say, "Father, my little sister has said everything she could." Avva finally shouts at them, "Then go eat with your friends!" While it may be less visible from the perspective of a Western viewer, the raised tone here is very exceptional, making visible the crisis of the moment and the depth of what is at stake.[41] The escalation is visible to Orulu, who also intervenes to disrupt the interaction, saying, "Daughter, don't say a word."

And so Apak stands, and walks towards the door. She stops there, turns to face her father, and poses the question that has been in the background all along: "So, the choice is mine to make?" No answer comes. She turns and bends to leave through the door, her brother shortly following. We are left with a shot that frames her father, looking ahead across the space, the gaze of his spirit helper focused on him.

In this refusal of speech, and assertion of the choice to live rather than follow the old ways, we are given even more space to consider the nature of the choice that is "hers to make." Her choice is not about strength of principle, but of the possibilities of continuing in life, and of not presuming too quickly that the meaning of a choice is straightforward. Clearly, the choice is both forced and constrained. The challenge is not simply to follow the old or the new ways, but takes us to questions about the coercion and possibility at the centre of the choice before her.

Our last moments in the film with Apak are drawn out through eleven minutes, as we consider her choice. We begin with a close-up of her face, standing outside of the igloo. We hear her tentatively and quietly hum a few notes of the Christian hymn that we overheard being sung (with mockery) in the opening shots of the film.[42] We then cut to a scene where the priest stands out in the bright light of day, his flock gathered before him, leading them in a version of that very song, one that sounds neither harmonious nor joyful. As they continue to sing, we gradually come to see Apak in the far distance, slowing walking across the snow towards the gathered group. Over an extended thirty seconds, the camera stays steady, with Umik and his followers singing in the foreground as she slowly approaches. It is another full minute before she is noticed, beckoned over, and drawn in to kneel with the other supplicants. We have many close-ups of her very blank face as she listens with the others, as they are told in the clearest of language that they are choosing to follow Jesus and thus must eat these meats to turn away from the old life. As viewers, we experience a deep feeling of disquiet and suspense as the meats are offered to everyone else, and finally to her. Her choice has been made. She puts the taboo meat into her mouth. The priest again leads the group in another song. Over three more minutes of screen time we hear the song, as the camera pans around the group, settling briefly on the many faces of Inuit and Danish explorers, faces that could be read as solemn or sorrowful, but whose lips continue to move in song (albeit disharmonious). It is only Apak, and the Danish explorer Therkel Mathiassen, whose lips remain still. One might ask whether non-Western viewers are invited to position themselves in some ways alongside Mathiassen, who has stood in solidarity and community with Avva's family as long as possible. While Mathiassen's silence might be an act of refusal or unfamiliarity with the song, we know that Apak does know the words (since we have seen her uttering them only minutes earlier as she stood outside the igloo). And so, we are again seeing the complexity of her choice. She will do what is necessary to live, but she will not sing the songs. In her refusal, she again lets us see her assertion of her own sovereignty, without explanation.[43]

## Wrapping Up

What then have we seen, in spending this time with Apak, in this story at the blurry edge of fact and fiction? She offers us an invitation to see the complexity in one Inuk woman's experience at a particular time in history. In spending time with Apak, we are given space to think deeply about her choices, her refusals, her sovereignty. We see a woman who chooses speech, chooses silence, chooses her own pleasure in the face of all the ways that she is also required to suffer. The language tells us she chooses to eat, and live. Both the script and the film also make visible the constraints within which her choices are made. We see that she has a lover chased away by her father, a husband murdered (by a man from another community who desired her), an arranged marriage forced upon her in response to avoid a blood feud. We see her conforming to some of the roles she carries. She accepts that the arranged marriage will serve the good of the community, but refuses to be warm to that husband and centres her own sexual desiring. When she miscarried, she hid the evidence rather than follow the taboos that would otherwise have been expected of her (taboos that would have limited not only the foods she could eat but the contact she could have with others). In these actions, she makes visible a refusal to fully follow rules others would impose on her body, her sexuality, her reproduction. When confronted with her choices (whether sex with her dead husband or hiding the evidence of the miscarriage), she acknowledges those choices without performing any sense of guilt or shame. Our time with her is an invitation to engage with the questions of sovereignty she raises, and to do so with generosity and curiosity. One might add that her choice at the end – to eat and live – is also one that calls to the future. She offers a kind of blueprint for sovereign refusals to come. In engaging with the multiple, shadowed, storied versions of her character, we have the opportunity to engage not simply with the past, but with the complex issues of our time. She invites us to return to the question of Theresa Spence's hunger strike, of the students' response to the public disregard of the personhood and sovereignty of Tina Lafontaine, and Colton Boushie, and Cindy Gladue. There is much in the storied power in Indigenous legal orders and Indigenous feminisms. They offer us space to learn how to engage with each other in more meaningful ways while doing less harm to each other in the process. It is a space worth taking up.

## NOTES

1 For more on this metaphor, see Rebecca Johnson, "The Persuasive Cartographer: Sexual Assault and Legal Discourse in *R v. Ewanchuk*" in Gayle MacDonald, ed, *Social Context and Social Location in the Sociology of Law* (Peterborough: Broadview, 2001) 247.

2 *Edwards v Canada (AG)* [1930] AC 124 [on whether women were "persons" eligible to sit on the Senate in Canada].

3 *R v Morgentaler,* [1988] 1 SCR 30 [the criminal code restrictions on abortion violated women's right to security of the person under the Charter]; or AA v BB, 2007 ONCA 2 [holding that the court can effectively recognize three legal parents to a child].

4 *Brooks v Canada Safeway Ltd*, [1989] 1 SCR 1219.

5 *R v Lavalee*, [1990] 1 SCR 852 [on reasonable force in the context of "battered woman syndrome"].

6 *Murdoch v Murdoch,* [1975] 1 SCR 423 [holding that a "farm wife" had no right to share in the family ranch following divorce].

7 *In re French* (1905), 37 NBR 359 (SC). [denying Mabel Penury French's application to the practice of law in New Brunswick, as her sex was a bar: "eligible persons" means exclusively "male persons"].

8 *Gauthier v Canada (Canadian Armed Forces),* [1989] CHRD No 3.

9 National Inquiry into Missing and Murdered Indigenous Women and Girls, *Reclaiming Power and Place: The Final Report of the National Inquiry into Missing and Murdered Indigenous Women and Girls* (Ottawa: MMIWG 2019), online: <https://www.mmiwg-ffada.ca/final-report/> [MMIWG].

10 The term "sovereign" here is not used in the sense of the European "sovereign" state, as in the ownership of territory. Here it connotes a sense of autonomy, self-determination, and agency.

11 For an example of a talk that attempts to tell these women's stories in a complex way, see Val Napoleon, "Cosmology and Law in the Spirit Respite Village" (Talk delivered at IdeaFest, March 2012, Victoria, BC), online: <https://www.youtube.com/watch?v=PEI0HsT2pag&t=20s>.

12 See the discussion of the importance and multiple uses of stories in Louis Bird, *Telling Our Stories: Omushkego Legends and Histories from the Hudson Bay* (Toronto: University of Toronto Press, 2005).

13 I am grateful here to Rachel Flowers for her re-articulation of this important question, which focused my attention on the processes of finding one's place (including one's place as a visitor) while ILRU was engaged in partnership work with the Secwépemc on laws related to membership and belonging. See Jessica Asch & Rebecca Johnson with Cheyenne Arnold-Cunningham (Indigenous Law Research Unit, Shuswap Nation Tribal Council, & Secwépemc Sna7a Elders Council), *Secwépemc Laws of Kwséltkten and Secwépemc-kt Report* (Victoria/ləkʷəŋən territory: Indigenous Law Research Unit, 2023), online: <https://ilru.ca/wp-content/uploads/2025/04/ILRU_SNTC_Report.pdf>.

14 See Audra Simpson, "The State Is a Man: Theresa Spence, Loretta Saunders and the Gender of Settler Sovereignty" (2016) 19:4 Theory & Event 17. I am particularly grateful for Julianna Hu Pegues's productive workshop with CIRCLE at University of Victoria, 1 March 2022, where she had us work with Simpson's engagement with Theresa Spence. For more on Simpson's extensive work on the politics of refusal, see her *Mohawk Interruptus: Political Life across the Borders of Settler States* (Durham: Duke University Press, 2014); see also Simpson, "The Ruse of Consent and the Anatomy of 'Refusal': Cases from Indigenous North America and Australia" (2017) Postcolonial Studies 20:1 18, where she further elaborates on the generative alternative that refusal may play not only as a political practice but also as a mode of analysis. It is this turn that I find so helpful in the context of work in law and film.

15 Simpson demands the depth of attention for Indigenous refusals as seen in Western scholarship's engagement with Antigone. See for example: Bonnie Honig, *Antigone, Interrupted* (Cambridge: Cambridge University Press, 2013); Honig, *A Feminist Theory of Refusal* (Cambridge, MA: Harvard University Press, 2021). Honig, like Simpson, focuses on the acts of self-governance that are at the core of refusal. For another powerful exploration of the power of refusal, see Rachel Flowers, "Refusal to Forgive: Indigenous Women's Love and Rage" (2015) 4:2 Decolonization: Indigeneity, Education & Society 32.

16 *R v Barton* 2017 ABCA 216; for the outcome on appeal to the Supreme Court, see *R v Barton*, [2019] 2 SRC 579.

17 The idea of Indigenous personhood is explored in Val Napoleon, "Gitxsan Legal Personhood: Gendered" in Austin Sarat, George Pavlich & Richard Mailey, eds, *Interrupting the Legal Person: Vol 87A* (Bingley, UK: Emerald, 2022) 19. On the disregard of Cindy Gladue's personhood in this case, see Sherene H. Razack, "Gendering Disposability" (2016) 28:2 Canadian Journal of Women and the Law 285.

18 See also <https://rebeccaj63.wordpress.com/2018/03/21/grief-protest-and-witnessing-reflections-on-the-deaths-of-colten-boushie-and-tina-fontaine/>.

19 Here, I honour my colleague Myron Gochnauer and Patricia Hughes at the University of New Brunswick Faculty of Law, who advocated for a class on women and the law and stewarded it through different iterations. My presumption is that there is never magic in the specific words we use to describe courses, but there is something important in ongoing conversations about the ways shifts in naming help us address the specific challenges of time and place.

20 See the dissent of Justice L'Heureux-Dube in *R* v *Seaboyer*: *R* v *Gayme*, [1991]2 SCR 577, as well as Elizabeth Sheehy, ed, *Sexual Assault in Canada: Law, Legal Practice and Women's Activism* (Ottawa: University of Ottawa Press, 2012).

21 In 2018 this was very much a part of the media discourse in the trials taking up the deaths of Cindy Gladue and Tina Fontaine. See *MMIWG, supra* note 10, which details many of the ways in which Indigenous women's lives lead to harm and death and Indigenous women's lives and choices are flattened. See also Val Napoleon, "An Imaginary for Our Sisters: Spirits and Indigenous Law" in Jeffery Hewitt, Beverly Jacobs & Richard Moon, eds, *Indigenous Spirituality and Religious Freedom* (Toronto: University of Toronto Press, 2025).

22 Because the two of us were teaching it at the same time (one in Israel, the other in Fredericton, NB), we had the opportunity to talk about what we were doing and to compare notes about what we were seeing in the different places. The films and insights from that course eventually took form in a book, which I highly recommend to anyone interested in law and film work: Orit Kamir, *Framed: Women in Law and Film: How Law on Screen Constructs Gender, Dignity and Honor* (Durham: Duke University Press, 2006). I speak more about this in Rebecca Johnson, "Judging Magic: Can You See the Sleight of Hand?" (2006) Michigan L Rev 1353.

23 On these storied methodologies, consider Joanne Archibald, *Indigenous Storywork* (Vancouver: UBC Press, 2008); Julie Cruikshank, *The Social Life of Stories: Narrative and Knowledge in the Yukon Territory* (Lincoln: University of Nebraska Press, 1998); Val Napoleon, "Did I Break It? Recording Indigenous (Customary) Law" (2019) 22 PER/PELJ, online: <http://dx.doi.org/10.17159/1727- 3781/2019/v22i0a7588>.

24 I take inspiration here from Edward W. Saïd, *Culture and Imperialism* (New York: Vintage, 1994). His argument focused on the nineteenth-century novel as a site for understanding empire, but his method is equally apt when applied to the popular cultural texts of the twenty-first century.

25 For more on this approach of exploring questions in film, and this film in particular, see Rebecca Johnson, "Questions about Questions: Law and Film Reflections on the Duty to Learn" (2020) 50 Northern Rev 83.

26 See, for example, the wonderful work done in Tasha Hubbard's film *Nîpawistamâsowin: We Will Stand Up*, Alanis Obamsawin's *We Can't Make the Same Mistake Twice*, or *Finding Dawn* (taken up by Cheryl Suzack in chapter 7).

27 I explore this idea with my friend Ruth Buchanan in Johnson & Buchanan, "Getting the Insider's Story Out: What Popular Film Can Tell Us about Legal Method's Dirty Secrets" (2001) 20 Windsor Yearbook of Access to Justice 87.

28 David R. Dow, "Fictional Documentaries and Truthful Fictions: The Death Penalty in Recent American Film" (2000) 17:3 Constitutional Commentary 511.

29 For more on the felt registers of film, see Ruth Buchanan & Rebecca Johnson, "Strange Encounters: Exploring Law and Film in the Affective Register" (2009) 46 Studies in Law, Politics, and Society 33.

30 For an exploration of the other two films, see Rebecca Johnson, "Intercultural Cinema and the (Re)Envisioning of Law: Exploring Life, Death and Law in *Atanarjuat* and *Before Tomorrow*" in Timothy D Peters & Karen Crawley, eds, *Envisioning Legality: Law, Culture and Representation* (Abingdon, UK: Routledge, 2018) 228.

31 Based in deep practices of collaboration, and with political commitments to Inuit ways of living, the film company plays an important part in the sustaining and transmission of Inuit knowledges and skills, involving a significant number of people on the production side, including dog teams, hunters, and artists working with skin and furs, and supporting construction techniques, language, storytelling practices and more. For more on the company, its history, and its works, see Michael Evans, *Isuma: Inuit Video Art* (Montreal/Kingston: McGill-Queen's University Press, 2008).

32 For a discussion of how the techniques of video produce these effects, see Norman Cohn & Joysanne Sidimus, "Norman Cohn Speaks with Joysanne Sidimus" in Gillian Robinson, ed, *The Journals of Knud Rasmussen: A Sense of Memory and High-Definition Inuit Storytelling* (Montreal: Isuma Distribution, 2008) 263.

33 Michael Robert Evans, *Frozen Light and Fluid Time: The Folklore, Politics and Performance of Inuit Video* (Bloomington: Indiana University, 1999); Sarah Best, "Time-Diffraction Stories: Inuit *Qaujimajatuqangit* and

Temporal Sovereignty in *The Journals of Knud Rasmussen* and *Split Tooth*" (2023) 10.1 Synoptique 5, online: <https://www.synoptique.ca/issue-10-1>.

34 Of particular interest is James Teit, in whose work the question "Who are we to each other?" is highly visible. See Wendy Wickwire, *At the Bridge: James Teit and an Anthropology of Belonging* (Vancouver: UBC Press, 2019).

35 Keavy Martin, *Stories in a New Skin: Approaches to Inuit Literature* (Winnipeg: University of Manitoba Press, 2012), particularly chap. 3.

36 "The Journals of Knud Rasmussen – Original Screenplay" in Gillian Robinson, ed, *The Journals of Knud Rasmussen: A Sense of Memory and High-Definition Inuit Storytelling* (Montreal: Isuma Distribution, 2008) 287. The volume also includes a version of the screenplay in Inuktitut.

37 In beginning to appreciate the shape of this life, a good resource is the five-volume series *Interviewing Inuit Elders.* Particularly helpful is Mariano Aupilaarjuk et al., *Interviewing Inuit Elders,* vol. 2: *Perspectives on Traditional Law,* ed Jarich Oosten, Frederic Laugrand & Wim Rasing (Iqaluit: Nunavut Arctic College, 1999).

38 For a full account of this story, see Shelagh Grant, *Arctic Justice: On Trial for Murder, Pond Inlet, 1923* (Montreal/Kingston: McGill-Queen's University Press, 2005). The back cover of the book recounts: "Although there was no Canadian law enforcement in the Eastern High Arctic when a crazed white fur trader was killed by an Inuk, authorities put

Nuqallaq and two other Baffin Island Inuit on trial. The Canadian government saw Robert Janes's death as murder; the Inuit saw it as removing a threat from their society according to custom. Nuqallaq was sentenced to ten years hard labour in Stony Mountain Penitentiary, where he contracted tuberculosis. He died shortly after being returned to Pond Inlet."

39 The song is "Uvnik" (human flesh), composed and performed by Tanya Tagak (from Sinaa, produced 2004).

40 There is a lovely discussion of the film by Maurie Alioff, "Falling Forward into an Icy World," *New York Times* (19 November 2006), online: <https://www.nytimes.com/2006/11/19/movies/19alio.html>.

41 For more on this, see Jean L Briggs, *Never in Anger: Portrait of an Eskimo Family* (Cambridge, MA: Harvard University Press, 1970).

42 This scene echoes an earlier one between Avva and one of his former shaman friends, who has lost his powers through eating the forbidden meats. The friend says to Avva, "The songs are not so hard to learn." After a long silence, Avva replies gently, "I have no room in my head for new songs." We see here that Apak, on the other hand, has retained some room in her head for things that must be learned if she is to be able to live.

43 In thinking about Apak's voice, and her narration, I find it interesting to compare film with script. In my own working with the film (prior to reading the script), I was curious about a film that sets up her voice at the beginning, but the voice never returns. She never gives us a closing to the story. There was thus surprise for me in reading the script and seeing that, initially, her voice did return at the end, to tell the reader what happened to various people (the death of her parents, the death of Kunuk, the trial for murder and eventual spread of tuberculosis to the north). The voice-over imagined in the script informs the viewer that she reaches the end of her life, seeing all that she had envisioned come to pass. In short, in the script Kunuk and Cohn give the viewers access to the visions she refused to tell her father. I appreciate the script, but find more power in the film, which withholds from us a narrative closure that suggests the future was already written in her dreams. There is something more open (from the point of view of of her sovereignty) in leaving that conclusionn unwritten.

## SOURCES CITED


Alioff, Maurie. "Falling Forward into an Icy World," *New York Times* (19 November 2006), online: <https://www.nytimes.com/2006/11/19/movies/19alio.html>

Archibald, Joanne. *Indigenous Storywork* (Vancouver: UBC Press, 2008).

Asch, Jessica & Rebecca Johnson with Cheyenne Arnold-Cunningham (Indigenous Law Research Unit, Shuswap Nation Tribal Council, & Secwépemc Sna7a Elders Council). *Secwépemc Laws of Ḱwséltkten and Secwépemc-kt Report* (Victoria/ləkʷəŋən territory: Indigenous Law Research Unit, 2023), online: <https://ilru.ca/wp-content/uploads/2025/04/ILRU_SNTC_Report.pdf>.

Aupilaarjuk, Mariano, Marie Tulimaaq, Akisu Joamie, Emile Imaruittuq & Lucassie Nutaraaluk. *Interviewing Inuit Elders*, vol. 2: *Perspectives on Traditional Law*, ed Jarich Oosten, Frederic Laugrand & Wim Rasing (Iqaluit: Nunavut Arctic College, 1999).

Best, Sarah. "Time-Diffraction Stories: Inuit *Qaujimajatuqangit* and Temporal Sovereignty in *The Journals of Knud Rasmussen* and *Split Tooth*." (2023) 10:1 Synoptique 5, online: <https://www.synoptique.ca/issue-10-1>.

Bird, Louis. *Telling Our Stories: Omushkego Legends and Histories from the Hudson Bay* (Toronto: University of Toronto Press, 2005).

Briggs, Jean L. *Never in Anger: Portrait of an Eskimo Family* (Cambridge, MA: Harvard University Press, 1970).

Buchanan, Ruth & Rebecca Johnson. "Strange Encounters: Exploring Law and Film in the Affective Register" (2009) 46 Studies in Law, Pol & Soc 33.

Canada, *Reclaiming Power and Place: The Final Report of the National Inquiry into Missing and Murdered Indigenous Women and Girls* (Ottawa: MMIWG, 2019).

Cohn, Norman & Joysanne Sidimus. "Norman Cohn Speaks with Joysanne Sidimus" in Gillian Robinson, ed, *The Journals of Knud Rasmussen: A Sense of Memory and High-Definition Inuit Storytelling* (Montreal: Isuma Distribution, 2008) 263.

Cruikshank, Julie. *The Social Life of Stories: Narrative and Knowledge in the Yukon Territory* (Lincoln: University of Nebraska Press, 1998).

Dow, David R. "Fictional Documentaries and Truthful Fictions: The Death Penalty in Recent American Film" (2000) 17:3 Constitutional Commentary 511.

Evans, Michael Robert. *Frozen Light and Fluid Time: The Folklore, Politics and Performance of Inuit Video* (Bloomington: Indiana University Press, 1999).

Evans, Michael Robert. *Isuma: Inuit Video Art* (Montreal/Kingston: McGill-Queen's University Press, 2008).

Flowers, Rachel. "Refusal to Forgive: Indigenous Women's Love and Rage" (2015) 4:2 Decolonization: Indigeneity, Education & Society 32.

Grant, Shelagh. *Arctic Justice: On Trial for Murder, Pond Inlet, 1923* (Montreal/Kingston: McGill-Queen's University Press, 2005).

Honig, Bonnie. *Antigone, Interrupted* (Cambridge: Cambridge University Press, 2013).

Honig, Bonnie. *A Feminist Theory of Refusal* (Boston: Harvard University Press, 2021).

Johnson, Rebecca. "Intercultural Cinema and the (Re)Envisioning of Law: Exploring Life, Death and Law in *Atanarjuat* and *Before Tomorrow*" in Timothy D. Peters & Karen Crawley, eds, *Envisioning Legality: Law, Culture and Representation* (Milton Park, UK: Routledge, 2018) 228.

Johnson, Rebecca. "Judging Magic: Can You See the Sleight of Hand?" (2006) Michigan L Rev 1353.

Johnson, Rebecca. "The Persuasive Cartographer: Sexual Assault and Legal Discourse in R v. Ewanchuk" in Gayle MacDonald, ed, *Social Context and Social Location in the Sociology of Law* (Peterborough: Broadview, 2001) 247.

Johnson, Rebecca. "Questions about Questions: Law and Film Reflections on the Duty to Learn" (2020) 50 Northern Rev 83.

Johnson, Rebecca & Ruth Buchanan. "Getting the Insider's Story Out: What Popular Film Can Tell Us about Legal Method's Dirty Secrets." (2001) 20 Windsor Yearbook of Access to Justice 87.

Kamir, Orit. *Framed: Women in Law and Film: How Law on Screen Constructs Gender, Dignity and Honor* (Durham: Duke University Press, 2006).

Kunuk, Zacharias & Norman Cohn. "The Journals of Knud Rasmussen – Original Screenplay" in Gillian Robinson, ed, *The Journals of Knud*

*Rasmussen: A Sense of Memory and High-Definition Inuit Storytelling* (Montreal: Isuma Distribution, 2008) 287.

Martin, Keavy. *Stories in a New Skin: Approaches to Inuit Literature* (Winnipeg: University of Manitoba Press, 2012).

Napoleon, Val. "Cosmology and Law in the Spirit Respite Village" (Talk delivered at IdeaFest, March 2012, Victoria BC), online: <https://www.youtube.com/watch?v=PEI0HsT2pag&t=20s>.

Napoleon, Val. "Did I Break It? Recording Indigenous (Customary) Law" (2019) 22 PER/PELJ, online: <http://dx.doi.org/10.17159/1727-3781/2019/v22i0a7588>.

Napoleon, Val. "Gitxsan Legal Personhood: Gendered" in Austin Sarat, George Pavlich & Richard Mailey, eds, *Interrupting the Legal Person, Studies in Law, Politics, and Society*, vol 87A (Bingley, UK: Emerald, 2022) 19.

Napoleon, Val. "An Imaginary for Our Sisters: Spirits and Indigenous Law" in Jeffery Hewitt, Beverly Jacobs and Richard Moon, eds, *Indigenous Spirituality and Religious Freedom* (Toronto: University of Toronto Press, 2025).

National Inquiry into Missing and Murdered Indigenous Women and Girls, *Reclaiming Power and Place: The Final Report of the National Inquiry into Missing and Murdered Indigenous Women and Girls* (Ottawa: MMIWG 2019), online: https://www.mmiwg-ffada.ca/final-report/>.

Razack, Sherene H. "Gendering Disposability" (2016) 28(2) Cdn J Women and the Law 285.

Robinson, Gillian, ed. *The Journals of Knud Rasmussen: A Sense of Memory and High-Definition Inuit Storytelling* (Montreal: Isuma Distribution International, 2008) 287.

Saïd, Edward W. *Culture and Imperialism.* (New York: Vintage, 1994)

Sheehy, Elizabeth, ed. *Sexual Assault in Canada: Law, Legal Practice and Women's Activism* (Ottawa: University of Ottawa Press, 2012).

Simpson, Audra. *Mohawk Interruptus: Political Life across the Borders of Settler States* (Durham: Duke University Press, 2014).

Simpson, Audra. "The Ruse of Consent and the Anatomy of 'Refusal': Cases from Indigenous North America and Australia" (2017) 20:1 Postcolonial Studies 18.

Simpson, Audra. "The State Is a Man: Theresa Spence, Loretta Saunders and the Gender of Settler Sovereignty" (2016) 19:4 Theory & Event 17.

Wickwire, Wendy. *At the Bridge: James Teit and an Anthropology of Belonging.* (Vancouver: UBC Press, 2019).

## FILMS

*Atanarjuat (The Fast Runner)* (dir. Zacharias Kunuk, 2001)

*Before Tomorrow* (dir. Marie-Hélène Cousineau and Madeline Ivalu, 2008)

*Finding Dawn* (dir. Christine Welsh, 2006)
*The Journals of Knud Rasmussen* (dir. Zacharias Kunuk, 2006)
*Nanook of the North* (dir. Robert Flaherty, 1922)
*Nîpawistamâsowin: We Will Stand Up* (dir. Tasha Hubbard, 2019)
*We Can't Make the Same Mistake Twice* (dir. Alanis Obamsawin, 2016)

## CASES

*R v Barton*, 2017 ABCA 216.
*R v Barton*, [2019] 2 SRC 579.
*Brooks v Canada Safeway Ltd*, [1989] 1 SCR 1219.
*Edwards v Canada (AG)* [1930] AC 124.
*Gauthier v Canada (Canadian Armed Forces)*, [1989] CHRD No 3.
*Murdoch v Murdoch*, [1975] 1 SCR 423.
*Murdoch v Murdoch*, [1975] 1 SCR 423.
*R v Lavalee*, [1990] 1 SCR 852.
*R v Morgentaler*, [1988] 1 SCR 30.
*R v Seaboyer: R v Gayme*, [1991]2 SCR 577.

# 9 Thoughts and Questions and Questions

KIM PATE AND VAL NAPOLEON

We offer an imagined conversation between twelve Indigenous women who have experienced violence, including sexual violence.[1] While the conversation is imagined, these women and their experiences are very real.[2] Through this conversation, we hope to create an opportunity to understand and reflect on the racist and gendered discrimination experienced by Indigenous women under the state legal system. We hope that this conversation will draw on the themes from the previous chapters to generate productive ways to think about the future and about finding ways forward in real women's lives.

We have reached a point in our history where it is banal to say that Indigenous women are often ill served by the Canadian legal system.[3] So instead of repeating that refrain, let's ask how an overhaul of the system – from policing to courtrooms to prisons and beyond – might address the dangerous racist, sexist, and misogynist biases that seem so firmly rooted in the current legal system. As the previous chapters have argued, we need to look beyond the state to the thoughtful and critical recognition of and engagement with Indigenous law. We must always ask, whether with state law or with Indigenous law, how might Indigenous women be guaranteed access to a system of real justice?

So where is the starting place? The extent of discrimination and inequality in the justice system faced by Indigenous women in Canada is staggering. For example, in 2022[4] Indigenous women accounted for half of the population in women's federal penitentiaries. Consider this against the fact that only one out of every twenty women in Canada is Indigenous. None of this is new. Read through the well-known 1999 SCC *Gladue* decision[5] where the court discussed the "Overrepresentation of Aboriginal Canadians in Penal Institutions" and reviewed the large number of commissions and inquiries that have tackled this issue.[6] The court concluded that the findings from those commissions and inquiries "cry out for recognition of the magnitude and gravity of the problem."[7] However, since then the situation has only worsened.

Senator Kim Pate authored and co-produced a national report that forms the basis of this chapter.[8] The report outlines the cases of twelve Indigenous women who experienced gross miscarriages of justice within the Canadian legal system. Its purpose is to advocate for a review of these cases and to lay the groundwork for the exoneration of these twelve women. Through their stories, ten interrelated elements of racist and gendered bias became evident, all of which "underlie the patterns of systemic inequality and violence experienced by each woman both prior to and while navigating the criminal legal system."[9] A summarized list of the elements is set out here to contextualize the women's conversation that follows.

1. Genocidal colonial forced removals from lands, institutionalization (from reserves, residential schools, mental asylums, and Indian hospitals to prisons) where Indigenous peoples were subjected to violence and forced assimilation, and exclusion from the safety of communities due to the federal *Indian Act*,[10] resulting in intergenerational trauma, marginalization, and lack of access to adequate economic, social, health, and other supports;
2. Victimization, hyper-responsibilization,[11] and deputization;[12]
3. Hyper-responsibilization and criminalization as a result of trying to survive and navigate marginalization and violence;
4. Bias with respect to police responses, particularly investigation and charging practices;
5. Bias in the exercise of prosecutorial discretion, exacerbated by the distortion of charging and plea-bargaining practices occasioned by mandatory minimum penalties;[13]
6. Lack of application of section 718.2(e) of the *Canadian Criminal Code*[14] and inadequate contextualization of racism, sexism, and violence in legal defences of Indigenous women;
7. Failure to consider alternatives to punitive sentences, in particular as a result of mandatory minimum penalties;
8. Discriminatory risk assessment and classification tools, practices, and policies, and consequently limited access to programs, services, and conditional release within the prison system;
9. Unending nature and ongoing impacts of life sentences; and
10. Perpetuation of the vicious circle of children in foster care, forced separation of Indigenous women from their children and communities, and a greater likelihood of them ending up in prison than in post-secondary education.

What might these women say to one another? How might they understand what has happened to them? What would have made a difference to their experiences? What if things had been different for them?[15] What they share is only a snippet of who they are as real Indigenous women, as whole human beings, and as legal agents. Most entered the legal system when they were very young. It is a given that their lives have borne the too often deadly brunt of Canada's colonial legacy.

**The Conversation**

Join us. We are going into a large airy room painted with a palette of soft pastels of blues, purples, yellows, and corals. Sunlight streams in through big windows, causing dust motes to dance gracefully. Delicate pale-green curtains move gently as they catch the light breezes allowed through the open door and windows. In the background, Mavis Staples is quietly singing "I'll Take You There."[16]

One by one, twelve Indigenous women enter the room, some moving hesitantly, others purposefully; some are joyful, others serene and gentle. As each steps into the room, her eyes scan the circle. Some recognize others with nods and smiles, others remain looking inward, seeing beyond the room. Women of all descriptions with all kinds of strength and beauty and grace, they are wearing vivid versions of the pastels that appear in the room so that they appear jewel like.

They each select a chair set out in a large circle. This is just a single moment, only one, captured from years that sometimes span decades. We know that some of these women have gone to the other side, and what we are seeing now is their spirits joining us across worlds. We know that some of these women have escaped incarceration and are now with their families. And we know that some of these women are still in prison or in some other form of custody.

Lastly, six ravens swoop in. They are Tricksters, the first law teachers from their respective peoples residing from across the great Turtle Island – north, south, east, and west, and two more, one from the sky and cosmos, the other from the earth. Some of these Indigenous Feminist Trickster Ravens are elderly, others young, the full spectrum really because they are ageless just as they are also all of LGBTQ+ and cis too. They perch on the remaining chairs. Mavis Staples finishes her song.

The Feminist Trickster Raven from the north is wearing a pink headscarf. She stands tall and opens her wings, and in a deep voice says, "Welcome all! Thank you for acting on the courage and strength it took for you to join this gathering." The other Trickster Ravens nod and hold up their wings in gratitude.

"We are here to create a public record with you and of you." The Feminist Trickster from the earth takes over. "What is most important today is that your public record acknowledge that all of you are more than your imprisonment. For those of you who have passed on, your story must be about more than your deaths. For those of you no longer incarcerated, your stories must be about your lives beyond prison. And for those of you still incarcerated, your stories must recognize the tensile strength you need every day to keep going." She is nodding, her white kerchief bright in the sunlight.

The Feminist Trickster from the Sky stands tall. Her kerchief is orange and yellow, shimmering. "Your stories cannot only be about despair and suffering. Nor can they only be about the failures of the Canadian legal system with its miscarriages of justice. Your memories cannot be forever captured, like amber, in a narrative of despair.[17] You are so much more than that. My sister Tricksters and I are here to honour you and your lives, your dignity, your strengths, and your families – and we are here to hold you up."

Raising her wings as if to hug everyone, Feminist Trickster from the west is perched on the back of her chair. "We will always need to feel the pain, but your daughters and granddaughters – and every other Indigenous daughter and granddaughter – also need the strength of hope." She is wearing a floral summer scarf of brightly coloured peonies. She hops back down to the chair seat.

Slowly, the Feminist Trickster from the east raises her head and looks around the room. She is ancient, with much white around her beak. Her steely dark eyes move across the room. Dressed in a beautiful turquoise scarf, she begins to speak. "This is a small step. There are many steps yet for us all to take if Indigenous women and girls are going to be safe and be accorded substantive equality and fairness in the Canadian legal system. Of course, we also know that women and girls are unsafe in some of our own communities as in urban centres – this means there are big challenges before Indigenous law too."

Finally, the Feminist Trickster from the south raises her head and looks down her long beak, and then she swoops around the outside of the circle of women – she flies around the circle twice, the air swooshing through her wing feathers. The fabric of her kerchief is woven with many shades of purple, so she appears dressed in shifting shadows. She returns to the back of her chair and begins to speak. "This the first time we are creating a gathering like this to do this work. Long overdue in my opinion." She shifts back and forth in her raven manner. "Here is how we will proceed. First, we invite you to briefly tell your story to each other. Then we will ask you how you would like to change your narratives, what stories you want your families and others to know. What do you want to add?"

She gazes around at the women. "Good? Ready?" She nods encouragingly. "Let's go. Who wants to go first?"

*Emma*

Emma looks up and clears her throat. "Where to start?" She is speaking softly. "Today, I am designated a dangerous offender. This means that my sentence is indeterminate, which is basically a life sentence without any possible parole eligibility period.

"First, I think I have to go back to how I got here. Before prison, I had a miscarriage 'cause of my partner, he was really violent so I lost that baby. Then I was twenty-one years old and pregnant again when I was first convicted. They got me for drug trafficking and assault with a weapon. I got three and half years.

"When I got to prison, I was so scared of losing another baby 'cause of the force used on me by the correctional staff. Then, while I was in jail, I used marijuana, and for that they took my daughter from me. They said I would never see her again."

Emma bows her head and takes a deep breath. "You know, I just gave up. Didn't give a damn about anything so I tried to escape. But ..." She stops, breathes, then starts, "But I assaulted a correctional officer when trying to do my escape." She looks down, studies her shoes.

She raises her eyes and looks around the room. The other women are nodding. She could hear some quiet mmms and hmms, and one "Yep, been there too."

Encouraged, Emma continues. "I was transferred to the segregated maximum-security unit in a penitentiary for men. Then there was some more fights, what they called 'altercations against staff.' I think I pled guilty. Anyway, I was found guilty of some charges. They called it 'forcible confinement' what I did.

"The problem was that some of the ..." –she stops to make air quotes – "'incidents.' These fights, they were started on purpose by some others. They were 'staged,' you know? As a way to get transferred to someplace else.

"Didn't matter though. I just pled guilty. I thought if I pled guilty, you know, taking responsibility, then I could see my girl. I thought I could lower my security rating so I could at least have contact with my daughter. Maybe even get to care for her."

Emma shakes her head. "Nobody has told me anything about how all this is going to affect my parole. I just don't know.

"So now I am out but on lifelong community supervision." Emma leans back in her chair and looks up at the ceiling shaking her head in seeming disbelief. "I was inside 2000 until 2018, and most of that time I was in segregation. I been on conditional release since 2018. Eighteen years! A lifetime, a whole friggin' lifetime."

*Winter*

Sitting beside Emma is Winter, who squirms a bit, then settles in, holds up her fingers, and begins ticking of the years. "Let's see. I was in and out of institutions from 1989 to 1992. Then in 1999, then in 2006. And since 2009, I been either in a federal prison or forensic hospital. That's where I am now."

Winter looks resigned. "It goes back, you know. I was abandoned. Then from when I was a baby and for my whole childhood, I was sexually abused." She is looking deep into her past; her voice becomes ragged.

"Lots of time I tried to kill myself. First time I did that I was thirteen." Winter pauses to gather her inner strength, and continues. "Since I was fourteen, I been in and out of jail. Sometimes while I was in prison, more time was added 'cause of 'incidents.'" Winter pauses again. "I tried to hurt myself lots of times. I had what they call 'disabling mental health issues.' Every time, they just added more sentence. They call these times incidents – sounds so clean and neat. Tidy."

Tears stream down Winter's face. Feminist Trickster from the south flies to stand on the back of her chair and places a wingtip on her shoulder. Winter smiles as she receives the small comfort. "I am still in custody. But you know what, it was not even called a sentence anymore. It became a custody. It was 'cause of my behaviour and then they found that I was not criminally responsible due to mental health issues. But I was still kept inside.

"It's cause when I was in segregation for so long, I kept banging my head against the wall. Now I will never be the same – they say physical, psychological, and neurological damage. When I tried to resist the staff, they tried to have me declared a 'dangerous offender.'" Tears continue to stream down her face.

From around the room, soft voices. "We hear you, girl. We are here with you."

Winter sounds exhausted, but keeps going. "So much kept happening. You know there was even a big review of my 'circumstances.' They reviewed that I had been held criminally responsible at the same time when I tried to hurt myself – at the same time they said I was mentally incompetent according to provincial law. The judge even refused the application! I don't understand it all."

Winter smiles as she looks into all the faces of the women listening to her. "I escaped anyway. Even though I was called 'incompetent' according to all the laws, I was able to apply for and consent to medical assistance in dying (MAiD). There was no external, independent intervention of any kind. I am free of it all now." Feminist Trickster from the south gently pats Winter's shoulder and swoops back to her chair.

*Vivi*

"I am on the other side too with Winter," Vivi begins. "My story began so long ago. Thirty years! Imagine, thirty years." Vivi shakes her head.

"I died on April 16, 2022. Cancer. When I died, I was still on conditional release and subject to lifelong community supervision by a parole officer. I could never get away from it. So crazy!"

Vivi smiles at everyone, and holds out her hands, palms up, "Where to start? I was nineteen years old. I got convicted of second-degree murder of a woman. She was inviting me, I should say 'procuring' me to be sexually exploited by a man that everyone knew was abusing young Indigenous women. He took photographs and videoed everything he did, all the abuse."

Vivi nods to herself. "Problem was that I didn't tell anybody about my childhood, the trauma an' all that. And I didn't tell anybody about what was all involved with what I did, the crime, you know? I didn't know it would have helped. I didn't tell my lawyer anything so I didn't get to explain my self-defence to the court, about how I tried to protect myself. Nothing. So I got convicted of second-degree murder, which resulted in a mandatory life sentence. But now I am free."

"Mmm, yes, you are free." Emma is holding up her hands.

*Olivia*

"My story started a long time ago now. Thirty years I spent in prison, lots in segregation. But the main thing is that I am out now, on parole, and I am living with family in my community.

"What a waste. As a kid, I was eleven years in a residential school. I suffered there like so many other thousands of us Indigenous Peoples[18] – physical, sexual, and psychological abuse. On top of that, they put down my language and we were not allowed to speak with family in community or follow our own ways. Nowadays, they call it 'cultural genocide.'

"I think somehow the residential school made me like prey to abusive men. I even married one when I was sixteen.

"Yep, lots of us did exactly that," Lily murmurs. Other voices quietly join in agreement.

Olivia stops to search her memories, her eyes looking inward. "At first I was considered an accomplice to my husband's drug dealing, so I got jail for that." She sighs. "It gets worse. When I was in prison, I pled guilty to the murder of a woman. But everybody knew that the death was actually a suicide. Both the staff and the other women inside were adamant about this fact."

Shifting slightly in her seat, Olivia continues. "She was like a sister to me and they said I killed her. She really suffered – terrible and disabling health issues. I used to help with her care, I wish I could have done more, that's what I feel guilty about, that I couldn't help her more."

"Of course there was this big investigation because of the six Indigenous women who committed suicide at Kingston.[19] There was an inquest and they said that the cause of death was unknown."

Olivia leans back and crosses her arms, then uncrosses them. "Four years after my friend died, I ended up confessing and pleading guilty to her murder. I had a lawyer but despite everything, you know, like the mismatch between my confession and the records of her death, I got convicted. I guess I pled this way because I felt intensely guilt. I felt personally responsible. I don't know really. But this meant that I got a mandatory life sentence. After ten years, even though I was eligible, I served way more time, like three times more time, before I was paroled to my community. That is my story for now."

*Lily*

Sitting tall, Lily smiles at the circle. "My story is similar to yours, Winter. The abuse since I was a wee one. By the time was twelve I was being trafficked and sexually exploited."

Lily stops for a couple of breaths. "There was this guy that we thought was abusing kids, his own children and others. Me and some others, we killed him. My role was limited, but I was still one among others who was responsible, and I was charged with first-degree murder. The others, my husband included, got lesser charges."

Smiling again, this time ruefully: "What them police and crown prosecutors said, and there was no evidence, was because I was the mother of one of the children believed to be victimized, and because I was a sexual abuse survivor, that I had the strongest motive. They said I should be held more responsible than the other accused, even my partner, my child's father."

"It got worse. They humiliated me and intimidated me at the trial. They called a guy who had sexually assaulted me as a witness against me. Can you believe it?" Lily is shaking her head in disbelief. "And they didn't consider my story, my history of abuse or trauma. The court didn't get to hear any of this stuff – I didn't get to tell my own story!"

"So sorry, Lily," Winter says gently. "We hear you now."

"Since 1991, I spent sixteen years in federal prison. I was found guilty of first-degree murder and that meant a mandatory life sentence. But I got the 'faint hope clause' so a jury reduced my mandatory twenty-five-year parole ineligibility to sixteen years that I already served. But like Emma, Vivi, and Olivia, the life sentence means I am on conditional release subject to life-long community supervision by a parole officer. The rest of our lives."

*Rose*

"What I am going to tell of my story is short," Rose states. "Right now, I am what is called assisted living in the community. When I was a teenager, I was hiding in a school – I was trying to get away from my dad. He was sexually abusing me, like some of your stories already." Rose sits back in her chair and continues, "I was convicted of breaking and entering. But I reacted badly to the treatment in prison, and I ended up with bunches more charges. I was also in isolation for a decade. After this, I was diagnosed with isolation-induced schizophrenia. All the long-standing segregation hurt me."

"Yes, that hurt so many of us, so sorry," Olivia smiles at Rose. "Yes, we hear you Rose," other voices chime in.

*Amy*

Amy runs her hands through her hair. "Let me start at the end. I have been living in the community for the past twenty-three years. I am fifty now."

She tips her head left, then right, stretching her neck. "I was adopted when I was three months old. It was the sixties scoop. I ended up in the child welfare system when I was twelve. This was 'cause of my first arrest – underage drinking with my friends. I refused to go home, such as it was, so the police handcuffed me and took me to a child services centre. I was forcibly strip-searched and penalized for resisting the search. This where the cycle started – institutionalization and segregation, but mostly segregation."

"Like you, Winter and Rose, I ended up with mental health issues, and a diagnosis of schizophrenia. And like you, Emma, I was designated a dangerous offender, I was twenty-one. But I was lucky and the Alberta Court of Appeal said I wasn't a dangerous offender!" Amy chuckles, "Get this, they said that I had been labelled for things I said or wrote, not for what I did!"

Amy claps her hands in delight, then looks serious again. "But get this, I spent most of my sentence in segregated maximum-security units in prisons for men! I got out July 1, 1999. That was the day."

"So glad you made it out, Amy," Sal smiles across the circle.

*Evangeline*

With a big sigh, Evangeline starts telling her story, "It's simple really. I was charged and convicted of second-degree murder when I was fifteen. Fifteen, but they still tried me as an adult – to a mandatory life sentence. I have been in jail since 1999. Just like you, I have been mostly in segregation. Now I have what they call 'significant' mental health issues. They say I have delusional paranoia. I know I have suicidal depression and extreme anxiety."

"Ahh, Evangeline, I am so sorry for your suffering," Amy speaks so gently. Other voices tune in quietly.

*Sal*

"Our stories are so similar." Sal looks down at the floor. "I was convicted of manslaughter and robbery and sentenced to life in prison. I spent fifteen years in prison, plus two years in a halfway house. Right now, I am on a conditional release – and like you, it means that I am subject to life-long community supervision by a parole officer. Sucks."

"And same as you, I didn't get to tell my story – my Indigenous history didn't get considered at trial. Just so I could get a conditional release, I gave up my possible avenues for appeal. I took responsibility for the robbery and death of a man who was robbed and shot by my co-accused. So I am here."

"Yeah, similar stories, can you believe it?" Annabelle is nodding. "We gotta stick together somehow," chimes in Madelaine.

*Madelaine and Annabelle*

Annabelle starts, "Me and Madelaine were residential school survivors along with our other sibs, our parents, and our grandparents. Like you, Olivia, we were sexually abused by residential school staff."

Madelaine picks up the thread: "I was nineteen when I was convicted of second-degree murder. This guy was a residential school caretaker and he propositioned me and my sister. I have been in federal prison since 1994. I got out for just a short time on a conditional release, but then I was returned to prison for breach of conditions. Right now, my application for conditional release and bail is pending a conviction review."

Annabelle takes over. "The guy, he was known to offer young people a place to party, alcohol, and money, and he usually expected sex. Our fourteen-year-old male cousin confessed to the murder, but the legal authorities fixated on us. And they decided that because Madelaine was older, she was likely more responsible. So the confession didn't matter. We were held at an RCMP detachment for several days of questioning – and this was in violation of a court order that we were supposed to be moved to a jail. There was no record of the questioning either. So what happened to all our rights?"

Annabelle continues, "I was convicted of second-degree murder along with my sister. Now she's on parole in the community, and she has a bail application pending, like she said. We were convicted by an all-white jury. Nobody talked about what happened at residential school. No other abuses were discussed."

Madelaine steps in. "Our appeal of our conviction was denied. On November 29, 2022, the province of Saskatchewan lost a bid to impose a publication ban about their attempts to reopen our case."

Annabelle looks thoughtful. "So stay tuned, everyone."

"We will," all the women say in unison.

*Jewel*

"Oh man. Where do I start? I was convicted of murder of my abusive partner. Like you all, I'm serving a mandatory life sentence. And now I'm on conditional release – and of course it is subject to lifelong community supervision by a parole officer."

"We hear you too, Jewel. Know we are here for you, however we can be," Evangeline smiles at Jewel.

The six Feminist Trickster Ravens nod their heads at the twelve women.

Feminist Trickster from the Sky hops to the back of her chair. "Our starting place has to be that you are legal agents, persons, and citizens who lived or are living within and against the constraints of the power relations that you are or were a part of, and that surrounded or surround you."

The Feminist Trickster Raven from the Earth nods. "Thank you all. Now we will turn to the questions we posed earlier: How would you like to change your narratives? What stories do you want your families and others to know? What do you want to add?"

Emma stands up and surveys the circle. "I can't undo the past. There is lots I wish I could have done differently. We all do. What we did at the time seemed to make sense at the time 'cause of what was happening to us. Like when I gave up and tried to escape. What I wish I knew is that I didn't deserve violence. I wish I didn't hate myself for losing my babies."

She pauses. "I want my family and everyone else to know that I did *not* deserve violence, that none of us deserved violence. We deserve love. I want people to know that." Emma sits back down.

Annabelle and Madelaine both stand up. They reach for each other's hands and hold tight as they face the circle. Annabelle begins, "I wish we had faith in justice – either from our own Indigenous law or from Canadian law. I wish we could have relied on others to protect us and to protect future children."

Madelaine looks at her sister. "Thank you, sis. I want people to know how alone we felt. How we couldn't see that we mattered to anyone. I want everyone to know that they matter, and that we matter too." Both Madelaine and Annabelle sit down.

Smiling shyly, Winter stands up. She is still for a minute. "My legal agency was only recognized when I decided to die. I want people to think about how things might have turned out for us all if our legal agency, our citizenry, and our dignity was accounted for by everyone making decisions about us and our lives. I mean for our whole lives." She nods at everyone and resumes her seat.

Vivi stands quietly. "I want people to think about the logics in our lives – yes, we did stupid things, but what was the context? How will that become visible? So I want people to think about our logics, from our perspectives and with our experiences."

Olivia takes her turn and stands, speaking softly and hesitantly. "I want everybody to think about why things kept getting worse for us, not better, in prison. What is wrong with a legal system that causes that? Why is it so hard to change the system – what is stopping the change?" Olivia holds out her hands in perplexity and then sits back down.

Lily jumps to her feet and raises a fist above her head. "I want people to ask themselves why they think we are disposable. Why we have a country that allows us to be abused and trafficked as babies, as children. I want people to think really, really, really hard about that."

Rose stands. "Here is what I want people to think about. How will rebuilding our laws create safety in our communities and in other places too? Look at what Canadian law has done – surely we can do better with rebuilding our own law. And yes, I know there is no room for idealization or romanticism, especially when it comes to violence."

Sal finds her feet; she kind of shuffles to stand. She looks out the windows to the beyond. "It won't be easy. All of us know that, but hey, it can't be harder than what we've already been through."

After a minute or two, Jewel smiles at the circle. "I am in. Count me in!"

Feminist Trickster from the Sky hops up to the back of her chair. "Thank you all. This is your new record for now. We know you will all have more to say as time goes on."

The other five Feminist Tricksters nod emphatically to indicate their agreement and support.

We are going to leave the conversation for now to return to this concluding chapter.

## Conclusion

The odds were stacked against these twelve women. Each one faced an impossible task in dealing with a legal system where they were given little respect. Further, these women had no idea how to navigate that system. Before they came anywhere near the legal system, their lives had already been impacted by alien policing, child welfare, education, and criminal legal systems – from the travails of colonization to the *Indian Act*[20] to imposed residential schools to social services agencies removing children from families and communities. In Canada, commissions and inquiries throughout preceding decades have recognized the fact that the criminal legal system has failed Indigenous people.[21]

So what is next? There are three broad categories within which to consider change. First, the existing systemic violence, racism, and sexism that is rooted in colonialism must be addressed. Second, there are the problems within the legal system as revealed in the stories. These two factors point to changes within the existing legal system. For example, Section 718.2(e) of the *Criminal Code* requires judges to take "the circumstances of Aboriginal offences" into account in sentencing, and especially to look at "all available sanctions, other than imprisonment, that are reasonable in the circumstances."[22] The latter is to include a consideration of alternative measures and community-based options, including appropriate restorative and/or Indigenous justice processes.

However, given the growing number of women incarcerated in federal prisons, it seems that the alternative measures tool has been inappropriately applied and/or underutilized.[23] Recently, in order to address the continuing over-representation of Indigenous people in the criminal legal system, the Department of Justice announced ten million dollars in funding[24] intended to support projects informed by s. 718.2(e) (also known as Gladue Principles)[25] as well as to address the education of criminal justice professionals. The project also asked for proposals regarding Indigenous community-led options for tackling crime, and Indigenous community-led efforts to change policies, practices, processes, and structures to address systemic barriers to and discrimination against Indigenous peoples. This latter approach exemplifies the important third category of change: looking for solutions in Indigenous law.

This approach puts legal change for Indigenous people in the hands of Indigenous people. In 2015, the summary of the Truth and Reconciliation Commission of Canada's *Final Report*[26] noted that Indigenous people continue to view Canadian law and Canada's legal institutions with suspicion,[27] and Canadian law continues to be a "significant obstacle to reconciliation."[28] The commission advised that "Aboriginal peoples must be able to recover, learn, and practice their own, distinct, legal traditions,"[29] and further that "establishing respectful relations ... requires the revitalization of Indigenous law and legal traditions."[30]

As Rose asked, in what ways could access to Indigenous law and legal institutions have changed the legal outcomes of these twelve women? Of course, different Indigenous societies have different law. The laws in different societies may vary but, like all legal systems, the law is rooted in and contextualized by each society. As discussed in this volume, legal principles may be found in stories or precedent that is passed down through generations, as is the nature of law. The legal principles in the oral histories and stories guide relationships, the governance and organization of the society, and the legitimate management of problems.

Hadley Friedland often uses the following published Cree story to demonstrate the application of Cree legal principles to a complex problem:[31]

> An old Cree man who was a powerful Shaman heard Sioux Woman laughing one day. He got mad because he thought she was making fun of him. He cursed her, and although she did not hear him, she became

> "sick and crazy" before Christmas, and began to turn into a *wetiko*. [Friedland describes the wetiko as a Cree legal construct for dealing with those who have become harmful. Wetiko are sometimes described as harmful humans or beings.] Her children grew scared of her.
>
> When Sioux Woman's mother saw [her daughter] was beginning to become a *wetiko*, she attempted to cure her daughter. While she worked to heal her, "all the children were taken away, and some of the grown people went away too. Only a few stayed there to watch her." When her daughter is cured "her grandchildren all came home, and they lived happily after that." The Shaman died within four days of the Sioux Woman being cured, and everyone was relieved.[32]

This seemingly simple story contains important Cree legal principles that govern appropriate legal responses in this situation, and potentially to other problems. Through her scholarship with Cree law, Hadley Friedland has argued that the wetiko is a comprehensive Cree legal construct that allows Cree people to legitimately deal with those that have become harmful to others. Then from her systematic analysis of numerous Cree stories, Friedland identified Cree key legal responses as healing, separation or avoidance, supervision, natural and spiritual consequences, acknowledging responsibility, and reintegration and incapacitation.[33] When looking again at the story, one can clearly see the application of these responses or principles with the exception of reintegration and incapacitation. One can then consider extrapolating the Sioux Woman story, along with others, to a present-day context with present-day problems – for example, think of the Shaman as a drug dealer and of Sioux Woman as suffering from addictions.

How might the experiences of the twelve women have been different if Cree legal principles had been applied to their situations and to the harms and injuries they caused to others and that were caused to them? We can see from Friedland's work that Cree law is also concerned with safety and fairness just as Canadian law is, so such a re-storying would not be about ignoring the harms and injuries that the twelve women caused, but rather contextualizing each situation fully and much more accurately than the courts did.

In 2020, a Cree teenager committed suicide in a group home far from his home and family. The recommendations of the coroner's jury focused on shifting the model of care for Indigenous children back into their families and communities. The statement of the boy's great-grandmother in response to the recommendations is a fitting ending to this volume. While she spoke about Indigenous children, her recommendation is just as valid for Indigenous women.

> We're realizing that the only way we can fix a broken system is to fix it for ourselves ... and it isn't for you people in the court, it isn't for the lawyers, it isn't for children's services, it isn't for your departments to help create a system that is going to work for us – it is our responsibility to ensure that our children are looked after in a manner that we understand.[34]

This volume brings together multiple perspectives and experiences of Indigenous women, Indigenous people, and of our allies. What should become immediately obvious is that the issues of Indigenous women create an enormous and complex field – from Sarah Deer rethinking tribal rape laws in the United States to how Darcy Lindberg explores how historic and present-day Cree ceremonies are integrally tied to contemporary governance and economic questions for Indigenous peoples. This volume gathers many conversations about invisible Indigenous male privilege, the consequences of romanticism and nationalisms, and the tensions within Indigenous law. We also have different disciplinary perspectives, including law, sociology, and political science – each with its own forms of analysis of the concerns and experiences of Indigenous women.

So, what if the twelve women in this chapter wrote the state laws that dealt with their cases? How might their experiences and insights have shaped the laws, the policies, and the institutions through which law acted? And further, if these same twelve women were at the local level and engaged in the hard work of rebuilding Indigenous laws governing safety, families, children, and harms and injuries, how might their work add to the depth, understanding, and practice of Indigenous law today? For one thing, Indigenous law would not be considered some philosophical woo-woo, but rather comprehended as a systematic, accountable, and critical problem-solving system.

The authors in this volume explore these important questions creatively through film, through stories, through Tricksters, through legislation and court decisions, through ceremony, and through both Indigenous and state law. At the end of the day, it is essential to listen to the voices of Indigenous women – this will be the basis of meaningful change. As Emily Snyder points out in chapter 1, this edited collection is not a special interest to "only be used in a gender and law course – rather, with this collection we aim to illustrate how analyses of Indigenous legal issues can change when gender is engaged *throughout*, rather than only occasionally in a chapter here and there." Indeed, in the future imaginary, Indigenous feminisms must be at the very core of rebuilding Indigenous law and governance.

NOTES

1 Kim Pate, Margaret Dawn Anderson & Yvonne Boyer, *Injustices and Miscarriages of Justice Experienced by 12 Indigenous Women: A Case for Group Conviction Review and Exoneration by the Department of Justice via the Law Commission of Canada and/or the Miscarriages of Justice Commission* (Ottawa: Office of Senator Kim Pate, 2022), online: <https://sencanada.ca/media/joph5la2/en_report_injustices-and-miscarriages-of-justice-experienced-by-12-indigenous-women_may-16-2022.pdf> [*Twelve Women*].

2 Kim Pate interviewed the women for the report. The twelve women knew each other, and read and offered comments on the report.

3 See for example National Inquiry into Missing and Murdered Indigenous Women and Girls, *Reclaiming Power and Place: The Final Report of the National Inquiry into Missing and Murdered Indigenous Women and Girls* (Ottawa: MMIWG, 2019), online: <https://www.mmiwg-ffada.ca/final-report/>.

4 Patrick White, "'Shocking and Shameful': For the First Time, Indigenous Women Make Up Half the Female Population in Canada's Federal Prisons," *Globe and Mail* (5 May 2022), online: <https://www.theglobeandmail.com/canada/article-half-of-all-women-inmates-are-indigenous/>. In 1995 Indigenous women comprised only 19 per cent of the population of federally sentenced women in prison. See Louise Arbour, *Commission of Inquiry into Certain Events at the Prison for Women in Kingston* (Ottawa: Commission of Inquiry, 1996) at para. 4.33, online: <https://epe.lac-bac.gc.ca/100/200/301/sgc-sgc/commission_inquiry_prison-e/199681-e.pdf> [Arbour Commission].

5 *R v Gladue* [1999] S.C.J No. 19, [1999]1 SCR 688.

6 *Ibid.* at para 59.

7 *Ibid.* at para 64.

8 *Twelve Women, supra* note 1.

9 *Ibid* at 7.

10 *Indian Act*, RSC 1985, c. I-5.

11 *Twelve Women, supra* note 1. The report defines hyper-responsibilization as racist and sexist biases and perceptions that led to the women's being held or viewed as more responsible and more at fault than others, including male co-accused and individuals who had inflicted violence on the women themselves. For an additional discussion of hyper-responsibility, see Canadian Association of Elizabeth Fry Societies & Native Women's Association of Canada, "Women and the Canadian Legal System: Examining Situations of Hyper-Responsibility" (2008) 26:3/4 Cdn Woman Studies 94, online: <https://cws.journals.yorku.ca/index.php/cws/article/view/22118>.

12 The term "deputizing" is defined at p. 11 of *Twelve Women, supra* note 1: "Any authorities with whom they were in contact ignored or minimized the abuse they lived. The National Inquiry into MMIWG noted a longstanding pattern of police failing to believe, open files or investigate, in addition to the propensity of police to dismiss sexualized violence as unfounded, and horrifically, to also be perpetrators of the sexualized violence. The result was a clear message that each was responsible for protecting herself and her children. They were effectively deputized to protect themselves and failure to do so was treated as their own fault and shame."

13 There are currently mandatory minimum sentences for convictions including murder, sexual offences, and impaired driving in Canada. In these circumstances, the court is unable to model a sentence based upon a consideration of the person and the circumstances of the offence.

14 *Criminal Code,* RSC 1985, c C-46, s 718.2 (e).

15 See *The IF Project: Incarcerated Women Documentary,* dir. Kathlyn Horan (2018), online: <https://www.documentary.org/project/if-project>. In 2008 a Seattle police officer, Kim Bogucki, walked into Washington Corrections Center for Women and asked, "If there was something someone could have said or done that would have changed the path that led you here, what would it have been?" This question struck a chord for women who had never had an opportunity to consider whether their life circumstances could have been different, and they began to respond to the question in writing. This was the genesis of *The IF Project.*

16 Mavis Staples and the Staple Singers' "I'll Take You There" was a hit song in 1972; online: <https://www.youtube.com/watch?v=DHpoGK1aX5Y>.

17 For an important discussion on this issue, see Hadley Friedland, "Navigating through Narratives of Despair: Making Space for the Cree Reasonable Person in the Canadian Justice System" (2016) 67 UNBLJ 269.

18 Co-author Kim Pate used the capitalized term "Indigenous Peoples" in the *Twelve Women* report upon which this chapter is based, and so that term is adopted here.

19 Between December 1988 and February 1991 six Indigenous women died by suicide while incarcerated at the Prison for Women in Kingston, Ontario. In 1994 a conflict between prisoners and guards led to a shameful incident where an all-male emergency response team strip-searched the women prisoners involved and left them shackled to the floor for hours. The prison was finally closed after the release of the 1996 *Arbour Report*: Arbour Commission, *supra* note 4.

20 *Indian Act*, RSC 1985, c I-5.

21 In *Bridging the Cultural Divide: A Report on Aboriginal People and Criminal Justice in Canada* (Ottawa: Minister of Supply and Services, 1996), the Royal

Commission on Aboriginal Peoples stated: "During its research phase, the Alberta task force on the criminal justice system assembled a list of 708 recommendations for reform from all the Aboriginal justice reports between 1967 and 1990. In its own 1991 report, *Justice on Trial*, the task force made 240 recommendations of its own. Several hundred additional proposals have since been made in other reports, bringing the total to as many as 1800 recommendations for reform" (284). For example, the vast over-representation of Indigenous people in the criminal justice system was considered by the Aboriginal Justice Inquiry of Manitoba (1991), The Royal Commission on Aboriginal Peoples (1996), Justice Frank Iacobucci in his report *Independent Review of First Nations Representation on Ontario Juries* (2013), and the Supreme Court of Canada in *R* v *Gladue* (1999).

22 The principles for this section were set out in *R* v *Gladue*, [1999] 1 SCR 688 and further refined in *R* v *Ipeelee*, 2012 SCC 13, [2012] 1 SCR 433.

23 For example see Renee Pelletier, "The Nullification of Section 718.2(e): Aggravating Aboriginal Over-Representation in Canadian Prisons" (2001) 39 2/3 Osgoode Hall LJ 469. The SCC cited this article in the *R* v *Ipeelee* decision.

24 Department of Justice Canada, News Release, "New Funding for Projects to Address Overrepresentation of Indigenous Peoples in Criminal Justice System" (30 June 2021), online: <https://www.canada.ca/en/department-justice/news/2021/06/new-funding-for-projects-to-address-overrepresentation-of-indigenous-peoples-in-criminal-justice-system.html>.

25 For a comprehensive discussion of the Gladue principles and their application, see Benjamin A Ralston, *The Gladue Principles: A Guide to the Jurisprudence* (Saskatoon: University of Saskatchewan, Indigenous Law Centre, 2021).

26 Truth and Reconciliation Commission of Canada, *Honouring the Truth, Reconciling for the Future: Summary of the Final Report of the Truth and Reconciliation Commission of Canada* (Ottawa: TRCC, 2015), online: <https://ehprnh2mwo3.exactdn.com/wp-content/uploads/2021/01/Executive_Summary_English_Web.pdf>.

27 *Ibid* at 202.

28 *Ibid*.

29 *Ibid* at 205.

30 *Ibid* at 16.

31 For example, Sioux Woman was one of the exercises employed in the Viens Commission; see Val Napoleon & Hadley Friedland, "Indigenous Laws as a Cornerstone for Concrete, Effective and Lasting Reconciliation: Testimony for the Public Inquiry Commission on Relations between Indigenous Peoples and Certain Public Services in Québec – Listening,

Reconciliation and Progress" (4–6 December 2017), online: <https://www.cerp.gouv.qc.ca/fileadmin/Fichiers_clients/Documents_deposes_a_la_Commission/P-250.pdf>; Also see Val Napoleon & Hadley Friedland, *Presentation for the National Inquiry into MMIWG Truth-Gathering Process, Expert & Knowledge-Keeper Panel on Indigenous Laws & Decolonizing Perspectives Part III, Vol I* (Delivered at the Canadian Human Rights Museum, Winnipeg, Manitoba, 22–24 August 2017). (*Note*: Recently, the website has removed information about or links to these three days of expert testimony.)

32 Ruth Landes cited in Morton Teicher, "Windigo Psychosis: A Study of a Relationship between Belief and Behavior among the Indians of Northeastern Canada" in Verne F Ray, ed., *Proceedings of the 1960 Annual Spring Meeting of the American Ethnological Society* (Seattle: University of Washington, 1960) at 58.

33 Hadley Louise Friedland, *The Wetiko Legal Principles: Cree and Anishinabek Responses to Violence and Victimization* (Toronto: University of Toronto Press, 2018); also see Hadley Friedland, "Cree Legal Traditions Report" (The Accessing Justice and Reconciliation Project, 2012) at 27–28, online: <www.ilru.ca>.

34 "Inquest into Cree Teen's Death at Abbotsford Group Home Makes 18 Recommendations," *Global News* (8 December 2022), online: <https://globalnews.ca/news/9335727/traevon-desjarlais-inquest-recommendations/>.

## SOURCES CITED

Canadian Association of Elizabeth Fry Societies and the Native Women's Association of Canada. "Women and the Canadian Legal System: Examining Situations of Hyper-Responsibility" (2008) 26:3/4 Cdn Woman Studies, 94, online: <https://cws.journals.yorku.ca/index.php/cws/article/view/22118>.

Department of Justice Canada. "New Funding for Projects to Address Overrepresentation of Indigenous Peoples in Criminal Justice System." News Release (30 June 2021), online: <https://www.canada.ca/en/department-justice/news/2021/06/new-funding-for-projects-to-address-overrepresentation-of-indigenous-peoples-in-criminal-justice-system.html>.

Friedland, Hadley. "Cree Legal Traditions Report" (The Accessing Justice and Reconciliation Project, 2012), online: ilru.ca

Friedland, Hadley. "Navigating through Narratives of Despair: Making Space for the Cree Reasonable Person in the Canadian Justice System" (2016) 67 UNBLJ 269.

Friedland, Hadley. The Wetiko Legal Principles: Cree and Anishinabek Responses to Violence and Victimization (Toronto: University of Toronto Press, 2018).

Iacobucci, Frank. *First Nations Representation on Ontario Juries* (Toronto: Ministry of the Attorney General, 2013).

IF Project: Incarcerated Women Documentary, Kathlyn Horan, director (2018), online: <https://www.documentary.org/project/if-project>.

Little, Simon. "Inquest into Cree Teen's Death at Abbotsford Group Home Makes 18 Recommendations," *Global News* (8 December 2022), online: <https://globalnews.ca/news/9335727/traevon-desjarlais-inquest-recommendations/>.

Manitoba Aboriginal Justice Inquiry. *Report of the Aboriginal Justice Inquiry of Manitoba* (Winnipeg: Aboriginal Justice Inquiry of Manitoba, 1991), online: <https://ajic.mb.ca/volume.html>.

Napoleon, Val & Hadley Friedland. "Indigenous Laws as a Cornerstone for Concrete, Effective and Lasting Reconciliation," Testimony for the public Inquiry Commission on Relations between Indigenous Peoples and Certain Public Services in Québec – Listening, Reconciliation and Progress (Val d'Or 4–6 December 2017), Doc P-250.

Napoleon, Val & Hadley Friedland. "Presentation for the National Inquiry into MMIWG Truth-Gathering Process, Expert & Knowledge-Keeper Panel on Indigenous Laws & Decolonizing Perspectives Part III, Vol I" (Delivered at the Canadian Human Rights Museum, Winnipeg, 22 August 2017), online: <https://www.mmiwg-ffada.ca/wp-content/uploads/2018/09/20170822_MMIWG_Winnipeg_Indigenous_Laws_Part_III_Vol_I.pdf>.

National Inquiry into Missing and Murdered Indigenous Women and Girls. *Reclaiming Power and Place: The Final Report of the National Inquiry into Missing and Murdered Indigenous Women and Girls* (Ottawa: MMIWG, 2019), online: <https://www.mmiwg-ffada.ca/final-report/>.

Pate, Kim, Margaret Dawn Anderson & Yvonne Boyer. *Injustices and Miscarriages of Justice Experienced by 12 Indigenous Women: A Case for Group Conviction Review and Exoneration by the Department of Justice via the Law Commission of Canada and/or the Miscarriages of Justice Commission* (Ottawa: Law Commission of Canada & Miscarriages of Justice Commission, 2022), online: <https://sencanada.ca/media/joph5la2/en_report_injustices-and-miscarriages-of-justice-experienced-by-12-indigenous-women_may-16-2022.pdf>.

Pelletier, Renee. "The Nullification of Section 718.2(e): Aggravating Aboriginal Over-representation in Canadian Prisons" (2001) 39 2/3 Osgoode Hall LJ 469.

Ralston, Benjamin A. *The Gladue Principles: A Guide to the Jurisprudence* (Saskatoon: University of Saskatchewan, Indigenous Law Centre, 2021).

Royal Commission on Aboriginal Peoples. *Bridging the Cultural Divide: A Report on Aboriginal People and Criminal Justice in Canada* (Ottawa: RCAP, 1996).

Teicher, Morton. "Windigo Psychosis: A Study of a Relationship between Belief and Behavior among the Indians of Northeastern Canada" in Verne F Ray, ed., *Proceedings of the 1960 Annual Spring Meeting of the American Ethnological Society* (Seattle: University of Washington, 1960).

Truth and Reconciliation Commission of Canada. *Honouring the Truth, Reconciling for the Future: Summary of the Final Report of the Truth and Reconciliation Commission of Canada* (Ottawa: TRCC, 2015), online: <https://ehprnh2mwo3.exactdn.com/wp-content/uploads/2021/01/Executive_Summary_English_Web.pdf>.

White, Patrick. "'Shocking and Shameful': For the First Time, Indigenous Women Make Up Half the Female Population in Canada's Federal Prisons," *Globe and Mail* (5 May 2022), online: <https://www.theglobeandmail.com/canada/article-half-of-all-women-inmates-are-indigenous/>.

## LEGISLATION

*Criminal Code*, RSC 1985, c C-46.

*Indian Act*, RSC 1985, c. I-5.

## JURISPRUDENCE

*R v Gladue* [1999]S.C.J No. 19, [1999]1 SCR 688.

*R v Ipeelee*, 2012 SCC 13, [2012]1 SCR 433.

# Contributors

**Sarah Deer** is distinguished professor at the University of Kansas and an enrolled citizen of the Muscogee (Creek) Nation of Oklahoma.

**Kahente Horn-Miller** is associate vice president, Indigenous Teaching, Learning and Research at Carleton University, associate professor in the Institute for Interdisciplinary Studies.

**Rebecca Johnson** is professor and associate director of the Indigenous Law Research Unit, Faculty of Law, University of Victoria.

**Julie Kaye** is associate professor, Faculty of Sociology, University of Saskatchewan.

**Darcy Lindberg** is assistant professor, Faculty of Law, University of Victoria.

**Val Napoleon** is a research chair and professor, Faculty of Law, University of Victoria.

**Kim Pate** is a member of the Canadian Senate and adjunct professor with the Faculty of Law, University of Ottawa.

**Emily Snyder** is associate professor of sociology, Department of History and Sociology, University of British Columbia, Okanagan.

**Cheryl Suzack** is professor of English and Indigenous studies, University of Toronto, and holds a non-budgetary cross-appointment to the Faculty of Law.

**waaseyaa'sin Christine Sy** is associate professor, Gender Studies, University of Victoria.

# Index

Printed and bound by CPI Group (UK) Ltd, Croydon, CR0 4YY

15/09/2026

14962404-0001